TELEVISION VIOLENCE:
A GUIDE TO THE LITERATURE
(2ND EDITION)

TELEVISION VIOLENCE:
A GUIDE TO THE LITERATURE
(2ND EDITION)

P.T. KELLY (ED.)

Nova Science Publishers, Inc.
Commack, New York

Editorial Production:	Susan Boriotti
Office Manager:	Annette Hellinger
Graphics:	Frank Grucci and Jennifer Lucas
Information Editor:	Tatiana Shohov
Book Production:	Donna Dennis, Patrick Davin, Christine Mathosian, Tammy Sauter and Lynette Van Helden
Circulation:	Maryanne Schmidt
Marketing/Sales:	Cathy DeGregory

Library of Congress Cataloging-in-Publication Data
available upon request

ISBN 1-56072-700-4

Contents

Introduction

This newly revised bibliography brings together sources on one of the crucial topics of our times - television violence. The media is filled each day with reports of how this and that serial killer and criminals of all stripes got their ideas from a TV program. One wonders how much of today's dumbing down and wanton violence and disregard for others is also triggered by TV and the movies. Is television helping train the school-boy killers popping up across America?

Citizens are told that the networks and cable TV will police themselves - thank you. And pigs will learn to fly! We are told that advertisers have a right to the highest ratings - a right mind you. The viewers have no rights of course. And if violence brings in sales for hamburgers, candy or laxatives better than any other kind of programming, then violence is what we and our children are to be fed according to the captains of our country. And why does violence seem to sell? One reason we are told is that America is a frontier country where early Americans had to shoot to survive. According to this train of thought, this violent streak somehow is being transferred through the soil 200 years later to the current inhabitants!

Another reason heard is that people just like to witness a good punch to the jaw or gut, especially when it is someone else's jaw or gut. Perhaps some do - but have they been programmed to think this way, or is it in their hearts, or do we, as a society, want to encourage such feelings? The answer, according to the captains, is if it sells more burgers, that's the way it is going to be. For more sales mean more money for the captains for themselves and, of course, for their political pals in Washington who most often function more as the protectors of the predators than of the citizens who elect them.

That there are active movements trying to do something about this violence attack on America is remarkable itself. Although it is often pointed out that no major wars have been fought in America with outside countries (if one forgets about the Revolutionary War), there have been a number of even more dangerous internal wars including the Civil War, the war against drugs and the violence war on America.

The violence war on America can be won. If sales and revenues are the engines of its birth and perpetuation, then sales and revenues can be its downfall. Negative publicity brings fear to the captains of America for negative publicity may threaten tomorrow's riches. It is hoped that this modest bibliography may serve as a useful tool for those who wish to research this war and make their contribution to the battles which loom before us.

P.T. Kelly
September 1999

General Studies

Abbott, M. & Disley, B. (1990)
1990 Media Watch Survey: A Report on Levels of Violence on New Zealand Television.
Auckland: Mental Health Foundation of New Zealand, 1990, 11 p.

Abrams, Floyd
Save free speech. (TV Violence: Survival vs. Censorship) (Column)
The New York Times, Nov 23, 1993, v. 143 p. A19(N) ppA
LC Call Number: Not in LC Collection
Magazine Index Micro Film: None
United States. Congress. Senate - Social policy / Violence in television - Social aspects /
Television programs - Censorship / Television and children - Laws, regulations, etc.

Advertisers vs. violence. (Association of National Advertisers)
Television Digest, Feb. 14, 1994, v. 34 n. n7 p. 5(1)
LC Call Number: May or May Not Be in LC. Search further.
Business Index Micro Film: 76Y0339
Assn. of National Advertisers (ANA) Chmn. Richard Garvey urged the organization's
members to do more with regard to the issue of TV violence before the government
imposes its own solution. Garvey expressed concern about the increasing levels of
graphic violence on TV. He stated that advertisers are primary stakeholders in
commercial TV and they have much to lose if the government imposes controls on the
industry. Garvey stated that the ANA supports all efforts designed to curb TV violence
and the development of devices designed to give parents control of what their children
watch.
Association of National Advertisers - Social policy / Violence in television -
Management

Alexander, Charles P.
Let's get tough on pop sex and violence.
Reader's Digest, (U.S. edition), Oct. 1990, v. 137 n. n822 p. 139(2)
LC Call Number: AP2.R255; Microfilm 02206 (1922-) MicRR
Magazine Index Micro Film: None
United States - Popular culture / Sex in mass media - social aspects / Violence in
television - psychological aspects / Censorship - United States

Alice Walker [videorecording] : a portrait in the first person / a ScreenTime Norflicks-Jillian
 production in association with Citytv... [et al.] ; produced by Jim Hanley, David Lee.
Princeton, NJ : Films for the Humanities, c1994.
1 videocassette (28 min.) : sd., col. ; 1/2 in.
PS3573.A425 Z56 1994x
VHS.
Interviewer: Jim Hanley; presenter: Moses Zaynor.
Photography, Ron Stannett; editor, Christopher
 Castelyn; music, Patricia Cullen.
Originally broadcast as a segment of: The originals.
Jim Hanley interviews Alice Walker, author of the novel The color purple. Her discussion touches on a variety of topics including family violence and the position of black women in America.

American Psychological Association. 1993. Violence & Youth: Psychology's Response. Volume I: Summary Report of the American Psychological Association Commission on Violence & Youth. Washington: American Psychological Association.
 Ammann, D. & Doelker, C. (Eds.) (1998)
Tatort Brutalo: Gewaltdarstellungen und ihr
Publikum. Zürich: Pestalozzianum Verlag, 1998, 219 p., ill., fig., bibl., ISBN 3-907526-32-5.

Anderson C
Violence in television commercials during nonviolent programming. The 1996 Major League Baseball playoffs.
Family Practice Department, Hennepin County Medical Center, Minneapolis, Minn 55408, USA.
JAMA, 278:1045-6, 1997 Oct 1
OBJECTIVE: To identify the frequency of violent television commercials aired during major league baseball playoffs, traditionally thought to be a family-oriented viewing time. DESIGN AND SETTING: All 6 World Series games televised on the Fox Television Network (Fox), all 5 American League Championship Series playoff games televised by the National Broadcasting Company (NBC), and 4 first-round playoff games televised by ESPN Sports Television Network (ESPN) were videotaped in October 1996. RESULTS: During the 15 televised games reviewed, 104 (6.8%) of the 1528 commercials contained violent content. Sixty-one commercials (10 per game) that included violent interactions were noted during the World Series, 30 (6 per game) during the American League Championship Series, and 13 (3 per game) during the 4 first-round playoff games for a total of 104. In these 104 violent commercials, 69 contained at least 1 violent act, 90 contained at least 1 violent threat, and 27 contained evidence of at least 1 violent consequence. Seventy (67.3%) of the violent commercials were promotions for television programs, 7 (6.7%) were cable television program advertisements, and 20 (19.2%) were big-screen movie promotions. Twenty (71.4%) of 28 big-screen movie

promotions were violent. Twenty-two (21.2%) of the 104 violent commercials and 7 "nonviolent" commercials contained blood or other graphic content, all of which were televised during the Fox presentation of the World Series. Fox also accounted for all 24 violent commercials that used a knife. Guns were involved in 25 violent commercials on NBC (5.0 per game), in 20 on Fox (3.33 per game), and in 7 on ESPN (1.75 per game). CONCLUSION: Overt violent content in commercials during the 1996 major league playoffs was common and consisted mainly of promotions for television programs and big-screen movies. It is counterintuitive to find such commercials in nonviolent programming and makes it difficult for parents to avoid exposing their children to this form of violence.

Andrews, Edmund L.
A chip that allows parents to censor TV sex and violence; it's cheap. It's easy. It's controversial: the broadcasters hate it. (computer chip installed in television could read electronic coding of offensive programs)
The New York Times, July 18, 1993, v. 142 p. F14(N) pF1
LC Call Number: Not in LC Collection
Magazine Index Micro Film: none
Television sets - Innovations / Television broadcasting industry - Social policy / Cable television broadcasting industry - Social policy / Violence in television - Standards

Antes, W. (Ed.) (1994)
Medien und Gewalt: Aktive Medienarbeit mit Kindern und Jugendlichen. Münster: Ökoia-Verlag, 1994, 120 p., ill., ISBN 3-925169-64-4.
Antiviolence chip. (has working counterpart in Europe) (Brief Article)
Television Digest, Sept. 6, 1993, v. 33 n. n36 p. 14(1)
LC Call Number: May or May Not Be in LC. Search further.
Business Index Micro Film: 73Q0893
Violence in television - Prevention / Television sets - Innovations / Consumer electronics industry - Innovations / Europe - Communication systems Europe

Arnaldo, C. (1996)
Television Violence Versus Viewer Power: The Power to Zap Away: A Synthesis of UNESCO IPDC Actions 1994-1996. Paris: UNESCO, 1996, 9 p.

Asamen, J.K. & Berry, G.L. (Eds.) (1998)
Research Paradigms, Television, and Social Behavior. Thousand Oaks: Sage Publications, 1998, X, 430 p., ill., bibl., ISBN 0-76190-655X.

Atkinson, D.; Gourdeau, M. & Sauvageau, F. (1991)
Synthèses et analyses de divers travaux relatifs à la violence à la télévision. Ottawa: Conseil de la Radiodiffusion et des Télécommunications Canadiennes, 1991, 55 p.

Attorney General addresses TV violence. (Janet Reno said she would support legislation curbing television violence if the industry does not regulate itself) (Brief Article)
Facts on File, Oct. 28, 1993, v. 53 n. n2761 p. 809(1)
LC Call Number: Not in LC Collection
Business Index Micro Film: None
Reno, Janet - Social policy
United States. Congress - Social policy / Violence in television - Laws, regulations, etc. /
Television broadcasting industry - Laws, regulations, etc.

Aufenanger, S.; Lampert, C. & Vockerodt, Y. (1996)
Lustige Gewalt? Zum Verwechslungsrisiko realer und inszenierter Fernsehgewalt bei Kindern durch humoreske Programmkontexte. München: Reinhard Fischer, 1996, 203 p., ill., fig., ISBN 3-88927-193-6.

Auletta, Ken
The electronic parent. New Yorker, v. 69, Nov. 8, 1993: 68-69, 72-75.
"The entertainment industry is scrambling for an answer to violence after Janet Reno's latest salvo, but a San Francisco radio show may already have one."
Crime prevention [San Francisco] / Violence in mass media [U.S.] / Television and children [U.S.] / Radio programs [San Francisco] / Business and social problems [U.S.]

Axe that axe! (violence on British television)
Economist (London), May 21, 1988, v. 307 n. n7551 p. 66(1)
LC Call Number: HG11.E2; Microfilm 03394 (1843-   ) MicRR
Magazine Index Micro Film: None
Programs containing violence: prime-time drama. (table) Calming down: violent acts per hour on television. (graph)
Television programs - Censorship / United Kingdom - Science and technology policy /
Crime in television - United Kingdom / Television broadcasting policy / Violence in television - United Kingdom
Great Britain

Baker Russell
Busby goes berserk. (television and motion pictures depict violence as if it were as harmless as a chorus line in a Busy Berkeley musical) (Column)
The New York Times, July 3, 1993, v. 142 p. 11(N) p19
LC Call Number: Not in LC Collection
Magazine Index Micro Film: None
Violence in motion pictures - Analysis / Violence in television - Analysis

Baker, Russell
Candidate for czar, censoring movie and TV violence. (Column)
The New York times, Oct. 26, 1993, v. 143 p. A15(N) ppA
LC Call Number: Not in LC Collection

Magazine Index Micro Film: None
Violence in motion pictures - Prevention / Violence in television - Prevention

Barlag, S. (1997)
Die Rolle der Medien bei der Ausbreitung Fremdenfeindlicher Gewalt seit Beginn der
90er Jahre. Osnabrück: Universität Osnabrück, 1997, 115 p., fig., Magisterarbeit.

Barongan, C. & Hall, G.C. (1995)
The Influence of Misogynous Rap Music on Sexual Aggression Against Women.
Psychology of Women Quarterly 16(1995)2, pp. 195-208, ISSN 0361-6843.

Barwick, H. (1990)
Research into Effects of Televison Violence: An Overview. Wellington: Broadcasting
Standards Authority, 1990, 82 p., bibl.

Bassett, G. & Shuker, R. (1994)
Attitudes and Perceptions of Television Violence. Wellington: Broadcasting Standards
Authority, 1994, 43 p., ill.

Bayles, Martha
Fake blood: why nothings gets done about media violence. Brookings review, v. 11, fall
1993: 20-23.
"Too often, the critics of media violence allow themselves to be intimidated by charlatans
wrapped in the protective cloak of 'art.' It is high time we ripped off that cloak and
exposed the philistinism underneath. Otherwise, the aesthetic of shock will continue to
provide the spiritual fodder for our children's self-destruction."
Violence in television [U.S.] / Censorship [U.S.]

Benson, Jim
Advisory fallout bruises TV biz: syndicators, local stations shy away from labeling issue.
(violence on television)
Variety, July 19, 1993, v. 351 n. n10 p. 25 (2)
LC Call Number: PN2000.V3 Folio; Microfilm 03722 (1905-   ) MicRR
Magazine Index Micro Film: None
Violence in television - Labeling / Television broadcasting industry - Analysis /
Television programs - Labeling

Benz, U. (1997)
Jugend, Gewalt und Fernsehen: Der Umgang mit bedrohlichen Bildern. Berlin: Metropol-
Verlag, 1997, 283 p., ill., fig., Diss., ISBN 3-926893-70-2.

Benz, U. (1998)
Warum sehen Kinder Gewaltfilme? München: C.H. Beck Verlag, 1998, 150 p., ill., ISBN
3-40642-045-1.

Berge, A.; Kihlbom, M. & Kjellqvist, E.B. et al. (1996)
Inre och yttre hotbilder: Psykoanalytiker ser på våld i media [Perceptions of Threat:
Psychoanalysts Discuss Violence in Media]. Stockholm: Våldsskildringsrådets
skriftserie, 1996, 118 p., ISSN 1102-447X.

Berger, G. (1989)
Violence and the Media. New York: Watts, 1989, 176 p., ISBN 0-531-10808-2.

Berkman, Dave
"If I don't like it, you can't see it." (criticism of religious fundamentalists who want to
censor television broadcasting)
USA Today (Magazine), March 1990, v. 118 n. n2538 p. 50(3)
LC Call Number: L11.S36
Magazine Index Micro Film: 54B0215
Rakolta, Terry - Political activity
United States. National Endowment for the Arts - Laws, regulations, etc. / United States.
Congress - Science and technology policy / United States. Federal Communications
Commission - Laws, regulations, etc. / Married… with Children (Television program) -
Criticism, interpretation, etc. / Sex in television - Laws, regulations, etc. / Mass Media -
Censorship / Violence in television - Laws, regulations, etc. / Fundamentals - Political
aspects

Berkowitz, L. (1990)
On the Formation and Regulation of Anger and Aggression: A Cognitive
Neoassociationistic Analysis. American Psychologist 45(1990)4, pp. 494-503, ISSN
0003-066X.

Berkowitz, L. (1993)
Aggression: Its Causes, Consequences, and Control. New York: McGraw-Hill, 1993,
XXIV, 485 p., ill., bibl., ISBN 0-07004-874-6.

Bernstein, Sid
Distorted reality can destroy us. (column from Advertising Age, Jan. 13, 1974 on
violence on television) (Considerations) (column)
Advertising Age April 22, 1991 v. 62, n. n17, p. 2(1) LC Call Number: HF5801. A276

Beschloss, Steven
TV's life of crime. (violent crime on television) (News)
Channels of communications, Sept. 24, 1990, v. 10 n. n13 p. 12(6)
LC Call Number: PN1992.6.C514
Magazine Index Micro Film: None
Crime in television - social aspects / Violence in television -'social aspects / Television
programs - Production and direction / Television broadcasting of news - management

Billingsley, Lloyd
TV: where the girls are good looking and the good guys win - but whose world view is this.
Christianity today (Washington), Oct. 4, 1985, v. 29 p. 36(6)
LC Call Number: BR1.C6418; Microfilm (0) 83/406 (1981-   ) MicRR
Magazine Index Micro Film: 30G0969
Stein, Ben - research / Gitlin, Todd - research violence in television - Moral and ethical aspects / popular culture - Moral and ethical aspects

Blangger, Tim;
Newsday Size: 6K; 01-07-1998; Page Number: C03; Section: Plugged In
Playing With Violence / Two gruesome games take dead aim at blood, guts and an apocalypse now
FOR A NUMBER of reasons, including the new breed of faster computers capable of rendering some remarkably realistic images, video games have gotten even more violent. The topic itself is not new, but as attention has shifted to controlling access t...

Bliwise, Robert J.
Searching for self-identity. Duke magazine, v. 80, Jan.-Feb. 1994: 14-18, 51.
"They're over-exposed to television and under-exposed to writing. They're driven to succeed, but they're worried about graduating into a failing economy. Are today's young adults, coined Generation X, hopelessly disengaged or merely misunderstood?"
Youth [U.S.] / Television and children [U.S.]

Bloome, David, Ripich, Danielle
Language in children's television commercials: a sociolinguistic perspective. Theory into practice, v. 28, Oct. 1979: 220-225.
Discusses how language in commercials aimed at children is used to promote the product, and how language is used to deceive young children.
Television and children [U.S.] / Deceptive advertising [U.S.] / Child psychology [U.S.]

Boe, S. (Ed.)
(1995)
Medievold: Barn och unge [Media Violence: Children and Youth]. Copenhagen: Kulturministeriet, 1995, 78 p.

Bohrmann, Th. (1997)
Ethik – Werbung – Mediengewalt: Werbung im Umfeld von Gewalt im Fernsehen: Eine Sozialethische Programmatik. München: Fischer, 1997, 309 p., Diss., ISBN 3-88927-211-8.

Bolin, G. (1998)
Filmbytare: Videovåld, kulturell produktion och unga män [Film Swappers: Video

Violence, Cultural Production and Young Men]. Umeå: Boréa Bokförlag, 1998, 288 p.,
Diss., ISBN 91-89140-00-1.

Boyd, William
Dying to make news. (realistic television violence in Great Britain)
New statesman (1975), Dec. 11, 1981, v. 102 p. 22(1)
LC Call Number: AP4.N64; Microfilm (0) 83/132 (1981-1983) MicRR
Magazine Index Micro Film: None
television broadcasting of news - Great Britain/ violence in television - Great Britain
Great Britain

Brady, F. (1996)
Violence in the Media. London: Macmillan, 1996, ISBN 0-33362-668-0.

Brady, Sarah
TV and the gun epidemic. (TV movie 'Strapped')
TV guide, August 21, 1993, v. 41 n. n34 . 14(2)
LC Call Number: Microfilm 06378 (1953-) MicRR
Magazine Index Micro Film: None
Firearms ownership - Media coverage / Violence in television - Portrayals, depictions,
etc.

Bratholm, A. (1992)
"Politivoldkomplekset" i Bergen: En rettstragedie og pressens svikt [The Coverage of
Police Violence in Bergen in the 80's in Norwegian Press]. In: Høyer, S.; Waldahl, R. &
Derby Hansen, S. (Eds.): Pressens Årbog 1991, pp. 161-177, København: C.A. Reitzel,
1992, 245 p., ISBN 87-7001-221-0.

Bridgman, G. (1995)
Turning Away From Television Violence: The 1995 Media Watch Survey. Auckland:
Mental Health Foundation of New Zealand, 1995, 27 p., ill., ISBN 0-90872-732-1.

Brinkmann, W. & Krüger, A. (Eds.)
(1998)
Kinder- und Jugendschutz: Sucht, Medien, Gewalt, Sekten. Stadtbergen: Kognos Verlag,
1998, 406 p., ill., ISBN 3-931314-10-3.

Broadcasting Standards Council (1995)
Violence in Broadcasting Worldwide: International Survey of Regulations in
Broadcasting with Specific Regard to Violence. Paris: UNESCO, 1995.

Brodie, John; Dempsey, John; Wharton, Dennis
Feting the oppressor. (Wexler Group fete for Sen. Paul Simon, who opposes television
violence) (Brief Article)

Variety, Sept. 6, 1993, v. 352 n. n4 p. 3(1)
LC Call Number: PN2000.V3 Folio; Microfilm 03722 (1905-   ) MicRR
Business Index Micro Film: None
Simon, Paul (Politician) - Political activity
United States. Congress. Senate - Officials and employees / Violence in television -
Political aspects - Public relations industry - Management

Brodie, John; Robins, J. Max
TV's year of living cautiously; advertiser-friendly skeds drop the wacky and weird.
(television programming)
Variety, May 24, 1993, v. 351 n. n4 p. 1(2)
LC Call Number: PN2000.V3 Folio; Microfilm 03722 (1905-   )MicRR
Business Index Micro Film: None
Television broadcasting industry - Analysis / Television programs - Planning / Violence
in television - Investigations

Brown, M. (1996)
The Portrayal of Violence in the Media. Canberra: Australian Institute of Criminology,
1996, ISBN 0-64224-015-9.

Browning, Graeme
Push-button violence. National journalism, v. 26, Feb. 26, 1994: 458-463.
"If any issue can be said to have captured the imagination of Capitol Hill in recent
months, it's the rising tide of murder and mayhem in motion pictures, television and
video games. But it's getting harder these days to tell where politics ends and true outrage
begins."
Violence in television [U.S.] / Television programs [U.S.] Law and legislation

Bryant, J. & Zillmann, D. (Eds.)
(1994)
Media Effects: Advances in Theory and Research. Hillsdale: Larence Erlbaum, 1994, IX,
505 p., ill., bibl., ISBN 0-80580-917-1.

Burr, Pat L., Burr, Richard M.
Parental responses to child marketing. Journal of advertising research, v. 17, Dec. 1977:
17-20.
The authors report results of interviews with 400 mothers whose children were in the 2 to
10 age range. The interviews concerned TV advertising directed to children.
Television and children [U.S.] / Television advertising [U.S.] /Market Surveys [U.S.]

Busch, Jackie S.
Television's effects on reading: a case study. Phi Delta Kappan, v. 59, June 1978: 668-671
The results of a study on the relationship between television viewing and reading indicated that "preschool and primary students benefited most from TV viewing. Then, around the age of 12, the saturation point was reached. The law of diminishing returns took effect, and students' total knowledge declined as they increased television viewing." Reading [Virginia] Research / Academic performance [Virginia] Research / Television and children [Virginia] Research

Büttner, C. & von Gottberg, J. (1995)
Jugendschutz und Fernsehen in Europa: Grenzenlose Fernsehgewalt? Frankfurt am Main: Hessische Stiftung, Friedens- und Konfliktforschung, 1995, II, 37 p., bibl., ISBN 3-92896-559-X.

Büttner, C. (1990)
Video-Horror: Schule und Gewalt. Weinheim: Beltz Verlag, 1990, 184 p., ISBN 3-40725-127-0.

Bybee, Carl; Robinson, Danny; Turow, Joseph
Determinants of parental guidance of children's television viewing for a special subgroup: mass media scholars. Journal of broadcasting, no. 3, summer 1982: 697-710.
"This study examines the level and nature of parental guidance regarding television exercised by mass media scholars. It also focuses on the relationship of that guidance to beliefs the scholar hold about the effects of television, to characteristics of their scholarship, and to basic demographic information.
Television and children [U.S.] Research / Social surveys [U.S.] / Parent and child [U.S.]
Cable violence described. (violence in cable television programs)
Television Digest, Feb. 1, 1993, v. 33 n. n5 p. 6(1)
LC Call Number: May or May Not Be In LC. Search further.
Business Index Micro Film: 69W0798
Professor George Gerbner of the University of Pennsylvania conducted a survey for the National Cable Television Assn. (NCTA) regarding violence on cable programs. The survey indicated that original cable programs have comparable amount of violence with broadcast television. NCTA, however, is still determined to implement a four-point scheme to lessen violence on cable programs. An industry policy statement on issues about violence will also be prepared.
National Cable Television Association - Planning/ Violence in television - Surveys / Television broadcasting policy - Planning/ Cable television - Social aspects

Cable, broadcast TV show equal amounts of violence. (study by University of Pennsylvania (Brief Article)
Jet, June 28, 1993, v. 84 n. n9 p. 56(1)
LC Call Number: E185.5.J4; Microfilm 07167 (1951-1979) MicRR

Magazine Index Micro Film: None
Violence in television - Reports

Canada seeks cooperation. (informal working relationships with US on resolving TV violence issue)
Television Digest, Feb. 14, 1994, v. 34 n. n7 p. 4(1)
LC Call Number: May or May Not Be in LC. Search further.
Business Index Micro Film: 76T0338
Violence in television - Evaluation / Television broadcasting industry - Management / Canada - Relations with the United States

Canada & TV violence, cooperation & consensus. Performing Org.: Canadian Radio-Television & Telecommunications Commission, Ottawa.
NTIS Order Number: MIC-95-04856INZ.
24p Publication Date: c1995.
Document Type: Technical Report
Country of Publication: Canada
Gender and violence in the mass media.
Performing Org.: Family Violence Prevention Division, Ottawa (Ontario).
NTIS Order Number: MIC-94-01624INZ.

Canadian coalition wants to bleep out rock video violence (music video)
Variety, Jan. 25, 1984, v. 313 p. 1(2)
LC Call Number: PN2000.V3 Folio; Microfilm 03722 (1905-   ) MicRR
Magazine Index Micro Film: None
Scott, David - political activity
Ontario. Censorship Board - social policy / Canadian Coalition Against Violent Entertainment - Management / Rock videos - censorship / subscription television - Canada / violence in television - sources
Ontario

Censorship in Sweden. (column)
America (New York, N.Y. 1909) Feb. 14, 1981, v. 144 p. 109(2)
LC Call Number: BX801.A5; Microfilm 02861 (1949-1968) MicRR
Magazine Index Micro Film: None
Censorship - Sweden /Sweden - censorship / violence in television - censorship / violence in motion pictures - censorship

Cerone, Daniel
A new effort under way to define violence on TV. (Mediascope and University of California, Los Angeles Center for Communication Policy retained by television industry to define violence)
The Los Angeles Times, Sept. 3, 1994, v. 113, p. F1
LC Call Number: Newspaper 7114-X

Business Index Micro Film: None
National Cable Television Association - Investigations / Violence in television -
Investigations / Television broadcasting industry - Investigations / Television programs -
Standards

Charlton, M. et al. (1995)
Zugänge zur Mediengewalt: Untersuchungen zu individuellen Strategien der Rezeption
von Gewaltdarstellungen im frühen Jugendalter. Abteilung für Klinische und
Entwicklungspsychologie, Psychologisches Institut der Universität Freiburg. Freiburg:
Universität Freiburg, 1995, 205 p., bibl.

Charren, Peggy
Children's TV: sugar and vice and nothing nice. Business and society review, no. 22,
summer 1977: 65-70.
Attacks the television advertising and children's products industries for disregarding the
vulnerability and social and human needs of children. Calls for the regulation of
commercial children's television.
Television advertising [U.S.] /Television and children [U.S.] / Action for Children's
Television

Charren, Peggy
What's missing in children's TV. World monitor, v. 3, Dec. 1990: 28, 30, 32-34.
"A powerful medium of persuasion is failing its promise. The US Congress demands
reform. Other nations watch in suspense. Cast your vote for the programs TV should
show."
Television and children [U.S.] / Television programs [U.S.]

Children and television: a challenge for education. Edited by Michael E. Manley-Casimir
and Carmen Luke. New York, Praeger, c1987, 311 p.
"Part I includes chapters that discuss theory and present empirical studies. The theme of
this section reflects a consensus among the researchers that the TV-child relationship is
interactive, that the child viewer is not a passive recipient of TV information but
cognitively acts upon incoming information... Part II moves from the theoretical and
empirical to practical educational questions, presenting approaches to curriculum design
for the teaching of critical and literate viewing skills... The chapters in Part III are policy
oriented... Finally, Part IV provides an annotated reference list of studies and position
papers published from 1975 to 1983."
Television and children [U.S.] Addresses, statements, etc. / Educational television [U.S.]
Addresses, statements, etc.

Clapp, Rodney
Forces combating TV smut flex their new muscle.
Christianity Today (Washington), March 13, 1981, v. 25 p. 74(2)
LC Call Number: BR1.C6418; Microfilm (0) 83/406 (1981-   ) MicRR

Magazine Index Micro Film: None
Wildmon, Donald - political activity
National Coalition for Better Television - political activity / violence in television -
political aspects / sex in mass media - political aspects / Moral Majority - political
activity / conservatism - political activity

Clark, Charles S.
TV violence: will Hollywood tone it down - or face regulation? CQ researcher, v. 3, Mar.
26, 1993: 165-188
"The average American child watches 8,000 murders and 100,000 acts of violence before
finishing elementary school - thanks to the miracle of television. Suggestions of a link
between make-believe TV violence and aggression in real life have been raised since
television's formative years in the 1950s - and always dismissed by the TV industry. But
recently the three major networks signed a first-ever joint statement outlining practices
aimed at reducing violence, and the cable, video and film industries are showing signs of
cooperating. Some in Congress are encouraged and maintain hopes that change will come
about voluntarily, without the need for federal regulation. But anti-violence activists and
scholars of television accuse the industry of merely paying lip service to the problem."
Violence in television [U.S.] / Television and children [U.S.] / Child psychology [U.S.] /
Violence research [U.S.]

Clemente, M. & Vidal Vázques, M.A. (1995)
Violencia y Televisión. Madrid: Nóesis, 1995, 165 p., ISBN 84-87462-21-9.

Clemente, M. & Vidal Vázquez, M.A. (1997)
Investigación de contenidos violentos emitidos por Tele Madrid y Onda Madrid
susceptibles de afectar a los menores. Madrid: Estudio solicitado por la Institución del
Defensor del Menor, 1997.

Clover, C.J. (1992)
Men, Women, and Chain Saws: Gender in the Modern Horror Film. Princeton: Princeton
University Press, 1992, 260 p., ill., bibl., ISBN 0-69104-802-9.

Clutterback, Richard
Terrorism and urban violence. In the communications revolution in politics. New York,
Academy of Political Science, 1982. (Proceedings, v. 34, no. 4, 1982) p. 165-175.
Surveys the effect rapid communications have had on the publicity given street violence,
riots, and terrorism, the potential for terrorist attacks against telecommunication and
computer systems, and the opportunities technological change has presented government
and business for dealing with terrorism.
Terrorism / Riots / Violence in television / Crime and the press / Television news /
Telecommunication - Security measures / Computer security measures

Coalition says violence on TV at record high.
Variety, Nov. 14, 1984, v. 317 p. 41(2)
LC Call Number: PN2000.V3 Folio; Microfilm 03722 (1905-   ) MicRR
Magazine Index Micro Film: None
Violence in television - reports / National Coalition on Television Violence - reports /
television programs - social aspects

Cockburn, Alexander
Beat the Devil. (Column)
The Nation (New York, NY) Jan. 17, 1994, v. 258 n. 2 p. 42(2)
LC Call Number: AP2.N2; Microfilm 03323 (1965-1979) MicRR
Magazine Index Micro Film: None
Talbott, Strobe - Management
Revolutionary Communist Party - Media coverage / Violence in television - Political
aspects / Censorship - Analysis

Cohen, Susan
Kidvideo games. Washington post, April 7, 1991: 17-24, 34-41.
"There are people in Washington who have high hopes for the Children's Television Act.
But the world in which children's programs are written and produced is far away from
the world in which they're regulated. If you want to find out why kid's TV is the way it is
- and whether there's any real chance it will change - it helps to spend some time in
Burbank."
Television and children [U.S.] / Television advertising [U.S.] Standards / Television
programs [U.S.]

Coldevin, Gary O.
Satellite television and cultural replacement among Canadian Eskimos: adults and
adolescents compared. Communications research, v. 6, April 1979: 115-134.
"The application of a satellite television distribution system in Canadian Arctic native
communities has precipitated a new form of electronic colonialism. As a test of its
influence, the degree of traditional culture replacement among Eskimo adults and their
adolescent offspring in a television community was examined after two and one-half
years of exposure to regular C.B.C. programming... The results demonstrated
significantly varied acculturation levels among the samples, with the greatest shift toward
Euro-Canadian structures accruing to television town adolescents, followed by settlement
students."
Eskimos [Canada] Social aspects / Television and children [Canada] / Communication
satellites [Canada] / Pluralism (Social sciences [Canada] / Social surveys [Canada]

Cole, J. (Ed.)
(1995)
The UCLA Television Violence Monitoring Report. Los Angeles: University of
California, Center for Communication Policy, 1995, 181 p.

Cole, J. (Ed.)
(1996)
The UCLA Television Violence Report 1996. Los Angeles: University of California, Center for Communication Policy, 1996, 220 p.

Cole, J. (Ed.)
(1998)
The UCLA Television Violence Report 1997. Los Angeles: University of California, Center for Communication Policy, 1998, 232 p., fig., chart.

Coles, Robert
What TV teaches children about politics. TV guide, v. 36, Feb. 6, 1988: 2-4
"A young person brought up in a strong and attentive family with its own explicitly acknowledged social, moral and political values is by no means a setup for the world's growing number of television scriptwriters and cameramen."
Television and children [U.S.] / Television in politics [U.S.] / Political socialization [U.S.] / Parent and child [U.S.]

Colford, Steven W.
TV ads to get violence exam. (Center for Communications Policy to monitor television commercials for violent content)
Advertising Age, July 4, 1994, v. 65 n. n28 p. 40(1)
LC Call Number: HF5801.A276
Business Index Micro Film: None
The Center for Communication Policy at the University of California in Los Angeles, CA, will check television commercials for violent content in the same way television programs are monitored. Sen. Paul Simon of Illinois, who has conducted a decade-long campaign against violent programming, announced the selection of the Center. The Association of National Advertisers objected to the concept of commercials as violent.
Simon, Paul (Politician) - Political activity
Violence in television - Measurement / Television advertising - Evaluation

College study finds 8-9 P.M. time slot is prime violence. (network television)
Variety, Sept. 17, 1986, v. 324, p. 1(2)
LC Call Number: PN2000.V3 Folio; Microfilm 03722 (1905-   ) MicRR
Magazine Index Micro Film: None
Gerbner, George - research
violence in television - research / television and children - research

Collins, W. Andrew; Wellman, Henry M.
Social scripts and developmental patterns in comprehension of televised narratives.
Communication research, v. 9, July 1982: 380-398.
"In the present research, second, fifth and eighth graders' recognition errors and recall of an action-adventure drama were examined jointly to determine how children represented

plots that they remembered inaccurately. Younger children's representations of the program were especially likely to reflect familiar actions and events sequences ('scripts'), cued by isolated, familiar occurrences in the televised portrayal."
Television programs [U.S.] / Television and children [U.S.]

Collure, Danny Duncan
Why murder in May brings good things to life for networks.
National Catholic Reporter, June 18, 1993 v29 n32 p18(1)
Comment of Steven Bochco. (violence on television program NYPD Blue)
Television Digest, Sept. 20, 1993, v. 33 n. n38 p. 5(1)
LC Call Number: May or May Not Be in LC. Search further.
Business Index Micro Film: 73T0386
Bochco, Steven - Attitudes
Violence in television - Censorship / Network-affiliated television stations - Social policy

Consejo Nacional de Television (1998)
Cinco estudio sobre violencia y television en Chile: Programa de investigacion: Violencia en television, percepciones y contenidos. Santiago: Consejo Nacional de Television, Departamento de Estudios, 1998, 264 p., fig., chart., tab., bibl.

Cooper, C.A. (1996)
Violence on Television: Congressional Inquiry, Public Criticism, and
Industry Response: A Policy Analysis. Lanham: University Press of America, 1996, IX, 201 p.

Cooper, Jim
From v-chip to hip hop. (broadcast content discussion at the National Association of Broadcasters 1994 convention)
Broadcasting and Cable, March 28, 1994, v. 124 n. n13 p. 22(1)
LC Call Number: TK6540B85
Business Index Micro Film: 77S2147
A panel of broadcasting industry executives, academics and consumer group representatives discussed broadcast content. The scientific basis for restricting violent and sexual content was disputed by the panelists, with some claiming that studies showed such content had a negative effect on children, while others argued that the evidence was not conclusive. Most panelists agreed that government intervention would not be welcome.
Violence in television - Analysis / Television broadcasting industry - Conferences, meetings, seminars, etc. / National Association of Broadcasters Convention - 1994

Cortes, Carlos E.
The societal curriculum and the school curriculum: allies or antagonists? Educational leadership, v. 36, April 1979: 475-479.
"Students learn from many sources. Educators need to become aware of what is being

taught by television and other societal 'teachers.' "
Learning [U.S.] / Social conditions [U.S.] / Television and children [U.S.]

Council on Children, Media and Merchandising
Edible TV: your child and food commercials. Washington, 1977, 102 p.
Presents excerpts from 1976-77 testimony before the FTC on the impact of food
commercials on children under 12, a synopsis of testimony of Robert Choate, and a report
of a developmental study on the use of graphics in conveying nutritional information.
Television advertising [U.S.] / Television and children [U.S.] / Nutrition [U.S.] /
Nutrition surveys [U.S.]

Cronström, J. & Höijer, B. (1996)
40 timmar i veckan: En studie av våld i sex svenska TV-kanaler [40 Hours a Week: A
Study of Violence Depictions in Six Swedish Television Channels]. Stockholm:
Kulturdepartementet, Våldsskildringsrådet, 1996, 153 p., tab., bibl, ISSN 1102-447X.

Cronström, J. (1994)
Skildringar av våld och våldets offer i televisionens nyhetsprogram: en kvantitativ-
kvalitativ innehållsanalys över tid och mellan aktörer i det svenska etermedieutbudet
[Depictions of Violence and Victims of Violence in Swedish Television Newscasts: A
Content Analysis of the Evening News on Public Service and Private Channels].
Stockholm: Stockholms universitet, Institutionen för journalistik, medier och
kommunikation, 1994, 22 p., tab., processed.

Crowell, Doris C.
Educational technology research: should we teach children how to learn from television?
Educational technology, v. 21, Dec. 1981: 18-22.
Examines techniques for improving the comprehension of videotaped material and
concludes that they "may have important implications for the improved application of
instructional television in schools where there is a heavy reliance on pre-programmed,
packaged teaching materials."
Television and children [U.S.] / Educational television [U.S.] Teaching [U.S.]

Culkin, John
Selling to children: fair play in TV commercials. Hastings Center report, v. 8, June 1978:
7-9.
Focuses on the debate between advertisers and public interest groups on the issue of T.V.
advertising aimed at children. Argues that "the battle is so unequal that federal regulatory
agencies have a responsibility to act on behalf of the interests of children and parents."
Television and children [U.S.] Television advertising [U.S.] / Independent regulatory
commissions / Child welfare [U.S.] / Freedom of speech [U.S.]

Culley, James D.; Lazer, William; Atkin, Charles K.
The experts look at children's television. Journal of broadcasting, v. 20, winter 1976: 3-21.
"The purpose of this research was to examine the attitudes of six key respondent groups towards the major issues in children's television advertising' including Action for Children's Television, advertising agency executives, members of government, and the general public.
Television and children [U.S.] / Television advertising [U.S.]

Cumberbatch, Guy
A measure of uncertainty: the effects of the mass media / Guy Cumberbatch with Dennis Howitt. - London: J. Libbey, c1989
vii, 88 p.; 25 cm. (Research monograph series /Broadcasting Standards Council, ISSN 0956-9073; 1) Includes bibliographical references.
Television broadcasting - Social aspects. Television - Psychological aspects. Violence in television. Sex in television. Howitt, Dennis. I Title. II Series: Research monograph series (Broadcasting Standards Council (Great Britain)); 1.

Cutler, Jonathan
Ready on the firing line. (UCLA Center for Communications Policy to study television violence)
Mediaweek, August 22, 1994, v. 4 n. n33 p. 22 (3)
Business Index Micro Film: None
The four television networks (ABC, CBS, Fox and NBC) hired the University of California at Los Angeles (UCLA) Center for Communications Policy for a study of television violence for $400,000-$500,000 per year. The research group, lead by UCLA professor Jeffrey Cole, will monitor network motion pictures, miniseries, and children's programs as well as four episodes of prime-time series. Researchers will analyze the context of violent actions, especially the emotional impact of depicted violence. Reports of the study will be made public at the end of each season of programming.
California, University of (Los Angeles). Center for Communications Policy - Contracts / Television broadcasting industry - Contracts / Violence in television - Research

Dalquist, U. (1998)
Större våld än nöden kräver? Medievåldsdebatten i Sverige 1980-1995 [More Violence than the Necessity of the Case Demands? The Media Violence Debate in Sweden 1980-1995]. Umeå: Boréa Bokförlag, 1998, 258 p., bibl., Diss., ISBN 91-89140-01-X.

Demkovich, Linda E.
Pulling the sweet tooth of children's TV advertising. National Journal, v. 10, Jan. 7, 1978: 24-26.
"The Federal Trade Commission is trying to decide how much protection children need from the advertisements they see on television. Critics say the ads for sugary cereals and other products shouldn't be shown to children, but the industry says the critics are off

base. The FTC may decide this month what it will do about the complaints."
Television advertising [U.S.] / Television and children [U.S.] / Independent regulatory
commissions / Sugar and sugar trade [U.S.] / U.S. Federal Trade Commission

Dempsey, John
Doing violence to sales: pols, professors preach pacifism; NATPE coin curbed. (National
Association of Television Program Executives; television violence)
Variety, Jan. 31, 1994, v. 353 n. n13 p. 23 (2)
LC Call Number: PN2000.V3 Folio; Microfilm 03722 (1905-   ) MicRR
Magazine Index Micro Film: None
Hundt, Reed - Addresses, essays, lectures
United States. Federal Communications Commission - Officials and employees /
National Association of Television Program Executives - Conferences, meetings,
seminars, etc. / Violence in television - Public opinion

Dempscy, John
Parental advisories okay by cablers - but what kind? (violence on television)
Variety, July 19, 1993, v. 351, n. 10 p. 25 (2
LC Call Number: PN2000.V3 Folio; Microfilm 03722 (1905-   ) MicRR
Magazine Index Micro Film: None
Television programs - Labeling / Violence in television - Labeling / Cable television
broadcasting industry - Social policy / Television broadcasting industry - Social policy

DeMuth, Christopher C.
The FTC tantrum against children's television. American spectator, v. 12, April 1979: 18-
21, 24.
The author considers questions of efficiency and values raised by the FTC's proposed
rule banning television advertising directed toward children, in this revised version of an
address to the Toy Manufacturers of America.
Television advertising [U.S.] / Television and children [U.S.]

Dennis, P.M. (1998)
Chills and Thrills: Does Radio Harm Our Children? The Controversy Over Program
Violence During the Age of Radio. Journal of the History of the Behavioral Sciences
34(1998)1, pp. 33-50, ISSN 0022-5061.

Det norske kulturdepartcmentet (1995)
Regjeringens handlingsplan mot vold i bildemediene [The Government's Action Plan
Against Violence in the Visual Media]. Oslo: Det norske kulturdepartementet, 1995, 50
p., ISBN 82-91565-00-7.

Diamond, Edwin
Gun and poses: Hollywood takes on violence. (media campaign to discourage gun use)
(Media)

New York (1968), Dec. 6, 1993, v. 26 n. n48 p. 32(3)
LC Call Number: F128.1.N4; Microfilm (0) 84/106 (1982-1983) MicRR
Magazine Index Micro Film: None
Winstein, Jay - Political activity
Violence in television - Moral and ethical aspects / Gun control - Social aspects

Dias, A.R.F. (1996)
O discurso da violência: As marcas da oralidade no jornalismo popular. Sâo Paulo:
Cortez Editora, 1996, 178 p., ill., ISBN 8-52490-660-X.

Diener, Ed; DeFour, Darlene
Does television violence enhance program popularity? Journal of personality and social
psychology, v. 36, March 1978: 333-341.
Results of two studies lead the authors to conclude that "there is presently little evidence
indicating that violence enhances program popularity."
Television programs [U.S.] / Violence in television [U.S.]
Diener, Ed; Woody, Lisa W.
Television violence, conflict, realism and action: a study in viewer liking.
Communication research, v. 8, July 1981: 281-306.
"The present experimental studies, using a variety of populations and methodologies,
found television violence to be either unpopular or regarded with indifference, thus
destroying the argument made by supporters of TV violence that viewers like and
actively seek out violent content in the shows they watch."
Television programs [U.S.] / Violence in television [U.S.]

Dines, G. & Humez, J.M. (Eds.) (1995)
Race and Class in the Media: A Text Reader. Thousand Oaks: Sage Publications, 1995,
648 p., ISBN 0-8039-5164-7.

Dirección General de Atención al Niño (1995)
Influencia de la televisión en la infancia y adolescencia Andaluza. Sevilla: Dirección
General de Atención, 1995, 233 p., ill., ISBN 84-7936-041-0.

Divergent Washington views on televised violence.
Television Digest, Sept. 20, 1993, v. 33 n. n38 p. 1(2)
LC Call Number: May or May Not Be in LC. Search further.
Business Index Micro Film: 73T0382
Three different opinions were presented concerning violence in television programs.
Surgeon Gen. Jocelyn Elders said that networks did not fulfill their promise to provide
warnings of violence content in their programs. Sen. Paul Simon said that segments of the
television broadcast industry blamed each other for the continuing violence in television,
while Motion Picture Assn. of America Pres. Jack Valenti said that politicians were
capitalizing on televised violence as a political issue.

Valenti, Jack - Social policy / Simon, Paul (Politician) - Social policy / Elders, Jocelyn - Social policy / Violence in television - Conferences, meetings, seminars, etc. / Television broadcasting industry - Laws, regulations, etc.

Dobson, Cathy
Children, television and advertising. FTC Library bulletin, v. 14, August 1977, suppl.: 1-7
A bibliography listing "books, government publications, useful indexes, [and] uncataloged materials available in the [FTC] library."
Television and children [U.S.] Bibliography / Television advertising [U.S.] Bibliography

Dobson, James
Let's do something about TV violence!
Christian herald (Chappaqua) Sept. 1982, v. 105 p. 57(2)
LC Call Number: B1.C63; Microfilm 01104 (1818-1845) MicRR
Magazine Index Micro Film: None
violence in television - social aspects

Docherty, D. (1990)
Violence in Television Fiction. London: John Libbey, 1990, 39 p., bibl., ISBN 0-86196-284-2.

Donahue, J. Christopher
What's right with television?
America, Oct 8, 1994 v171 n10 p25(1)

Donnerstein, E. & Linz, D. (1995)
The Media. In: Wilson, J.Q. & Petersilia, J. (Eds.): Crime, pp. 237-264, San Francisco: Institute for Contemporary Studies, 1995, XV, 631 p., ill., ISBN 1-55815-427-2.

Donohue, Thomas R.
Perceptions of violent TV newsfilm: an experimental comparison of sex & color factors.
Journal of broadcasting, v. 20, spring 1976: n185-195.
"Study relates viewer sex with perceptions of color and black-and-white Vietnam television newsfilm, finding that sex is a far more important factor in determining viewer reaction to such material than any differences in the film itself."
Television news [U.S.]/ Violence in television [U.S.] / Foreign news [U.S.] / Vietnamese Conflict

Donohue, Thomas R.; Henke, Lucy L.; Donohue, William A.
Do kids know what TV commercials intend? Journal of advertising research, v. 20, Oct. 1980: 51-57
Find that "children understand the intent of television commercials at a younger age than has been reported in the literature."

Television and children [U.S.] / Television advertising [U.S.]
Drevitch, Gary
Murder, she saw. (violence in mass media) (Cover Story)
Scholastic update, Feb. 11, 1994, v. 126 n. n9 p. 12 (2)
LC Call Number: Ap2.S477; Microfilm 02828 (1954-1974) MicRR
Magazine Index Micro Film: None
Violence in television - Social aspects / Mass media and youth - Social aspects

DuRant RH; Rich M; Emans SJ; Rome ES; Allred E; Woods ER
Violence and weapon carrying in music videos. A content analysis [see comments]
Department of Pediatrics, Bowman Gray School of Medicine, Wake Forest University,
Winston-Salem, NC, USA. rdurant@bgsm.edu
Arch Pediatr Adolesc Med, 151:443-8, 1997 May
BACKGROUND: The positive portrayal of violence and weapon carrying in televised
music videos is thought to have a considerable influence on the normative expectations of
adolescents about these behaviors. OBJECTIVES: To perform a content analysis of the
depictions of violence and weapon carrying in music videos, including 5 genres of music
(rock, rap, adult contemporary, rhythm and blues, and country), from 4 television
networks and to analyze the degree of sexuality or eroticism portrayed in each video and
its association with violence and weapon carrying, as an indicator of the desirability of
violent behaviors. METHODS: Five hundred eighteen videos were recorded during
randomly selected days and times of the day from the Music Television, Video Hits One,
Black Entertainment Television, and Country Music Television networks. Four female
and 4 male observers aged 17 to 24 years were trained to use a standardized content
analysis instrument. RESULTS: A higher percentage (22.4%) of Music Television videos
portrayed overt violence than Video Hits One (11.8%), Country Music Television
(11.8%), and Black Entertainment Television (11.5%) videos (P = .02). Rap (20.4%) had
the highest portrayal of violence, followed by rock (19.8%), country (10.8%), adult
contemporary (9.7%), and rhythm and blues (5.9%) (P = .006). Weapon carrying was
higher on Music Television (25.0%) than on Black Entertainment Television (11.5%),
Video Hits One (8.4%), and Country Music Television (6.9%) (P < .001). Weapon
carrying was also higher in rock (19.8%) and rap (19.5%) videos than in adult
contemporary (16.1%), rhythm and blues (6.9%), and country (6.3%) videos (P = .002).
The videos with the highest level of sexuality or eroticism were found to be less likely to
contain violence (P < or = .04). CONCLUSION: Because most music videos are between
3 and 4 minutes long, these data indicate that even modest levels of viewing may result in
substantial exposure to violence and weapon carrying, which is glamorized by music
artists, actors, and actresses.

Dwyer, Victor
Small-screen monsters.
Maclean's, March 30, 1992 v105 n13 p57(2)

Dwyer, Victor
Small-screen monsters. (violence in television movies) (Cover Story)
Maclean's, March 30, 1992, v. 105 n. n13 p. 57(2)
LC Call Number: AP5.M2; Microfilm (0) 84/200 (1909-1982) MicRR
Magazine Index Micro Film: 64F0268
Violence in television - Analysis

Eckert, R. & Steinmetz, L. (1991)
Grauen und Lust – die Inszenierung der Affekte: Eine Studie zum abweichenden
Videokonsum. Pfaffenweiler: Centaurus Verlag, 1991, 190 p., bibl., ISBN 3-89085-530-
X.

Edwards, Ellen
TV violence escalates sharply, study says; networks object to including news shows
(Center for Media and Public affairs study; includes related article)
The Washington Post, August 5, 1994, v. 117 p. C1
LC Call Number: Newspaper
Business Index Micro Film: None
Violence in television - Research / Television broadcasting industry - Management /
Television programs - Moral and ethical aspects

Egan, Lola M.
Children's viewing patterns for television news. Journalism quarterly, v. 55, summer
1978: 337-342.
Report on a survey of over 400 children in grades 2-6 in San Jose, Calif.
Television and children [San Jose, Calif.] / Television news [U.S.]

Egge, S. (1997)
Medievoldens innflytelse på utsatte barn og unge: ingen kommer ingensteds fra: alla
kommer hjemmefra [The Influence of Media Violence on Exposed Children and Youth].
Oslo: Institutt for medier og kommunikasjon, Oslo universitet, 1997, 100 p., processed.

Eldridge, John
War and peace news on British television. Current research on peace and violence, v. 6,
no. 1, 1983: 3-28.
An analysis of news bulletins on the coverage of defense and disarmament issues in
specific event news.
Television news [Great Britain] / Military intervention [Argentina] Falkland Islands /
Arms control / War and religion / Foreign news [Great Britain] / Violence in television
[Great Britain]

Elguren, A. (Ed.)
(1994)
Det skrekkelige: fra grøssere til splatter – seks essays om horror [From Horror Films to

Splatter Films: Six Articles on Horror]. Oslo: Aschehoug kursiv, 1994, 161 p., ISBN 82-03-26015-2.

Engelhardt, Tom
Saturday morning fever: the hard sell takeover of kids TV. Mother Jones, v. 11, Sept. 1986: 39-42, 44-48, 54.
Looks at the business world behind the screen of children's television - where toys are developed and marketed.
Television and children [U.S.] / Television and advertising [U.S.]

Enos, Sondra Forsyth
Living in truly tasteless times.
Ladies' Home Journal, Nov. 1984, v. 101 p. 129 (8)
LC Call Number: AP2.L135; Microfilm 05422 and 02626 (1884-1977) MicRR
Magazine Index Micro Film: 17F4641
Etzioni, Amitai - research
television - social aspects / sex in television - social aspects / violence in television - social aspects
Eron, Leonard D.; Reisman, Del
Should the television industry do more to curb depictions of violence? (At Issue)
CQ Researcher, March 26, 1993, v. 3 n. n12 p. 281 (1)
LC Call Number: H35.E35
Magazine Index Micro Film: None
Media representatives contends that regulation violates freedom of expression. They also argue that violence in television is primarily an attempt to portray the true state of society and involve audience in the stories. On the other hand, critics believe the industry should seriously pursue self-regulation against of violent scenes. This suggestion is anchored on the argument that portrayals of violence may be confirming children's views of violence as a normal occurrence, desensitizing them to the problems violence breeds in society.
Violence in television - Social aspects / Television broadcasting industry - Social policy / Violence in children - Social aspects

Ericson, R.V. (Ed.)
(1995)
Crime and the Media. Aldershot: Dartmouth, 1995, XXX, 429 p., ill., ISBN 1-85521-433-4.

Eron LD
Media violence.
Institute for Social Research, University of Michigan, Ann Arbor 48106, USA.
Pediatr Ann, 24:84-7, 1995 Feb

Etzioni, Amitai
Lock up your TV set. (violence on television)

National review (New York) Oct. 18, 1993, v. 45 n. n20 p. 50(3)
LC Call Number: AP2.N3545; Microfilm 06959 (1967-1974) MicRR
Magazine Index Micro Film: None
Violence in television - Social aspects / Television sets - Innovations / Television
programs - Safety and security measures

Faber, Ronald J.; Perloff, Richard M.; Hawkins, Robert P.
Antecedents of children's comprehension of television advertising. Journal of
broadcasting, v. 26, spring 1982: 575-584.
"Study compared the importance of role taking and logical operations stage in predicting
children's understanding of the purpose of television advertising. Role taking was found
to be the more critical variable."
Television advertising [U.S.] / Television and children [U.S.]

Fair, J.E. & Astroff, R.J. (1991)
Constructing Race and Violence: U.S. News Coverage and the Signifying Practices of
Apartheid. Journal of Communication 41(1991)Autumn, pp. 58-74, ISSN 0021-9916.

Finney, Angus
Gutter and gore. (tabloid television shows about "true crimes")
New statesman society, Sept. 9, 1988, v. 1 n. n14 p. 47(2)
LC Call Number: PAR
Magazine Index Micro Film: None
Crime - television use / Television programs - social aspects / America's Most Wanted
(television program) - criticism, interpretation, etc. / Unsolved Mysteries (television
program) - criticism, interpretation, etc. / Violence in television - public opinion / Crime
in television - public opinion / Talk shows - criticism, interpretation, etc. / The Morton
Downey Jr. Show (Television program) - criticism, interpretation, etc.

Fischer, H.D. (1996)
100 Jahre Medien-Gewalt-Diskussion in Deutschland: Synopse und Bibliographie zu
einer zyklischen Entrüstung. Frankfurt am Main: IMK, 1996, 347 p., ill., bibl., ISBN 3-
927282-45-6.

Fischer, Raymond L.
It is possible to regulate television violence?
USA Today (Magazine), July 1994, v. 123 n. n2590 p. 72(4)
LC Call Number: L11.S36
Magazine Index Micro Film: None
United States. Federal Communications Commission - Social policy/ Violence in
television - Prevention/ Television broadcasting industry - Laws, regulations, etc.

Fischer, Raymond L.
Sex, drugs and TV: stretching the limits of bad taste. (Mass Media)

USA Today (Magazine), March 1990, v. 118 n. n2538 p. 46(4)
LC Call Number: L11.S36
Magazine Index Micro Film: 54B0211
Helms, Jesse - Science and technology policy / Bush, George - Science and technology
policy / Sikes, Alfred - Selection, appointment, resignation, etc. United States. Congress.
House - Science and technology policy / United States. Federal Communications
Commission - Laws, regulations, etc. / United States. Congress. Senate - Science and
technology policy / National Association of Broadcasters - Standards / Married... with
Children (Television program) - Criticism, interpretation, etc. / Sex in television - Laws,
regulations, etc. / Violence in television - Laws, regulations, etc.

Flint, Joe
TV violence: what the market will bear. (TV news magazines tone down violence to
appease advertisers)
Broadcasting and Cable, Oct. 25, 1993, v. 123 n. n43 p. 18(1)
LC Call Number: TK6540B85
Business Index Micro Film: None
TV news magazines are toning down violent content to appease advertisers, and are
reaping the benefits. 'A Current Affair' has increased ad sales by discontinuing re-
enactments and curbing sensationalism. A new entry to the genre, Warner Bros'
'Entertainment News Television,' is billing itself as an 'advertiser friendly' alternative to
existing tabloids. Advertisers may have a special interest in sponsoring nonviolent
content: One bill currently in Congress would require sponsors of such shows to be listed.
Violence in television - Management / Sensationalism in television - Management /
Television advertising - Social aspects / Television broadcasting of news - Social aspects

Foster, Benjamin P.; Wuilleumier, Rudolph B.; Mullins, Bonnie E.
A sin tax on on-screen violence.
Tax Notes, Nov. 29, 1993, v. 61 n. n9 p. 1117-1118
LC Call Number: KF6272.T39
Business Index Micro Film: None
The Clinton administration should consider imposing a sin tax on the glorification of
violence by the television and movie industries. Sin taxes are imposed on guns, tobacco
and alcohol because these items are thought to have a direct effect on medical costs. The
glorification of violence has the same effect and so should be taxed. A tax based on shots
fired, accidental deaths and intentional murders in mass media would raise a lot of
money.
Violence in television - Taxation / Violence in mass media - Taxation / Violence in
motion pictures - Taxation

Fowles, Barbara R.
Teaching children to read: an argument for television. Urban review, v. 9, summer 1976:
114-120.
"The intention of this brief paper has been, in a sense, to account for the apparent success

of The Electric Company in setting children on the path to becoming readers. While this in part serves as a response for those who criticize The Electric Company for either its conception or its execution of reading instruction, this is certainly not the primary purpose. Rather, the point is to suggest that television has particular strengths for communicating some of the abstract principles underlying our writing system…"
Television and children [U.S.] / Reading - Study and teaching / Educational television [U.S.] / The Electric Company (Television program)

Fraser, Laura
Super Bowl violence comes home. (domestic violence and televised football)
Mother Jones, Jan. 1987, v. 12 p. 15(1)
LC Call Number: AP2.M79193
Magazine Index Micro Film: 37B6098
Football (professional) - social aspects / television broadcasting of sports - social aspects / domestic relations - social aspects / violence in television - social aspects

Frau-Meigs, D. & Jchel, S. (1997)
Les écrans de la violence: Enjeux éonomiques et responsabilités sociales. Paris: Economica, 1997, 264 p., bibl., ISBN 2-71783-349-8.

Frau-Meigs, D. (1997)
La violence sur les écrans, enjeux culturels de politiques économiques. Image et violence, actes du colloque BPI 3-4 octobre 1996. Paris: BPI en Actes, 1997.

Frazer, Charles F.
The social character of children's television viewing. Communication research, v. 8, July 1981: 307-322.
"This study considers some social dimensions of children's television viewing. Review of the literature shows a paucity of data on the subject and a tendency to focus research attention on television rather than children. This study is grounded on symbolic interactionist principles and utilizes naturalistic observation in data collection. Specimens of viewing behavior are offered and an argument for sociologically grounded investigation is made."
Television [U.S.] / Sociological research [U.S.] / Child psychology [U.S.] / Television and children [U.S.]

Freedman, Tracy; Weir, David
Polluting the most vulnerable. Nation, v. 236, May 4, 2983: 600-614.
Accuses the Reagan Administration of being unconcerned with children's welfare as environmental regulations are relaxed.
Child health [U.S.] / Lead poisoning [U.S.] / Carcinogens [U.S.] / Television and children [U.S.] / U.S. Environmental Protection Agency

Freeman, Mike
'Robocop' formula: humor, humanity, hormones. (television program)
Broadcasting and cable, Jan. 24, 1994, v. 124 n. n4 p. 67(2)
LC Call Number: TK6540B85
Business Index Micro Film: None
Television production company Skyvision Entertainment and program distribution
company Rysher Entertainment Inc will produce the program 'Robocop' with less
violence than the films upon which it was based, due to the present public concern over
television violence. The television show, scheduled for introduction in March 1994, will
instead emphasize humor and emotions. The original screenwriters will be employed.
News characters for the TV show version are described.
Robocop (Motion picture) - usage / Robocop (Television program) - Planning /
Television production companies - Planning / Television program distribution companies
- Planning / Violence in television - Planning

Freeman, Mike
Violence study targets first-run; networks credited with improvement; Capitol Hill asks
for copies of report. (Center for Media and Public Affairs)
Broadcasting and Cable, Feb. 14, 1994, v. 124 n. n7 p. 30(1)
LC Call Number: TK6540B85
Business Index Micro Film: 76S0674
The most violent television programs for 1993, based on the number of serious violent
acts portrayed, were identified in a study by the Center for Media and Public Affairs
(CMPA). Included in the list are 'Star Trek: The Next Generation' and 'Star Trek: Deep
Space Nine.' as well as 'Highlander' and 'seaQuest DSV.' The CMPA also reported that
1993 television show premiers had 28% less violence than did 1992 premiers. Six of the
10 programs were from syndicators, and these independents are being asked to police the
violence content of their programming. Syndicators oppose violence warnings as an
introduction to censorship.
Center for Media and Public Affairs - Research /Violence in television - Research /
Syndication of television programs - Reports

Freeman, Mike
Violence, late-night talk wars hijack promo panel. ('Broadcast Networks in the '90s'
panel, PROMAX/BDA conference)
Broadcasting and Cable, June 21, 1993, v. 123 n. n25 p. 28(2)
LC Call Number: TK6540B85
Business Index Micro Film: 71Z2416
A panel convened at the 1993 PROMAX/BDA Conference that was intended for
discussion on brand identity for television network programs was instead dominated by
talk of late night programming and violence on television. Panel members of the
'Broadcast Networks in the 90s' forum were concerned that congressional attempts to
stop television violence would eventually lead to censorship. Other panel members
discussed demographic merits of various late night television shows, including 'The Late

Show with David Letterman' and 'The Tonight Show with Jay Leno.'
Television broadcasting industry - Conferences, meetings, seminars, etc. / Violence in
television - Conferences, meetings, seminars, etc. / Television programs - Conferences,
meetings, seminars, etc.

Friedman, David
Ball games or brawl games?
TV Guide, March 27, 1982, v. 30 p. 17(2)
LC Call Number: Microfilm 06378 (1953-) MicRR
Magazine Index Micro Film: None
television broadcasting of sports - ethical aspects/ violence in television - psychological
aspects

Friedrichsen, M. & Vowe, G. (Eds.)
(1995)
Gewaltdarstellungen in den Medien: Theorien, Fakten und Analysen. Opladen:
Westdeutscher Verlag, 1995, 418 p., ill., fig., bibl., ISBN 3-531-12768-3.

Früh, W. (1995)
Die Rezeption von Fernsehgewalt: Eine empirische Studie zum wahrgenommenen
Gewaltpotential des Fernsehangebots durch verschiedene Zielgruppen. Media
Perspektiven (1995)4, pp. 172-185, ISSN 0170-1754.

Frydman, M. (1993)
Télévision et violence: Bilan et réponses aux questions des parents et éducateurs. Paris:
Montignies sur sambre, 1993, 142 p., bibl., ISBN 2-87133-008-5.

Gabree, John
Can 'Hill Street Blues' keep dodging the Nielsen bullet?
TV Guide, Oct. 31, 1981, v. 29 p. 27(5)
LC Call Number: Microfilm 06378 (1953-) MicRR
Magazine Index Micro Film: None
Hill Street Blues (television program) - rating / television serials - rating / violence in
television - analysis

Gadget censors TV sex & violence
Moneysworth (New York), May 1982, v. 12 p. 8(1)
LC Call Number: TX335.M65; Microfilm 06132 (1973-1982) MicRR
Magazine Index Micro Film: None
DiLorenzo, Mark - research
sex in television - censorship / violence in television - censorship

Gale, Bob.
Fans of sex and violence will love the V-chip.

Wall Street Journal, Feb 21, 1996 pA140(W) pA14(E) col 3 (18 col in)
Gan, S.L.; Hill, J.R.; Pschernig, E. & Zillmann, D. (1996)
The Hebron Massacre: Selective Reports of Jewish Reactions, and Perceptions of
Volatility in Israel. Journal of Broadcasting and Electronic Media 40(1996)1, Winter, pp.
122-131, ISSN 0883-8151.

Garbarino, Steven
A farewell to arms. (gun control)
Interview (New York, N.Y. 1977) March 1994, v. 24 n. n3 p. 108(4)
Magazine Index Micro Film: None
Gun control - Citizen participation / Violence in television - Prevention

Gardella, Kay
Violence on the home screen. (address to Tri-State Catholic Committee on Radio and
Television) (Transcript)
America (New York, NY 1909) Sept. 11, 1993, v. 169 n. n6 p. 4(1)
LC Call Number: BX801.A5; Microfilm 02861 (1949-1968) MicRR
Magazine Index Micro Film: none
Violence in television - Addresses, essays, lectures / Television viewers - Political
activity

Gauntlett, D. (1995)
Moving Experiences: Understanding Television's Influences and Effects. London: John
Libbey, 1995, VIII, 148 p., bibl., ISBN 0-86196-515-9.

Gauntlett, D. (1996)
Video Critical: Children, the Environment and Media Power. Luton: University of Luton
Press, 1996, VIII, 176 p., ill., bibl., ISBN 1-86020-513-5.

Gay, Verne
Acts of violence and crime tallied in Variety study. (primetime TV shows)
Variety, August 16, 1989, v. 336 n. n5 p. 39(3)
LC Call Number: PN2000.V3 Folio; Microfilm 03722 (1905-) MicRR
Magazine Index Micro Film: None
The 25 shows with the most crime and violence. (table) Death and injury by network.
(table) Top 10 rates shows by network. (table) Top 10 most violent shows by network.
(table) Top 10 shows without crime or violence. (table)
Violence in television - statistics / Television programs - research

Geen, R.G. (1994)
Television and Aggression: Recent Developments in Research and Theory. In: Zillmann,
D. & Bryant, J. (Eds.): Media, Children, and the Family: Social Scientific,

Psychodynamic, and Clinical Perspectives, pp. 151-162, Hillsdale: Lawrence Erlbaum Associates, 1994, XIII, 351 p., ISBN 0-80581-210-5.
Gendolla, P. & Zelle, C. (Eds.)
(1990)
Schönheit und Schrecken: Entsetzen, Gewalt und Tod in alten und neuen Medien. Heidelberg: Winter, 1990, 239 p., ill., bibl., ISBN 3-533-04215-4.

Gentikow, B. (1997)
Medievold og samfunnsvold [Violence in the Media and in the Society]. Bergen: Institutt for medievitenskap, Bergens universitet, 1997, 40 p., ill., ISBN 82-578-0370-7.

Gentikow, B. (1998)
Eksesser: et kulturkritisk blikk på sex- og voldstekster [Orgies: A Cultural Critical Prospective on Texts with Sex and Violence Contents]. Norsk Medietidsskrift 2(1998) Spec. Issue, pp. 32-53, ISSN 0804-8452.

Gerbner, G. (1992)
Violence and Terror In and By the Media. In: Raboy, M. & Dagenais, B. (Eds.): Media, Crisis, and Democracy: Mass Communication and the Disruption of Social Order, pp. 94-107, London: Sage Publications, 1992, 199 p., ISBN 0-8039-8640-8.

Gerbner, G. (1993)
Violence in Cable Originated Television Programs: A Report to the National Cable Television Association. Washington D.C.: National Cable Television Association, 1993, 15 p.

Gerbner, George and others.
The "mainstreaming" of America: violence profile no. 11. Journal of communication, v. 30, summer 1980: 10-29.
"In addition to bringing the Violence Profile up to date, we present a new formulation of our methodological and theoretical position based on new findings and relating to the work of these investigators."
Violence in television [U.S.] / Violence research [U.S.]

Gerbner, George and others.
Trends in network television drama and viewer conceptions of social reality 1967-1977. Philadelphia, Annenberg School of Communications, University of Pennsylvania, 1978. 1 v. (various pagings) (Pennsylvania. University. Annenberg School of Communications. Violence profile no. 9)
"Television violence dropped sharply in 1977 from the record high reached a year ago. But the evidence continues to indicate television's cumulative cultivation of viewer conceptions of danger, mistrust, and alienation. Moreover, new data suggest that heavy viewers of police and crime shows are more likely than light viewers to act on these

conceptions: they report acquiring locks, dogs and guns to protect themselves."
Television viewers [U.S.] / Violence in television [U.S.] / Social surveys [U.S.]
Gerbner, George
Death in prime time: notes on the symbolic functions of dying in the mass media.
Annals of the American Academy of Political and Social Science, Jan. 1980, v. 447 p.
64(7)
LC Call Number: H1.A4
Magazine Index Micro Film: None
Death - television use / violence in television - social aspects

Gilbert, W. Stephan
Mediations
New statesman society, Sept. 23, 1988, v. 1 n. n16 p. 42(1)
LC Call Number: PAR
Magazine Index Micro Film: None
Violence in television - analysis / Arts - Censorship / Theater - Censorship

Gillespie, Nick
Meek previews.
Reason, May 1994 v26 n1 p42(2)
Gilliam, Dorothy
Because violence is no fun.
The Washington Post, Feb 17, 1996 v119 pCl col 1 (22 col in)

Giroux, H.A. (1995)
Pulp Fiction and the Culture of Violence. Harvard Educational Review 65(1995)2,
Summer, pp. 299-314, ISSN 0017-8055.

Giroux, H.A. (1995)
Racism and the Aesthetic of Hyper-Real Violence: Pulp Fiction and Other Visual
Tragedies. Social Identities 1(1995)2, August, pp. 333-354, ISSN 1350-4630.

Giroux, H.A. (1996)
Fugitive Cultures: Race, Violence, and Youth. New York: Routledge, 1996, VIII, 247 p.,
bibl., ISBN 0-415-91578-8.

Gitlin, Todd
"The symbolic crusade against media violence is a confession of despair." (factors
influencing street violence)
The Chronicle of Higher Education, Feb. 23, 1994, v. 40 n. n25 p. B5(1)
LC Call Number: Not in LC Collection
Magazine Index Micro Film: None
Influential people crusading against television violence must realize that street violence
can also be attributed to existing social problems. Access to lethal weapons and the

absence of parental authority contribute to the increase in violence, and the public must pay more attention to social issues. Television violence deserves criticism, but it is not the root cause of street violence.
Violence - Social aspects / Violence in television - Influence

Gitlin, Todd
Imagebusters: the hollow crusade against TV violence. American prospect, no. 16, winter 1994: 42-49.
"The question liberal crusaders fail to address is just how much real-world violence can be blamed on the media."
Violence in television [U.S.] / Television and children [U.S.] / Censorship [U.S.] / Television industry [U.S.]

Glazer, Sarah
Preschool: too much too soon? Washington, Congressional Quarterly, 1988. 54-6 p. (Editorial research reports, 1988, v. 1, no. 5)
Partial contents - Debate over curriculum. The behaviorists rebut. Techniques defended. Divided developmentalists. Why so academic? Older kindergartners
Preschool education [U.S.] / Kindergarten [U.S.] / Child development [U.S.] / Day care [U.S.] / Television and children [U.S.]

Goldman, Kevin
Is it action or violence from MCA TV? (MCA Television to advertise its action/ adventure show 'Vanishing Son') (Column)
The Wall Street Journal, Nov. 18, 1993, p. B12 (W) ppB
LC Call Number: See Catalogs or Staff
Business Index Micro Film: None
Television production companies - Advertising / Advertising agencies - Contracts / Violence in television - Economic aspects

Goldman, Kevin
It is action or violence from MCA TV?(MCA Television to advertiser its action/ adventure show 'Vanishing Son') (Column)
The Wall Street Journal, Nov. 18, 1993, p. B12 (W) ppB
LC Call Number: See Catalogs or Staff
Magazine Index Micro Film: None
Television production companies - Advertising / Advertising agencies - Contracts / Violence in television - Economic aspects

Goldsborough, Robert
Beavis pales next to TV news: Ad Age reviewer takes a look at violent comment on the tube.
Advertising Age, Nov 1, 1993 v64 n46 p8(1)

Goldsborough, Robert
Beavis pales next to TV news: Ad Age reviewer takes a look at violent content on the
tube
Advertising Age, Nov. 1, 1993, v. 64 n. n46 p. 8(1)
LC Call Number: HF5801.A276
Business Index Micro Film: 74Y4290
There was more violence on television news than in either 'Beavis and Butt-Head' or
'NYPD BLUE' during a comparison of episodes of those programs on Oct. 22, 1993 and
Oct. 26, 1993 respectively. The news broadcast was analyzed on Oct. 26th. The 'Beavis
and Butt-Head' episode was not so much violent as vulgar. On 'NYPD Blue' there was
no more violence than on other detective programs, but there was more gratuitous sex.
The news program had stories about a child molester, a man who killed his former
girlfriend's new boyfriend and a 52 year old pedestrian who was severely injured by a
hit-and-run driver.
NYPD Blue (Television program) - Criticism, interpretation, etc. / Beavis and Butt-Head
(Television program) - Criticism, interpretation, etc. / Violence in television - Analysis /
Television broadcasting of news - Analysis

Goldstein, J. (1996)
Television Violence in America: Summary and Critique of Two Recent Studies.
Communicatio Socialis 29(1996)3, pp. 371-378, ISSN 0010-3497.

Goldstein, J. (Ed.) (1998)
Why We Watch: The Attractions of Violent Entertainment. Oxford: Oxford University
Press, 1998, 288 p., ill., bibl., ISBN 0-19-511821-9.

Gollin, Albert E.; Anderson, Thelma
Mass media in the family setting: social patterns in media availability and use by parents.
[New York] Newspaper Readership Project, 1980. 60 p.
"NRP: 80-01"
"Families that comprise a representative sample of American households with children
age 6 to 17 were interviewed as part of a nationwide study of the media habits and
attitudes of children and their mothers. Data for this report come from the sample of
mothers, who provided information on household characteristics and family media use."
Families [U.S.] / Mass media [U.S.] / Social surveys [U.S.] / Social classes [U.S.] /
Television and children [U.S.] / Reading [U.S.]

Gómes, L. (1997)
Violencia en la televisión. Caracas: Comité por una Radiotelevisión de Servicio Público,
1997, 32 p., bibl.

Goodman, Ellen
What the V-chip can't do.
The Washington Post, Feb 17, 1996 v119 pA25 col 5 (15 col in)

Goodman, Walter
Qualifying the quantity of on-screen violence. (the Center for Media and Public Affairs report 'A Day of TV Violence') (Living Arts Pages)
The New York Times, August 30, 1994, v. 143 p. B3 (N) pC20
LC Call Number: Not in LC Collection
Magazine Index Micro Film: None
Violence in television - Analysis

Goodnow, K. J. (1992)
Alien/Aliens: Analyzing the Forms and Sources of Horror. Bergen: Universitetet i Bergen, Institutt for massekommunikasjon, 1992, 162 p., ISSN 081-2814.

Goonasekera, A. (1990)
Lock, Yut, Kam: Violence on Television in Asia. Asian Journal of Communication 1(1990)1, pp. 136-146, ISSN 0129-2986.

Gosselin, A. (1993)
Violence et effet d'incubation de la télévision: La thèse de la cultivation analysis.
Québec: Département d'information et de communication, Université Laval, 1993, 69 p., bibl., ISBN 2-92138-305-5.

Gosselin, A. (1994)
Média et violence. Dimensions micro-macro des modèles d'explication. Québec: Département d'information et de communication, Université Laval, 1994, 45 p., bibl., ISBN 2-92138-307-1.

Green, Charlie
Do violent 'toons lead to violent teens? (study will evaluate network television programs for violence) (Brief Article)
Business Week, August 29, 1994, n. n3387 p. 6(1)
LC Call Number: HF5001.B89; Microfilm 01956 (1929-   ) MicRR
Business Index Micro Film: none
Violence in television - Research / Television broadcasting industry - Evaluation

Green, Michelle
Flying chairs and fists on his talk show give Geraldo Rivera a busted nose - and another rating break.
People (Chicago, 1974) Nov. 21, 1988, v. 30 n. n21 p. 60(2)
LC Call Number: AP2.P417
Magazine Index Micro Film: 47D0943
Geraldo Rivera (portrait)
Rivera, Geraldo - wounds and injuries / Violence in television - cases / Geraldo (Television program) - production and direction

Greenfield, Jeff
TV is not the world. Columbia journalism review, v. 17, May-June 1978: 29-34
Contends that the critics of television have overestimated its power and have not
addressed the fact that "our major instrument of entertainment and news is geared to the
direct financial interest of the largest corporations in the United States, and that the
possession of huge sums of money is the dominant method of access to this instrument."
Proposes governmental actions to reform the medium.
Television broadcasting [U.S.] / Television and children [U.S.] / Television advertising
[U.S.]

Greenfield, Meg
TV's true violence. (depictions of real and fictional violence) (Column)
Newsweek, June 21, 1993, v. 121 n. n25 p. 72(1)
LC Call Number: AP2.N6772; Microfilm 01125 (1933-) MicRR
Magazine Index Micro Film: None
Violence in television - Moral and ethical aspects

Gripsrud, J. (1993)
Skräck och fasa i kropp och själ: Om en historisk förflyttning i skräckfiktionens fokus
[Filled With Horror: On a Change in Focus of Horror Fiction]. In: von Feilitzen, C.;
Forsman, M. & Roe, K. (Eds.): Våld från alla håll: Forskningsperspektiv på våld i rörliga
bilder, pp. 227-248, Stockholm: Brutus Östlings Bokförlag Symposion, 1993, 383 p.,
ISBN 91-7139-123-1.

Grobel, Lawrence
The new violence patrol. (TV violence watchdogs March Kelly and Jeffrey Cole)
TV Guide, August 20, 1994, v. 42 n. n34 p. 22(4)
LC Call Number: Microfilm 06378 (1953-) MicRR
Magazine Index Micro Film: None
Kelly, Marcy - Research / Cole, Jeffrey - Research
Violence in television - Research

Groebel, J. & Gleich, U. (1993)
Gewaltprofil des deutschen Fernsehprogramms: Eine Analyse des Angebots privater und
öffentlich-rechtlicher Sender. Opladen: Leske und Budrich, 1993, 134 p. + app. 40 p.,
tab., fig., bibl., ISBN 3-8100-1093-6.

Groebel, J. & Smit, L. (1996)
Media en geweld: Inventariserend onderzoek [Media and Violence: Investigated Study].
Utrecht: Universiteit Utrecht, Vakgroep Massacommunicatie, 1996, 73 p., ISBN 9-
03463-364-0.

Groebel, J. & Smit, L. (1997)
Gewalt im Internet: Report für die Enquete-Kommission 'Zukunft der Medien' des

Deutschen Bundestages. Utrecht: Dept. Media Psychology, Universität Utrecht, 1997, 54 p., tab.

Groebel, J. (1998)
The UNESCO Global Study on Media Violence: A Joint Project of UNESCO, the World Organization of the Scout Movement and Utrecht University. Paris: UNESCO, 1998, 19 p., bibl.

Groller, Ingrid
TV & Family life: do they mix?
Parents, (Bergenfield), May 1987, v. 62 p. 32(1)
LC Call Number: HQ768.P33
Magazine Index Micro Film: 39A5287
Violence in television - surveys / Television and children - surveys / Television and family - social aspects

Grossberg, L.; Wartella, E. & Whitney, D.C. (1998)
Mediamaking: Mass Media in a Popular Culture. Thousand Oaks: Sage Publications, 1998, XVIII, 442 p., bibl., ISBN 0-76191-176-6.

Group of 64 organizations. (coalition formed to oppose antiviolence legislation)
Television Digest, Jan. 31, 1994, v. 34 n. n5 p. 8(1)
LC Call Number: May or May Not Be in LC. Search further.
Business Index Micro Film: 76N0178
Violence in television - Political aspects

Grube, Joel W., Wallack, Lawrence
Television beer advertising and drinking knowledge, beliefs, and intentions among school children. American Journal of Public Health, v. 84, Feb. 1994: 254-259.
"The findings suggest that alcohol advertising may predispose young people to drinking. As a result, efforts to prevent drinking and drinking problems among young people should give attention to countering the potential effects of alcohol advertising."
Television and children [U.S.] / Advertising [U.S.] / Alcoholic beverages [U.S.]

Guild, Hazel
Ghoulish TV news is a real turnoff for German chief. (Helmut Schmidt dislikes TV violence)
Variety, May 20, 1981, v. 303 p. 1(2)
LC Call Number: PN2000.V3 Folio; Microfilm 03722 (1905-) MicRR
Magazine Index Micro Film: None
Schmidt, Helmut - social policy
Television broadcasting of news - Germany, West / violence in television - Germany, West / German Reading Association - meetings / newspapers - Germany, West Germany, West

Gunter, B. & Harrison, J. (1998)
Violence on Television: An Analysis of Amount, Nature, Location and Origin of
Violence in British Programmes. London: Routledge, 1998, XIII, 330 p., bibl., ISBN 0-
415-17260-8.

Gunter, Barrie
Dimensions of television violence / Barrie Gunter. - New York: St. Martin's Press, 1985
ix, 282 p.: ill.; 23 cm. Bibliography: p. 263-274. Includes index.
Violence in television. Title. Bibliography: p. 263-274.

Gustafsson, ; Filipson, L. & Eckert, G. (1995)
TV – bundsförvant eller fiende? Om barn, föräldrar och tv-tittande [Television –
Companion or Enemy? On Children, Parents and Television Viewing]. Stockholm:
Kulturdepartementet, Våldsskildringsrådet, 1995, 134 p., fig., tab., ISSN 1102-447X.

Haden-Guest, Anthony
The man who's killing TV violence. New York, v. 10, July 11, 1977: 33-36.
Surveys efforts of George Gerbner to curb television violence. Notes that "for ten years,
Gerbner and a miniscule staff have been doing the only constant, systematic research on
TV violence."
Television programs [U.S.] / Violence in television [U.S.] / Gerbner, George

Hagell, A. & Newburn, T. (1994)
Young Offenders and the Media: Viewing Habits and Preferences. London: Policy
Studies Institute, 1994, XVI, 105 p., ill., bibl., ISBN 0-85374-614-1.

Haire, Kevlin C.
Is 'Homicide' scaring away visitors? (effect of television program on Maryland tourism
industry) (Special Report: Tourism)
Baltimore Business Journal, Feb. 11, 1994, v. 11 n. n38 p. 13(2)
LC Call Number: May or May Not Be in LC. Search Further.
Business Index Micro Film: 78Q4671
Homicide: Life on the Street (Television program) - Economic aspects / Violence in
television - Economic aspects / Tourist industry - Maryland / Maryland - Business and
industry / Baltimore, Maryland - Portrayals, depictions, etc.

Haire, Kevlin C.
WMAR promoting its policy of 'no body bags.' (television station; policy to delete
graphic violence)
Baltimore Business Journal, July 8, 1994, v. 12 n. n7 p. 9(1)
LC Call Number: May or May Not Be in LC. Search further.
Business Index Micro Film: None
WMAR, Baltimore, Maryland (Television) - Management / Violence in television -
Social aspects

Haldar, M. (1996)
"Leve lykkelig med sukker på": en studie av vold- og seksualitetsforestillinger i barns fjernsynsverden og i barns hverdagsverden [A Study on Ideas of Violence and Sex in Children's Television World and in Their Every Day World]. Oslo: Politihøgskolens forskningsavdeling, 1996, 179 p., ISBN 82-90019-14-9.

Hämäläinen, V. (1989)
Joukkoviestinnän ja väkivallan väliset yhteydet sekä lehtikirjoittelu väkivallasta: väkivaltaa vastaan -projektin julkisuustavoitteen kannalta [The connection between mass communication and violence, and press writing about violence from the point of view of publicity targets set in the project Against violence]. Helsinki: University of Helsinki, Department of Communication, 1989, 60 p. + app.

Hargrave, A.M. (1996)
Teenagers. London: Broadcasting Standards Council, 1996, 77 p., tab., chart.

Hargrave, A.M. (Ed.) (1993)
Violence in Factual Television. London: John Libbey, 1993, VIII, 151 p., ISBN 0-86196-441-1.

Harris, Mike
Oz PM slams TV violence. (Australian Prime Minister Paul Keating) (Brief Article)
Variety, Nov. 9, 1992, v. 349 n. n3 p. 40(2)
LC Call Number: PN2000.V3 Folio; Microfilm 03722 (1905-   ) MicRR
Magazine Index Micro Film: None
Keating, Paul - Social policy
Violence in television - Australia / Australia - Popular culture. Australia

Hart, Marion
Thea-trically. (television comedy 'Thea' is judged to be TV's tenth most violent show) (Brief Article)
Entertainment Weekly, Feb. 4,1994, n. n208 p. 13(1)
LC Call Number: PN1993.E59
Magazine Index Micro Film: None
Thea (Television program) - Social aspects / Violence in television - Statistics

Health & Human Services. (Secretary Donna Shalala)
Television Digest, Dec. 20, 1993, v. 33 n. n51 p. 7(1)
LC Call Number: May or May Not Be in LC. Search further.
Business Index Micro Film: 75P0696
Shalala, Donna E. - Social policy
Violence in television - Social aspects / Television broadcasting industry - Social policy

Heath, L. & Gilbert, K. (1996)
Mass Media and Fear of Crime. American Behavioral Scientist 39(1996)Fall, pp. 379-386, ISSN 0002-7642.
Herbert, Bob
Violence in real life. (legislators act like they have done something about crime by getting television executives to place a disclaimer on some programming, instead of dealing with everyday violence and crime in American cities) (Column)
The New York Times, July 11, 1993, v. 142 p. E19(N) pE1
LC Call Number: Not in L C Collection
Magazine Index Micro Film: None
United States. Congress. Senate - Social policy / Violence in television - Laws, regulations, etc. / Violent crimes - Statistics

Hertzberg, L.J.; Ostrum, G.F. & Field, J.R. (Eds.)
(1990)
Violent Behavior, Vol. 1: Assessment and Intervention. Great Neck: PMA Publishing Corporations, 1990, XII, 339 p., ill., ISBN 0893352209.

Hesse, P. & Mack, J.E. (1991)
The World is a Dangerous Place: Images of the Enemy on Children's Television. In: Rieber, R.W. (Ed.): The Psychology of War and Peace: The Image of the Enemy, pp. 131-153, New York: Plenum Press, 1991, XX, 282 p., ill., ISBN 0306435438.

Hickey, Neil
How much violence? (portrayal of violence on television) (includes an article on the effects of TV violence on children) (Cover Story)
TV Guide, August 22, 1992, v. 40 n. n34 p. 10(2)
LC Call Number: Microfilm 06378 (1953-) MicRR
Magazine Index Micro Film: None
Center for Media and Public Affairs - Reports / Violence in television - Statistics / Television programs - Social aspects

Hickey, Neil
New violence survey released. (violence on television)
TV guide, August 13, 1994, v. 42 n. n33 p. 37(3)
LC Call Number: Microfilm 06378 (1953-   ) MicRR
Magazine Index Micro Film: None
Violence in television - Reports / Television - Social aspects

Higgins, Patricia Beaulieu
Television's action arsenal: weapon use in prime time / by Patricia Beaulieu Higgins, Marla Wilson Ray. [Washington]: United States Conference of Mayors, c1978.
57 p.; 23 cm. Includes bibliographical references.

Violence in television - United States. Television programs - United States. Ray, Marla Wilson, joint author. I Title.

Hill, A. (1997)
Shocking Entertainment: Viewer Response to Violent Movies. Luton: University of Luton Press, 1997, 131 p., ill., bibl., ISBN 1-86020-525-9.

Hindu social reform. (Hindu social reform group campaigns against sex-and-violence culture cultivated by western TV networks)
Television Digest, Dec. 27, 1993, v. 33 n. n52 p. 6(1)
LC Call Number: May or May Not Be In LC. Search further
Business Index Micro Film: 75N0115
Violence in television - Evaluation / Sex in television - Evaluation / Hindus - Demonstrations, protests, etc. / New Delhi, India - Demonstrations, protests, etc.
New Delhi, India

Hirsch, Paul M.
Public policy towards television: mass media and education in American society. School review, v. 85, Aug. 1977: 481-512.
Traces the growth of mass communications in the United States from the first newspapers through the development of radio to the present dominant role of television. Points out that little is known about the effect of television viewing on the individual, but that for society as a whole television creates a commonly shared culture which unifies the many diverse elements of contemporary American society.
Mass media [U.S.] / Television programs [U.S.] / Television and children [U.S.] / Culture [U.S.]

Hoefer, G. & Janssen, S.R. (1995)
Gewalt als Unterhaltung im Kinderfernsehen? Analysen von Actionserien und Zeichentrickprogrammen. Coppengrave: Coppi-Verlag, 1995, 309 p., fig., bibl., ISBN 3-93025-807-2.

Hoefer, G. (1995)
Fernsehen für Kinder? Gewaltstrukturen und konservative Rollenbilder in den beliebtesten Kinderprogrammen. Coppengrave: Coppi-Verlag, 1995, 171 p., ISBN 3-930258-06-4.

Hoffman, A.M. (Ed.)
(1996)
Schools, Violence, and Society. Westport: Praeger Publishers, 1996, XIII, 357 p., bibl., ISBN 0-275-94978-8.

Höijer, B. & Andén-Papadopoulus, K. (Eds.) (1996)
Våldsamma nyheter: perspektiv på dokumentära våldsskildringar i media [Violent News:

Perspectives on Documentary Descriptions of Violence Media]. Stockholm/Stehag: Brutus Östlings Bokförlag Symposion, 1996, 238 p., ill., ISBN 91-7139-274-2.

Höijer, B. (1994)
Våldsskildringar i TV-nyheter: produktion, utbud, publik [Violence in Television News: Production, Content, Audience]. Stockholm: Kulturdepartementet, Våldsskildringsrådet, 1994, 98 p., tab., ISSN 1102-447X.

Höijer, B. (1996)
The Dilemmas of Documentary Violence in Television. The Nordicom Review (1996)1, pp. 53-61, ISSN 0349-6244.

Holland, Patricia
Thrills and bills. (violence in entertainment media)
New statesman society, April 22, 1994, v. 7 n. n299 p. 35(2)
LC Call Number: PAR
Magazine Index Micro Film: None
Violence in mass media - Analysis / Violence in television - Analysis / Violence in motion pictures - Analysis

Holland, Patricia.
Thrills and bills.
New Statesman & Society, April 22, 1994 v7 n299 p35(2)

Holm Sörensen, B.; Beckmann, J. & Bjerrum, B. et al. (1995)
Medievold: børn og unge [Media Violence: Children and Young People]. København: Kulturministeriet, 1995, 78 p., bibl., ISBN 87-601-4820-9.

Holman, Richard L.
France takes aim at TV violence. (World Wire)
The Wall Street Journal, Dec. 2, 1993, p. A10 (E)
LC Call Number: See Catalogs or Staff
Business Index Micro Film: None
Violence in television - France / France - Social policy

Honig, Bill
Should schools turn off channel one? Business and society review, no. 74, summer 1990: 11-14.
"This plan to convert our schools from an educational to a commercial purpose should be nipped in the bud. Educators in New York, California, North Carolina, and other states across the nation have sent that message loudly and clearly to Channel One."
Educational television [U.S.] / Cable television [U.S.] / Television advertising [U.S.] / Television and children [U.S.]

Hornik, Robert C.
Television access and the slowing of cognitive growth. American educational research journal, v. 15, winter 1978: 1-15.
Reviews the research literature concerning the effect of television on school performance, focusing on a study done in El Salvador. The effect of television access on three groups of junior high students was studied over a two to three year period. "There was no obvious effect on short-term achievement. There were, however, consistent negative effects on reading improvement for all three cohorts, and a significant negative effect on general ability growth for one."
Television and children [El Salvador] Research / Academic performance [El Salvador]

How violent is television?
Christian Herald (Chappaqua) Sept. 1982, v. 105 p. 58(1)
LC Call Number: BR1.C63; Microfilm 01104 (1818-1845) MicRR
Magazine Index Micro Film: None
Violence in television - social aspects / National Coalition on Television Violence - reports

Hughes, John
More sleaze on TV.
The Christian Science Monitor, Sep 12, 1996 v88 n202 p20 col 3 (14 col in)

Hurka, H.M. (1997)
Phantasmen der Gewalt: Die mediale Konstruktion des Opfers. Wien: Passagen Verlag, 1997, 179 p., ISBN 3-85165-262-2.
Husson, William
Theoretical issues in the study of children's attention to television. Communication's research, v. 9, July 1982: 323-351.
"Indicates that there are many factors that should be considered when evaluating the way children attend to the television screen. In particular, the effects of three factors - television stimulus attributes, the child's level of cognitive development, and the nature of the viewing environment - may have a significant impact on a child's overall pattern of attention."
Television and children [U.S.]

Huston, A.C.; Donnerstein, E.; Fairchild, H.; Feshbach, N.D.; Katz, P.A.; Murray, J.P.; Rubinstein, E.A.; Wilcox, B.L. & Zuckerman, D. (1992)
Big World, Small Screen: The Role of Television in American Society. Lincoln: University of Nebraska Press, 1992, VIII, 195 p., ISBN 0-80322-359-9.

Huston, Aletha C., and others
Communicating more than content: formal features of children's television programs.
Journal of communications, v. 31, summer 1981: 32-38.
"The origins, development, and evaluations of the Child Development Associate

Credential program are reviewed to provide the framework of its assumptions and implications for current practice. Several concerns are raised about the potential biases and narrowness inherent in the system."
Television and children [U.S.]

Hvitfelt, H. (Ed.)
(1994)
En studie i brott: Aktuellt, Rapport och TV4-Nyheterna granskade [A Study in Crime: The Television News Programmes "Aktuellt", "Rapport" and "TV4-Nyheterna" Reviewed]. Stockholm: Näringslivets Mediainstitut/NMI, 1994, 20 p., fig., tab., ISSN 1101-2587.

IDSA and SPA meet on ratings. (Interactive Digital Software Assn.; Software Publishers Assn.) (Consumer Electronics)
Television Digest, July 11, 1994, v. 34 n. n28 p. 13(1)
LC Call Number: May or May Not Be in LC. Search further.
Business Index Micro Film: 79X0176
Software Publishers Association - Conferences, meetings, seminars, etc. / Trade and professional associations - Conferences, meetings, seminars, etc. / Violence in television - Conferences, meetings, seminars, etc.

Independent Broadcasting Authority. Working Party on the Portrayal of Violence on Independent Television. The portrayal of violence on television: Working Party second interim report. London: Independent Broadcasting Authority, 1975.
8 p.; 23 cm. Cover title.
Violence in television. Title.

Industry to approve standard blocking violent TV shows. (technical standard for new television sets to block out shows parents don't want their children to see; Electronics Industry Association)
The Wall Street Journal, July 11, 1994, p. B6(W) pB5
LC Call Number: See Catalogs or Staff
Business Index Micro Film: None
Electronic Industries Association - Standards / Television sets - Safety and security measures / Violence in television - Rating

Is TV violence more harmful than we think?
Christianity Today (Washington), Dec. 11, 1981, v. 25 p. 66(1)
LC Call Number: BR1.C6418; Microfilm (0) 83/406 (1981-   ) MicRR
Magazine Index Micro Film: None
violence in television - research / television - moral and religious aspects

It's safer on TV. (decreasing number of violent incidences portrayed on TV) (Brief Article)
Time (Chicago), August 16, 1993, v. 142 n. n7 p. 17(1)
LC Call Number: AP2.T37; Microfilm 02914 (1923-) MicRR
Business Index Micro Film: None
Violence in television - Statistics

Jarlbro, G. & Jönsson, A. (1995)
Våldsbrott i svensk press: en jämförelse mellan åren 1983 och 1993 [Violent Crime in the Swedish Press: A Comparison between 1983 and 1993]. Göteborg: Göteborgs universitet, 1995, 41 p., tab., ISSN 1101-4679.

Jehel-Cathelineau S. (Ed.)
(1995)
Enquête sur la représentation de la violence dans la fiction à la télévision en France. Paris: Conseil Supérieur de l'Audiovisuel, 1995, 88 p. Tab., fig., ISBN 2-4-089435-0.

Jenish, D'Arcy
Prime-time violence: despite high ratings for violent shows, revulsion is growing over bloodshed on TV. (Cover Story)
Maclean's, Dec. 7, 1992, v. 105 n. n19 p. 40(4)
LC Call Number: AP5.M2; Microfilm (0) 84/200 (1909-1982) MicRR
Magazine Index Micro Film: None
Violence in television - Psychological aspects / Television programs - Production and direction / Canada - Social policy. Canada.

Jensen, Elizabeth
Networks pick UCLA to study violence, hoping to pre-empt government action. (University of California, Los Angeles' Center for Communication Policy picked to analyze violence on television programs)
The Wall Street Journal, June 30, 1994, p. B5(W) pB9
LC Call Number: See Catalogs or Staff
Business Index Micro Film: None
United States. Congress. Senate - Social policy / California, University of (Los Angeles) - Research / Television broadcasting industry - Research / Violence in television - Research

Jensen, Elizabeth
One-day study finds rise in violence on TV, but research method is disputed. (Center for Media and Public Affairs study for Harry Frank Guggenheim Foundation)
The Wall Street Journal, August 5, 1994, p. B10(W) pB1
LC Call Number: See Catalogs or Staff
Business Index Micro Film: None

Franks, Martin - Management
Violence in television - Reports / Television broadcasting industry - Management

Jensen, Elizabeth; Graham, Ellen
Stamping out TV violence: a losing fight. (includes related information)
The Wall Street Journal, Oct. 26, 1993, p. B1 (W) ppB1
LC Call Number: See Catalogs or Staff
Magazine Index Micro Film: None
United States. Congress - Social policy / Violence in television - Analysis / Television
broadcasting - Moral and ethical aspects / Television and children - Social aspects /
Violence research - Evaluation

Jensen, J.F. (1993)
Powerplay: maskulinitet, makt och våld i datorspel [Powerplay: Masculinity, Power and
Violence in Computer Games]. In: von Feilitzen, C.; Forsman, M. & Roe, K. (Eds.): Våld
från alla håll: Forskningsperspektiv på våld i rörliga bilder, pp. 151-
173, Stockholm: Brutus Östlings Bokförlag Symposion, 1993, 383 p., ISBN 91-7139-
123-1.

Jessell, Harry A.
Washington watch (includes multiple briefs on various topics)
Broadcasting and Cable, May 10, 1993   v. 123 n. n19 p. 37(1)
LC Call Number: TK6540B85
Business Index Micro Film: 71Q1506
Clinton, Bill - Science and technology policy / Neel, Roy - Selection, appointment,
resignation, etc. / Sikes, Alfred - Evidence / Fishel, Andy - Evidence / Brown, Bob -
Selection, appointment, resignation, etc.
United Stated. Federal Communications Commission - Cases / United States Telephone
Association - Officials and employees / Harry Frank Guggenheim Foundation - Reports /
Telecommunications policy - Analysis / Cable television - Prices and rates / Violence in
television - Reports

Jillette, Penn.
Warning: this is a violent article.
Playboy, Sept 1994 v41 n9 p46(2)

Johnson, J.D.; Adams, M.S.; Hall, W. & Ashburn, L. (1997)
Race, Media, and Violence: Differential Racial Effects of Exposure to Violent News
Stories. Basic and Applied Social Psychology 19(1997)1, pp. 81-90, ISSN 0197-3533.

Jones, Laurie
AMA: give parents tools to judge TV, video violence. (American Medical Association)
American Medical News, July 25, 1994, v. 37 n. n28 p.8(1)
LC Call Number: Microfilm 02679

Business Index Micro Film: None
American Medical Assn (AMA) Pres. Dr. Robert E. McAfee called for a uniform rating system for motion pictures, television programs and video games in testimony before the House Energy and Commerce Telecommunications and Finance Subcommittee. McAfee said that parents need an easily understandable system for judging the exposure of their children to violence. Subcommittee Chmn. Edward J. Markey is sponsoring a bill that would require television sets to contain a chip that would allow parents to block out certain programs. The subcommittee particularly is worried about violence in video games, which are unregulated.
Markey, Edward J. - Social policy / McAfee, Robert E. - Social policy
American Medical Association - Social policy / Violence in television - Social policy

Kalamas, A.D. & Gruber, M.L. (1998)
Electrodermal Response to Implied Versus Actual Violence on Television. Journal of General Psychology 125(1998)1, pp. 31-37, ISSN 0022-1309.

Kalis, P. & Neundorf, K.A. (1989)
Aggressive Cue Prominence and Gender Participation in MTV. Journalism Quarterly 66(1989)1, Spring, pp. 148-154, 229, ISSN 0196-3031.

Katzman, Solomon, Katzman, Nathan
Public television programming content by category fiscal year 1978. [Washington] Corporation for Public Broadcasting [1979] 106 p.
Contents. Definitions and categories. The PTV system in fiscal year 1978. Instructional television services. Sesame Street and the electric company. "General" and news/public affairs programs. Special or target audience programs. Local programming. PBS and prime-time programming.
Public television [U.S.] / Educational television [U.S.] / Television programs [U.S.] / Television and children [U.S.] / Television news [U.S.]

Kelly, P.T. (Ed.) (1996)
Television Violence: A Guide to the Literature. New York: Nova Science Publishers, 1996, 195 p., ISBN 1-56072-299-1.

Keppler, A. (1997)
Über einige Formen der medialen Wahrnehmung von Gewalt. Kölner Zeitschrift für Soziologie und Sozialpsychologie 37(1997)
Spec. supplement, pp. 380-400, ISSN 0023-2653.

Kepplinger, H.M. & Giesselmann, T. (1993)
Die Wirkungen von Gewaltdarstellungen in der aktuellen Fernsehberichterstattung: Eine konfliktteoretische Analyse. Medienpsychologie 5(1993)3, pp. 160-189, ISSN 0936-7780.

Kim, Stephen J.
"Viewer discretion is advised": a structural approach to the issue of television violence. University of Pennsylvania law review, v. 142, Apr. 1994: 1383-1441.
"This comment addresses the issue of television violence from a structural perspective which recognizes program content as the product of a complex web of market, organizational, legal and occupational, legal and occupational constraints that restrict creativity and innovation in the industry. Viewed from this perspective, the problem of television violence emerges as a symptom of a larger dilemma: the industry's reliance on the convention of violence is an example of how networks, advertisers, and producers have fallen into a cycle of dependence on formulae and routines to deal with uncertainty in the television market. Solutions to this problem require the removal of structural constraints rather than the imposition of additional content-based restrictions which, unfortunately, have recently gained public momentum."
Violence in television [U.S.] Research / Violence research [U.S.] / Television programs [U.S.] Economic aspects / Television industry [U.S.] Social aspects

Kinder, M. (1991)
Playing With Power in Movies, Television and Video Games: From Muppet Babies to Teenage Mutant Ninja Turtles. Berkeley: University of California Press, 1991, XI, 266 p., ISBN 0-52007-570-6.

Kliment, T. (1996)
Kollektive Gewalt und Massenmedien: Anmerkungen zur Forschungslage. Forschungsjournal Neue Soziale Bewegungen 9(1996)1, pp. 46-58, ISSN 0933-9361.

Knoll, J.H. (1993)
Gewalt und Spiele: Gewalt und Videospiel im Widerstreit der Meinungen. Düsseldorf: Livonia, 1993, 217 p., ill., bibl., ISBN 3-928795-08-2.

Kodaira, S. (1998)
A Review of Research on Media Violence in Japan. In: Carlsson, U. & von Feilitzen, C. (Eds.): Children and Media Violence: Yearbook from the UNESCO International Clearinghouse on Children and Violence on the Screen 1998, pp. 81-105, Göteborg: Nordicom, Göteborgs universitet, 1998, 387 p., ISBN 91-630-6358-1.

Kofler, G. & Graf, G. (Eds.) (1995)
Sündenbock Fernsehen? Aktuelle Befunde zur Fernsehnutzung von Jugendlichen, zur Wirkung von Gewaltdarstellungen im Fernsehen und zur Jugendkriminalität. Berlin: Vistas Verlag, 1995, 171 p., ISBN 3-89158-142-4.
Kolbert, Elizabeth
Study finds TV violence on the rise; compares stations in 1992 and 1994. (Center for Media and Public Affairs study) (National Pages)
The New York Times, August 5, 1994, v. 143 p. A9(N) pA13
LC Call Number: Not in LC Collection

Business Index Micro Film: None
Violence in television - Research / Television broadcasting industry - Social policy /
Cable television broadcasting industry - Social policy

Koontz, Dean; Carlson, Timothy
Why we love horror. (TV shows) (includes an article on TV shows during the week of
Halloween)
TV guide, Oct 23, 1993 v. 41 n. n43p. 22(5)
LC Call Number: Microfilm 06378 (1953-   ) MicRR
Magazine Index Micro Film: None
Horror television programs - Criticism, interpretation, etc. / Violence in television -
Criticism, interpretation, etc.

Koop, C. Everett
An epidemic of violence. In Representative American Speeches 1983-1984. New York
H.W. Wilson Company, 1984. (Reference Shelf, v. 56, no. 4, 1984) p. 164-175.
Keynote address by the U.S. surgeon general at a National Coalition on Television-
sponsored conference, Oct. 6, 1983 encouraging research into the motivations of the
audience "rather than to continue pounding away at the broadcaster."
Violence in television [U.S.] Addresses, statements, etc. / Television and children [U.S.]
Addresses, statements, etc.

Koritnik, Shirley
Documentary targets TV 'circle of blame.' (PBS documentary on TV violence, "The
Violence Factor")
National Catholic reporter, Sept. 21, 1984, v. 20 p. 8(1)
LC Call Number: Microfilm 04882 (1964-   ) MicRR
Magazine Index Micro Film: 24K6510
The Violence Factor (television program) - production and direction / violence in
television - analysis / violence - analysis

Kowalewski, M. (1993)
Deadly Musings: Violence and Verbal Form in American Fiction. Princeton: Princeton
University Press, 1993, X, 301 p., bibl., ISBN 0-6910-6973-5.

Kunkel, Dale
From a raised eyebrow to a turned back: the FCC and children's product-related
programming. Journal of communication, v. 38, autumn 1988: 90-108.
"Structural changes in the broadcasting industry, new ways of financing and distributing
programs, aggressive marketing by the toy industry, and most importantly, the
deregulatory climate at the FCC have together created a favorable environment for
children's program-length commercials, whose primary purpose is to sell toys through
the shows heroes."
Television and children [U.S.] / Television advertising / Television programs [U.S.]

Lacroix, J.M. (Ed.)
(1997)
Violence et télévision autour de l'exemple canadien. Paris: Presses de la Sorbonne Nouvelle, 1997, 269 p., bibl., ill., ISBN 2-87854-115-4.

Landers, Robert K.
Troubled teenagers. Washington, Congressional Quarterly, 1987. 346-359. p. (Editorial research reports, 1987, v. 2, no. 2)
"Drinking, drugs, sex and suicide by troubled teenagers are prompting efforts by parents to set limits on adolescent behavior."
Youth [U.S.] / Drugs and youth [U.S.] / Rock music [U.S.] / Television and children [U.S.] / Suicide [U.S.]
Landler, Mark; Smith, Geoffrey
The MTV tycoon. Business week, no. 3284, Sept. 21, 1992: 56-60, 62
Describes Sumner Redstone, owner of MTV and its parent Viacom International, Inc., and his plans to expand the cable company into a worldwide TV network.
Cable television [U.S.] / Television programs [U.S.] / Rock music [U.S.] Economic aspects / Redstone, Sumner / MTV Network

Lang, A.; Newhagen, J. & Reeves, B. (1996)
Negative Video as Structure: Emotion, Attention, Capacity, and Memory. Journal of Broadcasting and Electronic Media 40(1996)4, pp. 460-477, ISSN 0883-8151.

Laosa, Luis M.
Viewing bilingual multicultural educational television: an empirical analysis of children's behaviors during television viewing. Journal of educational psychology, v. 68, April 1976: 133-142
"Reports an empirical investigation of behaviors exhibited by early elementary school children while viewing two programs of a children's bilingual multicultural educational television series."
Television and children [U.S.] / Bilingual education [U.S.] / Elementary school students [U.S.] / Human behavior [U.S.]

Lapham, Lewis H.
Burnt offerings. (crime and violence in the entertainment media) (Editorial)
Harper's magazine, April 1994, v. 288 n. n1727 p. 11(5)
LC Call Number: AP2.H3; Microfilm 03395 (1867-) MicRR; Ultrafiche LAC (1850-1905) MicRR
Magazine Index Micro Film: None
Violence in motion pictures - Analysis / Violence in television - Analysis
Larsen, O.N. & Catton, W.R.Jr (1994)
Voicing Social Concern. Lanham: University Press of America, 1994, XI, 306 p., ISBN 0-81919-437-9.

Ledingham, J.E.; Ledingham, C.A. & Richardson, J.E. (1993)
La violence dans les médias: Ses effets sur les enfants. Ottawa: Santé et bien être social
Canada, 1993, 19 p., bibl., ISBN 0-662-98422-6.

Lees, Gail Ellen
Unsafe for little ears? The regulation of broadcast advertising to children. UCLA law
journal, v. 25, June 1978: 1131-1186.
"Comment contents that false and deceptive advertisements are rightly forbidden, but that
no comprehensive ban on advertising to children may issue without a definite showing of
harm. After focusing on children's advertising in general, the Comment discusses
commercials for specific products. In each context, the effects of television advertising on
children and the impact proposed regulations would have on children's programming and
on protected commercial speech are examined."
Television and children [U.S.] / Television advertising [U.S.] / Deceptive advertising
[U.S.]

Leims, Th. (1993)
Sensationsjournalismus, Sex und Gewalt im japanischen Fernsehen: Japanologische
Anmerkungen zu einem aktuellen Thema. Communications 18(1993)3, pp. 355-379,
ISSN 0341-2059.

Lemish, D. (1997)
The School as a Wrestling Arena: The Modelling of a Television Series. European
Journal of Development Research 22(1997)4, pp. 395-418, ISSN 0957-8811.

Lemish, D. (1998)
Fighting Against Television Violence: An Israeli Case Study. In: Carlsson, U. & von
Feilitzen, C. (Eds.): Children and Media Violence: Yearbook from the UNESCO
International Clearinghouse on Children and Violence on the Screen 1998, pp. 125-138,
Göteborg: Nordicom, Göteborgs universitet, 1998, 387 p., ISBN 91-630-6358-1.

Leo, John
Good drama, not the Krazy Kat kind.
U.S. News & World Report, Feb 26, 1996 v120 n8 p22(1)

Leonard, John.
Smoke and mirrors : violence, television, and other American cultures / John Leonard.
New York : New Press : Distributed by Norton, 1997.
290 p. : ill. ; 22 cm.
PN1992.6.L46 1997
156584226X

Leonard, John
TV and the decline of civilization.
The Nation, Dec 27, 1993 v257 n22 p785(5)

Leonard, John
Why blame TV?
Utne Reader, May-June 1994 n63 p90(5)

Lermack, Paul
TV: the interruptible medium. Dissent, spring 1978: 186-192.
Examines television programming to clarify the relationship between the viewer and the
TV. Contends that because TV viewing takes place in areas where other activities are
happening, programming must be interruptible, repetitious and simple so that a viewer
can follow the program while doing something else.
Television programs [U.S.] / Television advertising [U.S.] / Television news [U.S.] /
Violence in television [U.S.]

Less. (television violence)
Economist (London), Aug. 29, 1987, v. 304, p. 56(2)
LC Call Number: HG11.E2; Microfilm 03394 (1843-   ) MicRR
Magazine Index Micro Film: None
Violence in television - Social aspects / Television broadcasting policy - United Kingdom
Great Britain

Lichter, S.R.; Lichter, L.S.; Rothman, S. & Amundson, D. (1994)
Prime Time: How TV Portrays American Culture. Washington D.C.: Regnery Publishers,
1994, IX, 478 p., ISBN 0-89526-491-9.

Lieb, Rebecca
German pols can't digest heavy dose of reality. (politicians object to reality programs on
television)
Variety, March 15, 1993, v. 350 n. n7 p. 41(2)
LC Call Number: PN2000.V3 Folio; Microfilm 03722 (1905-   ) MicRR
Business Index Micro Film: NONE
Violence in television - Laws, regulations, etc. / Television broadcasting industry -
Germany

Lindell, E. (Ed.) (1989)
Med skolan mot våldet [With School Against Violence]. Stockholm: Utbildningsförlaget,
1989, 185 p., ill., fig., tab., ISBN 91-47-03190-5.

Link, David
Facts about fiction: in defense of TV violence.
Reason, March 1994 v25 n10 p22(5)

Link, David
Facts about fiction: in defense of TV violence. Reason, v. 25, Mar. 1994: 22-26.
"Despite millennia of moral teachings to the contrary, some people are going to murder, rape, mutilate and torture others, and there seems to be no certain way to predict who will, or to prevent them from doing so. But violence continues to be a story - both on the news and in drama - because it is unusual, something the vast majority of people do not engage in."
Violence in television [U.S.] / Television and children [U.S.] /Violence in mass media [U.S.]

Link, David
Facts about fiction: in defense of TV violence.
Reason, March 1994, v. 25 n. n10 p. 22(5)
LC Call Number: H1.R35
Magazine Index Micro Film: None
Violence in television - Analysis / Fictions, Theory of - Analysis

Linné, O. & Wartella, E. (1998)
Research about Violence in the Media: Different Traditions and Changing Paradigms. In: Dickinson, R.; Harindranath, R. & Linné, O. (Eds.): Approaches to Audiences: A Reader, pp. 104-119, London: Arnold, 1998, 318 p., ISBN 0-340-69225-1.

Linné, O. (1995)
Media Violence Research in Scandinavia. Nordicom Review (1995)2, pp. 1-11, ISSN 1403-1108.

Linné, O. (1998)
What Do We Know About European Research on Violence in the Media? In: Carlsson, U. & von Feilitzen, C. (Eds.): Children and Media Violence: Yearbook from the UNESCO International Clearinghouse on Children and Violence on the Screen 1998, pp. 139-154, Göteborg: Nordicom, Göteborgs universitet, 1998, 387 p., ISBN 91-630-6358-1.

Linz, D. & Donnerstein, E. (1989)
The Effects of Violent Messages in the Mass Media. In: Bradac, J.J. (Ed.): Message Effects in Communication Science, Newbury Park: Sage Publications, 1989, 320 p., ISBN 0-80393-224-3.

Lipman, Joanne
TV violence measured. (TV Guide survey) (Column)
The Wall Street Journal, August 17, 1992, p. B6 (W) pB4
LC Call Number: See Catalogs or Staff
Magazine Index Micro Film: None

TV Guide (Periodical) - Surveys / Violence in television - Surveys / Television
broadcasting - Surveys

Literacy and the future of print. Journal of communication, v. 30, winter 1980: 89-204
Partial contents. The emergence of print culture in the West, by E. Eisenstein. The
decline of literacy, by P. Cooperman. The changing reading habits of the American
public, by J. Robinson. Television viewing, children's reading, and related classroom
behavior, by D. Zuckerman, D. Singer and J. Singer. The evolution of televised reading
instruction, by J. Tierney. On the language and authority of textbooks, by D. Olson.
Technology and civilization / Printing - Future / Illiteracy - Future / Reading - Future /
Reading [U.S.] / Educational surveys [U.S.] / Television and children [U.S.] /
Educational television [U.S.] / Textbooks [U.S.]

Lloyd-Kolkin, Donna; Wheeler, Patricia; Strand, Theresa
Developing a curriculum for teenagers. Journal of communication, v. 30, summer 1980:
119-125.
Reports on a curriculum designed to help teenagers become critical television watchers.
Critical TV viewers are defined as those who "should be able to intelligently select the
programs they watch, evaluate their relation to TV, identify the possible effects of TV on
their daily lives, and recognize TV's persuasive appeal."
Television and children [U.S.] / Curriculum planning [U.S.] / Television viewers [U.S.]

Lode, S. (1998)
Gewalt im Fernsehen: Entwicklung und Wirkung von Gewalt im Fernsehen,
verfassungsrechtliche Vorgaben und bestehende Regularien. Münster: Münster
Universität, 1997, XVIII, 184 p., Diss.

Loftus, Jack
TV vigilantes rest crusade until fall: boycott is off, admen on leash.
Variety, July 1, 1981, v. 303 p. 43(2)
LC Call Number: PN2000.V3 Folio; Microfilm 03722 (1905-   ) MicRR
Magazine Index Micro Film: None
Wildmon, Don - social policy
Coalition for Better Television - social policy / violence in television - censorship / sex in
mass media - censorship / television programs - censorship
Löwander, B. (1997)
Rasism och antirasism på dagordningen: studier av televisionens nyhetsrapportering i
början av 1990-talet [Racism and Anti-Racism on the Agenda: Studies of Swedish
Television News in the Beginning of the 90s]. Umeå: Sociologiska institutionen, Umeå
universitet, 1997, 251 p., Diss., ISBN 91-628-2608-5.

Lowe, Carl, ed.
Television and American culture. New York, H.W. Wilson Company, 1981. 235 p. (The
Reference Shelf, v. 53, no. 2)

A compilation of articles about television and its effects on politics religion, education and other aspects of American culture.
Television [U.S.] / Television in politics [U.S.] / Cable television [U.S.] / Television programs [U.S.] Television and children [U.S.] / Mass media in religion [U.S.] / Television news [U.S.] / Public television [U.S.]

Luca, R. (1993)
Zwischen Ohnmacht und Allmacht: Unterschiede im Erleben medialer Gewalt von Mädchen und Jungen. Frankfurt am Main: Campus-Verlag, 1993, 221 p., ill., bibl., ISBN 3-593-34874-8.

Ludwig, H.W. & Marc Pruys, G. (1998)
"...So brauch' ich Gewalt": Wie Fernsehgewalt produziert und bekämpft wird. Baden Baden: Nomos Verlag, 1998, 130 p., ISBN 3-7890-5198-5.

Ludwig, H.W. (1995)
Die Jagd nach dem Zuschauer: Überlegungen zur inszenierten Gewalt auf dem Bildschirm. Tübingen: Eberhard-Karls-Universität, 1995, 35 p., ill.

Lukesch, H. & Brosius, H.B. (Eds.)
(1990)
Wenn Gewalt zur Unterhaltung wird...: Beiträge zur Nutzung und Wirkung von Gewaltdarstellungen in Audiovisuellen Medien. Regensburg: Roderer, 1990, 172 p., fig., ISBN 3-89073-494-4.

Lurcat, L. (1989)
Violence à la télé: l'enfant fasciné. Paris: Les éditions Syros/Alternatives, 1989, 198 p., ISBN 2-86738-399-4.

Lurcat, L. (1990)
Impact de la violence télévisuelle. Enfance 43(1990)1-2, pp. 167-172, ISSN 0013-7544.

Lurcat, L. (1995)
Le temps prisonnier: Des enfances volees par la television. Paris: Desclee De Brouwer, 1995, 184 p., ill., ISBN 2-220-03622-7.

Lynn, R.; Hampson, S. & Agahi, E. (1989)
Television Violence and Aggression: A Genotype-Environment, Correlation and Interaction Theory. Journal of Social Behaviour and Personality 17(1989), pp. 143-164, ISSN 0886-1641.

Maasø, A. (1997)
Voldens rolle i filmfortellingen: En analyse av Die Hard 2, Kickboxer IV og Natural Born Killers [The Role of Violence in Film Narrative: An Analysis of Die Hard 2,

Kickboxer IV and Natural Born Killers]. Oslo: Politihøgskolen, 1997, 191 p., ill., tab., fig., ISBN 82-7808-011-9.
MacBeth, T.M. (Ed.) (1996)
Tuning In To Young Viewers: Social Science Perspectives on Television. Thousand Oaks: Sage Publications, 1996, 282 p., ISBN 0-80395-825-0.

MacKie, Alexander
The children's advertising battle. [Columbia, Mo.] University of Missouri School of Journalism, 1979. 6 p. (Freedom of Information Center. Report no. 398)
"Cap'n Crunch meets the FTC this month, as hearings begin on a proposal to limit television advertising directed at children. Included in this report are the major arguments expected to be advanced by both pro- and antiregulation groups in what many observers consider the most controversial proceeding ever undertaken by a regulatory agency."
Television and children [U.S.] / Television advertising [U.S.] / Independent regulatory commissions / U.S. Federal Trade Commission

Macklin, M. Carole
Do children understand TV ads? Journal of Advertising research, v. 23, Feb.-Mar. 1983: 63-70.
Television and children [U.S.] / Television and advertising [U.S.]

Macklin, M. Carole
Do young children understand the selling intent of commercials? Journal of consumer affairs, v. 19, winter 1985: 293-304.
"Researchers interested in advertising effects on children are urged to consider the necessity and desirability of improved nonverbal measures in dealing with a subject population with limited language facility."
Television and children [U.S.] Research / Television advertising [U.S.]

Maio, Kathi
Hooked on hate? Unfunny comedians, MTV, tabloid television, fright films, and other media invasions.
MS. Sept.-Oct. 1990, v. 1 n. n2 p. 42(3)
LC Call Number:: HQ1101.M55; Microfilm (0) 84/2006 (1983-1984) MicRR
Magazine Index Micro Film: None
Violence in mass media - Analysis / Women - Portrayals, depictions, etc. / Violence in television - Analysis
Mandese, Joe; Jensen, Jeff
Marketers on TV warnings: yawn. (includes article on watchdog groups' views of violent-program warnings)
Advertising Age, July 5, 1993, v. 64, n. n28, p. 1(2)
LC Call Number: HF5801.A276
Business Index Micro Film: 72V4328
Marketers claim that the television networks' agreement to air parental-discretion

warnings for violent prime-time programs will not significantly impact their advertising choices. Ad agencies, the networks and media buyers continue to worry, however, that the warnings will result in ad spending cuts. Advertisers responding to a survey indicated that the planned warnings are less important to them than their in-house program - content guidelines.
Violence in television - Economic aspects / Television advertising - Surveys / Advertising industry - Analysis

Marks, Leonard M.
Broadcasters can curb TV violence - if viewers help. (Column)
Insight, Sept. 5, 1994, v. 10 n. n36 p. 38(2)
LC Call Number: AP2.I624
Magazine Index Micro Film: None
Violence in television - Social aspects / Television viewers - Services / Television programs - Social aspects / Television broadcasting industry - Social policy

Marshall, Tari; Norwood, Jennifer
[Music Videos], PTA Today, v 13, Apr. 1988: 26-29.
Contents - music videos - have they gone too far? by Jennifer Norwood. Music with explicit language: what can parents do? by Tari Marshall
Rock music [U.S.] / Violence in television [U.S.] / Pornography [U.S.]

Marshall, Thomas R.
The benevolent bureaucrat: political authority in children's literature and television.
Western political quarterly, v. 34, Sept. 1981: 389-398.
Presents a content analysis of the image of government in child-oriented mass media, finding "that government symbols, programs, and officials appear with a surprisingly high frequency on 'normal' (non-newcast) television and in children's books. When they do appear, government officials are typically presented as both benevolent and competent."
Political socialization [U.S.] / Television and children [U.S.] / Television in politics [U.S.] / Literature [U.S.] / National objectives [U.S.] / National emblems [U.S.] / Rating of public officials [U.S.]

Martel, Jay
No pain, no game. (television program 'American Gladiators')
Rolling Stone, May 17, 1990, n. n578 p. 37(1)
LC Call Number: AP2.R73; Microfilm (0) 82/105 (1967-1983) MicRR
Magazine Index Micro Film: None
American Gladiators (Television program) - criticism, interpretation, etc. / Violence in television - analysis

Martinez, A. (1991)
La violence à la télévision: État des connaissances scientifiques. Ottawa: Conseil de la Radiodiffusion télécommunications canadiennes, 1991, 64 p., bibl.

Mathews, Joseph
Should children be protected from TV commercials? Human rights, v. 8, fall 1979: 24-27, 48, 54.
Article looks at the problems caused by child directed TV commercials and notes some of the successes of the F.T.C. in controlling this type of advertising. Considers the implications of recent court decisions for regulation, focusing on the decision in Virginia Pharmacy which gave protection to the dissemination of commercial information.
Television and children [U.S.] / Television advertising [U.S.] / Government regulation [U.S.] / Freedom of information [U.S.] Legal cases / Supreme Court decisions

McAvoy, Kim
Clinton to weigh in on TV violence. (Brief Article)
Broadcasting and Cable, Dec. 6, 1993, v. 123, n. n49 p. 18(1)
LC Call Number: TK6540B85
Business Index Micro Film: 74X2648
Clinton, Bill - Social policy / Simon, Paul (Politician) - Political activity
Violence in television - Political aspects / Television broadcasting industry - Laws, regulations, etc.

McAvoy, Kim
Hillary Clinton decries excess violence in TV. (Brief Article)
Broadcasting and Cable, March 14, 1994, v. 124 n. n11 p. 47(1)
LC Call Number: TK6540B85
Business Index Micro Film: 77N1771
Clinton, Hillary Rodham - Addresses, essays, lectures. Violence in television - Moral and ethical aspects / Television broadcasting of news - Moral and ethical aspects / Television broadcasting industry - Moral and ethical aspects
McClellan, Steve
Programmers challenge violence survey. (Center for Media and Public Affairs)
Broadcasting and Cable, August 15, 1994, v. 124 n. n33 p. 14(2)
LC Call Number; TK6540B85
Business Index Micro Film: None
A survey of television violence conducted by the Center for Media and Public Affairs has provoked an angry response from programmers. The number of violent scenes on television has increased 40% since the previous study in April, 1992, according to the report. In each study, programs during a Thursday 18-hour broadcast schedule were evaluated for violent content. Critics of the study allege that its methodology was seriously flawed.
Center for Media and Public Affairs - Research / Violence in television - Surveys / Television broadcasting industry - Management

McConnell, Frank
Art is dangerous: 'Beavis & Butt-Head,' for example. (television program)
Commonwealth, Jan. 14, 1994, v. 121 n. n1 p. 28(2)
LC Call Number: AP2.C6897; Microfilm 06252 (1924-   ) MicRR
Magazine Index Micro Film: None
Beavis and Butt-Head (Television program) - Criticism, interpretation, etc. / Violence in television - Analysis

McManus, John; Berry, Jon
ANA sets initiatives on TV violence, policy research; outgoing president DeWitt Helm Jr. details plans to be announced at conference. (Association of National Advertisers) (Interview)
Brandweek, Oct. 18, 1993, v. 34 n. n42 p. 46(3)
LC Call Number: HF5801.A43
Business Index Micro Film: None
An interview of outgoing Association of National Advertisers' (ANA) Pres DeWitt Helm Jr. is presented. Helm discusses the ANA's planned initiatives on violence in the media and research bias, how advertising works, and the influence of share of voice and share of market on advertising market share. The ANA plans to research violence in television by initiating a task force to analyze and look for solutions to the problem.
Helm, DeWitt, Jr.   Interviews
Association of National Advertisers - Officials and employees / Violence in television - Laws, regulations, etc.

Media and the arts (anecdotes on rating system for TV violence and acquisition of the New York Post) (News Digest) (Brief Article)
Time (Chicago), July 12, 1993, v. 142 n. n2 p. 19(1)
LC Call Number: AP2.T37; Microfilm 02914 (1923-   ) MicRR
Magazine Index Micro Film: None
New York Post (Newspaper) - Acquisitions, mergers, divestments / Violence in television - Standards

Meirim, J.M. (Ed.) (1994)
A violência associada ao desporto: Ecolectânea de textos. Lisboa: Ministério da Educacao, 1994, 131 p.

Meirowitz, K. (1993)
Gewaltdarstellungen auf Videokassetten: Grundrechtliche Freiheiten und gesetzliche Einschränkungen zum Jugend- und Erwachsenenschutz; eine verfassungsrechtliche Untersuchung. Berlin: Duncker und Humblot, 1993, 432 p., fig., bibl., Diss., ISBN 3-428-07815-2.

Merrow, John
Children and television: natural partners. Phi Delta Kappan, v. 67, Nov. 1985: 211-214.

"Though attacks on television watching are all too common (and all too easy), TV is a fact of children's lives. Let us rethink how we use television in the schools, argues the creator of the PBS series, 'Your Children, Our Children.'" Suggests that "hands-on experience with television will make children better-educated, better-informed consumers of television, and that will lead them to demand better television - and to avoid inferior programming."
Television and children [U.S.]

Messaris, Paul; Kerr, Dennis
Mothers' comments about TV: relation to family communication patterns.
Communications research, v. 10, Apr. 1983: 175-194.
"The major findings were as follows: Concept orientation was associated positively with mothers' exploration of moral issues raised by TV programs in discussions with their children (but not with the giving of explicit directives about the implications of these issues for the children's own conduct). Concept orientation was also associated with mothers' use of TV as an occasion for giving their children information about historical, geographic or scientific details pertinent to a TV program."
Television and children [U.S.] / Parent and child [U.S.]

Metze-Mangold, V. (1997)
Auf Leben und Tod: Die Macht der Gewalt in den Medien. Berlin: Aufbau-Taschenbuch-Verlag, 1997, 127 p., ISBN 3-7466-8519-2.

Meumann, M. & Niefanger, D. (Eds.)
(1997)
Ein Schauplatz herber Angst: Wahrnehmung und Darstellung von Gewalt im 17. Jahrhundert. Göttingen: Wallstein Verlag, 1997, 272 p., ill., ISBN 3-89244-234-7.

Meyer, Timothy P.; Donohue, Thomas R.; Henke, Lucy L.
How Black children see TV commercials. Journal of advertising research, v. 18, Oct. 1978: 51-58.
Find that the "results of their survey may be roughly equivalent to saying that white children from middle-class to upper-middle-class backgrounds are about twice as aware of TV commercials and their intent as urban black children." Also find that "black children are more likely than white children to believe that TV commercials always tell the truth." Conclude that "those who advertise the children should seriously consider changing their biased and deceitful presentations."
Television advertising [U.S.] / Television and children [U.S.] / Black youth [U.S.]

Mifflin, Lawrie
A call for decency.
(Steve Allen and Shirley Jones are chairing Parents Television Council, a conservative group working to stop sex and riot once on TV) (Living Arts Pages).
The New York Times, Oct 14, 1998 v148 pBg(N) pE9(L) col 6. (9 col. in)

Miller, D. (1994)
Don't Mention the War: Northern Ireland, Propaganda and the Media. London: Pluto Press, 1994, XII, 368 p., ill., bibl., ISBN 0-74530-835-X.

Miller, M. Mark; Reeves, Byron
Dramatic TV content and children's sex-role stereotype. Journal of broadcasting, v. 20, winter 1976: 35-50.
Analyzes "prime-time TV drama to isolate counter-stereotypical sex role portrayals" and then 'conducted a survey to determine the impact of the counter-stereotypical portrayals on children's occupational sex-role perceptions."
Television and children [U.S.] / Sex discrimination [U.S.]

Miller, Mark Crispin
Black and white. New republic, v. 185, Oct. 28, 1981: 27-31.
Assesses the NBC documentary, "America - Black and White," on racial problems in the U.S. Judges that "although the program told us little about racism in our society, it revealed a lot about the subtle sort of racism that pervades television news." Charges the documentary producers with condescending and unprobing reporting and the television industry overall with contributing to illiteracy and feelings of powerlessness of many young Blacks.
Race relations [U.S.] Evaluation / Blacks in mass media [U.S.] / Television news [U.S.] / Television broadcasting [U.S.] /Television and children [U.S.] / American-Black and White (Television program)

Miller, T.; Hearth, L.; Molcan, J. & Dugoni, B. et al. (1991)
Imitative Violence in the Real World: A Re-Analysis of Homicide Rates Following Championship Prize Fights. Aggressive Behaviour 17(1991), pp. 121-134, ISSN 0096-140X.

Mills, Claudia
Children's television. QQ, v. 6, summer 1986: 11-14.
Addresses these questions: "how worried should we be about what our children are watching - and about what's being sold to them as they watch? And should we be trying to do something about it?"
Television and children [U.S.]

Mohr, Phillip J.
Parental guidance of children's viewing of evening television programs. Journal of broadcasting, v. 23, sprig 1979: 213-228.
Questionnaires were administered to 5,167 school children and their parents in Sedgwick County, Kansas to determine what guidance parents provide their children on the viewing of specific television programs. Answers revealed that little guidance is given.
Television and children [Kansas] / Parent and child [Kansas] / Social surveys [Kansas]

Mongin, O. (1997)
La violence des images, ou, Comment s'en debarrasser? Paris: Seuil, 1997, 183 p., ill., bibl., ISBN 2-02030-630-1.

Montalbano, William D.
Pope calls on TV to improve its image; the pontiff says television is 'a public trust.' He urges governments, viewers and the industry itself to police it. (Pope John Paul II)
The Los Angeles Times, Jan. 25, 1994, v. 113 p. A13
LC Call Number: Newspaper 7114-X
Business Index Micro Film: None
John Paul II, Pope - Addresses, essays, lectures - Television broadcasting industry - Addresses, essays, lectures / Violence in television - Addresses, essays, lectures

Morain, Claudia
Turning off the violence. (conference on violence on television)
American Medical News, August 23, 1993, v. 36 n. n32 p. 2(2)
LC Call Number: Microfilm 02679
Business Index Micro Film: None
Sen. Paul Simon gave the television industry 60 days to formulate a plan to reduce violence on television at a meeting of the National Council for Families and Television. If the industry fails to comply with his deadline, Simon said that he will seek federal legislation. Bowing to pressure, the industry has already agreed to broadcast frequent parental advisories. Scientific studies show a link between violence in television viewed by children and later violent behavior.
Violence in television - Social aspects / Physicians - Social policy / Television broadcasting industry - Social policy

Morgan, Michael; Gross, Larry
Television viewing, IQ and academic achievement. Journal of broadcasting, v. 24, spring 1980: 117-133.
Analyzes the relations between television watching and intellectual development.
Television and children [U.S.] / Academic performance [U.S.] / Intelligence levels [U.S.]

Morrison, Patricia; McCarthy, Margaret; Gardner, Howard
Exploring the realities of television with children. Journal of broadcasting, v. 23, fall 1979: 453-463.
"Approaches reality and fantasy discrimination as a classificatory ability: thus it focuses on how children arrive at such beliefs, the reasons they supply for their judgments, and the extent to which reality (and fantasy) function as a meaningful dimension for assessing television."
Television and children [U.S.] Research

Most violent TV show targets handguns.
American Rifleman, Jan. 1980, v. 128, p. N9 (2)

LLC Call Number: SK1.A52
Magazine Index Micro Film: None
Violence in television - political aspects / Hawaii Five-O (television program) - political aspects / firearms - law and legislation / National Citizens Committee on Broadcasting - political activity / National Rifle Association - political activity

Mouseler, V. (1997)
La violence dans les programmes de jeux. In: Image et violence, Actes du colloque BPI, 3-4 octobre 1996. Paris: BPI en Actes, 1997.

Mullin, C.R. & Linz, D. (1995)
Desensitization and Resensitization to Violence Against Women: Effects of Exposure to Sexually Violent Films on Judgements of Domestic Violence Victims. Journal of Personality and Social Psychology 69(1995)3, pp. 449-459, ISSN 0022-3514.

Muñoz, J.J. & Pedrero, L.M. (1994)
Efectos negativos de la televisión entre la población infantil. Salamanca: Facultad de Ciencias de la Información, Universidad Pontificia, 1994, 94 p., ill., ISBN 84-604-9498-5.

Murdock, G. (1994)
Visualizing Violence: Television and the Discourse of Disorder. In: Hamelink, C.J. & Linné, O. (Eds.): Mass Communication Research: On Problems and Policies: The Art of Asking the Right Questions: In Honour of James D. Halloran, pp. 171-187, Norwood: Ablex, 1994, XVIII, 417 p., ISBN 0-89391-738-9.

Murphy-Berman, Virginia; Whobrey, Linda
The impact of captions on hearing-impaired children's affective reactions to television. Journal of special education, v.17, spring 1983: 47-62.
"Results indicated that captions seemed to enhance hearing-impaired children's abilities to perceive the emotional complexity of presented information."
Television and children [U.S.] / Handicapped children [U.S.] / Deaf [U.S.]

Murray, J.P. (1997)
Media Violence and Youth. In: Osofsky, J.D. (Ed.): Children in a Violent Society, pp. 72-96, New York: Guilford Press, 1997, XIV, 338 p., ISBN 1-57230-183-X.

Murray, J.P. (1998)
Studying Television Violence: A Research Agenda for the 21st Century. In: Asamen, J.K. & Berry, G.L. (Eds.): Research Paradigms, Television, and Social Behavior, pp. 369-412, Thousand Oaks: Sage Publications, 1998, X, 430 p., ISBN 0-76190-654-1.

Murray, Karen
Striking out at violence on TV. (Canada) (Brief Article)

Variety, May 17, 1993, v. 351 n. n3 p. 61 (2)
LC Call Number: PN2000.V3 Folio; Microfilm 03722 (1905-   ) MicRR
Magazine Index Micro Film: None
Josephson, Wendy - Addresses, essays, lectures
Canadian Cable Television Association - Conferences, meetings, seminars, etc. /
Violence in television - Addresses, essays, lectures / Television broadcasting industry -
Social aspects

Mustonen, A. (1995)
TV-vaekivalta – Ramboja vai Rampoja? [Salience of Television: Violence on Finnish
Television]. Psykologia 30 (1995)1, pp. 28-34, ISSN 0355-1067.

National Coalition on Television Violence
http://www.nctvv.org/

National television violence study start here
Thousand Oaks; London: SAGE, c1997-1998
2 v. (xxi,568p;424p); 28cm (pbk)
Includes bibliographies
Violence on television--United States
[Univ. Lib.] 1997.11.3001-3002

National Television Violence Study, Volume 2; Executive Summary. Santa Barbara:
University of California, Center for Communication and Social Policy, 1997, 53 p., tab.

National Television Violence Study, Volume 3. Executive Summary. Santa Barbara:
University of California, Center for Communication and Social Policy, 1998, 59 p., fig.,
ill., tab., chart.

NCC opposes TV violence. (National Council of Churches) (News)
The Christian Century (1902) July 14, 1993, v. 110 n. n21 p. 704 (2)
LC Call Number: BR1.C45; Microfilm 01962 (1900-   ) MicRR
Magazine Index Micro Film: None
National Council of Churches - Social policy / Violence in television - Social aspects

Nelson, Scott A.
Crime-time television. FBI Law enforcement bulletin, v. 58, Aug. 1989: 1-9.
"Weekly 'crime-time' television shows have resulted in the apprehension of fugitives, the
solution of difficult cases and positive publicity for the law enforcement agencies
involved. This article discusses the development of crime-time television and its pros and
cons. It also offers suggestions to the law enforcement manager who may be approached
by a local or national network to participate in a crime-solving program."
Crime and the press [U.S.] / Violence in television [U.S.] / Television news [U.S.] /

Fugitives from justice [U.S.] / America's Most Wanted (Television program) / Unsolved mysteries (Television program)

Networks, cable. (criticism of television violence study)
Television Digest, August 8, 1994, v. 34 n. n32 p. 7(1)
LC Call Number: May or May Not Be in LC. Search further.
Business Index Micro Film: None
Violence in television - Reports

Nevius, John R. Jr.
The "Cookie Monster" and cognitive enculturation. Educational technology, v. 20, Sept. 1980: 57-60.
Argues that the richness in fantasy and make-believe of such television programs as Sesame Street, Mr. Rogers and Captain Kangaroo enable them, like the radio programs of the 1930s and 1940s and the classics of children's literature, to help "children become cognitively enculturated to society's definition of cultural reality."
Television and children [U.S.]
Newton, D.E. (1996)
Violence and the Media: A Reference Handbook, Santa Barbara: ABC-CLIO Inc., 1996, XIV, 254 p., bibl., ill., ISBN 0-87436-843-X.

O'Connor, John J.
TV likes to explore the violence that it may inspire. (television programs analyzing the medium's affect on its audience) (Living Arts Pages)
The New York Times, Dec. 9, 1993, v. 143 p. B3(N) pC22
LC Call Number: Not in LC Collection
Magazine Index Micro Film: None
Violence in television - Analysis / Television feature stories / Analysis

O'Donnell, H. & Boyle, R. (1996)
A Semiotics of Violent Actuality: Encoding Football Fan Behaviour during Euro'92.
Leisure Studies 15(1996)1, January, pp. 31-48, ISSN 0261-4367.

Ogles, R.M. & Sparks, G.G. (1989)
Television Violence and Viewer's Perceptions of Criminal Victimization. Mass Communication Review 16(1989)3, pp. 2-11, ISSN 0193-7707.

Oliver, M.B. (1994)
Portrayals of Crime, Race, and Aggression in 'Reality-Based' Police Shows: A Content Analysis. Journal of Broadcasting and Electronic Media 38(1994)Spring, pp. 179-192, ISSN 0883-8151.

One viewer's violence is another viewer's action.
CQ Researcher, March 26, 1993, v. 3 n. n12 p. 270(1)

LC Call Number: H35.E35
Magazine Index Micro Film: None
The subjective definition of violence and violent acts poses a difficulty for trained monitors to rate or index violence in television. Against accusations that even slapstick comedy routines are rated as violent, several media research organizations define violence as deliberate hostile acts, whether physical or with the use of a weapon, aimed to achieve specific goals and purposes. Some monitoring groups also assign weights to violent acts, serving to mitigate or aggravate ratings of the use of violence.
Violence in television - Research / Violence - Terminology

Oppenheim, Mike
TV isn't violent enough
TV Guide, Feb. 11, 1984, v. 32 p. 20(2)
LC Call Number: Microfilm 06378 (1953-   ) MicRR
Magazine Index Micro Film: 21D0732
Violence in television - evaluation

Ortega-Esteban, J. (1996)
Delincuencia juvenil y medios de communicación social. Letras de Deusto 26(1996)71.

Pally, Marcia
Dirty movies and rock don't cause violence. (response to article of May 12, 1993) (Letter to the Editor)
The Wall Street Journal, June 11, 1993, p. A11(W) pA1
LC Call Number: See Catalogs or Staff
Business Index Micro Film None
Violence - Causes of / Violence in motion pictures - Influence / Violence in television - Influence

Pape, H.; Isachsen, T. & Jessen, J. (1998)
Ungdom og vold i bildemediene [Youth and Violence on the Screen]. Oslo: Norsk institutt for forskning om oppvekst, velferd og aldring, 1998, 82 p., tab., bibl., ISBN 82-789-033-9.

Perl, S. (1994)
Kinder als Rezipienten von Gewaltdarstellungen im Fernsehen: Ein kritische Literaturbericht. Braunschweig: Technische Universität, 1994, 166 p.

Petersen, James R.
The curse of the boob tube: TV, socialization and violence. (The Playboy Forum)
Playboy (Chicago), Dec. 1992, v. 39 n. n12 p. 49(1)
LC Call Number: AP2.P69 Rare Bk.
Magazine Index Micro Film: None
Violence in television - Research / Television viewers - Social aspects

Petzal, David E.
Real life. (TV and police shootings, firearms ownership)
Field & Stream, Dec. 1988, v. 93 n. n8 p. 16(2)
LC Call Number: SK1.F45
Magazine Index Micro Film: 48M1687
Rowan, Carl T. - Cases
Violence in television - Analysis / Police - Assaults against / Firearms ownership - Cases

Pfarr, K. (1994)
Die Neue Zeitung: Empirische Untersuchung eines Informationsmediums der frühen
Neuzeit unter besonderer Berücksichtigung von Gewaltdarstellungen. Mainz: Mainz
Universität, 1994, 293 p., ill., bibl., Diss.

Plagens, Peter
Violence in our culture: as America bring on make-believe gore, you have to ask: what
are we doing to ourselves?
Newsweek, April 1, 1991, v. 117 n. n13 p. 46(6)
LC Call Number: AP2.N6772; Microfilm 01125 (1933-) MicRR
Magazine Index Micro Film: 59E0631
Violence in literature - Social aspects / Violence in mass media - Social aspects /
Violence in motion pictures - Social aspects / Violence in television - Social aspects /
Violence - Social aspects

Pooley, Eric
Cop stars. New York, v. 25, March 16, 1992: 42-49.
Describes "how police and gangsters are cashing in on today's mania for true-crime
entertainment."
Crime and the press [U.S.] / Police [U.S.] / Television programs [U.S.] / Violence in
television [U.S.] / Television news [U.S.]

Popper KR
A patent for making television
Pediatr Med Chir, 17:157-60, 1995 Mar-Apr

Porter, Kristen
Teaching peace. (North American Essay Contest Winner)
The Humanist (Buffalo, N.Y.) May-June, 1992, v. 52 n. n3 p. 32(2)
LC Call Number: B821.A1H8
Magazine Index Micro Film: 64E3608
Youth and peace - Social aspects / Violence in television - Social aspects

Postrel, Virginia
TV or not TV?
Reason, August-Sept 1993 v25 n4 p4(2)

Poundstone, Paula
Keeping my mouth shut: why I can't talk dirty, and other people get away with murder.
(comedian narrative) (Column)
Mother Jones, Jan.-Feb. 1994, v. 19 n. n1 p. 80(1)
LC Call Number: AP2.M79193
Magazine Index Micro Film: None
Violence in television - Anecdotes, cartoons, satire, etc. / Women comedians -
Anecdotes, cartoons, satire, etc.

Powers, Ron
The new 'holy war' against sex and violence. TV Guide, v. 29, April 18, 1981: 6-8, 10,
12.
Examines the campaign of Mississippi minister Don Wildmon's Coalition for Better
Television to lead a boycott of sponsors of television programs deemed offensive because
of their "violent, sexual, and profane content."
Mass media in religion [U.S.] / Television advertising [U.S.] / Boycott [U.S.] / Violence
in television [U.S.] / Pornography [U.S.] / Church and social problems [U.S.] / New
Right [U.S.] / Clergy [Mississippi] Political activities / Wildmon, Don / Coalition for
Better Television

Pressman, Steven
Congress expected to consider alcohol ad ban. Congressional quarterly weekly report, v.
43, Jan. 19, 1985: 122-126.
Discusses controversy over alcohol advertising on television. An accompanying article
by J. Calmes, "Kids' TV advocates lobby Congress for help - but broadcasters say
programs are adequate," focuses on the link of commercial television to advertisements.
Television advertising [U.S.] Law and legislation / Television and children [U.S.] /
Alcoholic beverage control [U.S.]

Prettyman, E. Barrett, Jr.; Hook, Lisa A.
The control of media-related imitative violence. Federal communications law journal, v.
38, Jan. 1987: 317-382.
Article concludes that "the extent to which there is a provable relationship between film
and television violence and imitative violence by viewers remains uncertain... For the
time being, the more fruitful area of control of imitative violence is the civil tort action
after broadcasts have been aired."
Violence in television [U.S.] / Compensation for victims of crime [U.S.] / Torts [U.S.]

Prime-time syndicated series. (action shows and other programs) (Fall Preview '93)
TV guide, Sept. 18, 1993, v. 14 n. n38 p. 67(1)
LC Call Number: Microfilm 06378 (1953-   ) MicRR
Magazine Index Micro Film: None
Violence in television - Production and direction / Science fiction television programs -
Criticism, interpretation, etc.

Prisuta, Robert H.
The adolescent and television news: a viewer profile. Journalism quarterly, v. 56, summer 1979: 277-282.
Study finds that "adolescents who view TV news feel family, friends and school think public affairs is important."
Political socialization [U.S.] / Television and children [U.S.]

Proffitt, Steve
Michael Moriarty; when fighting against censorship means defending television violence. (actor who went head to head with Attorney General Janet Reno over limits on violent programming) (Interview)
The Los Angeles Times, March 6, 1994, v. 113, p. M3
LC Call Number: Newspapers 7114-X
Business Index Micro Film: None
Moriarty, Michael - Interviews / Reno, Janet - Social policy
Actors - Interviews / Violence in television - Laws, regulations, etc.

Queenan, Joe
Get a grip, guys.
TV Guide, March 15, 1997 v45 n11 p19(1)

Quinn, Susan
Making children's television safe for children. Boston magazine, v. 69, Oct. 1977: 97-99, 163-171.
Surveys the activities of Action for Children's Television, a Boston-based group which has become "the single most effective consumer voice for better children's TV in the country."
Television and children [U.S.] / Action for Children's Television

Rabinowitz, Dorothy
The Attorney General as scriptwriter. (Janet Reno, violence in the media)
The Wall Street Journal, Nov. 1, 1993, p. A15 (W) ppA
LC Call Number: See Catalogs or Staff
Magazine Index Micro Film: none
Reno, Janet - Evaluation
United States. Department of Justice - Officials and employees / Attorneys general - Evaluation / Violence in television - Social aspects / Television broadcasting - Social policy / Censorships - Analysis

Rasmussen, H.A. (1989)
Actionfilm og drengekultur [Films of Action and Young Men's Culture]. In: Højbjerg, L. (Ed.): Reception af levende billeder, pp. 221-234, København: Akademisk Forlag, 1989, 245 p., fig., ill., bibl., ISBN 87-500-2869-3.

Rathmayr, B. (1996)
Die Rückkehr der Gewalt: Faszination und Wirkung medialer Gewaltdarstellung.
Wiesbaden: Quelle und Meyer, 1996, 168 p., ill., bibl., ISBN 3-494-01256-3.

Reed, Ishmael
Stats, lies & videotapes (network television's unflattering portrayal of African
Americans)
Emerge, April 1994, v. 5 n. n7 p. 50(4)
LC Call Number: E185.5.E45
Magazine Index Micro Film: None
African Americans in television - Portrayals, depictions, etc. / Racism in mass media -
Analysis / Violence in television - Social aspects

Reid, Leonard N.
Viewing rules as mediating factors of children's responses to commercials. Journal of
broadcasting, v. 23, winter 1979: 15-26.
Analyzes whether the "differences in children's responses to television advertising and
parents' handling of those responses are mediated by the parent's concern with their
child's consumer development and ascribed and enforced viewing rules."
Television and children [U.S.] / Television advertising [U.S.] / Parent and child [U.S.]

Reid, Leonard N.; Frazer, Charles F.
Children's use of television commercials to initiate social interaction in family viewing
situations. Journal of broadcasting, v. 24, spring 1980: 149-158.
"The observations of this study indicate that television viewing has an emergent character
consisting of many interacting and competing activities and events, and through these the
child viewer acts toward and through television commercials in relation to the total
interactional character of the family viewing situation."
Television and children [U.S.] / Parent and child [U.S.]

Reid, Leonard N.; Rotfeld, Herbert J.
How informative are ads on children's TV shows? Journalism quarterly, v. 58, spring
1981: 108-111.
An examination was made of 324 Saturday morning commercials to determine if they
were informative as well as persuasive. Results indicate "that Saturday morning network
commercials are probably no less informative than commercials broadcast in other
dayparts."
Television and children [U.S.] / Television advertising [U.S.]

Reporting on a riot. Washington journalism review, v. 14, July-August 1992: 20-30.
In the first of two articles Ron LaBrecque offers "a behind-the-scenes look at how KNBC
television news and the Los Angeles Times covered a city in turmoil. With sidebars on
racial resentment at the Times and on why viewers feel compelled to watch violent news
footage;" then Penny Bender discusses the risks reporters take in covering dangerous

stories like the Los Angeles riots.
Riots [Los Angeles] / Racial violence [Los Angeles] / Crime and the press [Los Angeles]
/ Television news [Los Angeles] / Black journalists [Los Angeles] / Violence in
television [Los Angeles] / Reporters and reporting [Los Angeles] Security measures / Los
Angeles Times / KNBC-TV (Los Angeles, Calif.)

Rice, Berkeley
The unreality of prime-time crime.
Psychology today, Aug. 1980, v. 14 p. 26(2)
LC Call Number: BF1.P855; Microfilm 06204 (1967-) MicRR
Magazine Index Micro Film: None
Haney, Craig - surveys / Manzolati, John - surveys violence in television - surveys /
crime in television - surveys

Rich, Frank
Coming to you dead from L.A.
The New York Times, May 2, 1998 v147 pA23(N) pAI2(L) col 6 (17 col in)

Richter, Paul
Clinton appeals to Hollywood on film, TV violence. (asks entertainment industry to
examine effects of violence on young people)
The Los Angeles Times, Dec. 5, 1993, v. 113, p. A1
LC Call Number: Newspaper 7114-X
Business Index Micro Film: None
Clinton, Bill - Addresses, essays, lectures
Entertainment industry - Addresses, essays, lectures / Violence in motion pictures -
Addresses, essays, lectures / Violence in television - Addresses, essays, lectures

Ricklefs, Roger and others
The television era. Wall Street Journal, Oct. 12, 1976, p. 1, 37; Oct. 15, p. 1, 24; Oct. 19,
p. 1, 23; Oct. 21, p. 1, 34; Oct. 26, p. 1, 37; Nov. 1, p. 1,; 22; Nov. 5, p. 1, 20.
Seven-part series on the impact of television on the ways Americans live.
Contents. Three families show how generation of TV has altered lifestyles, by R.
Ricklefs. Entertainment, action are major ingredients of the local TV news, by P. Revzin.
From bugs to batman, children's TV shows produce adult anxiety, by J. Lublin. Sporting
life on TV thrives on big stakes and a diverse lineup, by F. Klein. Electronic impresarios
cater to TV audiences with games, classics, by S. Grover. How TV commercials use
ploys and anxiety to try to win viewers, by H. Lancaster. Overcoming decades TV set
could become instrument for change, by J. Tannenbaum.
Television programs [U.S.] / Television and children [U.S.] / Television viewers [U.S.] /
Television news [U.S.] / Television advertising [U.S.] / Cable television [U.S.] /
Television broadcasting [U.S.]

Riding, Alan
TV in Spain is cutting back on prime-time sex and violence
The New York Times, May 10,1993, v. 142 p. C6(N) pD6
LC Call Number: Not in LC Collection
Magazine Index Micro Film: None
Television broadcasting - Spain / Sex in television - Spain / Violence in television - Spain
/ Spain - Social policy

Ridley-Johnson, Robyn; Cooper, Harris; Chance, June
The relation of children's television viewing to school achievement and Q. Journal of
educational research, v. 76, May-June 1983: 294-297.
"Results suggest that in this sample: children whose parents set rules for watching
television did better in school and had higher Q.'s than other children; amounts of
viewing of all types of shows were highly correlated, with the exception of sports
viewing; more television watching was associated with lower Q.'s; and higher math
grades were associated with a preference for sports, family, game and cartoon shows."
Television and children [U.S.] Research / Intelligence levels [U.S.] Research / Academic
performance [U.S.] Research

Robertson, Thomas S.; Rossiter, John R.; Gleason, Terry C.
Children's conceptions of proprietary medicines: the role of television advertising, [n.p.,
1978] 158 p.
"NSF/RA-780258"
"Report describes the results of an empirical research project specifically designed to
assess the effects of televised medicine advertising on children... The project objective is
to provide an analysis of the relationship between proprietary medicine advertising and
children's beliefs, attitudes and behavior toward proprietary medicines."
Television and children [U.S.] Research / Drug advertising [U.S.] Research

Roe, K. (1993)
Videovåldets första fans [The First Fans of Video Screen Violence]. In: von Feilitzen, C.;
Forsman, M. & Roe, K. (Eds.): Våld från alla håll: Forskningsperspektiv på våld i rörliga
bilder, pp. 111-128, Stockholm/Stehag: B. Östlings Bokförlag Symposion, 1993, 383 p.,
ISBN 91-7139-123-1.

Roeper, Richard
Religious sanctimony; do unto the Bible as you would to unto TV.
Playboy (Chicago), Dec. 1989, v. 36 n. n12 p. 48(1)
LC Call Number: AP2.P69 Rare Bk.
Magazine Index Micro Film: None
Sex in television - Moral and ethical aspects / Violence in television - Moral and ethical
aspects / Censorship - Moral and ethical aspects / Christian Leaders for Responsible
Television - Management

Rogers, Michael
The last TV taboos. (economic aspects of controversial programs)
Fortune, Oct. 1, 1984, v. 110 p. 8(1)
LC Call Number: HF5001.F7; Microfilm 02739 (1930-   ) MicRR
Magazine Index Micro Film: 24K6288
Violence in television - economic aspects / television programs - economic aspects

Rolston, B. & Miller, D. (Eds.)
(1996)
War and Words: The Northern Ireland Media Reader. Belfast: Beyond the Pale
Publications, 1996, XVII, 458 p., ill., bibl., ISBN 1-90096-000-1.

Roman, James
Dealing with the controversies over children's television, USA Today, v. 109, Sept.
1980: 62-64.
Looks at some of the objections made about children's television and discusses the
various plans which have been suggested as remedies. Concludes that marketplace forces
may offer the best hope for improvement. "If, in the future, more children are drawn
away from broadcast television to the competing technologies, the broadcasters will be
forced to change their approach to children's television."
Television and children [U.S.]

Rose, Frank
Celebrity victims: crime casualties are turning into stars on tabloid TV. New York, v. 22,
July 31, 1989: 38-44.
Chronicles several stories of people who were victims of violent crimes and the public's
thirst to see the victims or their surviving families on television shows or in print
discussing the attack and their feelings. Includes discussions of how victims have started
to help themselves through a variety of means, including self-help groups and therapy
sessions with other victims and their families.
Victims of crimes [U.S.] Trends / Crime and the press [U.S.] Trends / Violence in mass
media [U.S.] Trends / Violence in television [U.S.] Trends / Self-care [U.S.] Trends /
Group counseling [U.S.]

Rosen, Jay
A subtler kind of violence. (television violating propriety)
Channels of communications, May 1987, v. 7 p. 58(1)
LC Call Number: PN1992.6.C514
Magazine Index Micro Film: None
Television broadcasting - moral and ethical aspects / Violence in television - Social
aspects

Rosengren, K.E.; Johnsson-Smaragdi, U. & Sonesson, (1995)
For Better and for Worse: Effects Studies and Beyond. In: Rosengren, K.E. (Ed.): Media

Effects and Beyond: Culture, Socialization and Lifestyles, pp. 133-149, London:
Routledge, 1995, 336 p., ISBN 0-415-0914-1.

Rosenstiel, Thomas B.
Views on TV violence reflect generation gap.
The Los Angeles Times, March 25, 1993, v. 112 p. F2
LC Call Number: Newspaper 7114-X
Business Index Micro Film: NONE
Television viewers - Attitudes / Violence in television - Demographic aspects /
Television - Public opinion

Rossiter, John R.
Does TV advertising affect children? Journal of advertising research, v. 19, Feb. 1979:
49-53.
Summarizes "the research evidence pertaining to the general effects of TV advertising on
children, analyzed as cumulative-exposure effects (with age) and heavy-viewing effects
(within age groups)." Finds that "exposure to TV advertising does not make children
more cognitively or mentally susceptible to persuasion. Children's increasingly negative
expressed attitudes toward TV advertising do not mean much."
Television advertising [U.S.] / Television and children [U.S.]

Rossiter, John R.; Robertson, Thomas S.
Children's dispositions toward proprietary drugs and the role of television drug
advertising. Public opinion quarterly, v. 44, fall 1980: 316-329
"Findings indicate that children are exposed to TV drug advertising while watching
general or adult programs, and that this advertising may to a small extent influence their
attitudes and behaviors toward these products - at least on a short-run basis. In other
words, TV drug advertising does not seem to influence children to an extent that may be
regarded as socially harmful or worthy of further legislative attention."
Television advertising [U.S.] / Drug advertising [U.S.] / Television and children [U.S.]

Rowland, Willard D.
The politics of TV violence: policy uses of communication research / by Willard D.
Rowland, Jr.; foreword by Horace Newcomb. - Beverly Hills, Calif.: Sage, c1983.
320 p.; 23 cm (People and communication; v. 16). Bibliography: p. 308-319.
Television broadcasting - Social aspects - United States. Violence in television - United
States. Title. I Title: Politics of T.V. violence. II Title: Politics of television violence. IV.
Series.

Royal, S. (1989)
Le ras le bol des bébés zappeurs: Télé-massacre, l'overdose? Paris: Robert Laffont, 1989,
192 p., ISBN 2-221-05826-7.

Rubin, Alan M.
Child and adolescent television use and political socialization. Journalism quarterly, v. 55, spring 1978: 125-129.
This study, which is based on questionnaire responses from elementary, junior high and senior high school students in Champaign, Ill., considers the influence of television viewing on the political socialization process. Findings indicate that "television viewing is associated with political knowledge and more favorable attitudes toward government." Political socialization [Illinois] / Television and children [Illinois] / Television and politics [Illinois]

Rubin, Alan M.
Television in children's political socialization. Journal of broadcasting, v. 20, winter 1976: 51-60.
Survey of seventh grade students found that "television was the predominant source of political information about all three objects in the young person's political environment..."
Television and children [Illinois] / Political socialization [Illinois] / Secondary school students

Saltzman, Joe
Beating the same old deadhorse. (hypocrisy of attacking sex and violence only in TV programs) (Column)
USA Today (Magazine) Nov. 1993, v. 122 n. n2582 p. 61(1)
LC Call Number: L11.S36
Magazine Index Micro Film: None
Violence in television - Political aspects

Saltzman, Joe
Good, evil and the media (column)
USA Today (Magazine) Nov. 1985, v. 114 p. 21(1)
LC Call Number: L11.S36
Magazine Index Micro Film: 31F4022
Television broadcasting of news - Analysis / Violence in television - analysis

Sanchís Roca, V. (1996)
Violencia en el cine: Matones y asesinos en serie. Valencia: La Máscara, 1996, 223 p., bibl.

Sander, B. (1997)
How Violent is TV Violence? An Empirical Investigation of Factors Influencing Viewers Perceptions of TV Violence. European Journal of Communication 12(1997)1, pp. 43-98, ISSN 0267-3231.

Sanders, B. (1994)
A is for Ox: Violence, Electronic Media, and the Silencing of the Written Word. New
York: Pantheon Books, 1994, XII, 269 p., bibl., ISBN 0-67941-711-7.

Sandman, Peter M.
The fight over television violence ratings. More, v. 8, April 1978: 35-40.
Recounts the battle between George Gerbner and Roger Wagner over the amount of
violence on television.
Television programs [U.S.] / Violence in television [U.S.] / Gerbner, George / Wagner,
Roger

Sanmartín, J. (1997)
Violencia y medios de comunicación. Valencia: Centro Reina Sofía para el Estudio de la
Violencia, 1997.

Sanmartín, J.; Grisolía, J.S. & Grisolía, S. (Eds.) (1998)
Violencia, televisión y cine. Barcelona: Ariel, 1998, 158 p., ISBN 84-344-7465-4.

Scheungrab, M. (1990)
Die Abbildung von Beziehungen zwischen Medienkonsum und Delinquenz im Rahmen
kausalanalytischer Modelle. Archiv für Psychologie 142(1990)4, pp. 295-322, ISSN
0066-6475.

Scheungrab, M. (1993)
Filmkonsum und Delinquenz: Ergebnisse einer Interviewstudie mit straffälligen und
nicht-straffälligen Jugendlichen und jungen Erwachsenen. Regensburg: Roderer, 1993,
348 p., fig., Diss., ISBN 3-89073-675-0.

Schicht, Jack
Religious groups v. TV's sex, violence. Columbia, School of Journalism, University of
Missouri, 1980, 8 p. (Missouri, University, Freedom of Information Center. Report no.
416)
"Religious organizations - churches and special interest groups - have played an integral
role in the national movement to combat sex and violence in television programming.
This report presents an overview of their role in that movement."
Church and social problems [U.S.] / Lobbyists [U.S.] / Television programs [U.S.] /
Television and children [U.S.] / Violence in television [U.S.] / Sex [U.S.] / Pornography
[U.S.] / Telecommunication policy [U.S.]

Schlesinger, P.; Dobash, R.; Dobash, R. & Weaver, R. (1992)
Women Viewing Violence: How Women Interpret Violence on Television. London:
British Film Institute, 1992, ISBN 0-85170-327-5.

Schmolke, M. (1997)
Gewaltdarstellungen im Fernsehen und ihre Auswirkungen auf Kinder und Jugendliche. Hildesheim: Fachhochschule Hildesheim/Holzminden, 1997, 84 p., fig.

Schneider, B. (1995)
Cowabunga: Zu Darstellung von Konflikten und ihren Lösungen in Zeichentrickserien; eine Inhaltsanalyse. Münster, New York: Waxmann, 1995, 344 p., bibl., Diss., ISBN 3-89325-338-6.

Schneider, H.J. (1996)
Violence in the Mass Media. Studies on Crime and Crime Prevention 5(1996)1, pp. 59-71, ISSN 1102-3937.

Schooler, C. & Flora, J.A. (1996)
Pervasive Media Violence. Annual Review of Public Health 17(1996), pp. 275-298, ISSN 0163-7525.

Schorr, Daniel
Go get some milk and cookies and watch the minutes on television
The Washingtonian, Oct. 1981, v. 17 p. 190(9)
LC Call Number: F191.W37
Magazine Index Micro Film: None
violence in television - social aspects / crime in television - research

Schwantes, Dave
Taming your TV and other media / by Dave Schwantes; edited by Gerald Wheeler. - Nashville: Southern Pub. Association, c1979.
160 p.; 17 cm. Includes bibliographical references.
Television broadcasting Social aspects - United States. Sex in television. Violence in television - United States. Wheeler, Gerald. I Title.

Scully, Sean
V blocker is easy chip shot away. (TV equipment makers say technology needed to censor violent programs does not pose insurmountable obstacles; includes article about V block bill)
Broadcasting and Cable, August 23, 1993, v. 123 n. n34 p. 64(1)
LC Call Number: TK6540B85
Business Index Micro Film: 72Z1439
TV equipment makers say that violence blocker technology does not pose insurmountable obstacles, but problems do exist. This technology would be available in the form of a computer chip with an internal clock. The addition of a memory device to compensate for power loss would raise the chip's cost and would add to the size and complexity of remote controls. In the final analysis the viability of V blocker technology is contingent on the willingness of cable companies or networks to post violence ratings.

Markey, Edward J. - Social policy.
Violence in television - Censorship / Television equipment and supplies industry -
Innovations / Television sets - Laws, regulations, etc.

Selnow, Gary W.; Bettinghaus, Erwin P.
Television exposure and language development. Journal of broadcasting, v. 26, winter
1982: 469-479.
"Correlations between the language sophistication levels of the subjects and television
exposure showed a significant negative inverse relationship. Differential results between
types of programs viewed and language development suggest support for an
environmentalist theory of language development."
Television and children [U.S.] / Language and languages [U.S.] / Child development
[U.S.]

Seltzer, M. (1998)
Serial Killers: Death and Life in America's Wound Culture. New York: Routledge, 1998,
IX, 302 p., ill., bibl., ISBN 0-41591-480-9.

Sen. Simon. (views on violence on cable TV)
Television Digest, Jan. 17, 1994, v. 34, n. n3 p. 6(1)
LC Call Number: May or May Not Be in LC. Search further.
Business Index Micro Film: 75W0007
Simon, Paul (Politician) - Attitudes
Violence in television - Evaluation / Cable television broadcasting industry - Evaluation
Shales, Tom and others
Television: grasping for air. Skeptic, no. 22, Dec. 1977: 13, 15-18, 20-26, 50, 52-54.
Four people - the Washington Post TV critic, a former Aspen Institute researcher, a TV
producer and a Stanford psychologist - give contrasting views on what TV is and ought to
be and on its effects on viewers.
Television programs [U.S.] Pro and con / Television and children [U.S.]

Shaw, Irene S.
Violence on television: program content and viewer perception; projects carried out by
Irene S. Shaw and David S. Newell; under the direction of B.P. Emmett with the advice
and assistance of Elihu Katz. London, British Broadcasting Corporation, 1982.
viii, 220 p. 23 cm. "List in alphabetical order, of programs referred to in Part One of the
report" inserted.
Violence in television - Great Britain. Television viewers - Great Britain. Newell, David
S., joint author. I British Broadcasting Corporation. Audience Research Dept. II Title.

Shaw, Martin.
Civil society and media in global crises :representing distant violence / Martin Shaw.
New York : Pinter, 1996.
viii, 212 p. ; 25 cm.

PN4784.W37 S53 1996
1855673878 1855672243 (pbk.)
Includes bibliographical references (p. [202]-203) and index.
War -- Press coverage. Violence -- Press coverage. Television broadcasting of news.
Broadcast journalism -- Social aspects. International relations -- Social aspects. DLC
DLC YDX
33360204

Should Congress pass legislation regulating TV violence? (Pro and Con)
The Congressional Digest, Dec. 1993, v. 72 n. n12 p. 300(14)
LC Call Number: JK1.C65
Magazine Index Micro Film: None
Violence in television - Social aspects / Television broadcasting - Social aspects

Siano, Brian
Frankenstein must be destroyed: chasing the monster of TV violence
The Humanist (Buffalo, N.Y.)Jan-Feb. 1994, v. 54 n. n1 p. 20(6)
LC Call Number: B821.A1H8
Magazine Index Micro Film: None
Violence in television - Moral and ethical aspects

Signorielli, N.; Morgan, M. & Gerbner, G (1995)
Violence on Television: The Cultural Indicators Project. Journal of Broadcasting and
Electronic Media 32(1995)2, pp. 278-283, ISSN 0883-8151.

Signoriello, Nancy
Television and adolescents' perceptions about work. Youth and society, v. 24, Mar. 1993:
314-341.
Updates "current knowledge about the representation of occupations on prime-time
network dramatic television and begin to explore how these representations may be
related to adolescents' perceptions about the work they will do in the future."
Television and children [U.S.] / Youth [U.S.] / Labor [U.S.]

Silberstein, John
Deregulation and children's advertising. Annual survey of American law, v. 1985, May
1986: 603-620.
Comment examines television deregulation and changes in the FCC's and FTC's
regulatory posture toward children's advertising.
Television advertising [U.S.] /Government regulation [U.S.] / Television and children
[U.S.] / Judicial review of administrative acts [U.S.] / Telecommunication law and
legislation [U.S.] / U.S. Federal Trade Commission / U.S. Federal Communications
Commission

Silver, Marc
Sex, violence and the tube: the fall lineup has more of the first, less of the second. Most of the good TV is aimed at kids. (includes related article)
U.S. News & World Report, Sept. 20, 1993, v. 115 n. n11 p. 76 (4)
LC Call Number: JK1.U65; Microfilm 06106 (1933-   ) MicRR
Magazine Index Micro Film: None
Television programs - Evaluation / Violence in television - Analysis / Sex in television - Analysis / Television programs for children - Evaluation

Simic, P. (1994)
The Former Yugoslavia: The Media and Violence. RFE/RL Research Report 3(1994)4, Fall, pp. 40-47, ISSN 0941-505X.

Singer, Dorothy G.; Zuckerman, Diana M.; Singer, Jerome L.
Helping elementary school children learn about TV. Journal of communication, v. 30, summer 1980: 84-93.
"Third-, fourth-, and fifth-graders learned to understand and criticize television programs and commercials, but parental viewing habits and attitudes toward TV remained a strong influence on children's behavior."
Television and children [U.S.] / Curriculum planning [U.S.]

Siskel, Gene
Tuning out the violence.
Parenting, Dec-Jan 1993 v7 n1 1 p126(4)

Sizer, Theodore R.
What's missing. World monitor, v. 5, Nov. 1992: 20-24, 26-27.
"A master educator surveys America's urgent search for better schools and proposes some answers. Among them; serious attention to children's school away-from-school, the TV tube, and adults who teach by example - not hypocrisy."
Educational policy [U.S.] / Television and children [U.S.]

Smilgis, Martha; Pilcher, Joe; Cronin, Mary
Incredible? Or abominable? For now, at least, those "reality shows" are also really hot.
Time (Chicago) Oct. 13, 1980, v. 116 p. 90(2)
LC Call Number: AP2.T37; Microfilm 02914 (1923-   ) MicRR
Magazine Index Micro Film: None
Landsburg, Alan - production and direction / Sklar, Richard - psychology
That's Incredible (television program) - criticism, interpretation, etc. / Games People Play (television program) - criticism, interpretation, etc. / Those Amazing Animals (television program) - criticism, interpretation, etc. / No Holds Barred (television serial) - criticism, interpretation, etc. / That's My Line (television serial) - critics, interpretation, etc. / Real People (television serial) - criticism, interpretation, etc. / Speak Up America (television serial) - criticism, interpretation, etc. / Fantastic television programs - psychological aspects / television programs - psychological aspects / violence in television -

psychological aspects / violence in television - psychological aspects / realism in moving-pictures - psychological aspects

Smith, M.E. (1993)
Television Violence and Behaviour: A Research Summary. ERIC Digest. Eric Digest (1993)EDO-IR-93-8, Syracuse: ERIC Clearinghouse on Information and Technology, Syracuse University, 1993.

Sneed, C. & Runco, M.A. (1992)
The Beliefs Adults and Children Hold About Television and Video Games. Journal of Psychology 126(1992)3, pp. 273-284, ISSN 0022-3980.

Solons decry vid violence; webs deny link between it and aggression.
Variety, May 17, 1989, v. 335 n. n5 p. 50(1)
LC Call Number: PN2000.V3 Folio; Microfilm 03722 (1905-) MicRR
Magazine Index Micro Film: None
United States. Congress. House. Committee on the Judiciary - investigations / Violence in television - investigations / Television broadcasting policy - investigations

Some 59%. (entertainment industry members feel media violence is a serious problem)
Television Digest, May 9, 1994, v. 34 n. n19 p. 7(1)
LC Call Number: May or May Not Be in LC. Search further.
Business Index Micro Film: 78Q0253
U.S. News and World Report (Periodical) - Surveys / Violence in television - Surveys

Sonesson, (1989)
Vem fostrar våra barn – videon eller vi? TV, video och emotionell och social anpassning [Who Brings Up Our Children – the Video or We? Television, Video and Emotional and Social Adaption]. Stockholm: Esselte Studium, 1989, 168 p., fig., tab., ISBN 91-24-35377-9.

Sonesson, (1989)
Videovåld och forskning [Video Violence and Research]. In: Lindell, E. (Ed.): Med skolan mot våldet, pp. 43-54, Stockholm: Utbildningsförlaget, 1989, 185 p., ISBN 91-47-03190-5.

Sonesson, (1993)
TV- och videovåldets inverkan på barn och ungdomar [The Influence of Violence in Television and Video on Children and Youth]. In: von Feilitzen, C.; Forsman, M. & Roe, K. (Eds.): Våld från alla håll: Forskningsperspektiv på våld i rörliga bilder, pp. 49-67, Stockholm: Brutus Östlings Bokförlag Symposion, 1993, 383 p., ISBN 91-7139-123-1.

Sørensen, B.H. (1995)
Media Violence: Young People. Nordicom Review (1995)2, pp. 13-20, ISSN 1403-1108.

Sparks, G. & Ogles, R. (1989)
Television Violence and Viewers' Perceptions of Criminal Victimization. Mass
Communication Review 16(1989)3, pp. 2-11, ISSN 0193-7707.

Sparks, G. & Ogles, R. (1990)
The Difference Between Fear of Victimization and the Probalitity of Being Victimized:
Implications for Cultivation. Journal of Broadcasting and Electronic Media 34(1990)3,
pp. 351-358, ISSN 0883-8151.

Sparks, R. (1992)
Television and the Drama of Crime: Moral Tales and the Place of Crime
in Public Life. Buckingham: Open University Press, 1992, XIII, 185 p., ISBN 0-33509-
328-0.

Sparks, Richard, 1961-
Television and the drama of crime: moral tales and the place of crime in public life /
Richard Sparks. Buckingham [England]; Philadelphia: Open University Press, 1992
xiii, 185 p.; 24 cm. (New directions in criminology series). Includes bibliographical
references (p.[165]-179) and index.
Crime and television - United States. Violence in television - United States. Television
broadcasting - Social aspects - United States. Television serials - United States. Law
enforcement - United States. Criminology. Title. I Series.

Splaine, John E.
Television and its influence on reading. Educational technology, v. 18, June 1978: 15-19.
Contends that one literacy has the potential for developing other literacies; and, thus, the
viewing of television has the potential for stimulating reading.
Television and children [U.S.] / Reading [U.S.]

Srygley, Sara Krentzman
Influence of mass media on today's young people. Educational leadership, v. 35, April
1978: 526-529.
"Educators are challenged more seriously than ever before to teach young people to
evaluate media more critically and to grow in taste and discrimination as they use media
in school and at home."
Child development [U.S.] / Television and children [U.S.]

Standards go down as channels go up. (talk by Howard Stringer at Hollywood Radio &
Television Society luncheon) (Brief Article)
Broadcasting and Cable, May 10, 1993, v. 123 n. n19 p. 65 (1)
LC Call Number: TK6540B85
Business Index Micro Film: 71Q1534
Stringer, Howard - Addresses, essays, lectures
Television broadcasting industry - Forecasts / Violence in television - Analysis

Swedish National Commission for UNESCO (1996)
Violence on the Screen and the Rights of the Child: Report from a Seminar in Lund, Sweden, 26-27 September 1995. Stockholm: Swedish National Commission for UNESCO, 1996, 177 p., ISSN 0348-8705.

Sweeps violence & sex abound in ratings quest. (survey of local TV news special efforts during May ratings period)
Variety, May 31, 1989, v. 335, n. n7 p. 52(3)
LC Call Number: PN2000.V3 Folio; Microfilm 03722 (1905-) MicRR
Magazine Index Micro Film: None
Television broadcasting of news - innovations / Television programs - Rating / Sensationalism in television - innovations / Sex in television - innovations / Violence in television - innovations
Symposium on commercial speech. Held at Brooklyn Law School, November 10, 1979.
Brooklyn law review, v. 46, spring 1980: whole issue.
Partial contents. Regulation of lawyer advertising: in the public interest? by R. Brosnahan and L. Andrews. A rationale for protecting and regulating commercial speech, by B. Neuborne. The Federal Communications Commission's impact on product advertising, by R. Lee. The First Amendment: barrier or impetus to FTC advertising remedies? by T. Westen. The case for FTC regulation of television advertising directed toward children, by M. Pauker. The pursuit of access in the electronic forum: can such a right be wrong? by D. Lively.
Advertising [U.S.] Conferences / Freedom of speech [U.S.] / Freedom of the press [U.S.] / Trade regulation [U.S.] / Legal advertising and soliciting [U.S.] / Television and children [U.S.] / Fairness doctrine / U.S. Federal Trade Commission / U.S. Federal Communications Commission

Symposium on Television Violence, Queen's University, Kingston, Ont, 1975
Symposium on television violence = Colloque sur la violence a la television / organized by the Research Branch, Canadian Radio-Television Commission, Donald Gordon Centre for Continuing Education, Queen's University, Kingston, 24-26 August 1975. Ottawa: Canadian Radio-Television and Telecommunications Commission, 1976.
xvi, 252 p.; 23 cm. English or French Bibliography: p. 227-233.
Violence in television - Congresses. Canada. Radio-Television Commission. Research Branch. I Title. II Title: Colloque sur la violence a la television.

Tarasov, K.A. (1996)
From Violence in Movies to Violence "Like in the Movies"? Sotsiologicheskie Issledovaniya 23(1996)2, pp. 35-41, ISSN 0132-1625.

Telecommunications Policy Research Conference, 5th, Airlie, Va., 1977
[Papers and proceedings. Washington]
Urban Institute [available from NTIS] 1977, 2 v.
"PB-277 435-PB-277 436"

Conference sponsored by the FCC, NSF, the Office of Telecommunications Policy and others.
"NSF/RA-770398, NSF/RA-770399"
Conference topics included "Toward a system of communications indicators: Revising the 1934 Communications Act: common carrier issues; Limits of television: U.S. policy on international telecommunications; New dimensions in radio spectrum management; Domestic satellite policy; Television advertising and children; Politics and the media; Recent empirical work in common carrier regulation; Roles for telecommunications; Social service delivery; Regulation, invention and innovation."
Telecommunication policy [U.S.] Conferences / Telephone [U.S.] Conferences / Television [U.S.] Conferences / International cooperation in telecommunication - Conferences / Radio broadcasting [U.S.] Conferences / Communication satellites [U.S.] Conferences / Television and children [U.S.] Conferences / Common carriers [U.S.] Conferences

Television and Growing Up: The Impact of Televised Violence (1972). Surgeon Generals Scientific Advisory Committee on Television and Social Behavior (Washington, DC Government Printing Office, 1972) One of the most famous studies on violence and behavior.

Television and the social studies. Social education, v. 52, Sept. 1988: 348-372, 374-383.
Contents. Television and the social studies, by Lynn A. Fontana. TV and teens: television in adolescent social development, by Richard Luker and Jerome Johnston. A perspective on public broadcasting and education, by Douglas F. Bodwell. Connections between television and the social studies curriculum by James S. Eckenrod and Saul Rockman. Television in the social studies classroom, by Keith W. Mielke. Teleeducation: the future by Joseph N. Pelton. Social education resource list by Amy Grotevant. Television production in the political science classroom, by Peter C. Hovde
Television and children [U.S.] / Educational television [U.S.] / Social sciences [U.S.] Study and teaching

Thain, Gerald
Suffer the hucksters to come unto the little children? Possible restrictions of television advertising to children under section 5 of the Federal Trade Commission Act. Boston University law review, v. 56, July 1976: 651-684.
Article explores the nature of concerns for the possible adverse impact of television commercial on child viewers and considers "the feasibility of, as well as the theoretical justification for, action by the Federal Trade Commission (FTC) under section 5 of the Federal Trade Commission Act to limit or prohibit certain television advertisements simply because they are directed to and viewed by large numbers of children."
Television and children [U.S.] / Television advertising [U.S.] / Trade regulation [U.S.] / Federal Trade Commission Act

Thanks but no thanks for sponsoring the program. (television viewers that do not object to sex and violence in television programs still may shun sponsors of those programs) (Brief Article)
ADWEEK Eastern Edition, Nov. 15, 1993, v. 34 n. n46 p. 24 (1)
LC Call Number: May or May Not Be In LC. Search further.
Business Index Micro Film: None
Violence in television - Research / Sex in television - Research / Television advertising - Public opinion

The arts & media. (brief about cable and television network plan to reduce violence on television) (The Week) (Brief Article)
Time (Chicago), Feb. 14, 1994, v. 143 n. n7 p. 18(1)
LC Call Number: AP2.T37; Microfilm 02914 (1923-) MicRR
Magazine Index Micro Film: None
Violence in television - Management

The arts & media. (Brief about cable and television network plan to reduce violence on television) (The Week) (Brief Article)
Time (Chicago), Feb. 14, 1994, v. 143 n. n7 p. 18(1)
LC Call Number: AP2.T37; Microfilm 02914 (1923-) MicRR
Business Index Micro Film: None
Violence in television - Management

The News Hour with Jim Lehrer, Tuesday, June 23, 1998
 [videorecording] / a coproduction of MacNeil/Lehrer
 Productions & WETA in association with WNET/13.
[Alexandria, VA] : Distributed by PBS Video, [1998]
1 videocassette (57 min.) : sd., col. ; 1/2 in.
SII686.N482 1998
VHS.
Anchor, Jim Lehrer.
Originally broadcast on June 23, 1998 on PBS.
Reports include: David Gergen on violence as entertainment.
Closed-captioned.

The Portrayal of violence in television programs: suggestions for a revised note of guidance / [prepared for Alasdair Milne by a group of practitioners in the making of programs]. [London]: British Broadcasting Corporation, [1979]
35 p.; 26 cm. "March 1979" - Cover. Includes bibliographical references.
Violence in television. Television broadcasting - Great Britain. Milne, Alasdair. I British Broadcasting Corporation.

The Revolution wasn't televised : sixties television and social conflict / edited by Lynn Spigel and Michael Curtin.

New York : Routledge, 1997.
361 p. : ill. ; 24 cm.
PN1992.6.R47 1997
0415911214 (hc)
0415911222 (pbk.)
Includes bibliographical references.
Includes: / Mark Alvey -- Senator Dodd goes to Hollywood: investigating video violence

The true story of the Roman arena [videorecording] / Time Watch ; a BBC production in association with Lionheart Television International, Inc. Princeton, N.J. : Films for the Humanities & Sciences [distributor], 1994.
1 videocassette (50 min.) : sd., col. ; 1/2 in.
DG78.1.T74 1994 VHS format.
Originally produced in 1993.
Producer, Jonathan Stamp ; editor, Laurence Rees.
Narrator, Andrew Sachs ; extracts read by Martin Jarvis, Bob Peck.
Drawing on first-hand Roman accounts and modern research, this program traces the Roman origins of the use of violence as mass entertainment through the rise of the Roman arena and the Games associated with it.

The TV habit: what is it doing to our children? PTA Today, April 1981: whole issue.
Partial contents. Television: the American schoolchild's national curriculum day in and day out by G. Gerbner. How to help our teens become critical viewers by D. Lloyd-Kolkin. TV viewing can lead to poor reading habits, bad homework, and tired kids, by V. Penn. Family TV viewing can be a good experience for everyone involved by M. Ploghoft.
Television and children [U.S.]

The violence clip. (V-chip can scramble television programs that are too violent)
Popular mechanics (New York, 1959) May 1994, v. 171 n. n5 p. 114(1)
LC Call Number: TR1.P77; Microfilm 06103 (1952-1965, 1970-1974) MicRR
Magazine Index Micro Film: None
Violence in television - Prevention / Television sets - Innovations

Theunert, H. & Knodt, D. (1994)
Zwischen Vergnügen und Angst – Fernsehen im Alltag von Kindern: Eine Untersuchung zur Wahrnehmung und Verarbeitung von Fernsehinhalten durch Kinder aus unterschiedlichen Soziokulturellen Milieus in Hamburg. Berlin: Vistas Verlag, 1994, 230 p., ill., fig., ISBN 3-89158-077-0.

Theunert, H. & Schorb, B. (1995)
"Mordsbilder": Kinder und Fernsehinformation: Eine Untersuchung zum Umgang von Kindern mit realen Gewaltdarstellungen in Nachrichten und Reality-TV im Auftrag der Hamburgischen Anstalt für Neue Medien (HAM)

und der Bayerischen Landeszentrale für Neue Medien (BLM). Berlin: Vistas Verlag, 1995, 247 p., bibl., ill., fig., ISBN 3-89158-145-9.

Theunert, H. (1996)
Gewalt in den Medien – Gewalt in der Realität: Gesellschaftliche Zusammenhänge und pädagogisches Handeln. München: KoPäd-Verlag, 1996, 259 p., bibl., ISBN 3-929061-18-X.

This is what you thought: readers split on fault for poor student achievement; have violent TV cartoons and toys gone too far?
Glamour, Dec. 1986, v. 84 p. 101(2)
LC Call Number: TT500.G46
Magazine Index Micro Film: 36H0836
Education surveys / Toys - surveys / Violence in television - surveys
Toivonen, K. (1991)
Persianlahden sota, joukkotiedotus ja peruskoululaisten ahdistuneisuus [The Gulf War, Mass Communication and the Anxiety of Pupils of Basic School]. Rovaniemi: Lapin yliopisto, 1991, 108 p., ill., ISBN 951-634-248-5.

Try this for TV violence? (television broadcasting in Libya)
Time (Chicago), March 2, 1987, v. 129 p. 38(1)
LC Call Number: AP2.T37; Microfilm 02914 (1923-) MicRR
Magazine Index Micro Film: 38L0515
Muammar Gaddaf (portrait)
Qadhafi, Muammar - military policy
Violence in television - Libya / Libya - politics and government
Libya

TV mayhem. (Nat'l Coalition on TV Violence survey)
Changing times, March 1983, v. 37 p. 8(1)
LC Call Number: HC101.C47; Microfilm 07057 (1967-1974) MicRR
Magazine Index Micro Film: 16M1994
Violence in television - surveys / National Coalition on Television Violence - surveys

TV protest; church alarm over violence
Time (Chicago), Sept. 30, 1985, v. 126 p. 72(1)
LC Call Number: AP2.T37; Microfilm 02914 (1923-) MicRR
Magazine Index Micro Film: 30K1391
National Council of Churches - social policy / violence in television - Moral and ethical aspects

TV violence in Australia: report to the Minister for Transport and Communications / Australian Broadcasting Tribunal. Sydney: Australian Broadcasting Tribunal, 1990-
v. <1-4>: ill.; 25 cm. Contents: v. 1. Decision and reasons. Research findings. Summary

of submissions; appendixes. Conference of technical papers; appendixes.
Violence in television - Australia. Australian Broadcasting Tribunal. I Australia. Dept. of
Transport and Communications.

TV violence, boycotts & reality. (Federal Communications Commission nominees
Rachelle Chong, Susan Ness pay lip service to advertiser boycotts, but consumer boycotts
are more effective) (Brief Article) (Editorial)
Advertising Age, May 30, 1994, v. 65 n. n23 p. 20(1)
LC Call Number: HF5801.A276
Magazine Index Micro Film: None
Chong, Rachelle - Social policy / Ness, Susan - Social policy
United States. Federal Communications Commission - Officials and employees /
Violence in television - Laws, regulations, etc.

TV violence. New York, WNET/Thirteen, 1983. 8 p.
The MacNeil-Lehrer Report, Jan. 24, 1983
Interview with Dr. Thomas Radecki of the National Coalition on TV Violence. Dr. David
Pearl of the National Institute of Mental health, Dr. Alan Wurtzel of the American
Broadcasting Company and Eric Mink of the St. Louis Post-Dispatch.
Television programs [U.S.] / Violence in television [U.S.]

Twitchell, J.B. (1989)
Preposterous Violence: Fables of Aggression in Modern Culture. New York: Oxford
University Press, 1989, 338 p., ill., bibl., ISBN 0-19505-887-9.

Two separate efforts. (monitoring television violence)
Television Digest, April 18, 1994, v. 34 n. n16 p. 6(1)
LC Call Number: May or May Not Be in LC. Search further.
Business Index Micro Film: 77W0738
Violence in television - Social aspects / Cable television broadcasting industry - Social
policy / Television broadcasting industry - Social policy

Twomey, Steve
Horrific news judgement.
(violent crime is to often the lead story in broadcast news journalism)
The Washington Post, Ian 19, 1998 v120 n19 pB1 col 1 (23 col in)

U.S. Congress. House. Committee on Agriculture. Subcommittee on Domestic
Marketing, Consumer Relations and Nutrition.
Nutrition education, Hearings 95th Cong., 1st sess. Part 1. Washington, U.S. Govt. Print.
Off., 1977, 802 p.
"Serial no. 95-Z"
Hearings held in Washington, D.C., Sept. 27-28, and Oct. 6, 1977: Nov. 7, Boston

Nutrition [U.S.] Study and teaching / Nutrition policy [U.S.] / Television advertising [U.S.] / Television and children [U.S.] / Food relief [U.S.]

U.S. Congress. House. Committee on Interstate and Foreign Commerce. Subcommittee on Communications.
Broadcast advertising and children. Hearings, 94th Cong., 1st sess. July 14-17, 1975. Washington, U.S. Govt. Print. Off., 1976, 495 p.
"Serial no. 94-53"
Television advertising [U.S.] Law and legislation / Television and children [U.S.] Law and legislation / Radio broadcasting [U.S.]

U.S. Congress. Senate. Committee on Commerce, Science and Transportation. Subcommittee on Communications. Commercial time on children's cable TV. Hearing, 101st Congress, 1st session, Oct. 18, 1989. Washington, G.P.O., 1990, 40 p. (Hearing, Senate, 101st Congress, 1st session. S. Hrg. 101-426)
Television and children [U.S.] / Television advertising [U.S.] / Cable television [U.S.]

U.S. Congress. Senate. Committee on Governmental Affairs. Permanent Subcommittee on Investigations.
The role of the entertainment industry in deglamorizing drug use. Hearing, 99th Congress, 1st session. Mar. 20, 1985. Washington, G.P.O., 1985. 183, 1st session, S. Hrg. 99-107)
Drug abuse prevention [U.S.] / Drugs and youth [U.S.] / Television and children [U.S.] / Public service advertising [U.S.] / Entertainers [U.S.]

U.S. Congress. Senate. Committee on the Judiciary.
Cartoon All-Stars to the Rescue. Joint hearing before the Senate Committee on the Judiciary and the House Committee on the Judiciary, 101st Congress, 2nd session on an entertaining way of enlightening children about the dangers of substance abuse. April 19, 1990. Washington, G.P.O., 1991, 52 p. (Hearing, Senate, 101st Congress, 2nd session, S. Hrg. 101-1220)
"Senate Judiciary Committee Serial no. J-101-70: House Judiciary Committee Serial no. 139"
Drug abuse prevention [U.S.] / Drugs and youth [U.S.] / Television and children [U.S.] / Cartoon All-Stars to the Rescue (Television program)

UCLA Television Violence Monitoring Reports
http://ccp.ucla.edu/violence.htm
The UCLA study examines every series, television movie, theatrical film shown on television, children's program, special and advertisement aired during a television season. Over 3,000 hours of television are monitored every year. In a major difference from many previous studies, the UCLA report examines the context in which violence occurs thus distinguishing between violence which in its context raises concerns and that which does not.

Uddén, G. (1996)
Man ville vara hjälte: unga kriminella om faktiskt våld och filmvåld [I Wanted To Be A Hero: Young Criminals About Real Violence and Film Violence]. Stockholm: Ministry of Culture, Ministry of Justice, 1998, 130 p. + app. 8 p., ISBN 91-38-31263-8, ISSN 1102-447X.

van der Voort, T.H.A. (1997)
De invloed van televisiegeweld [The Influence of Television Violence]. Amsterdam: Swets & Zeitlinger, 1997, 212 p., ill., ISBN 90-265-1076-4.

van Loon, J. (1997)
Chronoes: Of/In the Televisualization of the 1992 Los Angeles Riots. Theory, Culture and Society 14(1997)2, pp. 89-104, ISSN 0263-2764.

Varma, V. (Ed.)
(1996)
Violence in Children and Adolescents. London: Jessica Kingsley Publishers, 1997, 217 p., ill., ISBN 1-85302-344-2.

Vedel, T. (1995)
Médias et violence. Paris: Institut des hautes etudes de la sécurité intérieure, 1995, 246 p., ISSN 1150-1634.

Video venom. (are TV addicts healthy?)
Time (Chicago), Oct. 20, 1980, v. 116 p. 81(1)
LC Call Number: AP2.T37; Microfilm 02914 (1923-   )MicRR
Magazine Index Micro Film: None
Television programs - sociological aspects / violence in television - research

Vidulich, Dorothy
Her 'literacy' campaign targets media violence. (Sister Elizabeth Thoman campaigns against television violence) (Column)
National Catholic reporter, March 18, 1994, v. 30 n. n20 p. 15(1)
LC Call Number: Microfilm 04882 (1964-   ) MicRR
Magazine Index Micro Film: None
Thoman, Elizabeth - Social policy / Violence in television - Management

Viemerö, V. & Paajanen, S. (1992)
The Role of Fantasies and Dreams in the TV Viewing-Aggression Relationship. Aggressive Behaviour 18(1992), pp. 109-116, ISSN 0096-140X.

Viles, Peter
Cuomo: let the people choose. (Mario M. Cuomo, violence in television) (Brief Article)
Broadcasting and Cable, Dec. 6, 1993, v. 123 n. n49 p. 18(1).

LC Call Number: TK6540B85
Business Index Micro Film: 74X2648
Cuomo, Mario M. - Addresses, essays, lectures
International Radio and Television Society - Conferences, meetings, seminars, etc./
Violence in television - Political aspects / Television broadcasting industry - Laws,
regulations, etc.

Violence on TV & you
Co-Ed, Oct. 1983, v. 29 p. 34 (7)
Magazine Index Micro Film: None
Violence in television - social aspects
Violence summit asked. (violence on TV)
Television Digest, Nov. 29, 1993, v. 33 n. n48 p. 6(1)
LC Call Number: May or May Not Be in LC. Search further.
Business Index Micro Film: 74W1297
Violence in television - United States / United States - Social aspects
United States

Violence, crime and Janet Reno. (US Attorney General) (American Survey) (Column)
Economist (London), Oct. 30, 1993, v. 329 n. n7835 p. A32 (1)
LC Call Number: HG11.E2; Microfilm 03394 (1843-   ) MicRR
Business Index Micro Film: None
Reno, Janet - Evaluation
Attorney general's - Evaluation / Crime prevention - Analysis / Violence in television -
Laws, regulations, etc.

Violence: can we outgrow it?
Engage/social action, v. 10, Mar. 1982: 9-40.
Articles discuss nuclear war preparations, spouse abuse, violence on television, the death
penalty and child abuse from a Christian perspective.
Violence in television [U.S.] / Nuclear weapons [U.S.] /War and religion [U.S.] /
Television and children [U.S.] / Capital punishment [U.S.] / Family violence [U.S.] /
Church and social problems [U.S.]

Vogelgesang, W. (1991)
Jugendliche Video-Cliquen: Action- und Horrorvideos als Kristallisationspunkte einer
neuen Fankultur. Opladen: Westdeutscher Verlag, 1991, VII, 313 p., fig., Diss., ISBN 3-
531-12226-6.

Volgy, Thomas J.; Schwarz, John E.
TV entertainment programming and sociopolitical attitudes. Journalism quarterly, v. 57,
spring 1980: 15-155.
Examines the "empirical relationships between exposure to entertainment programming

and the attitudes of the public viewing the programs."
Political socialization [U.S.] / Television programs [U.S.] / Television and children [U.S.]

Wall, M.A.A. (1997)
"Pernicions New Strain of the Old Nazi Virus" and an "Orgy of Tribal Slaughter": A
Comparison of U.S. News Magazine Coverage of the Crisis in Bosnia and Rwanda.
Gazette 59(1997)6, pp. 411-428, ISSN 0016-5492.

Walsh D
TV violence.
Fairview Behavioral Services, USA.
Minn Med, 78:14-5, 48, 1995 Jun

Walsh, Thomas
"Law & Order" star quits amid violence protests. (NBC television series; Michael
Moriarty)
Back Stage, Feb. 4, 1994, v. 35 n. n5 p. 1(2)
LC Call Number: Microfilm 83/411
Business Index Micro Film: 76P3553
Michael Moriarty, star of the NBC television series "Law & Order," has announced his
intentions to quit the show at the end of the season. Moriarty is quitting as part of his
personal protest campaign against Atty. Gen. Janet Reno's attacks on violence in the
television industry. Moriarty's campaign, which includes several full-page ads in national
trade periodicals, suggests heavy censorship in the network. Reports have it that Sam
Waterson is being considered to replace Moriarty.
Moriarty, Michael - Political activity / Reno, Janet - Social policy
Law and Order (Television program) - Censorship / Television broadcasting industry -
Social policy / Violence in television - Censorship

Ward, Scott
Compromise in commercials for children. Harvard business review, v. 56, Nov.-Dec.
1978: 128-136.
"The Federal Trade Commission's 'kidvid rule' is the heaviest attack to date on
children's television advertising. In the recent war between consumer activists and
regulatory agencies, on the one hand, and the TV advertisers, on the other, however, the
real issues underlying the various charges against TV advertising for children are far
from clear-cut, says this author. He points out that both sides of the controversy are
adopting a political-legal approach that involves a costly and protracted battle, and he
suggests a more rational alternative using research-based educational methods."
Television advertising [U.S.] / Television and children [U.S.] / U.S. Federal Trade
Commission

Wartella, E.; Whitney, C.; Lasorsa, D.; Danielson, W.; Olivarez, A.; Olivarez, R.; Lopez,
R.; Jennings, N. & Klijn, M. (1998)

Television Violence in 'Reality' Programming: University of Texas, Austin Study. In: Federman, J. (Ed.): National Television Violence Study. Volume 2, pp. 205-266, Thousand Oaks: Sage Publications, 1998, 424 p., ISBN 0-7619-1088-3.

Wass, H.; Raup, J.; Cerullo, K.; Martel, L.; Mingione, L. & Sperring, A. (1989) Adolescents' Interest in and View of Destructive Themes in Rock Music. Omega Journal of Death and Dying 19(1989)3, pp. 177-186, ISSN 0030-2228.

Wass, H.; Raup, J.L. & Sisler, H.H. (1989) Adolescents and Death on Television: A Follow-Up Study. Death Studies 13(1989), pp. 161-173, ISSN 0748-1187.

Waters, Harry F. TV's record crime wave: 'tis the season of cops, con men, pushers and pimps Newsweek, May 6, 1985, v. 105 p. 76(3) LC Call Number: AP2.N6772; Microfilm 01125 (1933-) MicRR Magazine Index Micro Film: 27G1887 Violence in television - analysis / detective and mystery television programs - evaluation / television programs - popular culture

Watne, O. (1992) Barn, film og sensur: filmsensurpraksis i Norge, Sverige og Danmark relatert til forskning om barn og film [Children, Film and Censorship in Norway, Sweden and Denmark]. Trondheim: Universitetet i Trondheim, 1992, 195 p., processed.

Watson, C. et al. (1991) Television Violence: An Analysis of the Portrayal of Violent Acts on three New Zealand Broadcasting Television Channels during the Week of 11th-17th February 1991. Palmerston North: Broadcasting Standards Authority, 1991, 69 p., ill.

Wattwood, Robert FTC regulation of TV advertising to children - they deserve a break today. University of Florida law review, v. 30, fall 1978: 946-978. Comment "discusses whether restrictions on children's advertising are socially, legally and economically justifiable. Initially, the public interest justification for the proposal and the statutory grounds upon which the Commission may base its proposed regulation are considered. Following this examination is a delineation of the potential constitutional and economic problems confronting the proposal and the possible resolution of these problems." Television and children [U.S.] / Television advertising [U.S.] / Independent regulatory commissions / U.S. Federal Trade Commission

Weaver, J.B. & Tamborini, R. (Eds.) (1996)
Horror Films: Current Research on Audience Preferences and Reactions. Mahwah:
Lawrence Erlbaum Associates, 1996, X, 206 p., ISBN 0-80581-173-7.

Webster, James G.; Coscarelli, William C.
The relative appeal to children off adult versus children's television programming.
Journal of broadcasting, v. 23, fall 1979: 437-451.
Find that "children's programs tended to be less preferred by children than the adult
programs they replaced, and the overwhelming majority of children would prefer to
watch their favorite adult program even if children's programming were available to
them."
Television programs [U.S.] / Television and children [U.S.]

Weibull, L. (1997)
Swedish Views on Violence in Society: How Important are the Media. In: Carlsson, U.
(Ed.): Beyond Media Uses and Effects, pp. 131-146, Göteborg: Göteborgs universitet,
1997, 147 p., ISSN 0349-1242.

Weimann, G. & Brosius, H-B. (1989)
Die Attraktivität von Gewalt: über welche internationalen Terroransclage berichten die
Medien? Publizistik 34(1989)3, pp. 329-339, ISSN 0033-4006.

Weiner, Stewart
Shock TV. (show 'I Witness Video')
TV guide, April 4, 1992, v. 40 n. n14 p. 30(3)
LC Call Number: Microfilm 06378 (1953-) MicRR
Magazine Index Micro Film: None
I Witness Video (Television program) - Criticism, interpretation, etc. / Television
programs - Criticism, interpretation, etc. / Violence in television - Social aspects

Weir, Walter
Advertisers hold solution to problem of TV violence. (Column)
Advertising Age, August 9, 1993, v. 64 n. n33 p. 14(1)
LC Call Number: HF5801.A276
Business Index Micro Film: 72Y4187
Studies have shown that television violence promotes violent behavior among youth.
Television executives continue to use violence, however, to improve ratings and attract
more advertising money. Advertisers, by telling their ad agencies to avoid placing
commercials on violent programs, could virtually end violent programming. The Bill
Cosby Show, Murphy Brown and other shows, though they are not violent, still attract
viewers.
Violence in television - Control / Television advertising - Social aspects

Weisman, John
TV and terrorism; when reporting can blow up in your face. (how to cover terrorist activities without encouraging others)
TV Guide, Feb. 23, 1985, v. 33 p. 2(4)
LC Call Number: Microfilm 06378 (1953-   ) MicRR
Magazine Index Micro Film: 28B0073
terrorism - television use / television broadcasting of news - analysis / violence in television - international aspects

Werner, A. (1994)
Barn i fjernsynsalderen: hva vet vi om medienes innflytelse? [Children in the Television Age]. Oslo: Ad Notam/Gyldendal, 1994, 156 p., fig., ill., ISBN 82-417-0260-4.

Werner, A. (1996)
Vold i mediene: hva skjer med publikum [Violence in the Media: What Happens With the Audicence?]. In: Pedersen, T.B. (Ed.): Kjønn i media: konferanse om utviklingen i mediene i et kjønnsperspektiv, pp. 142 150, Oslo: 1996, 271 p., ISBN 82-91242-04-6.

Wessely, C. (1997)
Von Star Wars, Ultima und Doom: Mythologisch verschleierte Gewaltmechanismen im kommerziellen Film und in Computerrollenspielen. Frankfurt am Main: Lang, 1997, 354 p., ill., fig., bibl., Diss., ISBN 3-631-31736-0.

Westin, C. (1994)
Våldet i bildmedierna: reflektioner utifrån en attitydundersökning [Violence in Visual Media: Reflections on an Attitude Survey]. Stockholm: Kulturdepartementet, Våldsskildringsrådet, 1994, 142 p., tab., ISSN 1102-447X.

What can be done? (violence in television) (Outlook)
CQ Researcher, March 26, 1993, v. 3 n. n12 p. 283 (2)
LC Call Number: II35.E35
Magazine Index Micro Film: None
Criticism of the media stemming from portrayals of sex and violence may be addressed with several individual and group efforts. For instance, parents may limit their children's viewing hours, monitor and discuss the shows with their children or turn off the television when programs they find objectionable are aired. Efforts such as complaining to television stations and political lobbying may also be necessary. However, the most effective control against violence may be to address the problem of poverty which is viewed as a root of violence in society.
Violence in television - Social aspects / Poverty - Psychological aspects / Violence - Causes of

What it does best. (television programming)
Life (Chicago), March 1989, v. 12 n. n3 p. 102 (10)

LC Call Number: AP2.L547 (1936-1978); AP2.L54715 (1978-   ); Microfilm 05422 and 06260 (1936-1972) MicRR
Magazine Index Micro Film: None
Nixon, Richard M. - Media coverage
Television broadcasting of sports - criticism, interpretation, etc. / Television and family - criticism, interpretation, etc. / Violence in television - criticism, interpretation, etc. / Television and politics - criticism, interpretation, etc. / Comedy programs - criticism, interpretation, etc.

White, Daniel R.
America's most wanted. American Bar Association journal, v. 75, Oct. 1989: 92-94, 96.
Profiles " 'America's Most Wanted', a half-hour weekly television show produced by Fox Broadcasting Co.," which uses re-enactments of vicious crimes as a vehicle to help authorities to capture fugitives. "As of this writing, 58 fugitives have been captured as a direct result of tips supplied by the show's viewers. Based on 76 episodes aired, this means over 76 percent of all episodes have resulted directly in a capture."
Crime and the press [U.S.] Trends / Violence in television [U.S.] / Television news [U.S.] / Fugitives from justice [U.S.]

Whitmer, B. (1997)
The Violence Mythos. Albany: State University of New York Press, 1997, XIV, 304 p., ill., bibl., ISBN 0-52021-571-0.

Whitney, C.; Wartella, E.; Lasorsa, D.; Danielson, W.; Olivarez, A.; Lopez, R. & Klijn, M. (1997)
Television Violence in 'Reality' Programming: University of Texas at Austin Study. In: Federman, J. (Ed.): National Television Violence Study. Volume 1, pp. 269-359, Thousand Oaks: Sage Publications, 1997, 568 p., ISBN 0-7619-0802-1.

Why we watch : the attractions of violent entertainment / edited by Jeffrey Goldstein.
New York : Oxford University Press, 1998. x, 270 p. : ill. ; 24 cm.
P96.V52 U68 1998
0195118219 (pbk. : alk. paper). 0195118200 (cloth : alk. paper)
The appeal of violent sports / Allen Guttmann – Death takes a holiday, sort of / Vicki Goldberg -- Immortal Kombat: war toys and violent video games / Jeffrey Goldstein -- Violent delights in children's literature / Maria Tatar -- Children's attraction to violent television programming / Joanne Cantor -- A test for the individual viewer: Bonnie and Clyde's violent reception / J. Hoberman -- When screen violence is not attractive / Clark McCauley -- The presence of violence in religion. / Maurice Bloch -- The psychology of the appeal of portrayals of violence / Dolf Zillmann -- Why we watch / Jeffrey Goldstein. Includes bibliographical references (p. 227-253) and indexes.

Wiegman, O.; Kuttschreuter, M. & Baarda, B. (1989)
Televisie, agressie en prosociaal gedrag: Een nadere beschouwing [Television,
Aggression, and Prosocial Behavior: A Closer Examination]. Nederlands Tijdschrift voor
de Psychologie en haar Grensgebieden 44(1989)2, pp. 49-61, ISSN 0028-2235.
Wiegman, O.; Kuttschreuter, M. & Baarda, B. (1992)
A Longitudinal Study of the Effects of Television Viewing on Aggressive and Prosocial
Behaviours. British Journal of Social Psychology 31(1992)2, pp. 147-164, ISSN 0144-
6665.

Wild at heart. (sex and violence in wildlife films)
The New Yorker, Nov. 9, 1992, v. 68 n. n38 p. 42(1)
LC Call Number: AP2.N6763; Microfilm 06192 (1925-1978) MicRR
Magazine Index Micro Film: None
Nature television programs - Criticism, interpretation, etc. / Violence in television -
Criticism, interpretation, etc. / Sex in television - Criticism, interpretation, etc.

Wilkinson, Francis
More Washington show talk; in today's episode, TV ruins everything (politics of
violence on television)
Rolling Stone, Dec. 9, 1993, n. n671 p. 38(1)
LC Call Number: AP2.R73; Microfilm (0) 82/105 (1967-1983) MicRR
Magazine Index Micro Film: None
Violence in television - Censorship / Censorship - Political aspects

Williams, Patricia A. and others
The impact of leisure-time television on school learning: a research synthesis. American
educational research journal, v. 19, spring 1982: 19-50.
"This synthesis of 23 research studies indicated that there is a slight negative relationship
between television viewing and achievement."
Television and children [U.S.] / Academic performance [U.S.]

Willis, E. & Strasburger, V.C. (1998)
Media Violence. Pedriatric Clinics of North America 45(1998)2, pp. 319-331, ISSN
0031-3955.

Wilson, B.J.; Kunkel, D.; Linz, D.; Potter, J.; Donnerstein, E.; Smith, S.L.; Blumenthal,
E. & Berry, M. (1998)
Violence in Television Programming Overall: University of California, Santa Barbara
Study. In: Federman, J. (Ed.): National Television Violence Study. Volume 2, pp. 3-204,
Thousand Oaks: Sage Publications, 1998, 424 p., ISBN 0-7619-1088-3.

Wistrand, M. (1992)
Entertainment and Violence in Ancient Rome: The Attidues of Roman Writers of the
First Century A.D. Göteborg: Acta Universitatis Gothoburgensis, 1992, 133 p., Diss.,
ISBN 91-7346-255-1.

Wober, M. (1992)
Violence and Appreciation: The Broken Chain. Medienpsychologie 4(1992)1, pp. 15-24,
ISSN 0936-7780.

Woiwode, Larry
Television: the cyclops that eats books.
USA Today (Magazine), March 1993, v. 121 n. n2574 p. 84 (2)
LC Call Number: L11.S36
Magazine Index Micro Film: None
Television - Social aspects / Violence in television - Analysis / Reading - Social aspects

Women viewing violence / Philip Schlesinger… [et al.]. London: British Film Institute,
1992.
xii, 210 p.: ill.; 22 cm. "Published… in associated with the Broadcasting Standards
Council" - T.p. verso. Includes bibliographical references (p. 183-184) and index.
Women - Crimes against - Great Britain. Violence in television - Great Britain.
Television and women - Great Britain. Schlesinger, Philip, 1948-

Women viewing violence / Philip Schlesinger... [et al.]
London : British Film Institute, 1992.
xii, 210 p. : ill. ; 22 cm.
PN1992.6.W67 1992
0851703275 (pbk.). 0851703305 (hbk.)
Published... in association with the Broadcasting Standards Council--T.p. verso.
Includes bibliographical references (p. 183-184)

Wood, Daniel B.
'Live' suicide in L.A. forces questions of broadcast ethics; a grisly shooting raises
concerns about media's hot pursuit of news via helicopters. by
The Christian Science Monitor, May 4, 1998 v90 n110 p3 col 1 (23 col in)

Wood, W.; Wong, F.Y. & Chachere, J.G. (1991)
Effects of Media Violence on Viewers' Aggression in Unconstrained Social Interaction.
Psychological Bulletin 109(1991)3, pp. 371-383, ISSN 0033-2909.

Worwode, Larry
Television: the cyclops that eats books.
USA Today (Magazine), March 1993 v121 n2574 p84(2)

Wurtzel, A. & Lometti, G. (1990)
The Television Violence: Viewer Aggression Debate. In: Surette, R. et al. (Eds.): The
Media and Criminal Justice Policy: Recent Research and Social Effects, pp. 23-33,
Springfield: Charles C Thomas Publisher, 1990, XX, 312 p., ISBN 0-39805-687-0.

Yuji, H. & Mori, S. (1995)
Gender and Violence on Computer Games (in Japanese). Journal of Child Study (1995)1,
pp. 93-104.
Zier, Julie A.
TV violence study released. (Center for Media and Public Affairs) (Brief Article)
Broadcasting and Cable, August 8, 1994, v. 124 n. n32 p. 56(1)
LC Call Number: TK6540B85
Business Index Micro Film: None
Violence in television - Statistics / Television programs - Surveys

Zillmann, D. & Weaver, J.B. (1997)
Psychoticism in the Effect of Prolonged Exposure to Gratuitous Media Violence on the
Acceptance of Violence as a Preferred Means of Conflict Resolution. Personality and
Individual Differences 22(1997)5, pp. 613-627, ISSN 0191-8869.

Zillmann, D.; Bryant, J. & Huston, A.C. (Eds.) (1994)
Media, Children, and the Family: Social Scientific, Psychodynamic, and Clinical
Perspectives. Hillsdale: Lawrence Erlbaum Associates, 1994, XIII, 351 p., ISBN 0-
80581-210-5.

Zimmerman, J.D. (1996)
A Prosocial Media Strategy: "Youth against Violence: Choose to De-Fuse". American
Journal of Orthopsychiatry 66(1996)3, pp. 354-362, ISSN 0002-9432.

Zoglin, Richard
A walk on the seamy side: new tabloid shows are thriving on sex and violent crime.
(television programming)
Time (Chicago), Oct. 31, 1988, v. 132 n. n18 p. 78(1)
LC Call Number: AP2.T37; Microfilm 02914 (1923-   ) MicRR
Magazine Index Micro Film: 46M0443

Geraldo Rivera. (portrait)
Rivera, Geraldo - production and direction
Crime in television - production and direction / Violence in television - production and
direction / Tabloid newspapers - television use / Television programs - popular culture

Zoglin, Richard
All the news that's fit. (G-rated news broadcasts)
Time (Chicago), June 20, 1994, v. 143 n. n25 p. 55(1)
LC Call Number: AP2.T37; Microfilm 02914 (1923-   ) MicRR
Magazine Index Micro Film: None
Television broadcasting of news - Social aspects / Violence in television - Social aspects

Zoglin, Richard
All the news that's fit. (G-rated news broadcasts)
Time (Chicago), June 20, 1994, v. 143 n. n25 p. 55(1)
LC Call Number: AP2.T37; Microfilm 02914 (1923-   ) MicRR
Business Index Micro Film: None
Television broadcasting of news - Social aspects / Violence in television - Social aspects

Zoglin, Richard
Oh, the agony! The ratings! (violence towards women on television)
Time (Chicago) Nov. 11, 1991, v. 138 n., n19 p. 88(1)
LC Call Number: AP2.T37; Microfilm 02914 (1923-   )
MicRR
Business Index Micro Film: 62C1255
Violence in television - Portrayals, depictions, etc. / Women in television - Portrayals,
depictions, etc.

Zoglin, Richard
The networks run for cover: to avoid a warning label, violent shows are getting toned
down - or dropped.
Time (Chicago), August 2, 1993, v. 142 n. n5 p. 52(2)
LC Call Number: AP2.T37; Microfilm 02914 (1923-   ) MicRR
Magazine Index Micro Film: None
Violence in television - Production and direction / Television programs - Rating /
Television producers and directors - Practice

Zuckerman, D.M. (1996)
Media Violence, Gun Control, and Public Policy. American Journal of Orthopsychiatry 66(1996)3, pp. 378-389, ISSN 0002-9432.

Zupanov, J. (1995)
Mass Media and Collective Violence. Javnost / Public 2(1995)2, Summer, pp. 77-84, ISBN 1318-3222.

TV Industry

ABC, CBS, FOX and NBC are searching for an outside expert to conduct an annual review of their programs for violent content. (Brief Article)
Broadcasting and Cable, April 11, 1994, v. 124 n. n15 p. 68(1)
LC Call Number: TK6540B85
Business Index Micro Film: 77U1335
Television broadcasting industry - Social policy / Violence in television - Prevention

Amid the aftershock of last Monday's earthquake in Los Angeles, the National Cable Television Association board met. (dealing with Congress' request to reduce violence on cable television) (Brief Article)
Broadcasting and Cable, Jan. 24, 1994, v. 124 n. n4 p. 154(1)
LC Call Number: TK6540B85
Business Index Micro Film: None
National Cable Television Association - Political activity / Cable television broadcasting industry - Political activity / Violence in television - Laws, regulations, etc.

Andrews, Edmund L.
4 networks agree to offer warnings of violence on TV: advisories for parents; on-the-air messages are seen as way to blunt demands for U.S. rating system. (ABC, CBS, NBC and Fox to provide cautions in hopes of discouraging regulations and technology that
The New York Times, June 30, 1993, v. 142 p. A1(N) pA1
LC Call Number: Not in LC Collection
Magazine Index Micro Film: NONE
Violence in television - Laws, regulations, etc. / Television programs - Rating / Television broadcasting industry - Social policy

Andrews, Edmund L.
Cable industry endorses ratings and devices to lock out violence. (in hopes of placating Federal lawmakers angry about violence on television)
The New York Times, Jan. 22, 1994, v. 143 p. 1(N) p11(L
LC Call Number: Not in LC Collection
Business Index Micro Film: None
United States. Congress - Social policy / Cable television broadcasting industry - Laws, regulations, etc. / Violence in television - Laws, regulations, etc.

Benson, Jim
Advisory fallout bruises TV biz: syndicators, local stations shy away from labeling issue.
(violence on television)
Variety, July 19, 1993, v. 351 n. n10 p. 25 (2)
LC Call Number: PN2000.V3 Folio; Microfilm 03722 (1905-)MicRR
Business Index Micro Film: None
Violence in television - Labeling / Television broadcasting industry - Analysis /
Television programs - Labeling

Bok, S. (1998)
Mayhem: Violence as Public Entertainment. Reading/Massachusetts: Addison Wesley,
1998, X, 194 p., ISBN 0-201-48979-1.

Boyatizis, C.J. (1995)
Effects of the 'The Mighty Morphin Power Rangers' on Children's Aggression With
Peers. Child Study Journal 25(1995)1, pp. 45-55, ISSN 0009-4005.

Braun, C. & Giroux, J. (1989)
Arcade Video Games: Proxemic, Cognitive and Content Analyses. Journal of Leisure
Research 21(1989)2, pp. 92-105, ISSN 0022-2216.

British report calls for more vid legislation
Variety, Oct. 23, 1985, v. 320 p. 1(2)
LC Call Number: PN2000.V3 Folio; Microfilm 03722 91905-) MicRR
Magazine Index Micro Film: None
Video tape industry - United Kingdom / Violence in television - United Kingdom /
Television broadcasting policy - United Kingdom

Broadcasters' reluctance. (House Telecom Subcommittee Chairman Markey addresses
National Information Infrastructure hearing)
Television Digest, Feb. 7, 1994, v. 34 n. n6 p. 9(1)
LC Call Number: May or May Not Be in LC. Search further.
Business Index Micro Film: 76R0170
Television broadcasting industry - Conferences, meetings, seminars, etc. / Violence in
television - Conferences, meetings, seminars, etc. / Television equipment and supplies
industry - Conferences, meetings, seminars, etc.

Brodie, John; Robins, J. Max
TV's year of living cautiously: advertiser - friendly skeds drop the wacky and weird
(Television programming)
Variety, May 24, 1993, v. 351 n. n4 p. 1(2)
LC Call Number: PN2000.V3 Folio; Microfilm 03722 (1905-) MicRR
Magazine Index Micro Film: None

Television broadcasting industry - Analysis / Television programs - Planning / Violence in television - Investigations

Brodie, John; Robins, J. Max
Webs mad as hell over Capitol crix. (legislation on television violence)
Variety, August 2, 1993, v. 351 n. n12 p. 1(2)
LC Call Number: PN2000.V3 Folio; Microfilm 03722 (1905-   ) MicRR
Business Index Micro Film: None
Violence in television - Political aspects / Television broadcasting industry - Political activity

Bunce, Alan
TV looks at violence, and looks and looks. (in the face of mounting pressure, television broadcasting industry promises to voluntarily reduce violence) (Column)
The Christian Science Monitor, (1983), Jan. 28, 1994, v. 86 n. n45 p. 17
LC Call Number: Newspaper
Business Index Micro Film: None
Television broadcasting industry - Standards / Violence in television - Standards / Cable television broadcasting industry - Standards

Cable backs violence controls, broadcasters monitoring. (television broadcasters and cable programmers)
Television Digest, Feb. 7, 1994, v. 34 n. n6 p. 1(2)
LC Call Number: May or May Not Be in LC. Search further.
Business Index Micro Film: 76R0162
Television broadcasters and cable operators expressed different opinions on the issue of controlling TV violence, with large cable companies supporting a broad program, while broadcasters decided to limit change only to monitoring. The cable programmer's plan endorses the use of V-chips in TV sets, providing parents with more information for controlling material viewed by children. On the contrary, broadcasters confirmed that they will only perform qualitative monitoring due to their opposition to several proposed bills prescribing ratings and defining violence of programs on TV.
Cable television broadcasting industry - Political activity / Television broadcasting industry - Political activity / Violence in television - Cases

Cable industry picks violence monitor (nonprofit MediaScope promotes "pro-social" entertainment)
The Los Angeles Times, May 17, 1994, v. 113 p. D2
LC Call Number: Newspaper 7114-X
Business Index Micro Film: None
Cable television broadcasting industry - Investigations / Violence in television - Investigations

Cable industry won't be ready to discuss violence on TV until next year.
Television Digest, Dec. 21, 1992, v. 32 n. n51 p. 7(1)
LC Call Number: May or May Not Be In LC. Search further.
Business Index Micro Film: 68Z0080
Cable television broadcasting industry - Social policy / Violence in television - Laws, regulations, etc.

Cable networks developing violence ratings system. (ratings system for television programs)
The Wall Street Journal, Jan. 24, 1994, p. B3(W) pB6
LC Call Number: See Catalogs or Staff
Business Index Micro Film: None
National Cable Television Association - Social policy / Cable television broadcasting industry - Social policy / Violence in television - Management / Television programs - Rating

Cable officials agree to outside monitor of network violence. (National Cable Television Association)
The Wall Street Journal, Jan. 10, 1994, p. B7(W) pB5
LC Call Number: See Catalogs or Staff
Business Index Micro Film: None
National Cable Television Association - Conferences, meetings, seminars, etc. / Cable television broadcasting industry - Laws, regulations, etc. / Violence in television - Laws, regulations, etc.

Cable picks Mediascope to watch violence.
Television Digest, May 23, 1994, v. 34 n. n21 p. 2(2)
LC Call Number: May or May Not Be in LC. Search further.
Business Index Micro Film: 78V0027
Mediascope has been selected by cable television industry officials to monitor television violence. The California-based firm will receive $1.2 million annually to conduct year-long studies of TV violence, which is expected to increase pressure on broadcasters. Mediascope will pass a final report to the National Cable Television Assn. in the fall of 1995 after monitoring 12 basic cable channels, 5 premiums and 3 local independent TV stations.
Violence in television - Management / Cable television broadcasting industry - management

Cable ratings on violence. (cable television industry developing rating system for violence)
The New York Times, Jan. 21, 1994, v. 143, p. D16 (L)
LC Call Number: Not in LC Collection
Magazine Index Micro Film: None

Cable television broadcasting industry - Social policy / Violence in television - Laws, regulations, etc.

Cable TV industry offers plan on violence. (National Cable Television Association announces rating system)
The New York Times, Feb. 2, 1994, v. 143 p. C5(N) pD5
LC Call Number: Not in LC Collection
Magazine Index Micro Film: None
Cable television broadcasting industry - Social policy / Violence in television - Laws, regulations, etc.

Cantor, J. & Harrison, K. (1997)
Ratings and Advisories for Television Programming: University of Wisconsin, Madison Study. In: Federman, J. (Ed.): National Television Violence Study. Volume 1, pp. 361-410, Thousand Oaks: Sage Publications, 1997, 568 p., ISBN 0-7619-0802-1.

Cantor, J.; Harrison, K. & Nathanson, A. (1998)
Ratings and Advisories for Television Programming. In: Federman, J. (Ed.): National Television Violence Study. Volume 2., pp. 267-322, Thousand Oaks: Sage Publications, 1998, 424 p., ISBN 0-7619-1088-3.

Carter, Bill
Networks start to tune out tabloid movies. (ABC, CBS, and NBC seem to cede sensational docudrama market to Fox Television) (Living Arts Pages)
The New York Times, July 27, 1994, v. 143 p. B1(N) pC9
LC Call Number: Not in LC Collection
Business Index Micro Film: None
Television broadcasting industry - Planning / Docudrama television programs - Planning / Violence in television - Evaluation

Carter, Bill
Uproar on TV violence frustrates the networks. (network executives claim violent programming predominates on cable and independent television stations)
The New York Times, July 5, 1993, v. 142 p. 25(N) p41
LC Call Number: Not in LC Collection
Magazine Index Micro Film: None
Television broadcasting industry - Social policy / Violence in television - Analysis

Cerone, Daniel
TV violence summit; a war of words. (meeting to discuss violence in television dissolves into finger-pointing blame game)
The Los Angeles Times, August 4, 1993, v. 112 p. F1
LC Call Number: Newspaper 7114-X
Business Index Micro Film: None

Television broadcasting industry - Conferences, meetings, seminars, etc. / Violence in television - Conferences, meetings, seminars, etc.

Cerone, Daniel
Valenti disputes research that TV sparks violence. (Jack Valenti, President of Motion Picture Association of America defends use of violence in television programming)
The Los Angeles Times, July 30, 1993, v. 112 p. D5
LC Call Number: Newspaper 7114-X
Business Index Micro Film: None
Valenti, Jack - Social policy
Violence in television - Social aspects / Television broadcasting industry - Social policy

Chermak, S.M. (1994)
Body Count News: How Crime is Presented in the News Media. Justice Quarterly 11(1994)4, pp. 561-582, ISSN 0741-8825.

Coakley, J. (1989)
Media Coverage of Sports and Violent Behavior: An Elusive Connection. Current Psychology Research and Review 7(1989)4, pp. 322-330, ISSN 1046-1310.

Coe, Steve
Pugnacious NBC jabs competitors. (television show competition and problems with legislators)
Broadcasting and Cable, August 1, 1994, v. 124 n. n31 p. 24(1)
LC Call Number: TK6540B85
Business Index Micro Film: None
NBC will keep 'Frasier' in its nine o'clock time slot, despite what competitive television networks will do to compete with the popular television program. NBC West Coast Pres. Don Ohlmeyer expressed his frustration with Congress over television violence issues at the Television Critics Assn. press tour. Ohlmeyer believes that independent television stations are just as much to blame on violence issues as national networks.
Ohlmeyer, Don - Attitudes
Television broadcasting industry - Management / Violence in television - Social aspects

Coe, Steve
Salhany supports violence - warning plan. (Fox CEO Lucie Salhany)
Broadcasting and Cable, July 19, 1993, v. 123 n. n29 p. 24(1)
LC Call Number: TK6540B85
Business Index Micro Film: 72S1119
Fox Broadcasting CEO Lucie Salhany says that the network will post viewer advisories on shows that contain violence, but only selectively. Salhany says that Fox is fortunate in having a lineup that consists largely of comedies, so that advisories will be limited to the films that comprise Fox Night at the Movies. Although she supports advisories, Salhany is opposed to the V-chip, a new technology that would allow parents to block out

programming, calling it an abrogation of parental responsibility.
Salhany, Lucie -. Attitudes
Violence in television - Censorship / Television broadcasting industry - Social policy

Cohen, A.A.; Adoni, H. & Bantz, C.R. (1990)
Social Conflict and Television News. Newbury Park: Sage Publications, 1990, 258 p.,
bibl., ISBN 0-80393-926-4.

Comedy Central seems to be going in a direction all its own on the TV violence issue.
(shows clips from ultra-violent movies on show called Drive-In Reviews) (Brief Article)
Broadcasting and Cable, Nov. 1, 1993, v. 123 n. n44 p. 57(1)
LC Call Number: TK6540B85
Business Index Micro Film: 74Z2034
Cable television broadcasting industry - Planning / Violence in television - Planning

Comstock, G.A. & Strasburger, V.C. (1990)
Deceptive Appearances: Television Violence and Aggressive Behavior. Journal of
Adolescent Health Care 11(1990)1, pp. 31-44, ISSN 0197-0070.

Condry, J. (1989)
The Psychology of Television. Hillsdale: Lawrence Erlbaum, 1989, XV, 324 p., ill.,
ISBN 0-89859-818-4.

Couloumbis, Angela E.
Wham! Bam! Cable networks plan to monitor own on-air violence.
The Christian Science Monitor (1983), Feb. 1, 1994, v. 86 n. n37 p. 3
LC Call Number: Newspaper
Business Index Micro Film: None
Simon, Paul (Politician) - Political activity. Cable television broadcasting industry -
Laws, regulations, etc. / Violence in television - Laws, regulations, etc.
Cumberbatch, G. & Howitt, D. (1989)
A Measure of Uncertainty: The Effects of the Mass Media. London: John Libbey, 1989,
VII, 88 p., ISBN 0-86196-231-1.

Dempsey, John
Parental advisories okay be cablers - but what kind? (violence on television)
Variety, July 19, 1993, v. 351 n. n10 p. 25(2)
LC Call Number: PN2000.V3 Folio; Microfilm 03722 (1905-   ) MicRR
Business Index Micro Film: None
Television programs - Labeling/ Violence in television - Labeling / Cable television
broadcasting industry - Social policy / Television broadcasting industry - Social policy

Edwards, Ellen
Broadcast and cable TV to name violence monitor.

The Washington Post, Feb. 2, 1994, v. 117 p. A1
LC Call Number: Newspaper
Business Index Micro Film: none
Cable television broadcasting industry - Social policy / Television broadcasting industry - Social policy / Violence in television - Prevention / Television programs - Evaluation

Edwards, Ellen
Cable leaders to develop violence ratings. (cable television industry)
The Washington Post, Jan. 11, 1994, v. 117 p. B1
LC Call Number: Newspaper
Business Index Micro Film: none
Cable television broadcasting industry - Social policy / Violence in television - Laws, regulations, etc.

Edwards, Ellen
Cable to air violence warnings; 15 networks agree to parental advisory
The Washington Post, July 30, 1993, v. 116 p. G1
LC Call Number: Newspaper
Business Index Micro Film: None
Cable television broadcasting industry - Social policy / Violence in television - Labeling

Edwards, Ellen
Study says syndicated shows are the real TV bad guys. (violence in television study by Center for Media and Public Affairs)
The Washington Post, Feb. 8, 1994, v. 117 p. C1
LC Call Number: Newspaper
Business Index Micro Film: None
Television broadcasting industry - Management / Violence in television - Research / Television programs - Research

Edwards, Ellen
TV networks agree to use of monitor; outsider to review program violence
The Washington Post, Jan. 22, 1994, v. 117 p. A1
Business Index Micro Film: None
Television broadcasting industry - Social policy / Violence in television - Evaluation / Television programs - Moral and ethical aspects

Edwards, Ellen
TV violence after the showdown. (Senator Paul Simon gives television networks two months to cut violence; in that time, little has happened)
The Washington Post, Sept. 30, 1993, v. 116 p. B1
LC Call Number: Newspaper
Business Index Micro Film: None

Simon, Paul (Politician) - Social policy / Violence in television - Laws, regulations, etc. / Television broadcasting industry - Social policy

Fifty ABC affiliates plan to pre-empt 'NYPD Blue' (Christian right influences new television show broadcast; Capital Cities/ ABC Inc.)
The Wall Street Journal, Sept. 22, 1993, p. B6(W) pA8
LC Call Number: See Catalogs or Staff
Business Index Micro Film: None
NYPD Blue (Television show) - Planning / Television broadcasting industry - management / Violence in television - Demonstrations, protests, etc.

Flint, Joe
Violence code could be economic scarlet letter. (code for violence on television programs could reduce advertising revenues)
Broadcasting and Cable, June 21, 1993, v. 123 n. n25 p. 33(2)
LC Call Number: TK6540B85
Business Index Micro Film: 71Z2421
Television broadcasters are worried that attempts to warn consumers about violence in television programs, such as a ratings system or a lock box for parents, will lead to decreased advertising revenues. Television advertising executives said advertisers often avoid buying time for television programs with advisory designations. Programmers believe that the US Congress may require the FCC to publish lists of violent programming, which may be subject to boycotts from special interest groups and advertising agencies.
Television advertising - Management / Violence in television - Laws, regulations, etc. / Television broadcasting industry - Finance

Forty cable networks. (will use channels to discuss violence on TV)
Television Digest, July 18, 1994, v. 34 n. n29 p. 8(1)
LC Call Number: May or May Not Be in LC. Search further.
Business Index Micro Film: None
Cable television broadcasting industry - Planning / Violence in television - Planning

Frankel, David H
US reel reform
Lancet (North American edition). v. 343 Feb. 12 1994 p. 408.
The television industry has responded in part to calls for a tighter regulation of television violence. Network companies have stated that they support independent monitoring but not violence ratings, broadcast-blocking technologies, or the limitation of violent programs to late-night scheduling as advocated by the National Cable Television Association. The networks maintain that self-regulation is the correct way to deal with the issue..

Frankel, Max
Live at 11: death.
The New York Times Magazine, June 15, 1997 p20 col 1 (21 col in)

Frau-Meigs, D. (1997)
Violence commise, violence subie. In: Lacroix, J-M. (Ed.): Télévision et violence,
authour de l'example canadien. Paris: Presses de la Sorbonne Nouvelle, 1997, 269 p.,
ISBN 2-87854-115-4.

Freeman, Mike
Syndicators eschew labels. (syndicators of first-run action dramas with violent content
will leave warning labels to stations) (special section: Action Hours) (Brief Article)
Broadcasting and Cable, August 23, 1993, v. 123 n. n34 p. 39(1)
LC Call Number: TK6540B85
Business Index Micro Film: 72Z1414
Violence in television - Censorship / Television programs - labeling / Television program
distribution companies - Social policy

Freeman, Patricia
As the 'clean TV' campaign heats up, ABC chills two new shows.
People (Chicago, 1974), May 22, 1989, v. 31 n. n20 p. 155(2)
LC Call Number: AP2.P417
Magazine Index Micro Film: 49L1934
Donald Wildmon. (portrait)
Wildmon, Donald E. - attitudes
Television programs - Moral and ethical aspects / Coalition of Christian Leaders for
Responsible Television - Management / Violence in television - public opinion / Sex in
television - public opinion / Crimes of Passion II (Television program) - production and
direction / Married … with Children (Television program) - production and direction

Gambardello, Joseph;
Newsday Size: 3K; 06-02-1992; Page Number: 0; Section: 0
Hasta La Vista to Violence? Cops seek Schwarzenegger for ad
Newspapers_&_Newswires Hasta La Vista to Violence? Cops seek Schwarzenegger for
ad By Joseph Gambardello. STAFF WRITER Possibly coming to a television screen near
you - Arnold Schwarzenegger in the role of peacemaker. That's the hope of the New
York Police Department,...

Gaouette, Nicole
Behind the networks' concern over TV rating: ad dollars.
by The Christian Science Monitor, June 27, 1997 v89 n149 pl col 1(18 col in)

Garbarino, Steve;
Newsday Size: 7K; 08-10-1992; Page Number: 0; Section:

DO MOVIES, MUSIC TRIGGER VIOLENT ACTS? Imitators Under The Influence of Art

Newspapers_&_Newswires DO MOVIES, MUSIC TRIGGER VIOLENT ACTS? Imitators Under The Influence of Art By Steve Garbarino. Staff writer Carolyn Brook contributed to this story. Steve Garbarino is a free-lance writer. A T A TIME when police groups are protesting Ice-T's heavy m...

Gay, Verne
How the networks set standards for portraying violent behavior. (TV programs)
Variety, August 15, 1989, v. 336 n. n5 p. 44(1)
LC Call Number: PN2000.V3 Folio; Microfilm 03722 (1905-) MicRR
Magazine Index Micro Film: None
Schneider, Alfred - attitudes
Violence in television - standards / Television broadcasting - standards / Television producers and directors - attitudes

Gerbner, G. (1996)
The Hidden Side of Television Violence. In: Gerbner, G.; Mowlana, H. & Schiller, H.I. (Eds.): Invisible Crisis: What Conglomerate Control of Media Means for America and the World, pp. 27-34, Boulder: Westview Press, 1996, 295 p., bibl., ISBN 0-81332-072-0.

Gitlin, T. (1994)
Imagebusters: The Hollow Crusade Against TV Violence. The American Prospect (1994)16, Winter, pp. 42-49, ISSN 1049-7285.

Gitlin, Todd
When the Right talks, TV listens. Nation, v. 237, Oct. 15, 1983: 333-340.
Reports on the efforts of Mississippi Methodist minister Don Wildmon's Coalition for Better Television "to clean up TV - and how the networks responded to the challenge." Television programs [U.S.] / Television industry [U.S.] / Television advertising [U.S.] / Boycott [U.S.] / Violence in television [U.S.] / Pornography [U.S.] / Church and social problems [U.S.] / New Right [U.S.] [U.S.] Clergy [Mississippi] - Political activities / Wildmon, Don / Coalition for Better Television

Gosselin, A.; De Guise, J. & Paquette, G. (1997)
Violence on Canadian Television and Some of its Cognitive Effects. Canadian Journal of Communication 22(1997)2, Spring, pp. 143-160, ISSN 0705-3657.

Gruenwald, Juliana
Panel approves bill to create TV ratings based on content, Congressional Quarterly Weekly Report. v. 55 May 3 1997 p. 1019.
On May 1, 1997, the Senate Commerce, Science and Transportation Committee approved legislation (S 363) that would require broadcasters to adopt a content-based television

ratings system or restrict violent programming to hours when children are least likely to be watching. The proposed legislation signals many lawmakers' disenchantment with the voluntary ratings system put in place in 1997 by the television industry. The industry's system, which was designed to be used with the v-chip technology that would enable parents to block out programs they do not want their children to see, rates programs on their suitability for certain age groups. The proposed legislation would require the Federal Communications Commission to define television violence and establish safe harbor viewing times for children.

Gunter, B. & Ward, K. (1997)
New Reporting of Television Violence in the British Press. Medienpsychologie 9(1997)4, pp. 253-270, ISSN 0936-7780.

Gunter, Barrie
Ethnicity and involvement in violence on television: nature and context of on-screen portrayals
Journal of Black Studies. v. 28 no 6 July 1998 p. 683-703.
A study was conducted to examine the nature and context of on-screen portrayals of ethnicity and involvement in violence. The contents of made-for television drama series and serials on British television were analyzed. A large-scale analysis was made of the findings, and separate results were analyzed for ethic profile of aggressors and victims, the nature of violence, the motivational context of TV violence, and the historical context.

Hamilton, J.T. (1998)
Channeling Violence: The Economic Market for Violent Television Programming.
Princeton: Princeton University Press, 1998, XIX, 390 p., bibl., ISBN 0-691-04848-7.
Hamilton, James T. (James Towler), 1961-
Channeling violence : the economic market for violent
television programming / James T. Hamilton.
Princeton, N.J. : Princeton University Press, c1998.
xix, 390 p. : ill. ; 25 cm.
PN1992.8.V55 H36 1998
0691048487 (cloth : alk. paper)

Hard-action skeins tired out, says 20th Fox TV's Katleman.
Variety, Nov. 7, 1984, v. 317 p. 80(1)
LC Call Number: PN2000.V3 Folio; Microfilm 03722 (1905-   ) MicRR
Magazine Index Micro Film: None
Katleman, Harris - interviews
violence in television - marketing / Twentieth Century - Fox Television - production and direction / television producers and directors - interviews

Harris, R.J. (1994)
A Cognitive Psychology of Mass Communication. Hillsdale: Lawrence Erlbaum
Associates, 1994, XV, 313 p., ill., ISBN 0-80581-264-4.

Hickey, Neil
TV's new plan to curtail street violence: "squash it!"
TV guide, Jan. 8, 1994, v. 42 n. n2 p. 34 (2)
LC Call Number: Microfilm 06378 (1953-   ) MicRR
Magazine Index Micro Film: None
Violence in television - Control / Television programs, Public service - Planning

Hift, Fred
Critics zero in on TV violence. (television networks agree to hold conference to discuss
ways to regulate quantity of violence incidents portrayed in television drama, in response
to government and public pressure)
The Christian Science Monitor (1983) May 4, 1993, v. 85 n. n110 p. 12
LC Call Number: Newspaper
Business Index Micro Film: None
Simon, Paul (Politician) - Social policy
Violence in television - Social aspects / Television broadcasting industry - Social policy

Hogben, M. (1998)
Factors Moderating the Effect of Televised Aggression on Viewer Behavior.
Communication Research 25(1998)2, pp. 220-247, ISSN 0093-6502.

Hollywood executives plan to curb violence on TV. (Writers Guild and other groups to
meet on television violence)
The Wall Street Journal, June 9, 1993, p. A9 (W)
LC Call Number: See Catalogs or Staff
Business Index Micro Film: None
United States. Congress. Senate. Committee on the Judiciary - Investigations / Television
broadcasting industry - Planning / Violence in television - Investigations

Hudson, T.J. (1992)
Consonance in Depiction of Violent Material in Television News. Journal of
Broadcasting and Electronic Media 36(1992)4, Fall, pp. 411-425, ISSN 0883-8151.

Hudson, T.J. (1992)
Graphic Depiction of Violent Material in Television News: News Directors' and
Producers' Perceived Acceptability Levels. Temple: Temple University, 1992, Diss.

Industry gathers to consider TV violence. (Entertainment industry)
Television Digest, August 2, 1993, v. 33, n. n31 p. 1(3)
LC Call Number: May or May Not Be in LC. Search further.

Business Index Micro Film: 72V0599
An entertainment industry-wide consultation on television violence will be held on
August, 2, 1993, in Los Angeles, CA. The House Telecom Subcommittee under Rep.
Edward Markey proposed legislation that would require 'V block technology' which
would prevent children from viewing television violence. The major broadcast networks
said that they would not use the 'V' rating but would instead issue parental warnings.
Various studies on television violence and industry policy on carrying advertisements in
violent television programs were discussed.
Violence in television - Conferences, meetings, seminars, etc. / Entertainment industry -
Conferences, meetings, seminars, etc. / Television broadcasting industry - Laws,
regulations, etc.

INTV has asked Justice Department. (Association of Independent Television Stations;
standards for violence on television)
Television Digest, Nov. 22, 1993, v. 33, n. n47 p. 9(1)
LC Call Number: May or May Not Be in LC. Search further.
Business Index Micro Film: 74V0386
Association of Independent Television Stations - Management / Violence in television -
Laws, regulations, etc.
Invisible crises : what conglomerate control of media means for America and the world /
edited by George Gerbner, Hamid Mowlana, Herbert I. Schiller.
Boulder, Colo. : Westview Press, c1996.
viii, 295 p. ; 25 cm.
Critical studies in communication and in the cultural industries.
P96.E25 I57 1996
0813320712 (hbk. : alk. paper)
0813320720 (pbk. : alk. paper)
Includes bibliographical references (p. 267-279) and index.
Includes/ Herbert I. Schiller -- The hidden side of television violence /

Jackson, Robert L.
Cable networks to unveil plan on violent programs.
The Los Angeles Times, Feb. 1, 1994, v. 113 p. A1
LC Call Number: Newspaper 7114-X
Business Index Micro Film: None
Cable television broadcasting industry - Social policy / Violence in television - Standards

Jackson, Robert L.
Cable vows to tackle issue of violence on TV. (cable television industry)
The Los Angeles Times, Jan. 28, 1993, v. 112, p. A14
LC Call Number: Newspaper 7114-X
Business Index Micro Film: NONE
Cable television broadcasting industry - Social policy / Violence in television - Standards

Jensen, Elizabeth
Networks pick UCLA to study violence, hoping to pre-empt government action.
(University of California, Los Angeles' Center for Communication Policy picked to
analyze violence on television programs)
The Wall Street Journal, June 30, 1994, p. B5(W) pB9
LC Call Number: See Catalogs or Staff
Magazine Index Micro Film: None
United States. Congress. Senate - Social policy / California, University of (Los Angeles)
- Research / Television broadcasting industry - Research / Violence in television -
Research

Jensen, Elizabeth
One-day study finds rise in violence on TV, but research method is disputed. (Center for
Media and Public Affairs study for Harry Frank Guggenheim Foundation)
The Wall Street Journal, August 5, 1994, p. B10(W) pB1
LC Call Number: See Catalogs or Staff
Magazine Index Micro Film: None
Franks, Martin - Management
Violence in television - Reports / Television broadcasting industry - Management

Jensen, Elizabeth
Simon imposes deadline on TV industry to take further steps on violence issue. (Senator
Paul Simon warns of congressional intervention against violence on television,
announces 60-day mandate)
The Wall Street Journal, August 3, 1993, p. B7 (W) pB7
LC Call Number: See Catalogs or Staff
Business Index Micro Film: None
Simon, Paul (Politician) - Social policy
Violence in television - Management / Television broadcasting policy - Social aspects /
Television broadcasting industry - Social policy

Johnson, R.N. (1996)
Bad News Revisited: The Portrayal of Violence, Conflict, and Suffering on Television
News. Peace and Conflict Journal of Peace Psychology 2(1996)3, pp. 201-216, ISSN
1078-1919.

Kaufmann, A. (1990)
Angst, Wahn, Mord: Von Psycho-Killern und anderen Film-Verückten. Münster: MakS
Publikationen, 1990, 228 p., ISBN 3-88811-543-4.

Kenigsberg, Abby;
Newsday Size: 5K; 08-26-1998; Page Number: A44; Section: Viewpoints
Commercial TV: Going Down the Tube

AS A BLUE-RIBBON panel in Washington deliberates on the obligations of the broadcasters who soon will begin profiting from the debut of digital television, it should take a critical look at what is happening now, right before its eyes. Ever since t...

Kirschke, Linda
Broadcasting genocide : censorship, propaganda & state-sponsored violence in Rwanda 1990-1994.
[London] : Article 19, 1996. xii, 180 p. ; 23 cm. DT450.435.B75 1996
1870798333 Written by, Africa Programme
researcher at Article 19.
October 1996.
Includes bibliographical references.
Radio-Télévision Libre des Mille Collines.

Kitman, Marvin;
Newsday Size: 7K; 08-16-1992; Page Number: 0; Section: 0
Newspapers_&_Newswires THE MARVIN KITMAN SUNDAY SHOW A Camcorder
Is the Star Marvin Kitman I'VE BEEN AMAZED at the vicious attacks by critics against
I Witness Video, which NBC ran as a series of three specials last spring and which starts
tonight as a series on Ch. 4 at...

Kolbert, Elizabeth
Study finds TV violence on the rise; compares stations in 1992 and 1994. (Center for Media and Public Affairs study) (National Pages)
The New York Times, August 5, 1994, v. 143 p. A9(N) pA13
LC Call Number: Not in LC Collection
Magazine Index Micro Film: none
Violence in television - Research / Television broadcasting industry - Social policy / Cable television broadcasting industry - Social policy

Kolbert, Elizabeth
The monitoring of violence in TV programs and video games may be a new growth industry. (Broadcasting industry creating panels to monitor violence in their media) (Column)
The New York Times, May 9, 1994, v. 143 p. C7(N) pD7
LC Call Number: Not in LC Collection
Business Index Micro Film: None
Violence in television - Management / Television broadcasting industry - Social policy / Video game industry - Social policy / Cable television broadcasting industry - Social policy

Kunkel, D.; Wilson, B.J.; Potter, J.; Donnerstein, E.; Smith, S.L.; Blumenthal, E.; Gray, T. & Linz, D. (1997)
Violence in Television Programming Overall: University of California, Santa Barbara

Study. In: Federman, J. (Ed.): National Television Violence Study, Volume 1, pp. 3-268, Thousand Oaks: Sage Publications, 1997, 568 p., ISBN 0-7619-0802-1.

Levine, M. (1996)
Viewing Violence: How Media Violence Affects Your Child's and Adolescent's Development. New York: Doubleday, 1996, XVI, 256 p., ISBN 0-385-47686-8.

Lippman, John
Trash, crash genres of past. (marketing of television programs at National Association of Television Program Executives Convention)
Variety, Jan. 24, 1990, v. 338 n. n3 p. 159 (1)
LC Call Number: PN2000.V3, Folio; Microfilm 03722 (1905-) MicRR
Magazine Index Micro Film: None
Television programs - marketing / Television production companies - marketing / National Association of Television Program Executives - Conferences, meetings, seminars, etc. / Violence in television - marketing

Lowry, Brian.
LOS ANGELES TIME; Size: 10K; 07-19-1998; Page Number: D12; Section: Fanfare
Newsday
TELEVISION / No More Kidding Around / THE `FAMILY HOUR' IS BECOMING A THING OF THE PAST AS NETWORK PROGRAMING FOR YOUNGER VIEWERS DISAPPEARS FROM PRIME TIME HOLLYWOOD THIS FIRST meeting with reporters after being named president of CBS Entertainment in 1995, Leslie Moonves was asked whether he'd be comfortable with his 12-year-old daughter watching a show in which a couple had sex in a dentist's chair...

Lowry, Brian
Webs plan one-two punch. (networks address violence on television)
Variety, Jan. 17, 1994, v. 353 n. n11 p. 33(2)
LC Call Number: PN2000.V3 Folio; Microfilm 03722 (1905-) MicRR
Business Index Micro Film: None
Television broadcasting industry - Management / Violence in television - Management

Makris, G. (1996)
The Myth of a Technological Solution to Television Violence: Identifying Problems with the V-Chip. Journal of Communication Inquiry 20(1996)2, Fall, pp. 72-91, ISSN 0196-8599.

Marano, Hara Estroff
A chip of fools? Augmented title: Norwegian campaign to educate against media violence
Psychology Today. v. 30 May/June 1997 p. 10.
Norway is the first country in the world to enact an education campaign against visual

violence. Rather than imposing censorship, Norway is seeking to breed individual responsibility through an innovative campaign that teaches school children skills for interpreting visual imagery. Students examine who makes a film, who it is intended for, and what gets omitted. In addition, by creating their own videos, they learn how media messages are fashioned. In contrast, by relying on the so-called V-chip to block violent programs in the home, the U.S. is, in effect, placing the blame on broadcasters for children's viewing habits.

Marshall, Tyler; Lippman, John
Big 3 networks agree to tone down TV violence.
The Los Angeles Times, Dec. 12, 1992, v. 112, p. A1
LC Call Number: Newspaper 7114-X
Business Index Micro Film: NONE
Television broadcasting industry - Social policy / Violence in television - Laws, regulations, etc.

Mason, Marilynne S.
Curbing TV violence; conference left unexplored the idea of an ethics code as an answer
The Christian Science Monitor (1983), August 10, 1993, v. 85 n. n178 p. 13
LC Call Number: Newspaper
Business Index Micro Film: None
Violence in television - Laws, regulations, etc. / Television broadcasting policy - Planning / Television broadcasting industry - Social policy

May TV sweeps programming. (less violence in television)
Television Digest, May 9, 1994, v. 34 n. n19 p. 5(1)
LC Call Number: May or May Not Be in LC. Search further.
Business Index Micro Film: 78Q0251
Cable television broadcasting industry - Moral and ethical aspects / Violence in television - Analysis

McAvoy, Kim
As part of a promise to Congress to curb violence on cable tv, the National Cable Television Association. (Mediascope to research the nature and quantity of violent programming on cable television through 1997) (Brief Article)
Broadcasting and Cable, May 23, 1994, v. 124 n. n21 p. 104(1)
LC Call Number: TK6540B85
Business Index Micro Film: 78V2766
National Cable Television Association - Contracts / Violence in television - Research / Cable television broadcasting industry - Research

McAvoy, Kim
Networks adopt violence warning. (television programs)
Broadcasting and Cable, July 5, 1993, v. 123 n. n27 p. 7(2)

LC Call Number: TK6540B85
Business Index Micro Film: 72P1498
The four major television networks announced, at a June 1993 Washington, DC press conference, that they will air the advisory 'due to some violent content, parental discretion advised' before some violent programs. Each network will be free to decide which programs will receive the warning. No current series will routinely include the warning, but some episodes of current series might.
Television broadcasting industry - Social policy / Violence in television - Management

McAvoy, Kim; Flint, Joe; Cooper, Jim; Eggerton, John
Violence debate heats up, shifts from D.C. to L.A.: on eve of conference, cable networks approve warnings, Markey blasts no-show advertisers... and more. (Washington D.C.; Los Angeles, CA; Congressman Ed Markey)
Broadcasting and Cable, August 2, 1993, v. 123 n. n31 p. 12(2)
LC Call Number: TK6540B85
Business Index Micro Film: 72V1383
Congressman Ed Markey held a hearing on violence in television on the eve of a scheduled violence summit to be held during the week of July 26, 1993, in Los Angeles, CA. Markey strongly criticized the advertisers who did not attend, but Motion Pictures Assn. of America Pres. Jack Valenti said that America must call for tougher gun control laws, create better schools and encourage more parental responsibility rather than blame television for violence in society. Fifteen cable networks have pledged to label violent programs, but many in the broadcasting industry do not believe that labels will make a difference.
Violence in television - Analysis / Television broadcasting - Moral and ethical aspects / Broadcasting industry - Management

Meyers, M. (1997)
News Coverage of Violence Against Women: Engendering Blame. Thousand Oaks: Sage Publications, 1997, XII, 148 p., ill., bibl., ISBN 0-8039-5635-5.

Mikami, S. (1993)
A Cross-National Comparison of the U.S.-Japanese TV Drama: International Culture Indicators (in Japanese). KEIO Communication Review (1993)15, pp. 29-44.

Mills, Mike
New bills make waves for broadcasters. (includes description of the bills)
Congressional Quarterly Weekly Report, Jan. 29, 1994, v. 52 n., n4 p. 161 (3)
LC Call Number: See Catalogs or Staff
Magazine Index Micro Film: None
Over-the-air broadcasters are facing a difficult year in 1994 because they are being closed out of the debate on reforming communication policy by telephone and cable lobbies while harmful bills have been introduced. Multiple bills concerning limits on television violence and mandates for health warnings on all alcoholic beverage ads are being

introduced into Congress and broadcasters believe they will adversely affect their
audience and advertising revenues.
Television broadcasting - Laws, regulations, etc. / Alcoholic beverages - Advertising /
Advertising law - Interpretation and construction / Violence in television - Laws,
regulations, etc.

Montgomery, Kathryn C. 1989.
Target: Prime Time. Oxford, New York, Toronto: Oxford University Press.

Moore, Simon R; Cockerton, Tracey
Viewers' ratings of violence presented in justified and unjustified contexts
Psychological Reports. v. 79 Dec. 1996 pt1 p. 931-5.
Viewers' ratings of violence were investigated in an independent groups design using 147
undergraduate students. A 10-min. film clip was introduced to one group (n=77) to
provide justification for the violent events. The second group (n=7O) acted as a control
with no justification given for the violence. Viewers of the justified violence rated that
violence as less extreme, and their interest and involvement in the program significantly
lower than viewers in the unjustified violence condition. Pre- to posttest increases in
anger were small and no significant difference was found between the two groups. These
results have important implications for reports of violence in the media. Reprinted by
permission of the publisher, 1996.
Violence in television; Situation Psychology.

Mustonen, Anu; Pulkkinen, Lea
Television violence: a development of a coding scheme, Journal of Broadcasting and
Electronic Media. v. 41 Spring 1997 p. 168-89.
Traditional analyses have treated TV violence as a homogenous entity disregarding the
nature and context of the violent acts. A new coding scheme was designed to examine the
amount of violence portrayed on TV; the degree to which it is obtrusive; and the
messages it conveys. The final, 37 item coding scheme is sensitive to features of televised
messages whether in fiction, or in non-fiction. It included contextual themes concerning
intensity (seriousness, realism, way of dramatization), and attractiveness (justification,
glamorization, efficacy) of TV violence. The coding scheme was applied to an analysis of
a program sample which consisted of all genres (N = 259) presented on Finnish network
television during one week. The analysis showed that television violence does not exist as
a homogenous entity, since portrayals of violence vary in amount, intensity, and
attractiveness.
Content analysis Communication; Violence in television; Television programs
Psychological aspects; Television programs Finland.

NAB says broadcasters will address TV violence. (National Association of Broadcasters)
(Brief Article)
Broadcasting and Cable, June 28, 1993, v. 123 n. n26 p. 64(1)
LC Call Number: TK6540B85

Business Index Micro Film: 72P1487
Violence in television - Management / Television broadcasting industry - Planning

Nationwide Communitarian Network. (special attention to violence in TV and movies)
Television Digest, August 30, 1993, v. 33 n. n35 p. 8(1)
LC Call Number: May or May Not Be in LC. Search further.
Business Index Micro Film: 73P0734
Television broadcasting industry - Social policy / Violence in television - Social aspects /
Violence in motion pictures - Social aspects

NBC fights accusation of violence. (Senator Kent Conrad accuses NBC of showing
movie with gratuitous violence) (Living Arts Pages)
The New York Times, Dec. 16, 1993, v. 143 p. B2(N) p20
LC Call Number: Not in LC Collection
Magazine Index Micro Film: None
Conrad, Kent - Social policy
Television broadcasting industry - Social policy / Violence in television - Political
aspects

NBC gets kudos for less violence, ABC ranks 'worst.'
Variety, March 24, 1982, v. 306 p. 259 (2)
LC Call Number: PN2000.V3 Folio; Microfilm 03722 91905-   ) MicRR
Magazine Index Micro Film: None
National Coalition on Television Violence - political activity / Coalition for Better
Television - political activity / violence in television - social aspects

Network TV termed not so violent. (network-affiliated TV stations)
Television Digest, July 26, 1993, v. 33 n. n30 p. 2(2)
LC Call Number: May or May Not Be in LC. Search Further.
Business Index Micro Film: 72V0582
CBS Inc. CBS Entertainment Pres. Jeff Sagansky believes that cable TV and independent
TV stations feature more violent programs than network-affiliated TV stations. Sagansky
also noted that the actions taken by Congress to regulate televised violence will not affect
the quality of TV programming and directed Congress to investigate other factors that
cause violence. Meanwhile, Home Box Office Inc and Showtime Entertainment Inc
officials expressed disagreement with some of the regulations featured under the Cable
Act.
Network-affiliated television stations - Management / Television broadcasting industry -
Management / Violence in television - Evaluation

Networks pick violence monitor. (television networks)
Television Digest, July 4, 1994, v. 34 n. n27 p. 6(1)
LC Call Number: May or May Not Be in LC. Search further.
Business Index Micro Film: 79V1515

Four broadcast TV networks selected the University of California at Los Angeles' Center for Communications Policy to monitor and analyze TV violence for two TV seasons. CBS Senior VP Martin Franks reported that the center will conduct a qualitative assessment of TV violence on network prime-time shows and children's programs. The programs will be assessed in terms of extent and nature of violence and its relevance to the plot.
California, University of (Los Angeles) - Contracts / Television broadcasting industry - Contracts / Violence in television - Investigations

Networks under the gun. Newsweek, v. 122, July 12, 1993: 64-66.
Broadcasters will include parental advisories before excessively violent programs and will send similar warnings to newspapers and magazines that carry TV listings. But critics say it is just hype.
Violence in television [U.S.] / Television and children [U.S.]

Networks vow TV violence warnings (television networks agree to put warnings on violent programs)
Facts on File, july 15, 1993, v. 53 n. n2746 p. 524 (1)
LC Call Number: Not in LC Collection
Magazine Index Micro Film: None
Violence in television - Laws, regulations, etc. / Television broadcasting industry - Laws, regulations, etc.

Oliver, M.B. & Armstrong, G.B. (1995)
Predictors of Viewing and Enjoyment of Reality-Based Fictional Crime Shows.
Journalism Quarterly 72(1994)3, pp. 559-570, ISSN 0196-3031.

Palmerton, P.R. & Judas, J. (1994)
Selling Violence: Television Commercials Targeted to Children. Sydney: International Communication Association, 1994, 39 p., processed.

Paridaen, P. (1990)
The Role of Language in Television News Violence. Australian Review of Applied Linguistics 14(1990)1, pp. 3-16, ISSN 0155-0646.

Price, M.E. (Ed.) (1998)
The V-Chip Debate: Content Filtering From Television to the Internet.
Mahwah: Lawrence Erlbaum Associates, 1998, XXV, 363 p., ill., bibl., ISBN 0-80583-061-8.

Rainie, Harrison; Streisand, Betsy; Guttman, Monika; Allman, William F.
Warning shots at TV. (violence on television; includes related articles)
U.S. News & World report, July 12, 1993, v. 115 n. n2 p. 48(3)
LC Call Number: JK1.U65; Microfilm 06106 (1933-   ) MicRR

Magazine Index Micro Film: None
Television broadcasting industry - Laws, regulations, etc. / Violence in television - Laws, regulations, etc.

Rajecki, D.W.; McTavish, D.G. & Rasmussen, J.L. et al. (1994)
Violence, Conflict, Trickery, and Other Story Themes in TV Ads for Food for Children.
Journal of Applied Social Psychology 24 (1994)19, pp. 1685-1700, ISSN 0021-9029.

Request to run antiviolence PSA: action-oriented PPV is among most popular programming. (public-service announcement, pay-per-view) (Brief Article)
Broadcasting and Cable, Feb. 21, 1994, v. 124 n. n8 p. 30(1)
LC Call Number: TK6540B85
Business Index Micro Film: 76U1252
Television broadcasting industry - Management / Pay-per-view television - Social aspects / Violence in television - Social aspects

Riding, Alan
TV in Spain is cutting back on prime-time sex and violence
The New York Times May 10, 1993, v. 142 p. C6(N) pD6
LC Call Number: Not in LC Collection
Business Index Micro Film: None
Television broadcasting - Spain / Sex in television - Spain / Violence in television - Spain / Spain - Social policy
Spain

Rist, Curtis;
Newsday Size: 3K; 08-06-1992; Page Number: 0; Section: 0
Did Robocop Movie Create a Monster?
Newspapers_&_Newswires In trying to explain his motive for killing six women, confessed killer Nathaniel White - like so many murder suspects before him - turned to the movies. In his case, it was the 1985 futuristic horror movie Robocop, which he said he saw just be...

Robichaux, Mark
The race is on. (sex and violence in programming) (Television)
The Wall Street Journal, Sept. 9, 1994, p. R10 (W)
LC Call Number: See Catalogs or Staff
Magazine Index Micro Film: None
Television broadcasting industry - Social aspects / Violence in television - Analysis / Sex in television - Analysis / Television programs - Moral and ethical aspects

Robins, J. Max
Webs put squeeze on small-screen sleaze. (television networks reduce sex and violence)
Variety, March 1, 1993, v. 350, n. n5 p. 1(2)

LC Call Number: PN2000.V3 Folio; Microfilm 03722 (1905-   ) MicRR
Magazine Index Micro Film: None
Television broadcasting industry - Moral and ethical aspects - Violence in television -
Planning / Sex in television - Planning

Rodriguez, Sutil C.; Esteban, JL.; Takeuchi, M.; Clausen, T; Scott, R.
Universidad Complutense de Madrid.
Televised violence: a Japanese, Spanish, and American comparison.
Psychol Rep, 77:995-1000, 1995 Dec
In Japan, Spain, and the USA during one week acts of violence (verbal and nonverbal)
were rated on the Index of Television Violence by 3 raters in each country. In all three
countries televised violence was more likely depicted in interpersonal conflict than
against property. Fewer scenes of physical or fatal injury appeared in Japan than in the
other two countries. Other observations were made.

Roth, Cliff
... commercials need to be rated too.
The Washington Post, Dec 30, 1996 v120 n25 pA11 col 1 (13 col in)

Russell, N. (1994)
Moral and the Media: Ethics in Canadian Journalism. Vancouver: UBC Press, 1994, XI,
249 p., ill., bibl., ISBN 0-77480-457-2.

Sabey, Rob
V-chips and ratings won't help and may hurt: TV takes on family values; stay tuned.
The Christian Science Monitor, March 12, 1996 v88 n73 pis col 1 (13 col in)

Saferstein, B. (1994)
Interaction and Ideology at Work: A Case of Constructing and Constraining Television
Violence. Social Problems 41(1994)2, pp. 316-345, ISSN 0037-7791.

Sandomir, Richard
Death is cheap: maybe it's just $14.95. (Semaphore Entertainment Group to offer 'The
Ultimate Fighting Championship II,' a cable sports broadcast of martial arts war which
could end in death for some of participants)
The New York Times, March 8, 1994, v. 143 p. B13 (L)
LC Call Number:: Not in LC Collection
Magazine Index Micro Film: None
Cable television broadcasting industry - Moral and ethical aspects / Television
broadcasting of sports - Moral and ethical aspects / Martial arts - Competitions / Violence
in television - Moral and ethical aspects

Say no to censors. (censorship of television network broadcasting) (Editorial)
Advertising Age, July 12, 1993, v. 64 n. n29 p. 16(1)

Television network broadcasters have already decided to place warnings on violent programs, but some pressure groups have threatened to boycott advertisers unless strict decency standards developed by physicians, psychologists, the viewing audience or the government are imposed on network programming. Such demands amount to censorship and are unconstitutional. Past pressure group boycotts have failed because advertisers base buying decisions on their own criteria. The networks should not be singled out for protests.
Censorship - Prevention / Television broadcasting industry - Management / Violence in television - Management

Schmuckler, Eric
The big four networks. (contract with UCLA's Center for Communication Policy to study television violence) (Brief Article)
Mediaweek, July 4, 1994, v. 4 n. n27 p. 5(1)
California, University of (Los Angeles) - Contracts / Network-affiliated television stations - Contracts / Violence in television - Research

Schmuckler, Eric
Violence study raises more questions than it answers.
MEDIAWEEK, Jan. 3, 1994, v. 4 n. n1 p. 1(2)
The recent study of television violence, sponsored by Sen. Byron Dorgan, claims that it is a successful example of how TV violence can be quantified and judged. The study evaluated programs on all four networks over a one-week period, rating them according to the number of violent acts per hour. Fox rated highest followed by ABC, NBC and CBS. Network executives complain that the study was too short, and that its definition of a violent act was too broad.
Violence in television - Reports / Television broadcasting industry - Political activity

Schorr, Daniel
TV violence - what we know but ignore. (in terms of economic incentives) (Column)
The Christian Science Monitor (1983) Sept. 7, 1993, p. 19
Violence in television - Economic aspects / Television broadcasting industry - Finance

Scully, Sean
Automated lockout for violent shows opposed. (television programs)
Broadcasting and Cable, July 5, 1993, v. 123 n. n27 p. 9(1)

LC Call Number: TK6540B85
Business Index Micro Film: 72P1500
Television broadcasters oppose a proposal to equip television sets with a device that would lock out all violent programs. The proposal was offered by House telecommunications subcommittee Chairman Ed Markey. NBC Entertainment Pres Warren Littlefield, in testimony to the subcommittee, said that the major networks would not support such a system but would back a system that would allow individual programs to be locked out.
United States. Congress. House. Subcommittee on Telecommunications - Investigations / Television broadcasting industry - Political activity / Violence in television - Investigations

Senator Paul Simon last week told a group of broadcasters that USA Network President Kay Koplovitz recently agreed in a private conversation to the cable industry's antiviolence plan. (Brief Article)
Broadcasting and Cable, March 7, 1994, v. 124 n. n10 p. 58(1)
LC Call Number: TK6540B85
Business Index Micro Film: 76X1294
Koplovitz, Kay - Political activity / Simon, Paul (Politician) - Political activity
Cable television broadcasting industry - Officials and employees / Violence in television - Laws, regulations, etc.

Shipman, John M. Jr.
Pressures on TV programs: Coalition for Better Television's case. Columbia, School of Journalism, University of Missouri, 1985. 7 p. (Freedom of Information Center. Report no. 504)
"The Coalition for Better Television used the economic boycott and the threat of the boycott against the networks in an effort to change programming. In the following report, the author contends that while the tactic might have had some success with advertisers, it was disregarded by viewers and had little effect on ratings."
Boycott [U.S.] /Television programs [U.S.] / Television industry [U.S.] / Television advertising [U.S.] / Consumer organizations [U.S.] / Violence in television [U.S.] / Pornography [U.S.] / Wildmon, Don / Coalition for Better Television

Signorielli, N. (1990)
Television's Mean and Dangerous World: A Continuation of the Cultural Indicators Perspective. In: Signorielli, N. & Morgan, M. (Eds.): Cultivation Analysis: New Directions in Media Effects Research, pp. 85-106, Newbury Park: Sage Publications, 1990, ISBN 0-80393-296-0.

Simon, Paul, 1928
Three U.S. senators speak out: why cleaning up television is important to the nation
The American Enterprise. v. 10 no2 Mar./Apr. 1999 p. 32-3.
The writer describes how he became involved in the effort to clean up TV and introduced

a bill that included an exemption in the antitrust laws for television violence. He contends that he is not proposing a ban on violence on television, but it should be on late at night, it should not be glorified, and it should provide a truthful representation of the hurt caused by violence.

Starker, S. (1989)
Evil Influences: Crusades Against the Mass Media. New Brunswick: Transaction Publishers, 1989, VI, 212 p., ISBN 0887382754.

Stevenson, Matthew
America unplugged. The American Enterprise. v.8 Sept./Oct. 1997 p. 60-2.
The writer considers the negative effect of television and discusses his decision on moving to Geneva, Switzerland, in the early 1990s to give up TV. He maintains that, more harmful than its nightly repetition of violence, television deprives small children of a life of the mind. He argues that not only does television promote dependence on the entertainment world, it also ends the divisions between children and adults, both of whom watch the same disturbing images at the same time. He states that, in the place of TV, his children devised a series of mythical worlds that can be visualized up as quickly as the changing of a channel. Television broadcasting United States; Television programs Social aspects.

Stonehill, Brian
Channel the appetite for gore. (separate cable television channels for violence accessible by adults only)
The Los Angeles Times, July 29, 1993, v. 112 p. B7
LC Call Number: Newspaper 7114-X
Business Index Micro Film: None
Violence in television - Analysis / Cable television broadcasting industry - Planning

Sukow, Randall M.
Cable turns down NAB violence invitation. (cable industry refused to attend National Association of Broadcasters meeting)
Broadcasting and Cable July 8, 1991, v. 121 n., n1 p. 28(2).
LC Call Number: TK6540B85
Business Index Micro Film: 59Y1475
National Association of Broadcasters - Conferences, meetings, seminars, etc. / Violence in television - Conferences, meeting, seminars, etc. / Cable television broadcasting industry - Social policy

Sukow, Randy
Nets adopt violence code. (major television networks) (Brief Article)
Broadcasting and cable, Dec. 14, 1992, v. 122 n. n51 p. 9(1)
LC Call Number: TK6540B85

Business Index Micro Film: NONE
Violence in television - Standards / Television broadcasting industry - Standards

Svoboda, M. (1997)
Aggressive Behavior Viewed in Programs for Children on Czech Public TV. Psychologia
a Pasychologia Dietata 32(1997)3, pp. 289-298, ISSN 0555-5574.

Talk of TV violence. (Cable television companies to monitor violent programs)
Television Digest, Jan. 31, 1994, v. 34 n. n5 p. 9(1)
LC Call Number: May or May Not Be in LC. Search further
Business Index Micro Film: 76N0179
Violence in television - Management / Cable television broadcasting industry - Social
policy

Telecomputers and helpful chaos. (new technologies and violent programs)
Christianity today (Washington), Feb. 7, 1994, v. 38 n. n2 p. 42(1)
LC Call Number: BR1.C6418; Microfilm (0) 83/406 (1981-   ) MicRR
Magazine Index Micro Film: None
Television broadcasting industry - Forecasts / Violence in television - Forecasts

Televised violence dominant issue at INTV-NATPE conventions. (Association of
Independent Television Stations; National Association of Television Program
Executives)
Television Digest, Jan. 31, 1994, v. 34 n. n5 p. 1(3)
LC Call Number: May or May Not Be in LC. Search further.
Business Index Micro Film: 76N0171
The INTV and NATPE conventions in Miami, Fl, were preoccupied with the issue of
televised violence and its effect on social behavior. FCC Chmn Hundt warned the
television industry that the FCC will implement legislative actions on televised violence.
While industry officials said that the government should not impose regulations on
violence, Motion Picture Association of America Pres. Jack Valenti said that the industry
should assume that televised violence is a cause of antisocial behavior.
Association of Independent Television Stations - Conferences, meetings, seminars, etc. /
National Association of Television Program Executives - Conferences, meetings,
seminars, etc. / Violence in television - Conferences, meetings, seminars, etc. / Television
broadcasting industry - Social policy

Television violence to be monitored. (by Center for Communications Policy, University
of California at Los Angeles; sponsored by major networks) (Living Arts Pages)
The New York Times, June 30, 1994, v. 143 p. B2(N) pC20
LC Call Number: Not in LC Collection
Magazine Index Micro Film: None
Violence in television - Research

Terry, Carol Burton;
Newsday Size: 2K; 03-11-1990; Page Number: 0; Section: 0
AS SEEN ON TV Viewers Speak Out
Newspapers_&_Newswires AS SEEN ON TV Viewers Speak Out Carol Burton Terry
There can be strength in numbers. That's what a couple of outraged Cagney & Lacey fans
discovered when they helped found Viewers for Quality Television a few years back: The
group's protests over...

The broadcast networks. (promise to control gratuitous violence on TV) (Brief Article)
Broadcasting and Cable, June 28, 1993, v. 123 n. n26 p. 64(1)
LC Call Number: TK6540B85
Business Index Micro Film: 72P1487
Television broadcasting industry - Planning / Violence in television - Management

The four networks took another step toward self-regulation by choosing the UCLA
Center for Communication Policy. (television violence analysis) (Brief Article)
Broadcasting and Cable, July 4, 1994, v. 124 n. n27 p. 36(1)
LC Call Number: TK6540B85
Business Index Micro Film: 79W2192
California, University of (Los Angeles). Center for Communication Policy - Contracts /
Television broadcasting industry - Contracts / Violence in television - Research

Trossman, M.S. (1995)
Just Images: Television News Coverage of High-Profile Criminal Trials. Chicago:
American Bar Association, 1995, 17 p., ISBN 1-57073-184-5.

Tulloch, J.C. & Tulloch, M.I. (1992)
Discourses about Violence: Critical Theory and the 'TV Violence' Debate. Text
12(1992)2, pp. 183-231, ISSN 0165-4888.
Under the gun. (violence in television) (Editorial)
The Los Angeles Times, August 3, 1993, v. 112 p. B6
LC Call Number: Newspaper 7114-X
Business Index Micro Film: None
Violence in television - Laws, regulations, etc. / television broadcasting industry - Social
policy / Cable television broadcasting industry - Social policy

Violence in factual television: annual review 1993/ edited by Andrea Millwood Hargrave
London: Libbey, c1993
viii,151p; 25cm
Public opinion and broadcasting standards; 4
On title page: Broadcasting Standards Council
IVF7 (YVG) (IVF)
Hargrave, Andrea Millwood

Broadcasting Standards Council
[Criminology Library] IVF7

Violence is key issue in critics tour. (violence on TV)
Television Digest, Jan. 17, 1994, v. 34 n. n3 p. 1(2)
LC Call Number: May or May Not Be in LC. Search further.
Business Index Micro Film: 75W0002
Violence on TV dominated the questions asked by participants to the annual critics tour
of the West Coast. However, TV network executives defended their industry, saying that
violence was not that pervasive on their shows. CBS Broadcasting Group Pres. Jeff
Sagansky stated that unlike cable, networks do not rely on feature films with hard action
scenes. Sagansky stated that violence on network TV has dramatically gone down over
the years.
Critics - Attitudes / Violence in television - Evaluation / Television broadcasting
industry - Evaluation

Violence was. (leading issue at the International TV Festival and Market)
Television Digest, Feb. 14, 1994, v. 34 n. n7 p. 10(1)
LC Call Number: May or May Not Be in LC. Search further.
Business Index Micro Film: 76Y0344
Violence in television - Evaluation / Television broadcasting industry - Conferences,
meetings, seminars, etc. / Europe - Business and industry

Warner, Gregory D.
Morals in the marketplace: the TV coalition in context. Christian century, v. 100, April
13, 1983: 342-345.
Examines the boycott of NBC and RCA for allegedly immoral television programming
by the Coalition for Better Television, headed by Mississippi minister Don Wildmon.
"Should Christians support a boycott as a method of influencing broadcasting? A boycott
is a last resort because it closes more doors than it opens."
Television programs [U.S.] / Television industry [U.S.] / Boycott [U.S.] / Violence in
television [U.S.] / Pornography [U.S.] / Church and social problems [U.S.] / New Right
[U.S.] / Clergy [Mississippi] Political activities / Wildmon, Don / Coalition for Better
Television / NBC Television Network / RCA Corporation

Waters, Harry F.
Networks under the gun: broadcasters have promised to clean up their act. Critics say
don't believe the hype (networks to issue parental advisories warning of violent
programs)
Newsweek, July 12, 1993, v. 122 n. n2 p. 64(3)
LC Call Number: AP2.N6772; Microfilm 01125 (1933-   ) MicRR
Magazine Index Micro Film: None
Television broadcasting industry - Standards / Violence in television - Standards

Weinraub, Bernard
Reno's warning shot has Hollywood circling the wagons. (Attorney General Janet Reno warns the television industry about violence on television) (Living Arts Pages)
The New York Times, Oct. 22, 1993, v. 143 p. B1 (N) ppC3
LC Call Number: Not in LC Collection
Magazine Index Micro Film: None
Reno, Janet - Social policy
Violence in television - Social aspects / Television broadcasting industry - Social policy / Television programs - Social aspects

Weinstein, Steve
Premium cable channels adopt content labels. (advisories on violence, sex and offensive language)
The Los Angeles Times, June 8, 1994, v. 113 p. F1
LC Call Number: Newspaper 7114-X
Business Index Micro Film: None
Cable television broadcasting industry - Laws, regulations, etc. / Violence in television - Laws, regulations, etc. / Sex in television - Laws, regulations, etc.

Wharton, Dennis
BET disarming vids. (Black Entertainment Television may ban guns in music videos) (Brief Article)
Variety, Sept. 6, 1993, v. 352 n. n4 p. 17(1)
LC Call Number: PN2000.V3 Folio; Microfilm 03722 (1905-) MicRR
Magazine Index Micro Film: None
Violence in television - Management / Cable television broadcasting industry - Social policy

Wharton, Dennis
Fox takes violence hit. (survey on violence in Fox Broadcasting's, other networks television shows)
Variety, Dec. 27, 1993, v. 353 n. n8 p. 38(1)
LC Call Number: PN2000.V3 Folio; Microfilm 03722 (1905-) MicRR
Magazine Index Micro Film: None
Violence in television - Surveys / Television broadcasting - Surveys

Winterhoff-Spurk, P. (1997)
Violence in TV News: The Cultivation of Emotions. In: Winterhoff-Spurk, P & van der Voort, T.H.A. (Eds.): New Horizons in Media Psychology: Research Cooperations and Projects in Europe, pp. 105-115, Wiesbaden: Westdeutscher Verlag, 1997, VI, 219 p., ISBN 3-53112-859-0.

Winterhoff-Spurk, P.; Heidinger, P. & Schwab, F. (1994)
Reality TV: Formate und Inhalte eines neuen Programmgenres. Saarbrücken: Logos

Verlag, 1994, 243 p., bibl., ill., tab., ISBN 3-928598-62-7.

With all the attention in Washington being paid to the issue of violence on television, cable MSO Continental Cablevision has decided to provide parents with a family viewing guide. (multiple system operator) (Brief Article)
Broadcasting and Cable, Feb 7, 1994, v. 124 n. n6 p. 49(1)
LC Call Number: TK6540B85
Business Index Micro Film: 76R1348
Cable television broadcasting industry - Services / Violence in television - Prevention

Wurth-Hough, Sandra
Network news coverage of terrorism: the early years. Terrorism, v. 6, no. 3, 1983: 403-421.
"Based upon the Vanderbilt Television News Archive, this study examines the image projected in reporting of terrorist activities by the three major national networks, the American Broadcasting Company (ABC), the Columbia Broadcasting System (CBS), and the National Broadcasting Company (NBC)."
Terrorism / Reporters and reporting [U.S.] / Violence in television / Violence in mass media [U.S.] / Television news [U.S.] / Radio journalism [U.S.] / ABC News / CBS News / NBC News

Wurtzel, Alan; Lometti, Guy
Determining the acceptability of violent program content at ABC. Journal of broadcasting, v. 28, winter 1984: 89-97.
"The following examination of how the ABC television network determines the acceptability of violent programming includes a description of their application of social science research methodology in the decision-making process."
Television programs [U.S.] / Violence in television [U.S.] / Television networks [U.S.]

Yablonsky, Linda
PBS censors AIDS allegory: 'Son of Sam and Delilah' is cited for violence and lack of clarity
The Advocate, Sept. 10, 1991, n. n585 p. 85(1)
LC Call Number: Not in LC Collection
Magazine Index Micro Film: None
Charles Atlas. (portrait)
Atlas, Charles - Production and direction. Son of Sam and Delilah (Television program) - Censorship / Documentary television programs - Censorship / AIDS (Disease) - Portrayals, depictions, etc. / Violence in television - Censorship / Public television - Censorship

Zbar, Jeffrey D.
Broadcasters brood over violence issue at NATPE convention. (National Association of Television Program Executives) (Brief Article)

Advertising Age, Jan. 31, 1994, v. 65 n. n5 p. 8(1)
LC Call Number: HF5801.A276
Business Index Micro Film: 76N3039
National Association of Television Program Executives - Conferences, meetings,
seminars, etc./ Violence in television - Addresses, essays, lectures / Television
broadcasting industry - Conferences, meetings, seminars, etc.

Zinsmeister, Karl
Wasteland: how today's trash television harms America
The American Enterprise. v. 10 no 2 Mar./Apr. 1999 p. 24-30.
The writer presents evidence from national newspapers drawing attention to the problem
and notes that a wide range of Americans are horrified by what is considered TV
entertainment today; they register sexual content as their main complaint, closely
followed by violence, and then crude language. He concludes that due to the amount of
time people spend watching television, it seems inevitable that they are influenced by it;
if it appeals to the worst in us, we may have to suffer the consequences in the future.

Zoglin, Richard
The networks run for cover: to avoid a warning label, violent shows are getting toned
down - or dropped.
Time (Chicago) August 2, 1993, v. 142 n. n5 p. 52 (2)
LC Call Number: AP2.T37; Microfilm 02914 (1923-   ) MicRR
Business Index Micro Film: None
Violence in television - Production and direction / Television programs - Rating /
Television producers and directors - Practice

Zoglin, Richard
Where are the censors? A titillating fall raises questions about network standards.
(television)
Time (Chicago) Dec. 12, 1988, v. 132 n. n24 p. 95(1)
LC Call Number: AP2.T37; Microfilm 02914 (1923-   ) MicRR
Magazine Index Micro Film: 47G0286
Television programs - standards / Television broadcasting - censorship / Sex in television
- censorship / Violence in television - censorship

Children and TV Violence

Abel, John D. Beninson, Maureen E.
Perceptions of TV program violence by children and mothers. Journal of Broadcasting, v.
20, summer 1976: 355-363.
Says there are clear differences in how both children and their mothers perceive and even
define violence.
Television and children - [U.S. / Television programs [U.S.] / Violence in television
[U.S.]

Abelman, Robert
Children and TV: the ABC's of TV literacy. Childhood education, v. 60, Jan.-Feb. 1984:
200-205.
"Children's television viewing habits are known to be a product of the quality and
quantity of parental mediation. This review establishes a clear rationale not only for those
efforts by parents but also such efforts by teachers. Children can be taught television
literacy as a part of the regular school curriculum."
Television and children [U.S.] / Teacher-student relationships [U.S.] / Parent and child
[U.S.]

Action Group on Violence on Television (AGVOT)
http://www.cab-acr.ca/about/tv/agvot_homepage.htm
AGVOT was created on February 22nd, 1993, following a conference sponsored by the
C.M. Hincks Institute, a Toronto-based organization with expertise in the area of
children's emotional health and development, and the Canadian Radio-television and
Telecommunications Commission, the federal agency responsible for the regulation of
broadcasting in Canada.
AGVOT's primary mandate was to coordinate broadcast and cable industry strategies and
initiatives to deal with the issue of violence on television. To that extent it is unique in the
world. There is no other country in which all the major segments of the broadcast, cable
and production industries have joined forces to address this important social issue.

Adeney, Miriam
'Mommie, why can't Jesus be Superman?' How to discuss violence with your
preschooler - and get a new perspective on Christ's sufferings
Christian Herald (Chappaqua) May 1982, v. 105 p. 14(4)

LC Call Number: BR1.C63; Microfilm 01104 (1818-1845) MicRR
Magazine Index Micro Film: None
Jesus Christ - teachings
violence in television - moral and religious aspects / children - religion

Adler, Richard P., and others.
Research on the effects of television advertising on children; a review of the literature
and recommendations for future research. [Washington, U.S. National Science
Foundation, for sale by the Supt. of Docs, U.S. Govt. Print. off, 1977] 229 p.
"NSF/RA 770115."
Concludes that television advertising does influence children and assesses "the current
state of knowledge about the effects of television advertising on children."
Television advertising [U.S.] / Television and children [U.S.]

Adolescence in the 1990s: risk and opportunity. Teachers College Record, v. 94, spring
1993: whole issue (453-672 p.)
Partial contents. - Changing views of adolescence in the contemporary society, by Rudy
Takanashi. - Schools as places for health, mental health, and social services. - Parent-
school involvement during the early adolescent years. - Improving the school-to-work
transition of American adolescents. - Adolescence and schooling in Germany and the
United States. - Adolescents and the mass media. - The Carnegie Conference on
Adolescent Health. - The need for a core, interdisciplinary, life-sciences curriculum in the
middle grades, by H. Craig Heler. - The potential effects of community organizations on
the future of our youth.
Youth [U.S.] / Middle schools [U.S.] / Junior high schools [U.S.] / Parent-school
relationships [U.S.] / School-to-work transition [U.S.] / Television and children [U.S.] /
Curricula [U.S.] / Community organization [U.S.] /Health education [U.S.]

Aidman, Amy.
SuDocs Call No.: ED 1.310/2:414078
Television violence content, context, and consequences
ERIC Clearinghouse on Elementary and Early Childhood Education.
Published: Champaign, IL : ERIC Clearinghouse on Elementary and Early Childhood
Education, University of Illinois, Date: [1997] Description: 1 v. Series: ERIC digest ;
EDO-PS-97-26 Item No.: 0466-A-03 (MF) Note: Microfiche.

Alperowicz, Cynthia
Toymakers takeover children's TV. Business and society review, no. 49, spring 1984; 47-
51.
Argues that programming on children's television has become program-length
commercials masquerading as programs.
Television and children [U.S.] / Toys [U.S.] / Television advertising [U.S.]

America's childhood.
Daedalus, v. 122, winter 1993: whole issue (308 p.)
Partial contents. Social movements for children. - Child poverty and public policy:
toward a comprehensive antipoverty agenda. - Towards sustainable development for
American families. - America's children and their elementary schools. - Thief of time,
unfaithful servant: television and the American child.
Children [U.S.] / Child welfare [U.S.] / Elementary education [U.S.] / Television and
children [U.S.] / Poor [U.S.]

Anderson, Daniel R.
How TV influences your kids.
TV Guide, March 3, 1990, v. 38 n. n9 p. 24(4)
LC Call Number: Microfilm 06378 (1953-) MicRR
Magazine Index Micro Film: 53J2439
Television programs for children - psychological aspects / Television and children -
social aspects / Violence in television - psychological aspects

Anker, Roy M.
Yikes! Nightmares from Hollywood. Christianity Today, v. 33, June 16, 1989: 18-23.
Anker argues that "in big cities and small towns, with at least one video store per
commercial half-mile, very young kids can rent virtually any film, from sex romps to
slasher and war-gore flicks." Suggests that parents watch the movies before they allow
their children to view them, watch the material with their children and then discuss the
content with them.
Motion pictures [U.S.] Trends / Pornography [U.S.] Trends / Violence in mass media
[U.S.] Trends / Television and children [U.S.] / Home video systems [U.S.] Standards /
Church and social problems [U.S.]

Appleyard, Bryan; Goddard, Peter
Curbing a culture of violence. (motion pictures) (includes related article on children and
television violence)
World press review, March, 1994, v. 41 n. n3 p. 24(2)
LC Call Number: AP2.A833
Magazine Index Micro Film: None
Violence in motion pictures - Social aspects / Violence in television - Social aspects /
Television and children - Social aspects

Atkin, Charles K.
Effects of campaign advertising and newscasts on children. Journalism quarterly, v. 54,
autumn 1977: 503-508.
Using data obtained from a sampling of elementary school children in Lansing, Mich.,
this study "examines the role of adult-oriented campaign news and commercials in the
political socialization of children." Findings indicate that "news exposure contributes to
children's knowledge about political candidates.

Political socialization [Michigan] / Television and children [Michigan] / Television in politics [Michigan] / Political advertising [Michigan]

Barry, David S.
Screen violence and America's children. Spectrum, v. 66, summer 1993: 37-42.
"Studies show that murder rates have risen in response to televised violence, not only in the United States, but elsewhere. Despite this correlation, the broadcast industry continues to saturate children's programming with violence."
Violence in television [U.S.] / Television children [U.S.] / Broadcasting [U.S.]

Belson, William A.
Television violence and the adolescent boy / William A. Belson. - Farnborough, Hants.: Saxon House, 1978. x, 529 p.: ill.; 23 cm. Includes bibliographical references.
Television and teenagers - United States. Violence in television - United States. Teenage boys. Television - United States - Psychological aspects.

Bernard-Bonnin, A.C.; Gilbert, S.; Rousseau, E.; Masson, P. & Maheux, B. (1991)
Television and the 3- to 10-Year Old Child. Pediatrics 88(1991)1, pp. 48-54, ISSN 0031-4005.

Berry, G.L. & Asamen, J.K. (Eds.) (1993)
Children and Television: Images in a Changing Sociocultural World. Newbury Park: Sage Publications, 1993, X, 332 p., ill., ISBN 0-80394-700-3.

Berry, Gordon L.
Television and the urban child: some educational policy implications. Education and urban society, v. 10, Nov. 1977: 31-54.
"Take[s] a look at the nature and needs of the inner-city child, the inner-city school, and the policy implications of television on the curriculum of both."
Television and children [U.S.] / Urban education [U.S.] / Curriculum planning [U.S.]

Black D; Newman M
Television violence and children [editorial]
BMJ, 310:273-4, 1995 Feb 4
Aggression; Child; Child Behavior; Child Psychology*; Child, Preschool; Human; Mental Health*; Television*; Violence*

Blurring the image. (television-watching effects)
Psychology Today (Magazine) July-August, 1992, v. 25 n. n4 p. 13(1)
LC Call Number: BF1.P855
Magazine Index Micro Film: 65A1316
Violence in television - Social aspects / Aggressiveness (Psychology) in children - Social aspects

Bok, Sissela
TV violence, children and the press: eight rationales inhibiting public policy debates. [Cambridge, Mass.] Joan Shorenstein Barone Center on the Press, Politics, and Public Policy. 1994. 21 p. (Discussion paper D-16)
"Although the depth of [the author's] concerns about televised violence is plain from this paper, she aims primarily not to make the case for only policy prescription or another. Rather, her goal is to expose some number of weak arguments whose dominance in current deliberation about the consequences of televised violence seems to her to be out of all proportion to their validity."
Television and children [U.S.] / Violence in television [U.S.] / Press [U.S.]

Boulard P; Arthuis M
Prevention of violence among adolescents and children
Bull Acad Natl Med, 180:1503-13, 1996 Jun-Jul

Bower, Bruce
Social channels tune in TV's effects. (research on television violence and children)
Science News (Washington), Sept. 14, 1985, v. 128 p. 166(1)
LC Call Number: Q1.S76
Magazine Index Micro Film: 29K2099
television and children - research / city and town life - Israel / violence in television - social aspects / country life - Israel

Braxton, Greg
A congressional call for return of 'family hour'.
Los Angeles Times, May 1, 1996 vl 15 pF1 col 5 (17 col in)

Brodkin, Margaret. 1993.
Every Kid Counts: 31 Ways to Save Our Children. San Francisco: HarperCollins Publishers.

Bryant, J. (Ed.) (1990)
Television and the American Family. Hillsdale: Lawrence Erlbaum Associates, 1990, 385 p., ISBN 0-80580-116-2.

Buckingham, D. & Allerton, M. (1996)
Fear, Fright and Distress: A Review of Research on Children's 'Negative' Emotional Responses to Television. London: Broadcasting Standards Commission, 1996, 67 p.

Cairns, E. (1990)
Impact of Television News Exposure on Children's Perceptions of Violence in Northern Ireland. Journal of Social Psychology 130(1990), pp. 447-452, ISSN 0022-4545.

Cannon, Carl M.
Honey, I warped the kids. Mother Jones, v. 18, July-Aug. 1993: 16-21
Discusses violence in Hollywood-made movies and television. A companion article,
"Passing the buck in Tinseltown," by Michael Krasny, gives personal comments by
producers, directors and actors on their thoughts about "excess violence in the movie
industry."
Violence in mass media [U.S.] / Television and children [U.S.] / Motion picture industry
[U.S.] / Social surveys [U.S.]

Cantor, J. (1998)
"Mommy, I'm Scared": How TV and Movies Frighten Children and What We Can Do to
Protect Them. New York, London: Harcourt Brace & Company, 1998, 249 p., ISBN 0-
15-100402-1.

Cantor, J. & Nathanson, A.I. (1996)
Children's Fright Reactions to Television News. Journal of Communication 46(1996)4,
Autumn, pp. 139-152, ISSN 0021-9916.

Cantor, J. (1996)
Television and Children's Fear. In: MacBeth, T.M. (Ed.): Tuning in to Young Viewers:
Social Science Perspectives on Television, pp. 87-115, Thousand Oaks: Sage
Publications, 1996, 282 p., ill., ISBN 0-80395-825-0.

Cantor, Joanne; Nathanson, Amy I
Predictors of children's interest in violent television programs, Journal of Broadcasting
and Electronic Media. v. 41 Spring 1997 p. 155-67.
Children's attraction to violent television was explored by comparing the relative
contributions of seemingly important predictors. A random sample of 285 parents of
children in kindegarten, second, fourth, and sixth grades was interviewed about their
children's television viewing habits. Analyses revealed that interest in classic cartoons,
which typically display violence for violence's sake, was predicted by grade, whereas
attraction to typically justice-restoring violent fare was predicted by grade, gender
aggression, and fright reactions to television.

Carlsson, U. & von Feilitzen, C. (Eds.) (1998)
Children and Media Violence: Yearbook from the UNESCO International Clearinghouse
on Children and Violence on the Screen 1998. Göteborg: Nordicom, Göteborgs
universitet, 1998, 387 p., fig., tab., chart., bibl., ISBN 91-630-6358-1.

Carlsson-Paige, Nancy, & Levin, Diane E. 1994. 'The Mighty Morphin Power Rangers:
Teachers Voice a Concern.' Cambridge, MA: Lesley College.

Carlsson-Paige, Nancy, & Levin, Diane E. 1994. 'Developmentally Appropriate
Television: Putting Children First.' Young Children, vol. 49 (5), pp. 38-44.

Carlsson-Paige, Nancy; Levin, Diane E.
Young children and war play. Educational leadership, v. 45, Dec. 1987-Jan. 1988: 80-84.
"In the classroom, teachers can use children's war play as an opportunity for instruction, but on a larger scale, children's television programming must become a matter of government policy."
Violence in television [U.S.] / Television and children [U.S.] / Television programs [U.S.]

Carthrane, Ardis
Medics say TV makes kids fat and violent.
Jet, May 21, 1990, v. 78 n. n6 p. 16 (2)
LC Call Number: E185.5.J4; Microfilm 07167 (1951-1979) MicRR
Magazine Index Micro Film: 55E0017
Television and children - psychological aspects / Violence in television - psychological aspects / Violence in children - causes of / Obesity in children - causes of

Charren, Peggy
It's 8 p.m. where are your parents? (controlling the amount of violence children watch on television) (Column)
The New York Times, July 7, 1993, v. 142 p. A13 (N) pA1
LC Call Number: Not in LC Collection
Business Index Micro Film: None
Violence in television - Laws, regulations, etc. / Television broadcasting industry - Laws, regulations, etc. / Television and children - Health aspects

Charren, Peggy
It's 8 p.m. where are your parents? (controlling the amount of violence children watch on television) (Column)
The New York Times, July 7, 1993 v. 142 p. A13(N) pA1
LC Call Number: Not in LC Collection
Magazine Index Micro Film: None
Violence in television - Laws, regulations, etc. / Television broadcasting industry - Laws, regulations, etc. / Television and children - Health aspects

Child's play; violent videos lure the young. (retail shops sell violent video cassettes)
Time (Chicago), June 1, 1987, v. 129 p. 31(1)
LC Call Number: AP2.T37; Microfilm 02914 (1923-   ) MicRR
Magazine Index Micro Film: 40E0628
Violence in television - Laws, regulations, etc. / Video recordings for children - Laws, regulations, etc. / Video tapes - marketing
Children, Media and Violence
http://interact.uoregon.edu/MediaLit/FA/MLmediaviolence.html
Media Literacy On-Line Project. College of Education - University of Oregon.

Introduction: This page provides a gateway to information on the ic of media and technology violence.

Clark, Charles S.
TV violence. (The Issues)
CQ Researcher, March 26, 1993, v. 3 n. n12 p. 267 (7)
LC Call Number: H35.E35
Magazine Index Micro Film: None
Youth exposure to violence is increasingly difficult to monitor with longer children's viewing hours and the variety of television broadcast formats available. The problem's relation to aggressiveness and violence in youth is not unnoticed, and several proposals to control violence in television have been presented by the political and public sectors. These proposals include a violence rating system and increased FCC regulation, although the latter raises fears of censorship. Broadcast networks showed their support with plans to minimize and properly present scenes containing violent materials.
Violence in television - Social aspects / Aggressiveness (Psychology) in children - Causes of / Television broadcasting industry - Social policy

Clarke-Pearson KM
Children--media violence--solutions.
N C Med J, 58:265-8, 1997 Jul-Aug

Coalition for Juvenile Justice (1997)
False Images? The News Media and Juvenile Crime, 1997 Annual Report. Washington D.C.: Coalition for Juvenile Justice, 1997, 72 p.

Comer, James P.
Sex, violence and the TV set. (As They Grow: 11 Through 13)
Parents (Bergenfield), Jan. 1993, v. 68, n. n1 p. 116(1)
LC Call Number: HQ768.P33
Magazine Index Micro Film: None
Teenagers - Conduct of life / Television and children - Psychological aspects / Violence in television - Psychological aspects.

Comer, James P.
Television, sex & violence. (11 through 13 years of age)
Parents (Bergenfield), July 1986, v. 61 p. 160(1)
LC Call Number: HQ768.P33
Magazine Index Micro Film: 34J3863
Sex in television - psychological aspects / Violence in television - psychological aspects / Television and children - psychological aspects / Parenting - technique

Comstock, G.A. & Paik, H. (1991)
Television and the American Child. San Diego: Academic Press, 1991, XIV, 386 p., ill.,
bibl., ISBN 0-12183-575-8.

Cooke, Patrick
TV or not TV. (influence of television) (includes related stories) (cover Story)
In Health, Dec.-Jan. 1991, v. 5 n. n7 p. 32(12)
LC Call Number: Not in LC Collection
Magazine Index Micro Film: None
The psychological effects of watching television are analyzed. The effect of TV on
children is debated, as are the effects of watching television violence.
Television - Influence / Television and children - Analysis / Television broadcasting -
Social aspects / Television viewers - Research / Violence in television - Research
Could kids defeat, (violence blockout systems)
Television Digest, August 16, 1993, v. 33 n. n33 p. 13 (1)
LC Call Number: May or May Not Be In LC. Search Further.
Business Index Micro Film: 72Z0514
Television equipment and supplies industry - Laws, regulations, etc. / Violence in
television - Laws, regulations, etc.

Davidson, John
Menace to society; worded about media violence? Cartoons may be the real culprit.
Rolling Stone, Feb 22, 1996 n728 p38(2)

Demers, David P.
Breaking your child's TV addiction / David Pearce Demers. - Minneapolis: Marquette
Books, c1989. 105 p.: ill.; 22 cm. Cover subtitle: A guide for parents. Bibliography: p.
[101]-102. Includes index. Television and children - United States. Violence in television
- United States. Television - United States - Psychological aspects. I. Title. II. Title: TV
addiction. Title: Breaking your child's television addiction.

Dennis PM
Chills and thrills: does radio harm our children? The controversy over program violence
during the age of radio.
Department of Psychology, Elizabethtown College, PA, USA.
J Hist Behav Sci, 34:33-50, 1998 Winter
A review of the popular and scientific periodical for the 1930s and 1940s revealed that
the controversy surrounding the radio "thriller" and its possible harmful effects on young
listeners was one of radio's most highly publicized issues during its golden years of
broadcasting. Many of the questions raised concerning this issue were similar to those
asked later during the age of television. Relying heavily upon the psychoanalytic
emphasis on emotion, catharsis, and intrapsychic dynamics, expert opinion voiced in
various popular periodicals and newspapers of the day suggested that the violence and
excitement portrayed in many of the crime and adventure programs was harmless, and

perhaps beneficial, for most listeners. However, research in support of this conclusion was sparse, and psychologists evidenced little interest in the issue. Not until the advent of television, and the emergence of social learning theory in the early 1960s, did psychologists direct significant research effort towards evaluating the effects of media violence.

Devore, Cynthia DiLaura, 1947-
Kids and media influence / by Cynthia DiLaura Devore. - Edina, Minn.: Abdo & Daughters, [1994] p. cm. - (Kids in crisis)
Includes bibliographical references and index.
Television and children - United States - Juvenile literature. Mass media and children - United States - Juvenile literature. Violence in television - United States - Juvenile literature.
[1. Violence in television. 2. Television - Psychological aspects.] I. Title. II. Series.

DiLorenzo, Francis
Courageous Christian love: a response to symbolic violence: pars dissertations ad lauream in Facultate S. Theologiae apud Pontificiam Universitatem S. Thomae de Urbe / Francis Di Lorenzo. - Romae: Pontificia Studiorum Universitas A.S. Thoma Aq. in Urbe, Facultas Theologiae, 1975.
73 p.; 24 cm. Bibliography: p. [51]-70.
Television and children. Violence in television - United States. Violence - United States. Love - Religious aspects - Christianity. Children - Religious life. I. Title.

Doerken, Maurine
Classroom combat, teaching and television / Maurine Doerken. - Englewood Cliffs, NJ.: Educational Technology Publications, c1983
xvii, 316 p.: ill.; 25 cm. Bibliography: p. 287-297. Includes index.
Television and children. Television and youth. Violence in television. Television advertising and children. Teachers - Attitudes. Television in education. I. Title.

Dorfman L; Woodruff K; Chavez V; Wallack L
Youth and violence on local television news in California.
Berkeley Media Studies Group, CA 94704, USA.
Am J Public Health, 87:1311-6, 1997 Aug
OBJECTIVES: This study explores how local television news structures the public and policy debate on youth violence. METHODS: A content analysis was performed on 214 hours of local television news from California. Each of the 1791 stories concerning youth, violence, or both was coded and analyzed for whether it included a public health perspective. RESULTS: There were five key findings. First, violence dominated local television news coverage. Second, the specifics of particular crimes dominated coverage of violence. Third, over half of the stories on youth involved violence, while more than two thirds of the violence stories concerned youth. Fourth, episodic coverage of violence was more than five times more frequent than thematic coverage, which included links to

broader social factors. Finally, only one story had an explicit public health frame. CONCLUSIONS: Local television news provides extremely limited coverage of contributing etiological factors in stories on violence. If our nation's most popular source of news continues to report on violence primarily through crime stories isolated from their social context, the chance for widespread support for public health solutions to violence will be diminished.

Dorr, A.; Kovaric, P. & Doubleday, C. (1990)
Age and Content Influences on Children's Perception of the Realism of Television Families. Journal of Broadcasting and Electronic Media 34(1990)4, Fall, pp. 377-397, ISSN 0883-8151.

Durenberger, David
"I see no reason we should not warn parents about the harmful effects that TV violence may have on their children." (Column)
Broadcasting and Cable, May 31, 1993, v. 123 n. n22 p. 74(1)
LC Call Number: TK6540B85
Business Index Micro Film: 71V1445
American television is a violence-strewn wasteland. Adults are wise enough to turn off programs saturated with mindless brutality and sadism, but children are not experienced or wise enough to understand that such violence harms them psychologically. The proposed Children's Television Violence Protection Act would require violent TV shows to supply parental warnings. These warnings would not infringe broadcasters' freedom-of-expression rights.
Violence in television - Laws, regulations, etc. / Television broadcasting industry - Laws, regulations, etc.

Early concerns. (Violence in television) (Background)
CQ Researcher, March 26, 1993, v. 3 n. n12 p. 274 (2)
LC Call Number: H351.E35
Magazine Index Micro Film: None
Violence in television was first recognized as a problem in 1952, when a Congressional subcommittee focused on media violence in relation to youth. However, media executives debunked social and political concerns with the argument that media was a factor in the rising incidence of juvenile arrests and that it was an advantage for the industry to be under self-regulation. Not even the results of a 1956 study linking violence in cartoons to increased aggressiveness and violence in children prevented the advent of more violent television programs and movies in the 1960s.
Violence in television - Analysis / Aggressiveness (Psychology) in children - Causes of / Television programs - Social aspects

Edgar, Patricia
Children and screen violence / Patricia Edgar. St. Lucia: University of Queensland Press, c1977.

ix, 275 p.; 22 cm. Aus. Bibliography: p. 265-270. Includes indexes.
Mass media and youth. Violence in motion pictures. Violence in television. Violence - Research. I. Title.

Edwards, Ellen
No tantrums at hearing on kids' TV. (Federal Communications Commission hearing on Children's Television Act of 1990)
The Washington Post, June 29, 1994, v. 117 p. D1
LC Call Number: Newspaper
Business Index Micro Film: None
United States. Federal Communications Commission - Investigations / Television and children - Laws, regulations, etc. / Violence in television - Laws, regulations, etc. / Television broadcasting industry - Laws, regulations, etc.

Emmens, Carol A.
Peggy Charren: ACT goals. (interview with president of Action for Children's Television)
School library journal, March 1993, v. 29 p. 129 (1)
LC Call Number: Z675.S3S29115
Magazine Index Micro Film: None
Charren, Peggy - interviews
Action for Childern's Television - Management / television and children - analysis / violence in television - analysis / cable television - public opinion / Calliope (television program) - production and direction

Faivelson, Saralie
Verdict on TV violence
Woman's Day, Oct. 1, 1987, p. 24(1)
LC Call Number: Not in LC Collection
Magazine Index Micro Film: 41B3817
Violence in television - psychological aspects / Violence in children - research / Aggressiveness (Psychology) in children - research / Television and children - psychological aspects

Fields, Suzanne
TV violence minus context numbs kids' sense of ethics. (Column)
Insight, August 2, 1993, v. 9 n. n31 p. 31 (2)
LC Call Number: AP2.I624
Magazine Index Micro Film: None
Violence in television - Moral and ethical aspects / Television and children - Social aspects / Violence in literature - Moral and ethical aspects

Freeman, Michael
Kids affected by seamy talk-show promos. (television show promotions intended for

adults reach children) (Brief Article)
Mediaweek, March 14, 1994, v. 4 n. n11 p. 4(1)
LC Call Number: HF6146.T42M43
Business Index Micro Film: 77Q1094
Television and children - Evaluation / Violence in television - Evaluation

French, J. & Pena, S. (1991)
Children's Hero Play of the 20th Century: Changes Resulting from Television's
Influence. Child Study Journal 21(1991)2, pp. 79-94, ISSN 0009-4005.
French, K. (Ed.)
(1996)
Screen Violence. London: Bloomsbury, 1996, VI, 250 p., ISBN 0-74752-549-8.

Friedlander, B.Z. (1993)
Community Violence, Children's Development, and Mass Media: In Pursuit of New
Insights, New Goals and New Strategies. Psychiatry 56(1993)1, pp. 66-81, ISSN 0031-
4005.

Funk, J.B. & Buchman, D.D. (1996)
Playing Violent Video and Computer Games and Adolescent Self-Concept. Journal of
Communication 46(1996)2, pp. 19-32, ISSN 0021-9916.
Gabriel RM; Hopson T; Haskins M; Powell KE
Building relationships and resilience in the prevention of youth violence.
RMC Research Corporation, Portland, OR 97204, USA. roy_gabriel@rmccorp.com
Am J Prev Med, 12:48-55, 1996 Sep-Oct
Self Enhancement, Inc., is a grassroots, community-service organization working in the
most disadvantaged high-risk community in Portland, Oregon. Its violence-prevention
program targets middle-school and high-school students by providing classroom and
community activities to these young people. These activities are designed to enhance
protective factors and build resilience in youths to enable them to attain healthy and
productive lives and to resist the threats of gangs, violence, and drugs. RMC Research
Corporation works in partnership with Self Enhancement, Inc., to conduct research and
evaluation on the effectiveness of its programs. The Self Enhancement, Inc., program
works primarily at the individual student and interpersonal relationship levels. Resilience
Theory and its culturally specific Relationship Model drive the formulation of specific
strategies and activities. Program staff mentor each student through his or her
preadolescent and adolescent years, promoting positive, prosocial norms and expectations
for behavior through their peer group activities. The Self Enhancement, Inc., program
consists of three major components: classroom, exposure, and proactive education.
Classroom education focuses on anger management, conflict resolution, and problem
solving. Exposure education consists of quarterly field trips to agencies and organizations
in the Portland area that deal with the causes and consequences of violence in the
community. Proactive education includes newsletters, student-run assemblies and
conferences, and radio/ television public service announcements that communicate

antiviolence messages. The evaluation plan is a longitudinal matched comparison group designed to assess the outcomes of the violence-prevention program. Key outcomes are protective factors, health-risk behaviors, and academic measures. Standardized assessment instruments (the Individual Protective Factors Index and the Youth Risk Behavior Survey) were administered to all students during winter 1994. The instruments will be readministered during the same period in the following two years of the project. School records were extracted to assess students' attendance and progress through their academic programs. Of the 326 seventh-, eighth-, and ninth-grade students participating in this study, 95% are African Americans and 51% are boys. The prevalence of fighting (56%) during the past 12 months is higher than that among African-American high-school students nationally, but weapon carrying (27%), alcohol use (30%), and marijuana use (18%) are the same or lower than national averages for this group. All baseline indicators are equivalent between the program and comparison groups with the exception of weapon carrying. Program students report carrying weapons more than do their comparison group counterparts. Baseline indicators of violence-related behaviors clearly indicate the need for intervention in this highly disadvantaged, African-American community. Through its historical presence and recent program development efforts, Self Enhancement, Inc., is well positioned to make a difference in the lives of these young people. The equivalence of program and comparison group students on baseline indicators of violence bodes well for an unequivocal assessment of program effectiveness over time.

Hopf H; Weiss RH
Viewing of horror and violence videos by adolescence. A study of speech samples of video consumers with the Gottschalk-Gleser Speech Content analysis
Prax Kinderpsychol Kinderpsychiatr, 45:179-85, 1996 May-Jun
In 1990 pupils of different schools in Württemberg were interviewed about their television and video consumption. It turned out that a high percentage of mainly male pupils of Hauptschulen (upper division of elementary schools) and special schools excessively and regularly consumed films which were on the index (X-rated) or seized depicting horror and violence. Subsequent to the inquiry through questionnaires and different personality tests, speech samples of 51 test persons were recorded on tape. 5 speech samples had to be excluded from further investigation since they contained less than 70 words. The transcribed and anonymized records were examined according to the Gottschalk-Gleser content analysis of verbal behavior, and two groups of so-called seldom lookers (n = 22) and frequent lookers (n = 24) were compared to each other. The frequent lookers significantly often reported about film contents which presumably means that their imagination is more restricted and less productive than that of the other group. In addition, this group of frequent lookers had significantly higher scores concerning death anxiety and guilt anxiety. With regard to hostility affects, their scores were also significantly raised concerning outward-overt hostility, outward-covert hostility, and ambivalent hostility. Probably the group of frequent lookers comprised more test persons with relationship disorders, with borderline risks, dissocial personality features, and problems to cope with their aggressiveness. So they show on the one hand a

raised affinity to watch such films, but simultaneously unconscious and conscious learning processes take place which stimulate further aggressive fantasies (and possibly also actions).

Gadow, K.D. & Sprafkin, J. (1989)
Field Experiments of Television Violence With Children: Evidence for an Environmental Hazard? Pediatrics 83(1989)3, pp. 399-405, ISSN 0031-4005.

Gadow, K.D. & Sprafkin, J. (1993)
Television "Violence" and Children with Emotional and Behavioral Disorders. Journal of Emotional and Behavioral Disorders 1(1993), pp. 54-63, ISSN 1063-4266.

Gardner, Marilyn
Media's message to children is, 'you're the problem.' (Children Now report on news coverage of young people)
The Christian Science Monitor (1983), March 10, 1994, . 86 n. n73 p. 13
LC Call Number: Newspaper
Business Index Micro Film: None
Youth - Media coverage / Mass media and teenagers - Reports / Violence in television - Reports / Television broadcasting - Reports

Gelman, Eric
MTV's message; parents worry about the sex and violence in music videos. Are they really bad for our kids?
Newsweek, Dec. 30, 1985, v. 106 p. 54(3)
LC Call Number: AP2.N6772; Microfilm 01125 (1933-   ) MicRR
Magazine Index Micro Film: 31K2349
Music videos - social aspects / television and youth - analysis / violence in television - analysis / sex in television - analysis

Gelman, Morrie
Hollywood gears to new style kidvid action. (TV shows)
Variety, Feb. 10, 1988, v. 330 n. n3 p. 1(2)
LC Call Number: PN2000.V3 Folio; Microfilm 03722 91905-   ) MicRR
Magazine Index Micro Film: None
Association of Independent Television Stations - surveys / Television programs for children - production and direction / Violence in television - public opinion / Syndication of television programs - marketing

Gerbner, G.; Gross, L. & Morgan, M. et al. (1994)
Growing Up with Television: The Cultivation Perspective. In: Bryant, J. & Zillmann, D. (Eds.): Media Effects: Advances in Theory and Research, pp. 17-42, Hillsdale: Lawrence Erlbaum Associates, 1994, IX, 505 p., ISBN 0-80580-917-1.

Gerbner, G.; Gross, L. & Morgan, M. et al. (1994)
Television Violence Profile No. 16: The Turning Point from Research to Action.
Philadelphia: The Annenberg School for Communications, University of Pennsylvania,
1994, 26 p.

Gerbner, George and others.
Trends in network television drama and viewer conceptions of social reality, 1967-1976.
Philadelphia, Annenberg School of Communications, University of Pennsylvania, 1977.
29, [74] p. (Pennsylvania, University. Annenberg School of Communications. Violence
profile no. 8)
Study found that "television violence increased sharply in all categories including 'family
viewing' and children's program time on all three networks."
Television programs [U.S.] / Violence in television [U.S.]

Gerbner, George and others.
Trends in network television drama and viewer conceptions of social reality 1967-1978.
Philadelphia, Annenberg School of Communications, University of Pennsylvania, 1979.
1 v. (various pagings) (Pennsylvania. University. Annenberg School of Communications.
Violence profile no. 10)
"Violence in weekend children' and late evening programming rose to near record levels
in the fall of 1978. All three major networks programmed more violence during weekend-
daytime (children's) hours than last year. The new findings also continue to show that
young people who watch more television are more apprehensive about their own safety
and are more likely to think that people are mean and selfish."
Television programs [U.S.] / Violence in television [U.S.] / Social surveys [U.S.] /
Television and children [U.S.]

Glucksmann, André, 1937-
Violence on the screen: a report on research into the effects on young people of scenes of
violence in films and television; translated [from the French] by Susan Bennett; with a
foreword by Paddy Whannel and an afterword by Dennis Howitt. London, British Film
Institute (Education Department), 1971
78 p. 23 cm. Originally published in Communications, 7, 1966. Includes bibliographical
references.
Violence in motion pictures. Violence in television. Motion pictures and children.
Television and children. I. Title.

Greenberg, Aurora
Parental behavior, TV habits, IQ predict aggression.
Science news (Washington), Sept. 3, 1983, v. 124 p. 148(1)
LC Call Number: Q1.S76
Magazine Index Micro Film: 19B5022
Criminal behavior, prediction of - social aspects / parent and child - social aspects /
violence in television - social aspects / television and children - social aspects /

intelligence levels - social aspects / child psychology - research / aggressiveness (psychology) - social aspects

Greiner, L.R. (1997)
Threatening Children: Mass Media and the Construction of a New Breed of Violent Youth Offender. Denver: University of Denver, 1997, 162 p., Diss.

Gross, Lynne Schafer, Walsh, R. Patricia
Factors affecting parental control over children's television viewing: a pilot study.
Journal of broadcasting, v. 24, summer 1980: 411-419.
"Investigate[s] various family factors that might relate to parental control over children's TV viewing."
Television and children [U.S.] / Parent and child [U.S.]
Heller, Melvin S.
Studies in violence and television / by Melvin S. Heller and Samuel Polsky. - New York: American Broadcasting Co., 1976
p. a-c, v, 503 p.: ill.; 28 cm. Includes bibliographical references.
Television and children. Violence in television. Aggressiveness (Psychology) in children.
I. Polsky, Samuel, joint author. II. American Broadcasting Company. Title.

Gulbenkian Foundation Commission (1995)
Children and Violence: Report of the Commission on Children and Violence convened by the Gulbenkian Foundation. London: Calouste Gulbenkian Foundation, 1995, VI, 313 p., index., ISBN 0-903319-75-6.

Gullotta, Th.P.; Adams, G.R. & Montemayor, R. (Eds.) (1998)
Delinquent Violent Youth: Theory and Interventions. Thousand Oaks: Sage Publications, 1998, VIII, 320 p., ISBN 0761913343.

Gunter, B. & McAleer, J. (1997)
Children and Television. London: Routledge, 1997, XIII, 260 p., bibl., ISBN 0-41514-451-5.

Halloran, J.D. & Gray, P. (1996)
Television in the Family. London: Broadcasting Standards Council, 1996, 108 p., tab.

Halse, J.A. & Krogh, I. (Eds.)
(1989)
Video og TV, vold mod børn??? [Video and Television, Violence Against Children???].
Hørsholm: Pædagogisk Psykologisk Forlag, 1989, 119 p., ill., ISBN 87-88101-45-2.

Hammarberg, Th. (1998)
Children and Harmful Influences from the Media. In: Carlsson, U. & von Feilitzen, C. (Eds.): Children and Media Violence: Yearbook from the UNESCO International

Clearinghouse on Children and Violence on the Screen 1998, pp. 21-30, Göteborg: Nordicom, Göteborgs universitet, 1998, 387 p., ISBN 91-630-6358-1.
Hart, A. (1996)
Television, Children and Violence. Communications 21(1996)4, pp. 433-445, ISSN 0341-2059.

Hoffner, C. & Haefner, M.J. (1994)
Children's News Interest during the Gulf War: The Role of Negative Affect. Journal of Broadcasting and Electronic Media 38(1994)2, pp. 193-204, ISSN 0883-8151.

Hollings, Ernest F.
TV violence: survival vs censorship; save the children. (Column)
The New York Times, Nov. 23, 1993, v. 143 p. A19(N) ppA
LC Call Number: Not in LC Collection
Magazine Index Micro Film: None
United States. Congress. Senate - Social policy / Violence in television - Psychological aspects / Children - Psychology and mental health / Television and children - Moral and ethical aspects

Horowitz, Roy and Susan Duff;
Newsday Size: 4K; 05-26-1990; Page Number: 0; Section: 0
Family Clinic Tuning In to the Issues of Kids' TV
Newspapers_&_Newswires Family Clinic Tuning In to the Issues of Kids' TV Dr. Roy Horowitz and Susan Duff Q. I find it almost impossible to get through the day without turning on the TV for my two boys, ages 2 1/2 and 5 years. Is television really so harmful for children...

Hough KJ; Erwin PG
Children's attitudes toward violence on television.
Manchester Metropolitan University, England.
J Psychol, 131:411-5, 1997 Jul
Children's attitudes toward television violence were studied. A 47-item questionnaire collecting attitudinal and personal information was administered to 316 children aged 11 to 16 years. Cluster analysis was used to split the participants into two groups based on their attitudes toward television violence. A stepwise discriminant function analysis was performed to determine which personal characteristics would predict group membership. The only significant predictor of attitudes toward violence on television was the amount of television watched on school days ($p < .05$), but we also found that the impact of other predictor variables may have been mediated by this factor.

Howe, Michael J.A.., 1940-
Television and children / Michael J.A. Howe. Hamden, Conn.: Linnet Books, 1977
157 p.; 23 cm.
Includes bibliographical references and index.

Television and children. Violence in television - Great Britain. Television programs for children - Great Britain. I. Title.

Hsieh, H.C. (1996)
The Effect of Cartoon and Noncartoon Violence on Aggression by Taiwanese School Children. Madison: University of Wisconsin, 1996, Diss.

Hudis, Mark
Beavis & Butt-Head fire tragedy prompts debate; the industry questions the effects of cartoons, violent or inane, on the nation's children.
ADWEEK Eastern Edition, Oct. 18, 1993, v. 34 n. n42 p. 10(1)
LC Call Number: May or May Not Be in LC. Search further.
Business Index Micro Film: None
The television industry was again forced to consider the effects of violent programming when a five year old boy set his house on fire, killing his younger sister, after watching an Oct. 1993 Beavis & Butt-Head cartoon on MTV Networks Inc. Psychologist Dr. Joyce Brothers said that young children are definitely affected by watching violent action on TV, but MTV insisted that it does not believe the cartoon caused the boy's actions. However, the network will remove the objectionable scene from the cartoon.
Cartoons and children - Social aspects / Television broadcasting industry - Social policy / Violence in television - Social aspects / Cartoon television programs - Influence.

Huesmann, L.R. & Miller, L.S. (1994)
Long-Term Effects of Repeated Exposure to Media Violence in Childhood. In: Huesmann, L.R. (Ed.): Aggressive Behavior: Current Perspectives, pp. 153-186, New York: Plenum Press, 1994, XIX, 305 p., ill., bibl., ISBN 0-306-44553-0.

Huesmann, L.R.; Moise, J.F. & Podolski, C.L. (1997)
The Effects of Media Violence on the Development of Antisocial Behavior. In: Stoff, D.M. & Breiling, J. (Eds.): Handbook of Antisocial Behavior, pp. 181-193, New York: John Wiley and Sons, 1997, XXII, 600 p., ISBN 0471124524.

Huston, Aletha, Donnerstein, Edward, et. al. 1992.
Big World, Small Screen. Lincoln & London: University of Nebraska Press.
Jeffrey, L. & Durkin, K. (1989)
Children's Reactions to Televised Counter-Stereotyped Male Sex Role Behaviour as a Function of Age, Sex and Perceived Power. Journal of Social Behaviour and Personality 4(1989), pp. 285-310, ISSN 0886-1641.

Jehel-Cathelineau, S. (1996)
L'impact de la violence televisee sur les enfants. Neuropsychiatrie de l'enfance et de l'adolescence 44(1996)3-4, pp. 108-114, ISSN 0222-9617.

Jehel-Cathelineau, S. (1997)
La rhétorique de la violence dans les programmes pour enfants. In: Image et violence, actes du colloque BPI 3-4 octobre 1996. Paris: BPI en Actes, 1997.

Jenkins, P. (1992)
Intimate Enemies: Moral Panics in Contemporary Great Britain. Hawthorne: Aldine de Gruyter, 1992, 262 p., ISBN 0-202-30435-3.

Jensen, Jeff
Violence still an issue in kids TV. (Special Report: Marketing to Kids)
Advertising Age, Feb. 14, 1994, v. 65 n. n7 p. S-6(1)
LC Call Number: HF5801.A276
Business Index Micro Film: 7S1564
A new plan by the National Cable Television Assn. would allow parents to scramble television shows they find objectionable because they contain violence or for other reasons. Due to public pressure, television violence may decrease, and broadcasters are feeling pressure from regulators to upgrade the amount of educational television they produce for children. However, educational children's television is difficult to sell successfully because there are many niches within the children's market. In addition, broadcasters do not feel that it is their job to become moral guides for children.
Violence in television - Analysis / Television and children - Analysis / Cable television broadcasting industry - Social policy

Johnson MO
Television violence and its effect on children.
Nursing PhD Collaborative Program, Medical University of South Carolina, Columbia, USA.
J Pediatr Nurs, 11:94-9, 1996 Apr
Television (TV) has become a large part of children's activities. Much discussion exists as to the level of violence on TV programs and its effect on children's behavior. This article reviews the literature, discusses social issues, and presents some interventions available to nursing professionals to assist children and families in coping with the impact of TV on children's lives.

Johnston, D.D. (1995)
Adolescents Motivations for Viewing Graphic Horror. Human Communication Research 21(1995)4, pp. 522-552, ISSN 0360-3989.

Josephson, W.L. (1995)
Étude sur les effets de la violence télévisuelle sur les enfants, selon leur âge. Ottawa: Ministère du patrimoine canadien et santé Canada, 1995, 74 p., bibl., ISBN 0-662-80121-0.

Kalamas AD; Gruber ML
Electrodermal responses to implied versus actual violence on television.
University of California School of Medicine, USA.
J Gen Psychol, 125:31-7, 1998 Jan
The electrodermal response (EDR) of children watching a violent show was measured. Particular attention was paid to the type of violence (actual or implied) that prompted an EDR. In addition, the impact of the auditory component (sounds associated with violence) of the show was evaluated. Implied violent stimuli, such as the villain's face, elicited the strongest EDR. The elements that elicited the weakest responses were the actual violent stimuli, such as stabbing. The background noise and voices of the sound track enhanced the total number of EDRs. The results suggest that implied violence may elicit more fear (as measured by EDRs) than actual violence does and that sounds alone contribute significantly to the emotional response to television violence. One should not, therefore, categorically assume that a show with mostly actual violence evokes less fear than one with mostly implied violence.

Katz, Lilian G.
How TV violence affects kids. (3 and 4-year-olds) (column)
Parents (Bergenfield) Jan. 1991, v. 66 n. n1 p. 113(1)
LC Call Number: HQ768.P33
Magazine Index Micro Film: 57M1952
Preschool children - psychology and mental health / Television and children - Psychological aspects/ Violence in television - Psychological aspects

Kettl P
The power of "Power Rangers" [editorial]
J Pediatr Health Care, 9:101-2, 1995 May-Jun

Kline, Stephen. 1993.
Out of the Garden: Toys, TV, and Children's Culture in the Age of Marketing. London, New York: Verso.

Knapp, Jane
Violence in children's lives: addressing the American tragedy. PTA today, v. 18, April 1993: 5-8.
Author describes four aspects of violence in the lives of children which concern her the most: "children are involved in violence; there are no safe harbors from violence, the larger issue of family violence; and our acceptance of violence as part of our culture." Television and children [U.S.] / Violence in television [U.S.] / Family violence [U.S.]

Kodaira, S.I. (1994)
Discussion for Further Development of Media for Children: Based on a Review of Research on Media Violence in Japan. Tokyo: NHK Broadcasting, 1994, 26 p.

Kolbert, Elizabeth
TV executives assess impact of the violence they portray. (conference on television violence and the impact of television on children sponsored by the National Council for Families and Television) (Living Arts Pages)
The New York Times, August 3, 1993, v. 142 p. B1 (N) pC13
LC Call Number: Not in LC Collection
Magazine Index Micro Film: None
Violence in television - Social aspects / Television broadcasting industry - Social policy / Cable television broadcasting industry - Social policy / Television broadcasting - Social aspects

Krcmar, M. (1998)
The Contribution of Family Communication Patterns to Children's Interpretations of Television Violence. Journal of Broadcasting and Electronic Media 42(1998)2, pp. 250-264, ISSN 0883-8151.

Krogh, T. (1994)
Non-Violence, Tolerance and Television: Report of the Chairman to the Intergovernmental Programme for the Development of Communication. Paris: UNESCO, 1994, IX, 89 p.

Krüger, U.M. (1994)
Gewalt in Informationssendungen und Reality TV. Media Perspektiven (1994)2, pp. 72-85, ISSN 0170-1754.

Krüger, U.M. (1996)
Gewalt in von Kindern genutzten Fernsehsendungen: Quantitative und qualitative Unterschiede im öffentlich-rechtlichen und privaten Programmangebot. Media Perspektiven (1996)3, pp. 114-133, ISSN 0170-1754.

Kunczik, M. (1994)
Violence and the Mass Media: A Summary of the Theories and Research. Bonn: Friedrich-Ebert-Stiftung, 1994, 232 p.

Kunczik, M. (1995)
Wirkungen von Gewaltdarstellungen: Zum aktuellen Stand der Diskussion. In: Mochmann, E. (Ed.): Gewalt in Deutschland: Sociale Befunde und Deutungslinien, pp. 1-30, München: Oldenbourg, 1995, 196 p., fig., bibl., ISBN 3-486-56110-3.

Kunczik, M. (1998)
Gewalt und Medien. Köln: Böhlau, 1998, X, 329 p., bibl., ISBN 3-412-06793-8.

Kunczik, M.; Bleh, W. & Matritzen, S. (1993)
Audiovisuellen Gewalt und ihre Auswirkungen auf Kinder und Jugendliche: Eine

schriftliche Befragung klinischer Psychologen und Psychiater. Medienpsychologie
(1993)1, pp. 3-19, ISSN 0936-7780.

Kuttschreuter, M.; Wiegman, O. & Baarda, B. (1989)
Television Vieweing Related to Aggressive and Prosocial Behaviour: A Longitudinal
Study in the Netherlands Compared With That in Five Other Countries. In: Pulkkinen, L.
& Ramirez, J.M. (Eds.): Aggression in Children, pp. 113-147, Sevilla: Publicaciones De
La Universidad De Sevilla, 1989, 155 p., ISBN 8-47405-434-6.

Langley, T.; O'Neal, E.C.; Craig, K.M. & Yost, E.A. (1992)
Aggression-Consistent, -Inconsistent, and -Irrelevant Priming Effects on Selective
Exposure to Media Violence. Aggressive Behavior 18(1992)5, pp. 349-356, ISSN 0096-
140X.

Lazar, B.A. (1996)
Old Battles, New Frontiers: A Study of Television Violence and Social Work with
Children. Child and Adolescent Social Work Journal 13(1996)6, pp. 527-540, ISSN
0738-0151.

Lazar, B.A. (1998)
The Lull of Tradition: A Grounded Theory Study of Television Violence, Children and
Social Work. Child and Adolescent Social Work Journal 15(1998)2, pp. 117-131, ISSN
0738-0151.

Leishman, Katie
When is television too scary for children? TV Guide, v. 29, Jan. 10, 1981: 4-6, 8
"Experts offer some guidelines to help parents and youngsters cope with the 'fright
factor.'"
Television and children [U.S.] / Child development [U.S.]
Levine, Suzanne Braun
Caution: children watching; when it comes to violence on TV, what's a parent to do?
MS. July-August 1994, v. 5, n. n1 p. 22(4)
LC Call Number: HQ1101.M55; Microfilm (0) 84/2006 (1983-1984) MicRR
Magazine Index Micro Film: None
Violence in television - Psychological aspects / Television and children - Psychological
aspects / Parent and child - Social aspects

Liebert, R.M., & Sprafkin, J. 1988.
The Early Window: The Effects of Television on Children and Youth. New
York:Pergamon Press.

Loftus, Jack
Webs back off violence in Saturday kidvid sked; ABC goes for education
Variety, Oct. 5, 1983, v. 312 p. 42(2)

LC Call Number: PN2000.V3 Folio; Microfilm 03722 (1905-   ) MicRR
Magazine Index Micro Film: None
Television programs for children - evaluation / television and children - analysis / United
States. Federal Trade Commission - Laws, regulations, etc. / Violence in television -
analysis

Mayes, Sandra L.; Valentine, K.B.
Sex role stereotyping in Saturday morning cartoon shows. Journal of broadcasting, v. 23,
winter 1979: 41-50.
"The results of this study indicate that child viewers of television cartoon programs
perceived that the characters they viewed possessed sex-typed attributes. That is, the
cartoon characters, who can serve as role models for children, clearly exhibited
stereotypical sex role behaviors to the subjects."
Television and children [U.S.] / Sex discrimination against women [U.S.]

McCormack, Thelma
TV and the child savers. (TV censorship)
Canadian forum, Nov. 1993, v. 72 n. n824 p. 29(3)
LC Call Number: AP5. C125
Magazine Index Micro Film: None
Television and children - Social aspects / Violence in television - Censorship / Children -
Psychology and mental health

McCoy, Elin
What TV is doing to your kids.
Parents (Bergenfield) June 1981, v. 56 p. 55(6)
LC Call Number: HQ768.P33
Magazine Index Micro Film: None
Child rearing / television and children - psychological aspects / violence in television -
psychological aspects / Television - Advertising - psychological aspects

McDaniel, P.J. (1997)
The Effects of Humorous Cartoon Violence on a Cognitive Learning Task. Beaumont:
Lamar University, 1997, 54 p., processed, Master Thesis.

McNair, P. & Oliver, P. (1993)
The Effects of Multimedia Advertising of Violent Toys in New Zealand: Children's and
Parents' Perceptions. Community Mental Health in New Zealand 8(1993)1, pp. 26-41,
ISSN 0112-3599.

Media Studies Journal. 1994. Children and the Media. Volume 8 (4). New York:
Columbia University.

Methvin, Eugene H.
TV violence: the shocking new evidence
Reader's digest (U.S. edition), Jan. 1993, v. 122 p. 49(5)
LC Call Number: AP2.R255; Microfilm 02206 (1922-) MicRR
Magazine Index Micro Film: None
Television and children - research / violence in television - research

Meyer, Marianne
Kidvid: locking out sex and violence on cable.
Video Magazine, April 1989, v. 13 n. n1 p. 61(2)
LC Call Number: Not in LC Collection
Magazine Index Micro Film: None
Cable television - standards / Violence in television - psychological aspects / Sex in
television - psychological aspects / Television and children - psychological aspects /
Motion pictures - Rating

Miller, Nancy L.
Media liability for injuries that result from television broadcasts to immature audiences.
San Diego law review, v. 22, Jan.-Feb. 1985: 377-400.
"This comment examines the tort liability of broadcasters for injuries that result from
children's imitating acts of television violence. The comment proposes a cause of action
in negligence derived from tort doctrines that recognize a special duty to preclude
liability and illustrates how any effect on free speech would be minimal."
Television and children [U.S.] / Television programs [U.S.] / Television industry [U.S.] /
Violence in television [U.S.] / Liability (Law) [U.S.]

Minow, Newton N.
How to zap TV violence. (television violence and children) (Column)
The Wall Street Journal, August 3, 1993, p. A14(W) pA1
LC Call Number: See Catalogs or Staff
Magazine Index Micro Film: None
Markey, Edward J. - Political activity
Violence in television - Social aspects / Television and children - Social aspects /
Television sets - Innovations / Electronic control - Political aspects

Mukerji, Rose
TV's impact on children: a checkerboard scene. Phi Delta Kappan, v. 57, Jan. 1976: 316-
321.
Television and children [U.S.]

Murray, John P. (1980),
Catharsis and Televised Violence, Boys Town Center for the Study of Youth
Development, television & youth 25 Years of Research & Controversy, Washington:
Boys Town Press, p.38.

Nathanson, Amy I.
Identifying and explaining the relationship between parental mediation and children's aggression
Communication Research. v. 26 no 2 Apr. 1999 p. 124-43.

Neff, David
Shootout at the Not-So-OK corral. (television violence) (Editorial)
Christianity Today (Washington) Nov. 9, 1992, v. 36 n. n13 p. 12(2)
LC Call Number: BR1.C6418; Microfilm (0) 83/406 (1981-   ) MicRR
Magazine Index Micro Film: None
Violence in television - Research / Television and children - Psychological aspects / Parenting- Moral and ethical aspects

Noble, Grant
Children in front of the small screen/ Grant Noble. - London: Constable; Beverly Hills, Calif.: Sage Publications, 1975.
256 p.; 23 cm. (Communication and society; 5) Bibliograph: p.[243]-250. Includes index.
Television and children. Violence in television. I. Title.
Ontario. Royal Commission on Violence in the Communications Industry.
Learning from the media. Toronto: Royal Commission on Violence in the Communications Industry: available from the Publications Centre, Ministry of Govt. Services, [1977]
313 p.; 26 cm. (Report of the Royal Commission on Violence in the Communications Industry; v. 5). Includes bibliographies.
Television and children. Television and youth - Canada. Television viewers - Canada. Violence in television - Canada. I. Title.
Office of Educational Research and Improvement, U.S. Dept. of Education, SuDocs Call No.: ED 1.308/2:10 Title: TV viewing and parental guidance. United States. Office of Educational Research and Improvement. Published: Washington, D.C.? : Date: 1994
Internet Access: http://www.ed.gov/pubs/OR/ConsumerGuides/tv.html Description: [4] p. ; 28 cm. Series: Education research consumer guide ; Item No.: 0455-G-04
0455-G-04 (online) Subject: Television and children -- United States.
Violence in television -- United States. Entry No.: 98-04717

Ontario. Royal Commission on Violence in the Communications Industry.
Vulnerability to media effects. Toronto: Royal Commission on Violence in the Communications Industry: available from the Publications Centre, Ministry of Govt. Services, [1977].
401 p.; 26 cm. (Report of the Royal Commission on Violence in the Communications Industry; v. 6). Includes bibliographical references.
Television and youth - Canada. Violence in television - Canada - Public opinion. Canada - Public opinion. Television viewers - Canada - Statistics. I. Title.

Osborn, D. Keith; Osborn, Janie D.
Television violence revisited. Childhood education, v. 53, April-May 1977: 309-311.
Compares 1976 figures of violence on television with 1969 figures and finds "that the
death rate has been reduced by approximately 50 percent over the intervening years' but
that "the number of violent acts is approximately the same for both time periods."
Television programs [U.S.] / Violence in television [U.S.] / Television and children
[U.S.]

Osofsky, J.D. (Ed.) (1997)
Children in a Violent Society. York: Guilford Press, 1997, 328 p., ISBN 1-57230-183-X.

Palmer, Edward L.; Dorr, Aimée
Children and the faces of television: teaching, violence, selling
New York: Academic Press, c1980, xvii, 360 p.; 24 cm. Includes bibliographies and
index
Television and children - Addresses, essays, lectures. Television programs for children -
Addresses, essays, lectures. Television advertising and children - Addresses, essays,
lectures. Violence in television - Addresses, essays, lectures. Television in education -
Addresses, essays, lectures. I. Palmer, Edward L. II. Dorr, Aimée.

Phillips, Catherine
Is TV good or bad for your child?
Chatelaine, Oct. 1987, v. 60 p. 38(1)
LC Call Number: AP5.C5
Magazine Index Micro Film: 41E5314
Television and children - research / Education - psychological aspects / Violence in
television - psychological aspects

Post, Jory
Into adolescence. Stopping violence: a curriculum for grades 5-8 / Jory Post. - Santa
Cruz, CA: Network publications, 1991.
viii, 116 p.: ill.; 28 cm. (Contemporary health series)
"Title no. 384" - T.p. verso
Violence - United States. Violence - Prevention - Study and teaching (elementary).
Violence in television - Study and teaching (Elementary). Conflict management - Study
and teaching (Elementary). Nonviolence - Study and teaching (Elementary). I. Title. II.
Title: Stopping violence. Title: Stopping violence. IV. Series.

Potter, W.J. & Warren, R. (1996)
Considering Policies to Protect Children from TV Violence. Journal of Communication
46(1996)4, pp. 116-138, ISSN 0021-9916.

Potter, W.J. & Warren, R. (1998)
Humor as Camouflage of Televised Violence. Journal of Communication 48(1998)2, pp.
40-57, ISSN 0021-9916.

Potts, R. & Henderson, J. (1991)
The Dangerous World of Television: A Content Analysis of Physical Injuries in
Children's Television Programming. Children's Environments Quarterly 8(1991)3-4, pp.
7-14., ISSN 0886-0505.

Powell, Stewart
What entertainers are doing to your kids. (controversy over freedom of expression in
entertainment)
U.S. News and World Report, Oct. 28, 1985, v. 99 p. 46(4)
LC Call Number: JK1.U65; Microfilm 06106 (1933-   ) MicRR
Magazine Index Micro Film: 30A1577
Parents Music Resource Center - political activity / Children's Television Workshop -
political activity / television and youth - investigations / sex in mass media -
investigations / Entertainment industry - public opinion / popular culture - television use /
United States. Federal Communications Commission - investigations / television
broadcasting / censorship

Prasad, V.K. & Smith, L.J. (1994)
Television Commercials in Violent Programming: An Experimental Evaluation of Their
Effects on Children. Journal of the Academy of Marketing Science 22(1994)4, pp. 340-
351, ISSN 0092-0703.

Prieto Rodriguez MA; March Cerdá JC; Argente del Castillo A
Violence and sexism in television cartoons for children. Analysis of the contents
Escuela Andaluza de Salud P´ublica, Granada.
Aten Primaria, 17:382-8, 1996 Apr 15
OBJECTIVE. To detect features of violence and sexism in cartoons in the children's
programmes of Spanish television companies. DESIGN. Analysis of the content of
cartoons broadcast by TV-1, TV-2, Canal Sur, Antena 3 and Tele 5 during one week.
MEASUREMENTS AND MAIN RESULTS. The programmes recorded were viewed by
two independent observers, first separately and then together. All those scenes with
violent contents or sexist messages were noted. The main findings were: a) violent
contents were very common; b) roles and jobs linked to gender were found; c) advertising
accompanied and was inserted within children's programming. CONCLUSIONS. The
points identified show the need for both school and family to encourage children to
develop a critical attitude to the messages they receive.

Pulkkinen, L. & Ramirez, J.M. (Eds.) (1989)
Aggression in Children. Sevilla: Publicaciones de la Universidad de Sevilla, 1989, 115 p.,
ISBN 8-47405-434-6.

Quigley, Mary W.
Kids watch television news and it scares them. Washington Journalism Review, v. 11, Oct. 1989: 46-48.
"Television's effect on children has been a source of controversy ever since the first kid sat down and watched glassy-eyed as Mighty Mouse roared down from outer space. But recently parents' concern has focused on news, perhaps because of the graphic 'adult' content of many news shows and the sizable number of children watching those shows."
Television news [U.S.] / Television and children [U.S.]

Quindlen, Anna
TV guide. (discussions of television violence and children are ignoring the issue of parental control) (Column)
The New York Times, Oct. 28, 1993, v. 143 p. A19 (N) ppA
LC Call Number: Not in LC Collection
Magazine Index Micro Film: None
Violence in television - Social aspects / Television and children - Social aspects / Child rearing - Moral and ethical aspects / Parent and child - Moral and ethical aspects

Raspberry, William
Parent-programmed TV? Get serious. (new plan to control how much violent television children watch) (Column)
The Washington Post, July 2, 1993, v. 116 p. A19
LC Call Number: Newspaper
Business Index Micro Film: None
Violence in television - Laws, regulations, etc. / Television and children - Social aspects / Television broadcasting policy - Analysis

Reassuring children (war's impact on children)
People (Chicago. 1974) Feb. 4, 1991, v. 35 n. n4 p. 13(1)
LC Call Number; AP2.P417
Magazine Index Micro Film: 58F1468
Television and children - Psychological aspects / Children and war - Psychological aspects / Violence in television - Psychological aspects

Rich M; Woods ER; Goodman E; Emans SJ; DuRant RH
Aggressors or victims: gender and race in music video violence.
Division of Adolescent/Young Adult Medicine, Children's Hospital, Harvard Medical School, Boston, Massachusetts 02115, USA.
Pediatrics, 101:669-74, 1998 Apr
OBJECTIVE: To examine portrayals of violence in popular music videos for patterns of aggression and victimization by gender and race. DESIGN AND SETTING: Content analysis of 518 music videos broadcast over national music television networks, Black Entertainment Television (BET), Country Music Television (CMT), Music Television (MTV), and Video Hits-1 (VH-1) during a 4-week period at randomly selected times of

high adolescent viewership. MAIN OUTCOME MEASURES: Differences in the genders and races portrayed as aggressors and victims in acts of violence. RESULTS: Seventy-six (14.7%) of the analyzed music videos contained portrayals of individuals engaging in overt interpersonal violence, with a mean of 6.1 violent acts per violence-containing video. Among the 462 acts of violence, the music video's main character was clearly the aggressor in 80.1% and the victim in 17.7%. In 391 (84.6%) of the violence portrayals, the gender of the aggressor or victim could be determined. Male gender was significantly associated with aggression; aggressors were 78.1% male, whereas victims were 46.3% female. This relationship was influenced by race. Among whites, 72.0% of the aggressors were male and 78.3% of the victims were female. Although blacks represent 12% of the United States population, they were aggressors in 25.0% and victims in 41.0% of music video violence. Controlling for gender, racial differences were significant among males; 29.0% of aggressors and 75.0% of victims were black. A logistic regression model did not find direct effects for gender and race, but revealed a significant interaction effect, indicating that the differences between blacks and whites were not the same for both genders. Black males were more likely than all others to be portrayed as victims of violence (adjusted odds ratio = 28.16, 95% confidence interval = 8.19, 84.94). CONCLUSIONS: Attractive role models were aggressors in more than 80% of music video violence. Males and females were victims with equivalent frequency, but males were more than three times as likely to be aggressors. Compared with United States demographics, blacks were overrepresented as aggressors and victims, whereas whites were underrepresented. White females were most frequently victims. Music videos may be reinforcing false stereotypes of aggressive black males and victimized white females. These observations raise concern for the effect of music videos on adolescents' normative expectations about conflict resolution, race, and male-female relationships.

Richters, J.E. (1996)
Disordered Views of Aggressive Children: A Late Twentieth Century Perspective.
Annals of the New York Academy of Sciences 20(1996)794, pp. 208-223, ISSN 0877-8923.

Roberts, Churchill
Children's and parents' television viewing and perceptions of violence. Journalism quarterly, v. 58, winter 1981: 556-564, 581.
Tries "to determine the extent to which children's viewing behavior and their notions about violence may be predicted by parental viewing and parental views of violence."
Television programs [U.S.] / Violence in television [U.S.] / Television and children [U.S.]

Rosenberg, Howard
The TV violence proposal: let's get cynical. (networks' plan for parental advisories on violent content in programs)
The Los Angeles Times, July 1, 1993, v. 112, p. F1
LC Call Number: Newspaper 7114-X

Business Index Micro Film: None
Violence in television - Laws, regulations, etc. / Television broadcasting - Social policy /
Television and children - Analysis

Rosengren, K.E. & Windahl, S. (1989)
Media Matter: TV Use in Childhood and Adolescence. Norwood, New Yersey: Ablex
Publishing Corp., 1989, 299 p., fig., tab., bibl., ISBN 0-89391-570-X.

Ross, Robert K.
Video violence. (column)
Essence, June 1988, v. 19 n. n2 p. 140(1)
LC Call Number: E185.86.E7
Magazine Index Micro Film: 45A3911
Television and children - Social aspects / Violence in television - Social aspects

Roth, Morry
Govt. kidvid report expected to equate viewing and violence
Variety, March 31, 1982, v. 306 p. 68(1)
LC Call Number: PN2000.V3 Folio; Microfilm 03722 (1905-   ) MicRR
Magazine Index Micro Film: None
television and children - psychological aspects / Untied States. National Institutes of
Health - research / violence in television - research

Rubinstein, Eli A.
Television and the young viewer. American scientist, v. 66, Nov.-Dec. 1978: 685-693.
"The pervasive social influence of television on children is being increasingly
documented, but has yet to be translated into a continuing and effective social policy."
Television and children [U.S.] / Television programs [U.S.] / Violence in television
[U.S.] / Television advertising [U.S.]

Salk, Lee
Are some TV characters bad for kids?
McCall's, Jan. 1991, v. 118 n. n4 p. 50(1)
LC Call Number: TT500.M2
Magazine Index Micro Film: 57M0699
Television and children - Analysis / Television - psychological aspects / Violence in
television - Influence

Sanson, A. & Muccio, C. (1993)
The Influence of Aggressive and Neutral Cartoons and
Toys on the Behaviour of Preschool Children. Australian Psychologist 28(1993)2, pp. 93-
99, ISSN 0005-0067.

Santos, R. & Albornoz, L. (1995)
Violencia en la programación televisiva infantil Argentina. Quilmes: Universidad
Nacional Quilmes, 1995.

Sawin, D.B. (1990)
Aggressive Behavior Among Children in Small Playgroup Settings with Violent
Television. Advances in Learning and Behavioral Disabilities 6(1990), pp. 157-177,
ISSN 0735-004X.

Schneider, L.B. (1994)
Warning: Television Violence May Be Harmful to Children: But the First Amendment
May Foil Congressional Attempts to Legislate Against It. University of Miami Law
Review 49(1994)2, pp. 477-530, ISSN 0041-9818.

Schorr, Daniel
Go get some milk and cookies and watch the murders on television. Washingtonian, v.
17, Oct. 1981: 190-196, 198-199.
Focuses on television's contribution towards fostering an American culture of violence.
Television and children [U.S.] / Violence in television [U.S.]

Schwarzberg, Neala S.
What TV does to kids.
Parents (Bergenfield), June 1987, v. 62 p. 100(5)
LC Call Number: HQ768.P33
Magazine Index Micro Film: 39G2987
Violence in television - psychological aspects / Television and children - psychological
aspects

Scully, Sean
Anti-violence tools for TV. (lock-out mechanism would allow parents to control TV
viewing, but is there a market for it?) (Brief Article)
Broadcasting and Cable, May 17, 1993, v. 123 n. n20 p. 44(1)
LC Call Number: TK6540B85
Business Index Micro Film: 71S1854
Violence in television - Censorship / Scrambling systems (Telecommunication) -
Innovations

Sege, R.D. & Dietz, W. (1995)
Television Viewing and Violence in Children: Pediatrician as Agent for Change. Journal
of the Mississippi State Medical Association 36(1995)10, pp. 318-327, ISSN 0026-6396.

Sege, R.D. (1998)
Life Imitating Art: Adolescents and Television Violence. In: Gullotta, Th.P. & Adams,

G.R. et al. (Eds.): Delinquent Violent Youth: Theory and Interventions, pp. 129-143, Thousand Oaks: Sage Publications, 1998, VIII, 328 p., ISBN 0-76191-334-3.

Sheff, David. 1994.
Video Games: A Guide for Savvy Parents. New York: Random House.

Silver, Marc
Sex, violence and the tube: the fall lineup has more of the first, less of the second. Most of the good TV is aimed at kids.
U.S. News & World Report, Sept 20, 1993 v1 15 n1 1 p76(4)

Simonson, H. (1992)
Interaction Effects of Television and Socioeconomic Status on Teenage Aggression. International Journal of Adolescence and Youth 3(1992)3-4, pp. 333-343, ISSN 0267-3843.

Singer, D.G.; Singer, J.L. & Zuckerman, D.M. (1990)
The Parent's Guide: Use TV To Your Child's Advantage. Reston: Acropolis, 1990, 203 p., ill., bibl., ISBN 0-87491-964-9.

Singer, Dorothy; Singer, Jerome
Protecting your child from TV violence
TV Guide, Sept. 5, 1981, v. 29 p. 35(2)
LC Call Number: Microfilm 06378 (1953-   ) MicRR
Magazine Index Micro Film: None
television and children - evaluation / violence in television - psychological aspects / children - education

Siskel, Gene
Tuning out the violence. (children's television and film viewing)
Parenting Magazine, Dec.-Jan. 1993, v. 7 n. n11 p. 126 (4)
LC Call Number: Not in LC Collection
Magazine Index Micro Film: None
Violence in motion pictures - Analysis / Violence in television - Analysis / Motion pictures and children - Analysis / Television and children - Analysis

Slaby, Ronald G.
Closing the education gap on TV's "entertainment" violence. (role of educators in exposing harmful effects on children)
The Education digest, April 1994, v. 59 n. n8 p. 4(4)
LC Call Number: L11.E265
Magazine Index Micro Film: None

Violence in television - Prevention / Television and children - Analysis / Television - Psychological aspects / Educators - Practice

Stack, S. (1990)
The Impact of Fictional Television Films on Teenage Suicide, 1984-85. Social Science Quarterly (1990)2, pp. 391-399, ISSN 0038-4941.

Stein, Harry
Mom, what does rape mean? (effects of TV sex and violence on children)
TV Guide, May 18, 1984, v. 32 p. 41(2)
LC Call Number: Microfilm 06378 (1953-) MicRR
Magazine Index Micro Film: None
Television and children - moral and ethical aspects / sex in television - moral and ethical aspects / violence in television - moral and ethical aspects

Stern, Loraine
A TV guide for parents. (television viewing habits of children) (Column)
Woman's Day, Feb. 1, 1994, v. 57 n. n4 p. 14(1)
LC Call Number: Not in LC Collection
Magazine Index Micro Film: None
Television and children - Social aspects / Violence in television - Social aspects
Strasburger VC; Donnerstein E
Children, adolescents, and the media: issues and solutions.
Department of Pediatrics, University of Mexico School of Medicine, Albuquerque, New Mexico, USA.
Pediatrics, 103:129-39, 1999 Jan

Strasburger VC; Hendren RL
Rock music and music videos.
Division of Adolescent Medicine, University of New Mexico School of Medicine, Albuquerque 87131, USA.
Pediatr Ann, 24:97-103, 1995 Feb

Strasburger VC
Children, adolescents, and television. A call for physician action.
Department of Pediatrics, University of New Mexico School of Medicine, Albuquerque, USA.
West J Med, 166:353-4, 1997 May

Study of violence on cable TV has been commissioned by NCTA, with completion due next year. (National Cable Television Association
Television Digest Oct. 7, 1991 v. 31 n., n40p. 7(1)
LC Call Number: May or May Not Be in LC. Search further.
Business Index Micro Film: 61T0404

National Cable Television Association - Social policy / Violence in television - Research / Cable television - Social aspects

Television and behavior
Children today, Sept.-Oct. 1982, v. 11 p. 28(1)
LC Call Number: HV741.C5362
Magazine Index Micro Film: None
violence in television - research / television and children - research / United States.
National Institute of Mental Health - reports

Television and the aggressive child: a cross-national comparison / edited by L. Rowell Huesmann, Leonard D. Eron. - Hillsdale, N.J.: L. Erlbaum Associates, 1986.
xv, 314 p.: ill.; 24 cm. (Communication). Includes bibliographies and indexes.
Television and children - Cross-cultural studies. Violence in television - Cross-cultural studies. Aggressiveness (Psychology) in children - Cross cultural studies. I. Huesmann, L. Rowell. II. Eron, Leonard D. Series: Communication (Hillsdale, N.J.)

Television at the crossroads. Society, v. 21, Sept.-Oct. 1984: 6-40
A collection of articles assesses the impact of television on children, focusing particularly on academic achievement, reading and violence.
Television and children [U.S.] Evaluation / Violence in television [U.S.]
The UNESCO International Clearinghouse on Children and Violence on the Screen
http://www.nordicom.gu.se/unesco.html

Toivonen, K. & Cullingford, C. (1997)
The Media and Information: Children's Responses to the Gulf War. Journal of Educational Media 23(1997)1, pp. 51-64, ISSN 1358-1651.

Tulloch, J.C. & Tulloch, M.I. (1992)
Tolerating Violence: Children's Responses to Television. Australian Journal of Communication 19(1992)1, pp. 9-21, ISSN 0811-6202

Turow, Joseph
Non-fiction on commercial children's television: trends and policy implications. Journal of broadcasting, v. 24, fall 1980: 437-448.
"The aim is to chart systematically the number and nature of nonfiction children's series broadcast over ABC, CBS and NBC from 1949 through 1979. A related goal is to determine whether such 'educational and informational'' programs broadcast from the time of the FCC hearings and report (beginning in January 1971 and ending in November 1974) were appreciably different from those telecast in the years prior to the Commission's active interest."
Television and children [U.S.] Trends / Television programs [U.S.] Trends

TV's sickos, shooters - and kids. (2 main stations agree to warning system for violent programming) (Editorial)
The New York Times, July 1, 1993, v. 142 p. A12 (N) pA1
LC Call Number: Not in LC Collection
Magazine Index Micro Film: None
Television broadcasting - Laws, regulations, etc. / Violence in television - Laws, regulations, etc. / Television and children - Laws, regulations, etc.
Uberos DJ; Gómez A; Muñoz A; Molina A; Galdó G; Pérez FJ
Television and childhood injuries: is there a connection?
Research Group 114, University of Granada, Spain. uberos@ctv.es
Arch Pediatr Adolesc Med, 152:712-4, 1998 Jul

United States. Congress. Senate. Committee on the Judiciary. Subcommittee on Juvenile Justice.
Media violence: hearing before the Subcommittee on Juvenile Justice of the Committee on the Judiciary, United States Senate, Ninety-eighth Congress, second session, on oversight on alleged media violence as it may affect children, October 25, 1984.
Washington: U.S. G.P.O. 1985.
iii, 121 p.: ill.; 24 cm. (S. hrg.; 98-1283) Distributed to some depository libraries in microfiche. Includes bibliographies. "Serial no. J-98-147." Item 1042-A, 1042-B (microfiche). Supt. of Docs. no.: Y 4.J 89/2: S.hrg.98-1283
Violence in television - Social aspects - United States. Television and children - United States. Television and youth - United States. I. Title. II. Series: United States. Congress. Senate. S. hrg.; 98-1283.
United States. Congress. Senate. Committee on Commerce, Science, and Transportation.
Television violence: hearing of the Committee on Commerce, Science, and Transportation, United States Senate, One Hundred Fourth Congress, first session, July 12, 1995.
SuDocs Call No.: Y 4.C 73/7:S.HRG.104-369
Title: Published: Washington: U.S. G.P.O. : For sale by the U.S. G.P.O., Supt. of Docs., Congressional Sales Office, Date: 1996 [i.e. 1996] Description: iv, 489 p. : ill. ; 23 cm. Series: S. hrg. ; 104-369 Item No.: 1041-A 1041-B (MF)

United States. Congress. Senate. Committee on Commerce, Science, and Transportation.
SuDocs Call No.: Y 1.1/5:105-89
Children's Protection from Violent Programming Act : report of the Committee on Commerce, Science, and Transportation on S. 363. Published: Washington : U.S. G.P.O., Date: 1997. Description: ii, 32 p. ; 23 cm. Series: Report / 105th Congress, 1st session, Senate ; 105-89 Item No.: 1008-C
1008-D (MF) Subject: Children -- Legal status, laws, etc. -- United States.
Violence in television -- Law and legislation -- United States.
Video recordings -- Law and legislation -- United States.
Children and violence -- United States -- Prevention. Entry No.: 98-04007

United States. Congress. Senate. Committee on Commerce, Science, and Transportation.
SuDocs Call No.: Y 1.1/5:104-171
Children's Protection from Violent Programming Act of 1995 : report of the Committee
on Commerce, Science, and Transportaton together with additional and minority views
on S. 470. Published: Washington : U.S. G.P.O., Date: 1995. Description: ii, 32 p. ; 23
cm. Series: Report / 104th Congress, 1st session, Senate ; 104-171 Item No.: 1008-C
1008-D (MF)
Children -- Legal status, laws, etc. -- United States. Violence in television -- Law and
legislation -- United States. Video recordings -- Law and legislation -- United States.
Children and violence -- United States -- Prevention. Entry No.: 96-06145

United States. Office of Educational Research and Improvement.
TV viewing and parental guidance.
SuDocs Call No.: ED 1.308/2:10 Published: Washington, D.C.? : Office of Educational
Research and Improvement, U.S. Dept. of Education, Date: 1994! Description: 4! p. ; 28
cm. Series: Education research consumer guide ; Item No.: 0455-G-04

Valkenburg, P.M. & van der Voort, T.H.A. (1995)
The Influence of Television on Children's Daydreaming Styles: A 1-Year Panel Study.
Communication Research 22(1995)3, pp. 267-287, ISSN 0093-6502.

Valkenburg, P.M.; Vooijs, M.W. & van der Voort, T.H.A. et al. (1992)
The Influence of Television on Children's Fantasy Styles: A Secondary Analysis.
Imagination, Cognition and Personality 12(1992/1993)1, pp. 55-67, ISSN 0276-2366.

Van Evra, J. (1997)
Television and Child Development. Mahwah: Lawrence Erlbaum Associates, 1997, 218
p., ill., bibl., ISBN 0 80580 573-3.

Vann, Allan S.
Kids, media, and family values.
Education Digest, March 1996 v61 n7 p23(3)

Video violence and children / edited by Geoffrey Barlow and Alison Hill. New York,
N.Y.: St. Martin's Press, 1985.
ix, 182 p.: ill; 23 cm. Includes bibliographies and index.
Television and children. Violence in television. I. Barlow, Geoffrey. II. Hill, Alison.

Videodrome (video violence)
Economist (London) August 13, 1994, v. 332 n. n7876 p. 73(2)
LC Call Number: HG11.E2; Microfilm 03394 (1843-   ) MicRR
Magazine Index Micro Film: None
Violence in children - Causes of / Violence in motion pictures - Social aspects / Violence

in television - Social aspects / Violence research - Analysis / Violent crimes -
Psychological aspects

Viemerö, V. (1996)
Factors in Childhood That Predict Later Criminal Behavior. Aggressive Behavior
22(1996)2, pp. 87-97, ISSN 0096-140X.

Violence on TV. TV Guide, v. 40, Aug. 22, 1992: 8-23.
"In this special issue, the editors of TV Guide present the results of a special study on
how much violence is out there, what leading experts think about its effects, and what can
be done."
Violence in television [U.S.] / Television and children [U.S.] / Child psychology [U.S.] /
Violence research [U.S.]

Vooijs, M.W. & van der Voort, T.H.A. (1993)
Learning About Television Violence: The Impact of a Critical Viewing Curriculum on
Children's Attitudinal Judgements of Crime Series. Journal of Research and
Development in Education 26(1993)3, pp. 133-142, ISSN 0022-426X.

Voort, T.H.A. van der
Television violence: a child's-eye view / T.H.A. van der Voort - Amsterdam; New York:
North-Holland; New York, N.Y., U.S.A.: Sole distributors for the U.S.A. and Canada,
Elsevier Science Publ. Co., 1986.
xiii, 440 p.: ill.; 23 cm. (Advances in psychology; 32). Bibliography: p. 403-423. Includes
indexes.
Television and children - United States. Violence in television - United States.
Aggressiveness (Psychology) in children. I. Title. II. Series: Advances in psychology
(Amsterdam, Netherlands); 32.

Vukelich MS
The media violence.
Minn Med, 78:16-8, 1995 Jun

Walker, K.B. & Morley, D.D. (1991)
Attitudes and Parental Factors as Intervening Variables in the Television Violence-
Aggression Relation. Communication Reports 8(1991)1-2, pp. 41-47, ISSN 0893-4215.

Warning from Washington: violence on television is harmful to children
Time (Chicago) May 17, 1982, v. 119 p. 77(1)
LC Call Number: AP2.T37; Microfilm 02914 (1923-   ) MicRR
Magazine Index Micro Film: None
Rubinstein, Eli A. - research
United States. National Institute of Mental Health - reports / television programs for
children - psychological aspects / violence in television - psychological aspects

Wartella, E. (1995)
Media and Problem Behaviour in Young People. In: Rutter, M. & Smith, D. (Eds.)
Psychological Dosorders in Young People's Time Trends and ther Causes, pp. 296-323,
Chichester: J. Wiley, 1995, XVIII, 843 p., ISBN 0-47195-054-8.

Wartella, E.; Heintz, K.E.; Aidman, A.J. & Mazzarella, S.R. (1990)
Television and Beyond: Children's Video Media in One Community. Communication
Research 17(1990)1, Spec. Issue, pp. 45-64, ISSN 0093-6502.

Wartella, E. & Middlestadt, S. (1991)
Mass Communication and Persuasion: The Evolution of Direct Effects, Limited Effects,
Information Processing, and Affect and Arousal Models. In: Donohew, L. & Sypher,
H.E. (Eds.): Persuasive Communication and Drug Abuse Prevention Communication, pp.
53-69, Hillsdale: Lawrence Erlbaum, 1991, XXI, 349 p., ISBN 0-80580-693-8.

Wartclla, E.; Olivarez, A. & Jennings, N. (1998)
Children and Television Violence in the United States. In: Carlsson, U. & von Feilitzen,
C. (Eds.): Children and Media Violence: Yearbook from the UNESCO International
Clearinghousc on Children and Violence on the Screen 1998, pp. 55-62, Göteborg:
Nordicom, Göteborgs universitet, 1998, 387 p., ISBN 91-630-6358-1.

Watts, Meredith W.; Sumi, David
Desensitization of children to violence? Another look at television's effects.
Experimental study of politics, v. 5, August 1976: 1-24.
Reports the results of a study "designed to test explicitly whether the predispositions of
the viewer were more closely associated with autonomic arousal than a gross measures of
television exposure of exposure to violent programs."
Television and children [U.S.] / Violence in television [U.S.]

Weiss, Stefanie
Stop, don't shoot. (National Education Association and DIC Entertainment L.P.'s new
programming standard)
NEA today, March, 1994, v. 12 n. n7 p. 3(1)
Magazine Index Micro Film: None
The National Education Assn. (NEA) and DIC Entertainment LP (DIC) have developed a
new guideline for children's television programming. NEA and DIC hope that the new
guideline will help reduce violence on children's television programs. The new code will
help guide animators, script writers and directors in developing new programs. A brief
discussion of the key items on the 12-point guideline is presented.
National Education Association - Social policy / Television broadcasting industry -
Social policy / Violence in television - Prevention

Weissbourd, Bernice
How much are children aware of? (2-year-old) (column)

Parents (Bergenfield) June 1985, v. 60 p. 124(1)
LC Call Number: HQ768.P33
Magazine Index Micro Film: 27K5033
child psychology - research / violence in television - psychological aspects

Wham! Pow! Bam! Violent acts per hour on cartoon shows. (illustration)
Knight, Marianna I.; Tooley, Jo Ann
U.S. News & World Report, June 13, 1988, v. 104 n. n23 p. 71(1)
LC Call Number: JK1.U65; Microfilm 06106 (1933-) MicRR
Magazine Index Micro Film: 45B0618
Violent acts per hour on cartoon shows. (graph) Violence in television - statistics /
Television programs for children - statistics

Wiley, Richard E.
Violence, the media, and the school. NASSP [National Association of Secondary School
Principals] bulletin, v. 60, May 1976: 19-25.
"States that the role of the FCC should be to provide direction and encouragement for the
television networks to adopt self-regulatory reforms, rather than to provide strict
regulation itself. The 'family viewing' plan is a result of the networks' attempts at self-
regulation."
Television and children / Violence in television [U.S.]

William M. Young & Associates
Violence on TV: the effects of television on children and youth: a report on the findings
of the public hearings conducted by the National PTA Television Commission, 1976-77 /
[text prepared by William M. Young & Associates] [Chicago]: National PTA [c1977]
[8] p.; 28 cm. Cover title.
Television and children. Violence in television - United States. Television and youth -
United States. I. National PTA Television Commission. II. Title. Title: Effects of
television on children and youth.

Williams, Jill
The drive to clean up television. Saturday Evening Post, v. 253, Nov. 1981: 74-77
Profiles Reverend Donald Wildmon and his Coalition for Better TV.
Television programs [U.S.] / Television and children [U.S.] / Sex [U.S.] / Violence in
television [U.S.] / Boycott [U.S.] / Wildmon, Don / Coalition for Better Television

Willis E; Strasburger VC
Media violence.
Department of Pediatrics, Medical College of Wisconsin, Milwaukee, USA.
Pediatr Clin North Am, 45:319-31, 1998 Apr
American media are the most violent in the world, and American society is now paying a
high price in terms of real life violence. Research has confirmed that mass media
violence contributes to aggressive behavior, fear, and desensitization of violence.

Television, movies, music videos, computer/video games are pervasive media and represent important influences on children and adolescents. Portraying rewards and punishments and showing the consequences of violence are probably the two most essential contextual factors for viewers as they interpret the meaning of what they are viewing on television. Public health efforts have emphasized public education, media literacy campaign for children and parents, and an increased use of technology to prevent access to certain harmful medial materials.

Wilson, B.J. & Smith, S.L. (1998)
Children's Responses to Emotional Portrayals on Television. In: Andersen, P.A. & Guerrero, L.K. et al. (Eds.): Handbook of Communication and Emotion: Research, Theory, Applications, and Contexts, pp. 533-569, San Diego: Academic Press, 1998, XXXII, 590 p., ISBN 0-1205-7770-4.

Wilson, B.J. & Weiss, A.J. (1991)
The Effects of Two Reality Explanations on Children's Reactions to a Frightening Movie Scene. Communication Monographs 58(1991), pp. 307-326, ISSN 0363-7751.

Zimmerman JD
A prosocial media strategy: "youth against violence: choose to de-fuse".
New York City Health and Hospitals Corporation, New York, USA.
Am J Orthopsychiatry, 66:354-62, 1996 Jul
The role of television in encouraging youth violence, and its potential as a prosocial teaching tool are examined. A media strategy developed by New York City in collaboration with inner-city youth exposed to violence, which focused on positive peer pressure for choosing nonviolent solutions to conflict is then delineated, along with the community and media coverage that followed. The effectiveness of the televised public service announcements appeared to be associated with the use of emotionally charged, real-life situations, speech, and body language by characters culturally appropriate to the target audience of at-risk youth.

Zuckerman, Diana M.; Zuckerman, Barry S.
Television's impact on children.
Design for arts in education. July-Aug. 1985, v. 86 p. 39(7)
LC Call Number: NK1160.D4
Magazine Index Micro Film: None
television and children - psychological aspects / television advertising and children - research / violence in television - psychological aspects

Zuckerman, Mortimer B.
The victims of TV violence. (controlling the amount of television violence children view) (Editorial)
U.S. News and World Report, August 2, 1993, v. 115 n. n5 p. 64(1)
LC Call Number: JK1.U65; Microfilm 06106 (1933-   ) MicRR

Magazine Index Micro Film: None
Violence in television - Standards / Television broadcasting industry - Standards /
Television and children - Social aspects

Behavioral Links

Acland, C.R. (1995)
Youth, Murder, Spectacle: The Cultural Politics of 'Youth in Crisis'. Boulder: Westview Press, 1995, XII, 176 p., ill., bibl., ISBN 0-81332-236-3.

Alienated America: racial division and youth violence. Spectrum, v. 66, summer 1993; 4-6, 8-43, 46-50.
First, Roger Wilson outlines the challenge facing States over repairing race relations; then James A. Mercy recommends a public health approach to youth violence; next Attorney General Janet Reno speaks about delinquency prevention; David S. Barry discusses the impact of television violence on children; and finally Ron LaBrecque examines diversity issues in the press, particularly at the Los Angeles Times.
Race relations [U.S.] States / Juvenile delinquency [U.S.] - Health aspects / Violence [U.S.] - Health aspects / Delinquency prevention [U.S.] / Television and children [U.S.] / Violence in television [U.S.] / Black journalists [Los Angeles] / Los Angeles Times

Almeida, Pamela M.
Children's television and the modeling of proreading behaviors. Education and urban society, v. 10, No. 1977: 55-60.
Concludes that "television as a vehicle for developing positive attitudes toward reading has been underutilized. By including peer role-modeling of proreading behaviors in children's television, a renewed interest in love for reading may be sparked in the children of the electronic generation."
Television and children [U.S.] / Reading [U.S.]

Anderson, C.A. & Morrow, M. (1995)
Competitive Aggression without Interaction: Effects of Competitive Versus Cooperative Instructions on Aggressive Behavior in Video Games. Personality and Social Psychology Bulletin (1995)21, pp. 1020-1030, ISSN 0146-1672.

Anderson, C.A. (1997)
Effects of Violent Movies and Trait Hostile Feelings and Aggressive Thoughts. Aggressive Behavior 23(1997)3, pp. 161-178, ISSN 0096-140X.

Andison, F. Scott
TV violence and viewer aggression: a cumulation of study results, 1956-1976.
Public opinion quarterly, v. 41, fall 1977: 314-331.
"Although there do exist several problems with the results cumulated, it seems quite clear that according to the findings of the studies collected there is at least a weak positive relationship between watching violence on television and the subsequent aggression displayed by viewers of that violence. In light of these findings, one would assume that the violence aired on television requires some curtailment, at least until the time that a definite conclusion is reached."
Violence in television [U.S.] / Violence research [U.S.] / Television viewers

Andreasen, M.S. (1990)
Evolution in the Family's Use of Television: Normative Data from Industry and Academy. In: Bryant, J. (Ed.): Television and the American Family, pp. 3-55, Hillsdale: Lawrence Erlbaum Associates, 1990, XVII, 385 p., bibl., fig., chart., ISBN 0-80580-116-2.

Atkin, Charles, and others.
Selective exposure to televised violence. Journal of broadcasting, v. 23, winter 1979: 5-13.
"This panel survey provides supportive evidence for selective exposure to aggressive television entertainment programming which is compatible with aggressive attitudinal predispositions. Even with a conservative regression analysis that controls for grade, sex, and initial viewing patterns, a significant relationship remains between prior orientations and subsequent program choices."
Television programs [U.S.] / Violence in television [U.S.]

Auter, Philip J.
"The relationship between watching violent programming and acting in a socially destructive manner is dubious at best." (Column)
Broadcasting and Cable, August 15, 1993, v. 123 n. n33 p. 58(1)
LC Call Number: TK6540B85
Business Index Micro Film: None
The relationship between destructive behavior in society and violence on television has not been satisfactorily proven, and legislation to put warning labels on violent programs will do little good. Congress would do better to try and solve problems of US violence in other ways, such as resisting National Rifle Association pressures.
Violence in television - Analysis

Balon, Robert E.
TV viewing preferences as correlates of adult dysfunctional behavior. Journalism quarterly, v. 55, summer 1978: 288-294, 318.
Questionnaires were used to determine the television preferences of inmates in two Ohio prisons. The results were correlated with type of crime committed. The findings were

nonconclusive and suggest that more research is needed to determine the link between television violence and criminal behavior.
Prisoners [Ohio] Research / Violence in television [U.S.] /Criminal psychology [U.S.] Research

Barry David S.
Screen violence and America's children
Spectrum: The Journal of State Government, Summer 1993, v. 66 n. n3 p. 37(6)
LC Call Number: JK2403.S7
Business Index Micro Film: None
Research by medical organizations in the US indicate that violence depicted on TV influences the occurrence of real crimes. The study further reveals that despite these research findings, the intensity and frequency of violent scenes depicted on TV are increasing. Members of the TV and motion picture industry in the US have expressed hesitation in accepting these findings concerning media influenced violence. As a result, shows depicting violence continues to be the staple of TV network programming.
Violence in television - Research / Television programs - Analysis

Barry, David
Screen violence: it's killing us. Harvard Magazine, v. 96, Nov.-Dec. 1993: 38-43
Argues that the written record shows that "exposure to violent images is associated with anti-social and aggressive behavior." Posits that violent films and cartoons alike teach children that violence is funny and is a way to solve problems.
Violence in television [U.S.] /Violence research [U.S.] /Television and children [U.S.] / Juvenile delinquency [U.S.] / Violence in mass media [U.S.]

Baxter, Leslie A., Kaplan, Stuart J.
Context factors in the analysis of prosocial and antisocial behavior on prime time television. Journal of broadcasting, v. 27, winter 1983: 25-36.
"A growing body of research evidence suggests that television plays an important role in socialization, especially for the young viewer. Social learning theory provides the dominant theoretical framework in accounting for television's socialization effects. Central to social learning is a focus on behaviors."
Television programs / Sex role / Human behavior / Television and children

Betsch, T. & Dickenberger, D. (1993)
Why Do Aggressive Movies Make People Aggressive? An Attempt to Explain Short-Term Effects of the Depiction of Violence on the Observer. Aggressive Behavior 19(1993)2, pp. 137-149, ISSN 0096-140X.

Brady, Diane
The power of 'cowabunga': does TV violence influence behavior? (Cover Story)
Maclean's, Dec. 7, 1992, v. 105 n. n49 p. 50(1)
LC Call Number:: AP5.M2; Microfilm (0) 84/200 (1909-1982) MicRR

Magazine Index Micro Film: None
Violence in television - Psychological aspects

Browne, K.D. & Pennell, A.E. (1998)
The Effects of Video Violence on Young Offenders. Birmingham: Home Office Research
and Statistics Directorate, 1998, 107 p., fig., tab., bibl.

Bryant, J. & Zillmann, D. (Eds.)
(1991)
Responding to the Screen: Reception and Reaction Processes. Hillsdale: Lawrence
Erlbaum Associates, 1991, XIV, 407 p., ill., ISBN 0-80580-033-6.

Buckingham, D. (1996)
Moving Images: Understanding Children's Emotional Responses to Television.
Manchester: Manchester University Press, 1996, 325 p., bibl., ISBN 071904-595-9.

Buckley, William F., Jr.
Don't blame violence on the tube. (television)
TV guide, March 19, 1994, v. 42 n. n12 p. 38(4)
LC Call Number: Microfilm 06378 (1953-   ) MicRR
Magazine Index Micro Film: None
Violence in television - Portrayals, depictions, etc. / Television viewers - Psychological
aspects

Bushman, B.J. & Geen, R.G. (1990)
Role of Cognitive-Emotional Mediators and Individual Differences in the Effects of
Media Violence on Aggression. Journal of Personality and Social Psychology 58(1990)1,
pp. 156-163, ISSN 0022-3514.

Bushman, B.J. (1995)
Moderating Role of Trait Aggressiveness in the Effects of Violent Media on Aggression.
Journal of Personality and Social Psychology 69(1995)5, pp. 950-960, ISSN 0022-3514.

Bushman, B.J. (1998)
Priming Effects of Media Violence on the Accessibility of Aggressive Constructs in
Memory. Personality and Social Psychology Bulletin 24(1998)5, pp. 537-545, ISSN
0146-1672.

Calvert, S.L. & Tan, S.L. (1994)
Impact of Virtual Reality on Young Adults' Physiological Arousal and Aggressive
Thoughts: Interaction versus Observation. Journal of Applied Developmental Psychology
15(1994)1, pp. 125-139, ISSN 0193-3973.

Cantor, J. (1994)
Confronting Children's Fright Responses to Mass Media. In: Zillmann, D. & Houston, A.C. (Eds.): Media, Children, and the Family: Social Scientific, Psychodynamic, and Clinical Perspectives, pp. 139-150, Hillsdale: Lawrence Erlbaum Associates, 1994, 351 p., ISBN 0-80581-210-5.

Carlson, James M.
Crime show viewing by preadults: the impact on attitudes toward civil liberties.
Communication research, v. 10, Oct. 1983: 529-552.
"Examines the impact of viewing television crime shows on preadults' attitudes toward civil liberties. The data analyzed were the result of a survey of [Providence, R.I.] school children in grades six through twelve. Generally, heavy viewers of crime shows were more likely to have anti-civil libertarian attitudes."
Television and children [U.S.] / Suspects' rights [U.S.] Public opinion / Political socialization [U.S.] / Public opinion [Providence] / Television viewers [Providence] Research.
Carlsson-Paige, Nancy, & Levin, Diane E. 1990. Who's Calling the Shots. Philadelphia: New Society Publishers.

Censor entertainment? Teens, parents speak up. (panel discussion)
U.S. News & World Report, Oct. 28, 1985, v. 99 p. 52(2)
LC Call Number: JK1.U65; Microfilm 06106 (1933-   ) MicRR
Magazine Index Micro Film: 30A1587
Popular culture - psychological aspects / parent and child - psychological aspects / sex in mass media - public opinion / violence in television - public opinion / television and youth - psychological aspects / adolescence - social aspects / rock music - social aspects

Centerwall, B.S. (1994)
Television and the Development of the Superego: Pathway to Violence. In: Chiland, C.; Young, J.G. & Kaplan, D. (Eds.): Children and Violence: The Child in the Family: The Monograph Series of the International Association for Child and Adolescent Psychiatry and Allied Professions, pp. 178-197, Northvale: Jason Aronson, 1994, XIII, 217 p., ISBN 1-56821-235-6.

Centerwall, Brandon S.
Our cultural perplexities (V): television and violent crime.
The Public Interest, Spring 1993, n. n111 p. 56 (16)
LC Call Number: H1.P86
Business Index Micro Film: NONE
Several studies showing the high correlation between TV exposure and violence tendencies pose the need to control TV viewing among children. Since the TV industry cannot be expected to change their programs for the sake of society's welfare, parents must manage their children's viewing habits. Certain strategies such as the use of time-channel locks, program rating systems and viewer education could be helpful in

controlling the surge of violence in society.
Television and children - Psychological aspects / Violence in television - Research /
Television broadcasting - Social aspects

Centerwall, Brandon S.
Television and violence: the scale of the problem and where to go from here. JAMA
[Journal of the American Medical Association], v. 267, June 10, 1992: 3059-3063.
Psychiatrist purposes to "discuss television's effects within the context of normal child
development; given an overview of natural exposure to television as a cause of
aggression and violence; summarize [his] own research findings on television as a cause
of violence; and suggest a court of action."
Television and children [U.S.] Research / Violence in television [U.S.] Research / Child
psychology [U.S.] Research / Violence research [U.S.]

Chaffee, Steven H.; Gerbner, George; Hamburg, Beatrix, A.; Pierce, Chester M.;
Rubinstein, Eli A.; Siegel, Alberta E.; Singer, Jerome L.
Society (New Brunswick) Sept.-Oct. 1984, v. 21 p. 30(6)
LC Call Number: H1.T72
Magazine Index Micro Film: 24G3684
United States. National Institute of Mental Health - research / television and children -
research / aggressiveness (psychology) - research / violence in television - psychological
aspects

Chamberlin, Leslie J.; Chambers, Norman
How television is changing our children. Clearing house, v. 50, Oct. 1976: 53-57.
"The exact nature of the effects of television on children depends on many limiting
conditions: the nature of the individual child's temperament, intelligence and needs, the
quality of his/her personal adjustment, the amount of information a child has, the strength
of his/her existing beliefs and values, and the opportunities which occur in real life for the
child to put into practice what he/she has learned from mass media."
Television and children [U.S.]

Cline, Victor B.
The child before the TV; the impact of television viewing on children's behavior and
values. Police chief, v. 43, June 1986: 22, 26, 28-29.
Television and children [U.S.] / Violence in television [U.S.]

Comstock, G.A. & Strasburger, V.C. (Eds.)
(1993)
Adolescents and the Media. Philadelphia: Hanley and Belfus, 1993, 182 p., Spec. Issue.,
ISBN 1-56053-101-0.

Cook, Thomas D.; Kendzierski, Deborah A.; Thomas, Stephen V.
The implicit assumptions of television research: an analysis of the 1982 NIMH report on

Television and Behavior. "Also examine[s] the conditions under which the findings must be used to modify programming."
Television and children [U.S.] / Television programs [U.S.] / Violence in television [U.S.]

Cooke,Patrick(1993),
TV Causes Violence? Says Who?, The New York Times, August 14,1993, p. L19.

Cripps, Edward J.
Violence and children's TV. America, v. 135, Sept. 11, 1976: 116-118.
Disputes the idea that there is an absence of proof to the negative effect of televised violence on child viewers.
Television and children [U.S.] / Violence in television [U.S.] / Child development [U.S.]

Curbing television's violent streak. (Editorial)
American Medical News, Sept. 6, 1993, v. 36 n. n33 p. 15(1)
LC Call Number: Microfilm 02679
Business Index Micro Film: None
The American Medical Assn. opposes violence in television and has endorsed a bill that would mandate a device installed in all new television sets allowing households to screen out violent television shows. The AMA believes that children imitate what they see on television and that viewing such violence on television may encourage aggressive behavior.
American Medical Association - Social policy / Violence in television - Analysis

Davidson, R.J.; Ekman, P. & Saron, C. et al. (1990)
Approach Withdrawal and Cerebral Asymmetry: Emotional Expression and Brain Physiology I. Journal of Personality and Social Psychology 58(1990)2, pp. 330-341, ISSN 0022-3514.

Davie, W.R. & Lee, J.S. (1995)
Sex, Violence, and Consonance/Differentiation: An Analysis of Local TV News Values. Journalism and Mass Communication Quarterly 72(1995)1, Spring, pp. 128-138, ISSN 1077-6990.

De Cordoba, Joseph
Streets are murder, but the tube is safe; Colombia tames TV; out: Rambo and the A-Team; in: Placido Domingo hits; in a coma: lots of viewers. (Colombia tries to purge violence from television programs, in reaction to high level of violent crime, murder
The Wall Street Journal, May 12, 1993, p. A1 (W) pA1
LC Call Number: See Catalogs or Staff
Business Index Micro Film: None
Violence in television - Colombia / Homicide - Colombia / Television broadcasting

policy - Colombia / Colombia - Social aspects
Colombia

Desmond, Roger Jon
Cognitive development and television comprehension. Communication research, v. 5,
April 1978: 202-220.
Examines the function of television as a teacher of social behavior, problem solving and
character motivation. The results of a study conducted with ninety children in three grade
levels indicate that age is the best predictor of learning, but that role-playing skills and
program-linking are also important.
Television and children [U.S.] Research / Learning [U.S.]

Dillin, John
Senate hearings lambaste high level of TV violence.
The Christian Science Monitor (1983) June 10, 1993, v. 85 n. n136 p. 1
LC Call Number: Newspaper
Business Index Micro Film: None
Simon, Paul (Politician) - Social policy
United States. Congress. Senate - Investigations / Motion Picture Association of America
- Political activity / Violence in television - Investigations / Television and children -
Psychological aspects

Dominick, Joseph R.
Videogames, television violence, and aggression in teenagers. Journal of communication,
v. 34, spring 1984: 136-147.
"Heavy videogame players were not necessarily more aggressive, but boys who played a
lot of arcade videogames had significantly lower self-esteem."
Video games [Georgia] / Violence in television [Georgia] / Television and children
[Georgia] / Youth [Georgia]

Dominick, Joseph R.; Richman, Shanna; Wurtzel, Alan
Problem-solving in TV shows popular with children: assertion vs. aggression. Journalism
quarterly, v. 56, autumn 1979: 455-463.
Focuses on a sample of the television programs most watched by 6 to 11 year olds, noting
the incidence of aggressive problem solving versus that of assertive problem solving.
Finds that prime time programming "is less violent and contains more of what might be
termed pro-social behavior than does Saturday programming."
Television and children [U.S.]

Donnerstein, E.; Slaby, R.G. & Eron, L.D. (1994)
The Mass Media and Youth Aggression. In: Eron, L.D.; Gentry, J.H. & Schlegel, P.
(Eds.): Reason to Hope: A Psychosocial Perspective on Violence and Youth, pp. 219-
250, Washington D.C.: American Psychological Association, 1994, XVIII, 492 p., ISBN
1-55798-272-4.

Dorfman, L.; Woodruff, K.; Chavez, V. & Wallack, L. (1997)
Youth and Violence on Local Television News in California. American Journal of Public Health 87(1997)8, pp. 1311-1316, ISSN 0090-0036.

Dubow, E.F. & Miller, L.S. (1996)
Television Violence and Aggressive Behavior. In: MacBeth, T.M. (Ed.): Tuning in to Young Viewers: Social Science Perspectives on Television, pp. 117-147, Thousand Oaks: Sage Publications, 1996, 282 p., ISBN 0-80395-825-0.

Durkin, K. & Low, J. (1998)
Children, Media and Aggression: Current Research in Australia and New Zealand. In: Carlsson, U. & von Feilitzen, C. (Eds.): Children and Media Violence: Yearbook from the UNESCO International Clearinghouse on Children and Violence on the Screen 1998, pp. 107-124, Göteborg: Nordicom, Götcborgs universitet, 1998, 387 p., ISBN 91-630-6358-1.

Ekman, P.; Davidson, R.J. & Friesen, W.V. (1990)
The Duchenne Smile: Emotional Expression and Brain Physiology II. Journal of Personality and Social Psychology 58(1990)2, pp. 342-253, ISSN 0022-3514.

Eron, L.D.; Gentry, J.H. & Schlegel, P. (Eds.)
(1994)
Reason to Hope: A Psychosocial Perspective on Violence and Youth. Washington D.C.: American Psychological Association, 1994, XVIII, 492 p., ill., bibl., ISBN 1-55798-272-4.

Eron, L.D.; Huesmann, L.R.; Lefkowitz, M.M. & Waldcr, L.O. (1996)
Does Television Violence Cause Aggression? In: Greenberg, D.F. (Ed.): Criminal Careers: The International Library of Criminology, Criminal Justice and Penology (11 Vols.), pp. 311-321, Aldershot: Dartmouth, 1996, ill., ISBN 1-85521-493-8.

Escalona-R., M.J. (1996)
Violencia televisada y niños una mirada periodística. Caracas: Universidad Catolica Andres Bello, Facultad de Humanidades y Educación, 1996, 147 p., bibl., Diss.

Espinoza-G., P.D. (1993)
La violencia comunicacional de la publicidad en la TV y su influencia en el comportamiento docente en el aula de clase la 2a etapa de educación básica 'Menca de Leoni' Guarenas. Caracas: Universidad Central de Venezuela, Facultad de Humanidades y Educación, 1993, 279 p., ill., bibl., Diss.

Feingold, Murray; Johnson, G. Timothy
Television violence - reactions from physicians, advertisers and the networks. New England journal of medicine, v. 296, Feb. 24, 1977: 424-427.

"Maintain[s] that the burden of proof that television violence does no harm lies with those who introduce it into society. Advertisers and networks will respond, we believe, to the problem of television violence if continuous public pressure is maintained."
Television programs [U.S.] / Violence in television [U.S.] / Human behavior [U.S.]

Feshbach, Seymour
Television and aggression; [an experimental field study, by] Seymour Feshbach and Robert D. Singer. [1st ed.] San Francisco, Jossey-Bass, 1971.
xviii, 186 p. 24 cm. (The Jossey-Bass behavioral science series) Bibliography: p. 175-180.
Violence in television. Aggressiveness (Psychology) I. Singer, Robert D., 1931- joint author. II. Title.

Fling, S.; Smith, L.; Rodriguez, T. & Thornton, D. (1992)
Video Games, Aggression, Self-Esteem: A Survey. Journal of Social Behavior and Personality 20(1992)1, pp. 39-45, ISSN 0886-1641.

Fowles, Barbara R.
A child and his television set: what is the nature of the relationship? Education and urban society, v. 10, Nov. 1977: 89-102.
"Suggests that while the impact of television on children's cognitive development can be favorable, it is probably limited by the child's linguistic capacity because much of human information is ultimately verbal."
Television and children [U.S.] / Child development [U.S.]

Fowles, J. (1992)
Why Viewers Watch: A Reappraisal of Television's Effects. Newbury Park: Sage Publications, 1992, X, 281 p., ISBN 0-80394-076-9.

Fowles, Jib
Could 'Dallas' and 'The Love Boat' actually be good for you?
TV Guide, Sept. 4, 1982, v. 30 p. 39(3)
LC Call Number: Microfilm 06378 (1953-) MicRR
Magazine Index Micro Film: None
Feshbach, Seymour - research
television programs - psychological aspects / violence in television - research

Freedman, J.L. (1992)
Television Violence and Aggression: What Psychologists Should Tell the Public. In: Suedfeld, P. & Tetlock, P.E. (Eds.): Psychology and Social Policy, pp. 179-189, New York: Hemisphere Publishing Corporations, 1992, XVII, 370 p., ill., ISBN 1-56032-063-X.

Geen, R.G. (1990)
Human Aggression. Pacific Grove: Brooks/Cole Pub. Co., 1990, XIII, 241 p., ISBN 0-53415-630-4.

Gerbner,G., Gross, L.P., Melody, W.H. (1982),
Violence and Aggression, Television and Behavior: Ten Years of Scientific Progress and Implications for the Eighties, Vol. #1, pp.36-44.

Grant, Paul J.
The risk in entertainment. (the quality of television programs and their liability) (Quality and the Law)
Quality, Dec. 1993, v. 32 n. n12 p. 56 (1)
LC Call Number: TS156.A1Q35
Business Index Micro Film: None
Television programs have been known to influence viewers to a large extent. There are numerous cases of juveniles or adults committing crimes or actions previously seen on television. Because of this, the question of liability for the effects of television programs arises. Although paying for cable or buying a ticket to watch a program may make it a product. The 'assumption of risk' defense gives emphasis to voluntary choice of behavior that poses a danger to life.
Violence in television - Analysis / Television programs - Laws, regulations, etc. / Products liability - Laws, regulations, etc.

Green, Charlie
Do violent 'toons lead to violent teens? (study will evaluate network television programs for violence) (Brief Article)
Business Week, August 29, 1994, n. n3387 p. 6 (1)
LC Call Number: HF5001.B89; Microfilm 01956 (1929-   ) MicRR
Magazine Index Micro Film: None
Violence in television - Research / Television broadcasting industry - Evaluation

Greeson, Larry E.; Williams, Rose Ann
Social implications of music videos for youth: an analysis of the content and effects of MTV. Youth & society, v. 18, Dec. 1986: 177-189.
"Although the content of music videos is often suggestive, the extent to which music videos influence adolescent attitudes, values and concerns has not yet been thoroughly researched. The present study was designed to address this research gap."
Rock music [U.S.] / Violence in television [U.S.] Research

Hall J
An unending parade of mayhem.
Iowa Med, 86:95, 1996 Mar

Halloran, J.D. (1990)
Mass Media and Violence. In: Bluglass, R. & Bowden, P. (Eds.): Principles and Practice of Forensic Psychiatry, pp. 571-575, Edinburgh: Churchill Livingstone, 1990, XXI, 1405 p., ISBN 0-44303-578-4.

Harvey, Susan E.; Sprafkin, Joyce N.; Rubinstein, Eli
Prime time television: a profile of aggressive and prosocial behaviors. Journal of broadcasting, v. 23, spring 1979: 179-189.
Examine the impact of Family Viewing Time on the level of violent activity on television during the first and only season in which the FVT code was in effect. Find that violence was lower in the FVT time slot, but that high violence shows were sifted to later times. "There is little evidence that the FVT policy resulted in any alterations of program format."
Television and children [U.S.] / Violence in television [U.S.]

Heller, Melvin S.; Polsky, Samuel
Studies in violence and television. New York, American Broadcasting Co., 1976, 503 p.
Partial contents. Responses of emotionally vulnerable children to television. Responses to cartoon and human portrayed television violence in emotionally vulnerable children. Television studies with youthful and violent offenders (pilot). Television viewing, anti-social development and violent behavior - an examination of one hundred young male offenders. Measurements of aggression in responses of adolescent and young adult offenders to television violence. Prosocial behavior, violence and television viewing habits: a pilot comparative study of non-offender adolescents and young adults. Responses of children to action-adventure television dramas with and without prosocial content. Cognitive style and its relationship to perception of violent or prosocial aspects in television programs. Responses of susceptible children to violent vs. prosocial television programs. Behavioral aggression and television viewing in children: psychological, developmental and clinical factors.
Television and children [U.S.] / Violence in television [U.S.] Television programs [U.S.]

Hogben, Matthew
Factors moderating the effect of televised aggression on viewer behavior ,
Communication Research. v. 25 no 2 , Apr. 1998 p. 220-47.
A study was conducted to investigate the effect of televised aggression on viewer aggression. Findings indicated that the overall relationship between televised aggression and viewer aggression was positive and significantly different from zero. An asymptotic effect was observed for the overall findings and across exposure and outcome measures. In addition, the existence of a number of prespecified social learning-based moderators was supported.

Holden, Constance
TV report affirms violence- aggression link.
Science (Washington, D.C), June 18, 1982, v. 216 p. 1299(1)

LC Call Number: Q1.S35; Microfilm 02916 (1883-   ) MicRR
Magazine Index Micro Film: None
violence in television - psychological aspects/ television programs - psychological
aspects / Television and Behavior (report) - publishing / United States National Institute
of Mental Health - investigations

Holicki, S. & Sonesson, I. (1991)
TV in the Socialization Process. A Study of Preschool Children in Sweden and Germany.
Nordicom Review (1991)1, pp. 15-23, ISSN 1403-1108.

Huesmann, L.R. (1995)
Screen Violence and Real Violence: Understanding the Links. Auckland: Media Aware,
1995, 37 p., ill., ISBN 0-47303-151-5.

Huesmann, L.R. (Ed.) (1994)
Aggressive Behavior: Current Perspectives. New York: Plenum Press, 1994, XIX, 305 p.,
ISBN 0-30644-553-0.

Huesmann, L.R.; Eron, L.D.; Berkowitz, L. & Chaffee, S. (1992)
The Effects of Television Violence on Aggression: A Reply to a Skeptic. In: Suedfeld, P.
& Tetlock, P.E. (Eds.): Psychology and Social Policy, pp. 191-200, New York:
Hemisphere Publishing Corporations, 1992, XVII, 370 p., ISBN 156032063X.

Huesmann, L.R.; Guerra, N.G.; Miller, L. & Zilla, A. et al. (1992)
The Role of Social Norms in the Development of Aggression. In: Zumkley, H. &
Fraczek, A. (Eds.): Socialization and Aggression, pp. 139-152, New York; Berlin:
Springer Verlag, 1992, XVII, 246 p., ill., ISBN 3-54054-799-1.

Hughes, J.N. & Hasbrouck, J.E. (1996)
Television Violence: Implications for Violence Prevention. School Psychology Review
25(1996)2, pp. 134-151, ISSN 0279-6015.

Huston, Aletha C.
Television and human behavior. Washington, Federation of Behavioral, Psychological
and Cognitive Sciences, 1985. 13 p.
Edited transcript of seminar presented July 26, 1985. Discusses the pervasiveness of
television, especially in children's lives. Comments on negative and positive effects of
TV viewing and the effects of advertising directed at children.
Television programs [U.S.] / Television and children [U.S.] / Television advertising
[U.S.] / Educational television [U.S.]

Intons-Peterson, M.J.; Roskos-Ewoldsen, B. & Thomas, L. et al. (1989)
Will Educational Materials Reduce Negative Effects of Exposure to Sexual Violence?
Journal of Social and Clinical Psychology 8(1989), pp. 256-275, ISSN 0736-7236.

Irwin, A.R. & Gross, A.M. (1995)
Cognitive Tempo, Violent Video Games and Aggressive Behavior in Young Boys.
Journal of Family Violence (1995)10, pp. 337-350, ISSN 0885-7482.

Iwao, Sumiko; Pool, Ithiel de Sola; Hagiwara, Shigeru
Japanese and U.S. media: some cross-cultural insights into TV violence. Journal of
communication, v. 31, spring 1981: 28-36.
"This study seeks to answer a small question that may help in answering a larger
question. The small question is how violence on Japanese television differs from violence
on U.S. television. The larger question is whether the relationship between TV viewing
and behavior in any culture is a function of sheer quantity of television violence or a
function of the treatment of violence in that culture's dramatic formulae."
Violence in television [U.S.] / Violence in television [Japan]

James, Caryn
If Simon says, 'Lie down in the road,' should you (entertainment industry ramifications
of viewers imitating dangerous activities portrayed in films and on television)
The New York Times, Oct. 24, 193, v. 143 p. E2(N) ppE2
LC Call Number: Not in LC Collection
Magazine Index Micro Film: None
The Program (Motion picture) - Influence / Violence in motion pictures - Influence /
Violence in television - Influence / Television viewers - Psychology and mental health /
Motion picture industry - Standards / Television broadcasting industry - Standards

Jenish, D'Arcy; Brady, Diane; Doyle, Kevin; Came, Barry
Prime-time TV: too much murder and mayhem. (includes related article)
Readers digest (Canadian edition) April 1993, v. 142 n. n852 p. 145 (5)
LC Call Number: AP5
Magazine Index Micro Film: None
Violence in television - Social aspects / Violence - Media coverage / Aggressiveness
(Psychology) in children - Causes of

Johnson, J.D.; Jackson, L.A. & Gatto, L. (1995)
Violent Attitudes and Deferred Academic Aspirations: Deleterious Effects of Exposure to
Rap Music. Basic and Applied Social Psychology 16(1995)1-2, pp. 27-41, ISSN 0197-
3533.

Kalamas, Alicia D; Gruber, Mandy L
Electrodermal responses to implied versus actual violence on television. The Journal of
General Psychology. v. 125 no1 Jan. 1998 p. 31-7.
A study was conducted to examine children's electrodermal responses (EDRs) to implied
and actual violence in a television program. In addition to whether actual or implied
violence prompted an EDR, the impact of the sounds associated with the violence in the
program was evaluated. Results revealed that children demonstrated the strongest EDRs

in response to implied violent stimuli, such as grave digging, grave opening, the villain's face, or the victim's face. The weakest EDRs were elicited by actual violent stimuli, such as stabbing. In addition, the background noise and voices of the program sound track increased the total number of EDRs. These findings suggest that implied violence might elicit more fear, as measured by EDRs, than actual violence would and that sounds alone contribute significantly to the emotional response to violence on television.

Kang, N. (1991)
A Critique and Secondary Analysis of the NBC Study on Television and Aggression. Syracuse: Syracuse University, 1991, Diss.

Kapoor, S.K.; Kang, J.G.; Kim, W.Y. & Kim, K. (1994)
Televised Violence and Viewers: Perceptions of Social Reality: The Korean Case. Communication Reports 11(1994)2, pp. 189-200, ISSN 0893-4215.

Karlen, Neal
A copycat assault. (murder patterned after a television program plot)
Newsweek, Oct. 22, 1984, v. 104 p. 38(1)
LC Call Number: AP2.N6772; Microfilm 01125 (1933-   ) MicRR
Magazine Index Micro Film: 17C1605
Sharon Brandt, (portrait) Farrah Fawcett. (portrait)
Brandt, Sharon - biography / Fawcett, Farrah - performances / Hughes, Francine - Portrayals, depictions, etc.
The Burning Bed (television program) - production and direction / violence in television - social aspects

Kellner, Hella
Television as a socializing factor. EBU review, v. 27, Nov. 1976: 16-21
"Initial results of a study concerning the effects of television violence on viewers' behavior."
Violence in television [West Germany] / Television programs [West Germany] / Television viewers [West Germany]

Klapper, Hope Luntin
Children's perceptions of televised fiction. California management review, v. 22, winter 1979: 36-49.
Concludes that "children of the ages studied can and do make judgments about the realism of televised fiction."
Television and children [U.S.] / Television programs [U.S.]

Kleiter, E.F. (1997)
Film- und Aggression – Aggressionspsychologie: Theorie und empirische Ergebnisse mit einem Beitrag zur allgemeinen Aggressionspsychologie. Weinheim: Studien-Verlag, 1997, XXVII, 668 p., ill., fig., bibl., ISBN 3-89271-700-1.

Krcmar, Marina
The contribution of family communication patterns to children's interpretations of television violence.
Journal of Broadcasting and Electronic Media. v. 42 no2 Spring 1998 p. 250-64.
In this study, children were shown one of three violent TV clips. Each clip showed an identical act of aggression, but the perpetrator's motivation and punishment for the violent act were manipulated. Children also filled out a questionnaire that asked about their family communication patterns (FCP). Overall, children who rated higher on the communication dimension were more likely to see motivated violence as more justified, whereas children who rated higher on the control dimension were likely to see punished violence as less justified.

Lamson, Susan R.
TV Violence: does it cause real-life mayhem? (includes related article)
American rifleman, July 1993, v. 141, n. n7 p. 32(3)
LC Call Number: SK1.A52
Magazine Index Micro Film: None
Violence in television - Influence / Crime - Causes of

Leonard, John
Why blame TV? (television and violence) (includes related article) (excerpt from The Nation)
UTNE Reader, May-June 1994, n. n63 p. 90(5)
LC Call Number: PN4784.U53U88
Magazine Index Micro Film: None
Violence in television - Analysis / Crime in television - Analysis / Television programs - Psychological aspects / Television viewers - Psychology and mental health / Mass media criticism - Analysis

Liebert, Robert M.; Sprafkin, Joyce
The early window: effects of television on children and youth. 3rd ed. New York, Pergamon Press, c1988. 306 p. (Pergamon general psychology series, v. 34)
Partial contents. TV violence: early politics, theories and research. The surgeon general's report [LRS72-589]. Aftermath of the report. Twenty years of TV violence research. Television advertising and children. Race and sex on TV.
Television and children [U.S.] Research / Violence in television [U.S.] Research / Television advertising [U.S.] Research / Minorities in mass media [U.S.] Research / Women in mass media [U.S.] Research / Violence research [U.S.] History / U.S. Surgeon General's Scientific Advisory Committee on Television and Social Behavior

Ling, Peter A.
T.V. Violence and aggressive behavior among Maori and European children / Peter A. Ling - Hamilton, N.Z.: University of Waikato, [1977?]

67 p.: ill.; 30 cm. (Psychology research series; no. 6) Bibliography: p. 51-67.
Television and children. Violence in television. Children, Maori. I. Title. II. Series.

Loye, David
TV's impact on adults: it's not all bad news. Psychology today, v. 11, May 1978: 87-88, 90, 93-94.
"The studies up to now have focused largely on how violent programs affect the young. In one of the first field studies on adults, groups of Los Angeles men watched TV at home - while their wives watched them." Study of 183 couples for a one week period finds that TV had some good and some bad effects on the behavior of viewers.
Television programs [U.S.] / Violence in television [U.S.] / Social surveys [U.S.]

Lukesch, H. (1989)
Video Violence and Aggression. The German Journal of Psychology 13(1989)4, pp. 293-300, ISSN 0705-5870.
Mackey, Aurora
Television and you: are you tuning into trouble?
Teen, Sept. 1983, v. 27 p. 4(3)
Magazine Index Micro Film: None
Television and youth - psychological aspects / violence in television - psychological aspects

Mann, James
What is TV doing to America? U.S. News & World Report, v. 93, Aug. 2, 1982: 27-30.
"In its 43 years, television has been praised as a miracle and damned as a distorter of reality. Now, new evidence is emerging about the medium and how it affects the people who watch it."
Television programs [U.S.] / Television and children [U.S.]

Martin, Jay
Caught in Fantasyland: electronic media's hold on society
USA Today (Magazine), July 1988, v. 117 n. n2518 p. 92(2)
LC Call Number: L11.S36
Magazine Index Micro Film: 45G0647
Mass media - Influence / Aggressiveness (Psychology) in children - Analysis / Television - Psychological aspects / Violence in television - Social aspects

Media violence and antisocial behavior. Journal of social issues, v. 42, no. 3, 1986: whole issue (197 p.)
Partial contents. The immediate effects of media violence on behavior by Russell G. Geen and Susan L. Thomas. The effects of media violence on attitudes, emotions, and cognitions by Brendan Gail Rule and Tamara J. Ferguson. Naturalistic studies of the long-term effects of television violence, by Charles W. Turner, Bradford W. Hesse, and Sonja Peterson-Lewis. Sexual violence in the media: indirect effects on aggression

against women, by Neil M. Malamuth and John Briere. Family experiences and television viewing as predictors of children's imagination, by Jerome L. Singer and Dorothy G. Singer. Issues bearing on the legal regulations of violent and sexually violent media by Daniel Ling, Steven Penrod and Edward Donnerstein.
Violence in television [U.S.] / Violence research [U.S.] / Television and children [U.S.]

Meierding, G. (1993)
Psychokiller: Massenmedien, Massenmörder und alltägliche Gewalt. Reinbeck bei Hamburg: Rowohlt Verlag, 1993, 152 p., ill., bibl., ISBN 3-499-19390-6.

Mink, Eric
Bum rap for the box: the TV violence theory down the tube. Washington Journalism review, v. 5, Jan.-Feb. 1983: 34-37, 59.
Argues against the idea that violence on television has caused a violent society.
Television programs [U.S.] / Violence in television [U.S.]

Mitchard, Jacquelyn
'Kids Killing Kids.' (TV special on teenage violence)
TV guide, April 23, 1994, v. 42 n. n17 p. 22(2)
LC Call Number: Microfilm 06378 (1953-) MicRR
Magazine Index Micro Film: None
Kids Killing Kids (Television program) - Criticism, interpretation, etc. / Television specials - Criticism, interpretation, etc. / Violence in television - Portrayals, depictions, etc.

Moise JF; Huesmann LR
Television violence viewing and aggression in females.
Institute for Social Research, University of Michigan, Ann Arbor 48109-1248, USA.
jmoise@umich.edu
Ann N Y Acad Sci, 794:380-3, 1996 Sep 20

Molitor, F. & Hirsch, K.W. (1994)
Children's Toleration of Real-Life Aggression After Exposure to Media Violence: A Replication of the Drabman and Thomas Studies. Child Study Journal 24(1994)3, pp. 191-207, ISSN 0009-4005.

Murray, J.P. (1997)
Neuroimaging and TV Violence Viewing. San Antonio: Kansas State University, 1997, 8 p.

Muson, Howard
Teenage violence and the telly. Psychology today, v. 11, Mar. 1978: 50-51, 53-54.
Reports the results of William Belson's study of television violence which "found that

some forms of violence on TV produce more real-life violence than others, including: physical and verbal violence between people in the story who have a close personal relationship... stories that present violence in a very realistic fashion, [and] violence committed by good guys in pursuit of good causes."
Television and children [Great Britain] / Violence in television [Great Britain] / Youth [Great Britain]

Mustonen, A. & Pulkkinen, L. (1993)
Aggression in Television Program in Finland. Aggressive Behavior 19(1993)3, pp. 175-183, ISSN 0096-140X.

Mustonen, A. (1997)
Nature of Screen Violence and its Relation to Program Popularity. Aggressive Behavior 23(1997)4, pp. 281-292, ISSN 0096-140X.

Notterman, J.M. (Ed.) (1997)
The Evolution of Psychology: Fifty Years of the American Psychologist. Washington D.C.: American Psychological Association, 1997, XXXV, 783 p., ISBN 1-55798-473-5.

Paik, H. & Comstock, G. (1994)
The Effects of Television Violence on Antisocial Behavior: A Meta-Analysis. Communication Research 21(1994)4, pp. 516-546, ISSN 0093-6502.

Paik, Haejung and Comstock, George (1994),
The Effects of Television Violence on Antisocial Behavior: A Meta-Analysis, Communication Research, Vol.#21,pp.526-542.

Palermo, G.B. (1995)
Adolescent Criminal Behavior: Is TV Violence One of the Culprits? International Journal of Offender Therapy and Comparative Criminology 39(1995)1, pp. 11-22, ISSN 0306-624X.

Palmer, C. (1991)
Effects of Modeled/Support of Media Violence and Need for Approval on Aggression. Current Psychology 10(1991)1-2, pp. 121-128, ISSN 1046-1310.

Pearl, David
Violence and aggression
Society (New Brunswick) Sept.-Oct. 1984, v. 21 p. 17(6)
LC Call Number: H1.T72
Magazine Index Micro Film: 24G3671
Violence in television - psychological aspects / aggressiveness (psychology) - causes of

Phillips, David P.
The behavioral impact of violence in the mass media: a review of the evidence from laboratory and nonlaboratory investigations. Sociology and social research, v. 66, July 1982: 387-398.
"Reviews the literature on the behavioral impact of aggressive messages in the mass media, particularly television. Laboratory experiments are briefly reviewed, but more extensive coverage is devoted to field experiments, of both the 'hands on' and 'hands off' variety. The paper also discusses the advantages and disadvantages of the various designs used to investigate this topic."
Violence in television [U.S.] / Violence research [U.S.]

Philo, G.; Henderson, L. & McLaughlin, G. (Eds.) (1996)
Media Representations of Mental Health/Illness. London: Longman, 1996, XV, 135 p., bibl., ISBN 0-58229-219-0.

Posch, Robert
What you do emerges from who you are. (Legal outlook) (Column)
Direct Marketing, July 1993, v. 56 n. n3 p. 43(4)
LC Call Number: HF5861.R4
Business Index Micro Film: 72U1064
Television has a potent ability to corrupt young minds. Numerous studies have shown that long-term childhood exposure to television is a contributing factor to such social ills as homicides, rapes and injurious assaults. Nevertheless, its defenders argue that television does not have such psychological effects. Their contention, however, runs counter to the main assumption behind television commercials. Critics explain that there would be no advertisements in television at all if the medium does not make an impact on the individual mental make-up, as its supporters claim. The damaging effects of sex and violence in the boob tube show that television is the junk medium. Direct mails and telemarketing calls, thus, should not be identified as junk mail and junk calls. Junk is the sole property of television.
Advertising, Direct-Mail - Evaluation / Violence in television - Evaluation / Sex in television - Evaluation

Potter, W. James; Warren, Ron
Humor as camouflage of televised violence, Journal of Communication. v. 48 no 2 Spring 1998 p. 40-57.
A study was conducted to investigate content-based explanations for why television viewers might not appear to be concerned with violence portrayed in comedy programs. Results suggest that the rate of violence, particularly of verbal forms of violence, is very high on comedy programs but that this rate is largely a result of high numbers of acts among the relatively minor forms of violence.

Potter, W.J. & Warren, R. (1995)
How Real Is the Portrayal of Aggression in Television Entertainment Programming?
Journal of Broadcasting and Electronic Media 39(1995)4, pp. 496-516, ISSN 0883-8151.

Potter, W.J. (1997)
The Problem of Indexing Risk of Viewing Television Aggression. Critical Studies in
Mass Communication 14(1997)3, pp. 228-248, ISSN 0739-3180.

Raffa, Jean Benedict
Television and values: implications for education. Educational forum, v. 49, winter 1985:
189-198.
Summarizes "the prevailing concerns about the impact of television on the formation of
values in youth, and some resultant implications for curriculum and instruction."
Television and children [U.S.] / Ethics [U.S.] / Education [U.S.]

Reeves, Byron
Perceived TV reality as a predictor of children's social behavior. Journalism quarterly, v.
55, winter 1978: 682-689, 695.
Study investigates "whether accounting for children's perceived reality of television will
contribute to the relationship between pro- and anti-social TV content and pro- and antisocial behavior."
Television and children [U.S.]

Regan, P.M. (1994)
War Toys, War Movies, and the Militarization of the United States, 1900-1985. Journal
of Peace Research 31(1994)1, pp. 45-58, ISSN 0022-3433.

Reith, M. (1996)
The Relationship between Unemployment in Society and the Popularity of Crime Drama
on TV. Journal of Broadcasting and Electronic Media 40(1996)2, pp. 258-264, ISSN
0883-8151.

Research International New Zealand (1990)
Survey of Community Attitudes and Perception of Violence on Television. Auckland:
Broadcasting Standards Authority, 1990, 81 p., ill.

Rich, M.; Woods, E.R.; Goodman, E.; Emans, S.J. & DuRant, R.H. (1998)
Aggressors or Victims: Gender and Race in Music Video Violence. Pediatrics
101(1998)4, pp. 669-674, ISSN 0031-4005.

Ridley-Johnson, R.; Surdy, T. & O'Laughlin, E. (1991)
Parent Survey on Television Violence Viewing: Fear, Aggression and Sex Differences.
Journal of Applied Developmental Psychology (1991)12, pp. 63-71, ISSN 0193-3973.

Rodriguez Sutil, C.; Esteban, J.L.; Takeuchi, M.; Clausen, T. & Scott, R. (1995)
Televised Violence: A Japanese, Spanish, and American Comparison. Psychological
Reports 77(1995)3, pp. 995-1000, ISSN 0031-2941.

Roe, K. (1989)
Notes on the Concept of Aggression and Its (Mis)use in Media Research. Göteborg:
Göteborgs universitet, Statsvetenskapliga institutionen, avdelning för
masskommunikation, 1989, 25 p., ISSN 0283-6696.

Roussou, N. (1996)
Factors of Humanitarian and Mass Culture and Aggression in Children and Young
People. Cyprus Review 8(1996)2, pp. 38-78, ISSN 1015-2281.

Russell, G.W. & Pigat, L. (1991)
Effects of Modelled Censure/Support of Media Violence and Need for Approval on
Aggression. Current Psychology 10(1991)1-2, pp. 121-128, ISSN 1046-1310.
Santos, G.A. (1998)
Medo e exclusâo social um estudo sobre a morte, o medo dos pobres e omedo de pobres.
Sâo Paulo: Psicologia Escolar e do Desenvolvimento Humano, 1998, 282 p., ill., Diss.

Signorielli, N; Gerbner, G. & Morgan, M. (1995)
Violence on Television: The Cultural Indicators Project. Journal of Broadcasting and
Electronic Media 39(1995)2, pp. 278-283, ISSN 0883-8151.

Silverman, Ronald E., 1946-
Short term effects of television viewing on aggressive and psychophysiological behavior
of adults and children [microform] / by Ronald E. Silverman.
1972. vii, 109 leaves : ill.
PN1992.6.S5 1972
Microform reproduction: Ann Arbor, Mich. : University Microfilms, 1972. 1 microfilm
reel ; 35 mm.
Thesis (Ph.D.)--State University of New York at Buffalo. Bibliography: leaves 99-109.

Simons, Marlise
A French mother fights TV violence; sues Paris aide, blaming U.S. program for son's
death. (Marine Laine sues government officials Herve Bourges and Jacques Boutet for
manslaughter after son tests explosive technique he saw on 'MacGyver') (International
The New York Times, August 30, 1993, v. 142 p. A5 (N) pA5
LC Call Number: Not in LC Collection
Magazine Index Micro Film: None
Violence in television - France / Homicide - Cases / France - Social aspects
France

Singer, Dorothy G.; Singer, Jerome L.
Television and the developing imagination of the child. Journal of broadcasting, v. 25, fall 1981: 373-387.
"Examines whether television enriches a child's imagination, leads to distortions of reality, and whether adult mediation while a child views a program or immediately after can evoke constructive changes or stimulate make-believe play."
Television and children / Child psychology / Child development

Singer, Jerome L.; Singer, Dorothy G.; Rapaczynski, Wanda S.
Family patterns and television viewing as predictors of children's beliefs and aggression. Journal of communication, v. 34, spring 1984: 73-89.
Report on a study which "reflects an effort to examine the ways in which children's family life and television viewing combine to predict aspects of their conscious experience as well as their social interaction patterns and behavior."
Television and children [U.S.] / Child development [U.S.]

Singer, M.I.; Anglin, T.M.; Song, L.Y. & Lunghofer, L. (1995)
Adolescents' Exposure to Violence and Associated Symptoms of Psychological Trauma. JAMA 273(1995)6, pp. 477-482, ISSN 0098-7484.

Singer, M.I.; Slovak, K.; Frierson, T. & York, P. (1998)
Viewing Preferences, Symptoms of Psychological Trauma, and Violent Behaviors Among Children Who Watch Television. Journal of the American Academy of Child and Adolescent Psychiatry 37(1998)10, pp. 1041-1048, ISSN 0890-8567.

Sixteen Russian roulette deaths linked to TV violence
Jet, March 5, 1981, v. 59 p. 7(1)
LC Call Number: E185.5.J4; Microfilm 07167 (1951-1979) MicRR
Magazine Index Micro Film: None
Violence in television - psychological aspects / firearms - accidents / National Coalition on Television Violence - reports / Deer Hunter (moving-picture) - influence

Slaby, Ronald G.
Combating television violence
The Chronicle of Higher Education, Jan. 5, 1994, v. 40 n. n18 p. B1(2)
LC Call Number: Not in LC Collection
Magazine Index Micro Film: None
A commission appointed by the American Psychological Association to collect scientific proof of the influence of violence in television on increasing violence in America, reported that television programs induce viewers' acts of crime. William Abbott, president of the National Foundation to Improve Television, appealed to the Federal Communications Commission to upgrade the standard of television programs.
Violence in television - Influence / United States - Social aspects
United States

Somers, Anne R.
Violence, television and the health of American youth. New England Journal of Medicine, v. 294, April 8, 1976: 811-817
Argues that one of the contributing factors to a youth culture of violence is television's daily diet of symbolic crime and violence and urges that the medical profession concern itself with this health hazard.
Television programs [U.S.] / Television and children [U.S.] / Violence in television [U.S.]

Sons of violence. (effects of television)
Psychology Today (Magazine) July-August 1992, v. 25 n. n4 p. 13(1)
LC Call Number: BF1.P855
Magazine Index Micro Film: 65A1316
Violence in television - Psychological aspects / Behavioral assessment of children - Psychological aspects

Special effects. (posttraumatic stress)
Psychology today, May-June 1992, v. 25 n. n3 p. 12(1)
LC Call Number: BF1.P855; Microfilm 06204 (1967-   ) MicRR
Magazine Index Micro Film: 64E0955
Post-traumatic stress disorder - Causes of / Violent crimes - Psychological aspects / Video tapes in courtroom proceedings - Psychological aspects / Violence in television - Psychological aspects / Crime in television - Psychological aspects

Sprafkin, Joyce N.
Children's television viewing habits and prosocial behavior: a field correlational study. Journal of broadcasting, v. 23, summer 1979: 265-276.
"Examine[s] the relationship between children's television viewing habits and the degree to which they exhibit prosocial behavior in school."
Television and children [U.S.] / Human behavior [U.S.]

Stack, S. (1989)
The Effect of Publicized Mass Murders and Murder-Suicides on Lethal Violence, 1968-1980: A Research Note. Social Psychiatry and Psychiatric Epidemiology 24(1989)4, pp. 202-208, ISSN 0933-7954.

Strasburger, V.C. (1995)
Adolescents and the Media: Medical and Psychological Impact. Thousand Oaks: Sage Publications, 1995, XI, 137 p., ill., ISBN 0-80395-499-9.

Suedfeld, P. & Tetlock, P.E. (Eds.) (1992)
Psychology and Social Policy. New York: Hemisphere Publishing Corporations, 1992, XVII, 370 p., ISBN 1-56032-063-X.

Sullivan, David B.
Commentary and viewer perception of player hostility: adding punch to televised sports.
Journal of broadcasting and electronic media, v. 35, fall 1991: 487-504.
"This study explored the impact of television commentary on viewers' perceptions and enjoyment of player hostility, including violent behavior, in the context of a less combative sport. Effects of fanship, gender, and varying levels of commentary (dramatic, neutral and no commentary) were tested in a 3 x 2 x 2 experimental design. A videotape of a heated Georgetown versus Syracuse men's college basketball game provided stimulus material, with the dramatic commentary treatment contradicting the visual evidence as to which team was the aggressor. Strong medium effects were revealed, with viewers of the dramatic commentary treatment perceiving Syracuse players as being significantly more hostile, in line with the manipulation. Men were more likely than women to enjoy the fighting in the game segment, but fans' perceptions of opponent hostility were as vulnerable to the biased commentary as those of nonfans."
Violence in sports [U.S.] Mathematical models / College sports [U.S.] Mathematical models / Basketball [U.S.] / Violence research [U.S.] Mathematical models / Violence in television [U.S.] Mathematical models / Television broadcasting of sports [U.S.] Mathematical models / Television viewers [U.S.] Research

Swerdlow, Joel
What is television doing to real people? Today's education, v. 70, Sept.-Oct. 1981: 51-54, 56-57.
Reviews the impact of television on learning, politics, selling and violence.
Television programs [U.S.] / Human behavior [U.S.] / Television in politics [U.S.] / Learning [U.S.] / Television advertising [U.S.] / Violence in television [U.S.]

Teevan, James J. Jr.; Hartnagel, Timothy F.
The effect of television violence on the perceptions of crime by adolescents. Sociology and social research, v. 60, April 1976: 337-348.
Violence in television [U.S.] / Violence [Maryland] / Youth [Maryland] / Television and children [U.S.]

Television and aggression: a panel study / J. Ronald Milavsky... [et al.]. New York: Academic Press, 1982
xvi, 505 p.: ill.; 24 cm. (Quantitative studies in social relations)
Bibliography: p. 491-499. Includes index.
Television broadcasting - Social aspects - United States. Violence in television - Social aspects - United States. Aggressiveness (Psychology). I. Milavsky, J. Ronald. II. Series.

Television and aggression : a panel study / J. Ronald Milavsky... [et al.]. New York : Academic Press, 1982. xvi, 505 p. : ill., charts ; 24 cm.
Quantitative studies in social relations.
HE8700.8.T335

0124959806 : $37.50
Includes index.
Bibliography: p. 491-499.

Television and social behavior: beyond violence and children: a report of the Committee
on Television and Social Behavior Social Science Research Council / edited by Stephen
B. Withey, Ronald P. Abeles. Hillsdale, N.J.: L. Eribaum Associates, 1980.
x, 356 p.; 24 cm. "Sponsored by the Social Science Research Council." Includes
bibliographies and indexes.
Television broadcasting - Social aspects - Addresses, essays, lectures. Television -
Psychological aspects - Addresses, essays, lectures. Violence in television - Addresses,
essays, lectures. I. Withey, Stephen Bassett, 1918- . II. Abeles, Ronald P., 1944-   . III.
Social Science Research Council (U.S.)

Television linked to youths' depression: expert. (Penn State University's Paul Kettle)
(Brief Article)
Jet, June 20, 1994, v. 86 n. n7 p. 27(1)
LC Call Number: E185.5.J4; Microfilm 07167 (1951-1979) MicRR
Magazine Index Micro Film: None
Television and youth - Psychological aspects / Depression in children - Causes of /
Violence in television - Psychological aspects

The mean machine? (violence on television and violence in society)
The Nation (New York, NY), August 13, 1988, v. 247 n. n4 p. 140(3)
LC Call Number: AP2.N2; Microfilm 03323 (1965-1979) MicRR
Magazine Index Micro Film: 46B0077
Violence in television - criticism, interpretation, etc. / Television and children - analysis /
Social problems - causes of

Toufexis, Anastasia
Our violent kids: a rise in brutal crimes by the young shakes the soul of society
Time (Chicago), June 12, 1989, v. 133 n. n24 p. 52(6)
LC Call Number: AP2.T37; Microfilm 02914 (1923-   ) MicRR
Magazine Index Micro Film: 50B0597
Survey: causes of teenage violence. (table) Survey: methods of reducing teenage
violence. (table)
Juvenile delinquency - causes of / Sadism in motion pictures - Social aspects / Rock
music - Social aspects / Violence in television - Social aspects / Rape - causes of

TV said to cause aggression. (TV violence)
Television Digest, March 2, 1992, v. 32 n., n9 p. 5(1)
LC Call Number: May or May Not be in LC. Search further.
Business Index Micro Film: 63Y0471

American Psychological Association - Reports / Violence in television - Psychology aspects

TV that's bad for your health; televised violence can have violent consequences; does anyone care? (Editorial)
The Los Angeles Times, May 30, 1993, v. 112 p. M4
LC Call Number: Newspaper 7114-X
Business Index Micro Film: None
United States. Congress - Social policy / Violence in television - Social aspects / Children - Psychology and mental health / Television broadcasting industry - Social policy

U.S. National Institute of Mental Health
Television and behavior: ten years of scientific progress and implications for the eighties: vol. 2: technical reviews. Rockville, Md. [1982] 362 p. (U.S. Dept. of Health and Human Services) DHHS publication no. (ADM) 82-1196)
Partial contents. The forms of television: effects on children's attention, comprehension, and social behavior, by M. Rice, A. Huston and J. Wright. Television viewing and arousal, by D. Zillmann. Television violence and aggressive behavior, by L. Huesmann. Violence in television programs: ten years later by N. Signorielli, L. Gross and M. Morgan. Television and role socialization: an overview, by B. Greenberg. Television and social relations: family influences and consequences for interpersonal behavior by J. McLeod, M. Fitzpatrick, C. Glynn and S. Fallis. Health campaigns on television by D. Solomon
Television programs [U.S.] / Violence in television [U.S.] / Violence research [U.S.]

United States. Congress. House. Committee on Energy and Commerce. Subcommittee on Telecommunications, Consumer Protection and Finance.
Social/behavioral effects of violence on television: hearing before the Subcommittee on Telecommunications, Consumer Protection, and Finance of the Committee on Energy and Commerce, House of Representatives, Ninety-seventh Congress, first session, October 21, 1981. Washington: U.S. G.P.O., 1982
iii, 248 p.: ill.; 24 cm. Includes bibliographies. "Serial no. 97-84." Item 1019-A, 1019-B (microfiche) Supt. of Docs. no.: Y 4.En 2/3:97-84
Television - United States - Psychological aspects. Television - Social aspects - United States. Violence in television - United States. I. Title.

United States. Congress. Senate. Committee on Commerce. Subcommittee on Communications. Scientific Advisory Committee on TV and Social Behavior. Hearing, Ninety-Second Congress, first session, on progress report, Surgeon General's Scientific Advisory Committee on Television and Social Behavior, September 28, 1971. Washington, U.S. Govt. Print. Off., 1971.
ii, 80 p. 24 cm. "Serial no. 92-32." Includes bibliographies. Supt. of Docs. no.: Y 4.C73/2:92-32

Television and children. Violence in television - United States. I. United States. Surgeon General's Scientific Advisory Committee on Television and Social Behavior. II. Title.

United States. Congress. Senate. Committee on Commerce. Subcommittee on Communications. Surgeon General's report by the Scientific Advisory Committee on Television and Social Behavior: hearings before the Subcommittee on Communications of the Committee on Commerce, United State Senate, Ninety-second Congress, second session... Washington: U.S. G.P.O., 1972.
2 v. (v, 526 p.); 24 cm. Hearings held Mar. 21-24, 1972. "Serial no. 92-52." Vol. [2]: Appendix A. Supt. of Docs. no.: Y 4.C73/2:92-52.
Television and children. Violence in television - United States. I. United States. Surgeon General's Scientific Advisory Committee on Television and Social Behavior. II. Title.

Use of mass media: patterns in the life cycle. American behavioral scientist, v. 23, Sept.-Oct. 1979: whole issue.
Contents. Media use and the life span by J. Dimmick, T. McCain and W. Bolton. Children's media environment by E. Wartella, A. Alexander and D. Lemish. Adolescents' use of media by R. Avery. Media use by adults by A. Morrison. Uses and gratifications among the elderly by C. Swank. Media use by older adults by T. Young. Mass media [U.S.] / Television [U.S.] / Social surveys [U.S.] / Television and children [U.S.] / Aged [U.S.]

van Raay, B.A.M. (1998)
Jongeren en geweld: Een onderzoek naar de beeldvorming van de Tilburgse politie, media, horeca en politiek [Youth and Violence: A Study of Tilburgian Police, Media and Politics]. Tilburg: Wetenschapswinkel Tilburg, 1998, IV, 138 p., ill.

VanHoose, John J.; Riddle, Denise
Television: a major cause of undesirable behavior. NASSP [National Association of Secondary School Principals] bulletin, v. 67, May 1983: 97-100.
"Television has the potential to make a substantial contribution to the development of young people, say these writers, who argue that this contribution cannot be realized unless middle level educators help young people develop the types of skills and insight they need to use the medium wisely."
Television and children [U.S.] / Secondary school students [U.S.] / Curriculum planning [U.S.]

Videodrome. (video violence)
Economist (London), August 13, 1994, v. 332 n. n7876 p. 73(2)
LC Call Number: HG11.E2; Microfilm 03394 (1843) MicRR
Business Index Micro Film: None
Violence in children - Causes of / Violence in motion pictures - Social aspects / Violence in television - Social aspects / Violence research - Analysis / Violent crimes - Psychological aspects

Violence front-burner issue. (debate on impact of televised violence on viewers)
Television Digest, Nov. 15, 1993, v. 33 n. n46 p. 5(1)
LC Call Number: May or May Not Be In LC. Search further.
Business Index Micro Film: 74T0694
The issue of televised violence's effects on viewers will continue to be hotly debated in
the near future. Senior US officials continue to press the issue but the Entertainment
Industries Council is working for self-regulation of the movie an TV industries. In
Canada, the Radio-TV Telecommunications Commission and Canadian Assn. of
Broadcasters have adopted voluntary regulations prohibiting the depiction of 'gratuitous
violence' in television.
Violence in television - Laws, regulations, etc. / Television broadcasting industry - Social
policy / Motion picture industry - Social policy

Violence in American life: a Center report. Center magazine, v. 14, Nov.-Dec. 1981: 13-
44.
Discussions among California's Commission on Crime Control and Violence Prevention,
staff at the Hutchins Center, and invited participants focused on prediction of violence in
children, television and learning of aggressive behavior, cultural roots of violence against
women, suggestions for neighborhood, state, and national policies, discipline and abuse
of children, and prevention of violence.
Violence research [U.S.] Conferences / Crime prevention [U.S.] Conferences / Children's
rights [U.S.] / Family violence [U.S.] / Crimes against women [U.S.] / Violence in
television [U.S.] / California. Commission on Crime Control and Violence Prevention.

Violence in American society. American behavioral scientist, v. 23, May-June 1980: 637-
776.
Partial contents. Crime and violence in American society by E. Flynn. Violence by youth;
violence against youth by E. Duxbury. Victims and aggressors in marital violence, M.
Straus. Television violence, victimization, and power, by G. Gerbner, L. Gross, N.
Signoriello and M. Morgan. From conflict theory to conflict resolution by E. Flynn
Violence [U.S.] / Crime and criminals [U.S.] / Juvenile delinquency [U.S.] / Family
violence [U.S.] / Violence in television [U.S.]

Violence on TV.
Science New (Washington), Sept. 5, 1981, v. 120 p. 151 (1)
LC Call Number: Q1.S76
Magazine Index Micro Film: None
television and youth - psychological aspects / violence in television - psychological
aspects / crime in television - psychological aspects

Violence, crime and Janet Reno. (US Attorney General) (American Survey) (Column)
Economist (London), Oct 30, 1993, v. 329 n. n7835 p. A33 (1)
LC Call Number: HG11.E2; Microfilm 03394 (1843-   )MicRR
Magazine Index Micro Film: None

Reno, Janet - Evaluation
Attorneys general - Evaluation / Crime prevention - Analysis / Violence in television - Laws, regulations, etc.

Violent family hour. (8-9 PM is most violent hour on TV)
Society (New Brunswick) Jan.-Feb. 1987, v. 24 p. 2(1)
LC Call Number: H1.T72
Magazine Index Micro Film: 37L3582
Violence in television - psychological aspects / Pennsylvania, University of. Annenberg School of Communications - surveys / television programs for children - psychological aspects

von Feilitzen, C. (1989)
Spänning, rädsla, aggression och våld [Excitement, Fear, Aggression and Violence]. In: von Feilitzen, C.; Filipson, L.; Rydin, I. & Schyller, I. (Eds.): Barn och unga i medieåldern: fakta i ord och siffror, pp. 188-208, Stockholm: Rabén & Sjögren, 1989, 287 p., tab., ISBN 91-29-59298-4.

von Feilitzen, C. (1994)
Media Violence: Research Perspectives in the 1980s. In: Hamelink, C. J. & Linné, O. (Eds.): Mass Communication Research: On Problems and Policies. The Art of Asking the Right Questions: In Honour of James D. Halloran, pp. 147-170, Norwood: Ablex Publishing Company, 1994, 417 p., ISBN 0-89391-951-9.

von Feilitzen, C. (1996)
Barn och de realistiska våldsskildringarna [Children and Realistic Depictions of Violence]. In: Andén-Papadopoulos, K. & Höijer, B. (Eds.): Våldsamma nyheter: Perspektiv på dokumentära våldsskildringar i media, pp. 203-222, Stockholm/ Stehag: Brutus Östlings Bokförlag Symposion, 1996, 238 p., ill., bibl., ISBN 91-7139-274-2.

von Feilitzen, C.; Forsman, M. & Roe, K. (Eds.) (1993)
Våld från alla håll: forskningsperspektiv på våld i rörliga bilder [Violence From All Directions: Fourteen Researchers Discuss Violence in Motion Pictures]. Stockholm: Brutus Östlings Bokförlag Symposion, 1993, 383 p., ill., bibl., ISBN 91-7139-123-1.

Walsh, John
Wide world of reports. (ABC rejects TV violence link to aggression)
Science (Washington, D.C.) May 20, 1983, v. 220 p. 804(2)
LC Call Number: Q1.S35; Microfilm 02916 (1883-   ) MicRR
Magazine Index Micro Film: None
Violence in television - social aspects / United States. National Institute of Mental health - reports / Television and Behavior (report) - publishing / A Research Perspective on Television and Violence (report) - publishing

Watch that first step. (linking television violence to child behavior) (Editorial)
Broadcasting and Cable, May 16, 1994, v. 124 n. n20 p. 74(1)
LC Call Number: TK6540B85
Business Index Micro Film: 78S1720
Television and children - Laws, regulations, etc. / Violence in television - Laws,
regulations, etc. / Television broadcasting industry - Laws, regulations, etc.

White, G.F.; Katz, J. & Scarborough, K.E. (1992)
The Impact of Professional Football Games upon Violent Assaults on Women. Violence
and Victims 7(1992)2, pp. 157-171, ISSN 0886-6708.

Williams, Wenmouth Jr., Wotring C. Edward
Mediated violence and victim consequences: a behavioral measure of attention and
interest. Journal of broadcasting, v. 20, summer 1976: 365-372.
Attempts to determine the effects of television violence on viewers by analyzing
differences in media violence wen consequences of that violence to the victim are shown
or not shown.
Violence in television [U.S.] / Television programs [U.S.] / Television viewers [U.S.]

Wurtzel, Alan; Lometti, Guy
Researching television violence
Society (New Brunswick), Sept.-Oct., 1984 v. 21 p. 22 (9)
LC Call Number: H1.T72
Magazine Index Micro Film: 24G3676
Violence in television - psychological aspects / aggressiveness (psychology) - research /
United States.
National Institute of Mental Health - research

Wurtzel, Alan; Lometti, Guy
Smoking out the critics.
Society (New Brunswick), Sept.-Oct. 1984, v. 21 p. 36(5)
LC Call Number: H1.T72
Magazine Index Micro Film: 24G3690
United States. National Institute of Mental Health - research / violence in television -
psychological aspects / aggressiveness (psychology) - causes of

Yukawa, S. & Yoshida, F. (1998)
The Effects of Media Violence on Affective, Cognitive, and Physiological Reactions of
Viewers. Japanese Journal of Psychology 69(1998)2, pp. 89-96, ISSN 0021-5236.

Zuger, Abigail ,
A fistful of hostility is found in women,
New York Times (Late New York Edition).July 28, 1998. p. F1+.
Recent studies into aggression by women were discussed at this month's meeting of the

International Society for Research on Aggression at Ramapo College, New Jersey. John Archer of the University of Central Lancashire, U.K., reported his findings from a large-scale review of studies of physical hostility in heterosexual relationships. Although most instances of serious violence and injuries that required medical attention were attributable to men, women actually tended to have a slightly higher rate of physical aggression. This discovery ties in with an emerging picture of women responding aggressively to certain environmental stresses, as can be seen in patterns of crime, including instances of domestic homicide.

Key words: Sex differences; Violence ; Women; Aggressiveness

Public Opinion

Anderson, David
The television time bomb; violence on the tube, a public health issue. (Editorial)
The New York Times, July 27, 1992, v. 141 p. A12 (N) pA1
LC Call Number: Not in LC Collection
Magazine Index Micro Film: None
Violence in television - Social aspects

Atkin, Charles K., Gantz, Walter
Television news and political socialization. Public opinion quarterly, v. 42, summer 1978: 183-198.
"Elementary school children frequently watch child-oriented news segments on Saturday morning television, and occasionally view network newscasts. News viewing is mildly associated with both political knowledge and public affairs interest for older children, but younger viewers learn little. Parent-child discussion of news is also related to newscast exposure."
Political socialization [U.S.] / Television news [U.S.] / Television and children [U.S.]

Bang, pow, ho, ho, ho. (violence in cartoons) (editorial)
America (New York, N.Y. 1909) Dec. 20, 1980 v. 143 p. 389(1)
LC Call Number: BX801.A5; Microfilm 02861 (1949-1968) MicRR
Magazine Index Micro Film: None
violence in television - public opinion / television and children - public opinion / National Coalition on TV. Violence - reports / cartoons and children - public opinion

Baruch, Rhoda
Why the fuss about television violence? (Commentary) (Special section: Action Hours)
Broadcasting and Cable, August 29, 1994, v. 124 n. n35 p. 40(2)
LC Call Number: TK6540B85
Business Index Micro Film: None
To remove violence from TV is to deny the phenomenon exists. It is far better to make it an instructive experience for viewers. Gratuitous violence should be eliminated entirely, and other violent displays should be depicted as a last-resort option, something socially undesirable. Broadcasters should concentrate on conveying constructive methods for

dealing with anger.
Violence in television - Standards / Television broadcasting - Censorship.

Bellafante, Ginia
Freedom of speech. (actor Michael Moriarty rants against Janet Reno for her anti-TV
violence campaign) (Brief Article)
Time (Chicago), Feb. 14, 1994, v. 143 n. 7 p. 75(1)
LC Call Number: AP2.T37; Microfilm 02914 (1923-) MicRR
Magazine Index Micro Film: None
Moriarty, Michael - Attitudes / Reno, Janet - Public opinion
Actors - Attitudes / Violence in television - Public opinion

Benton, Sarah
In praise of canceling TV violence
New statesman (1975), Sept. 4, 1987, v. 114 p. 10(1)
LC Call Number: AP4.N64; Microfilm (0) 83/132 (1981-1983) MicRR
Magazine Index Micro Film: None
Grade, Michael - Management
Television broadcasting - United Kingdom / Violence in television - Public opinion
Great Britain

Berman, David R., Stookey, John A.
Adolescents, television, and support for government. Public opinion quarterly, v. 44, fall
1980: 330-340.
Using data from a 1978 study of 600 teenagers in Phoenix, Ariz., the authors find "a
negative relationship between the amount of television watching and support for all levels
of government." Suggests that content analysis is necessary to judge the relationship
between viewing of entertainment programs and youths' affective orientations toward
government, and that local news contributes more to political malise than does network
news.
Political socialization [U.S.] / Television and children [U.S.] / Politics and government
[U.S.] Public opinion / Television news [U.S.] Evaluation / Youth in politics [U.S.] /
Public opinion [Phoenix, Arizona]

Biocca, F.; Brown, J.; Shen, F.; Bernhardt, J.M.; Batista, L.; Kemp, K.; Makris, G.; West,
M.; Lee, J.; Straker, H.; Hsiao, H. & Carolone, E. (1997)
Assessment of Television's Anti-Violence Messages: University of North Carolina at
Chapel Hill Study. In: Federman, J. (Ed.): National Television Violence Study. Volume
1, pp. 413-530, Thousand Oaks: Sage Publications, 1997, 568 p., ISBN 0-7619-0802-1.

Buck, Rinler
Coming battle over TV violence (Editorial)
Brandweek, August 9, 1993, v. 34 n. n32 p. 14(1)
LC Call Number: HF5801.A43

Business Index Micro Film: None
Television programmers need to address the issue of violence in children's shows. More parents and political groups are protesting violence in children's shows. While broadcasters claim that advertisements influence viewers, they deny that violence influences viewers. In the 1990s, television programmers who want to run effective advertisements will need to move away from violent shows and target quality audiences. Violence in television - Analysis / Television broadcasting industry - Moral and ethical aspects

Bunce, Alan
The bottom line on TV violence. (networks must face reduction of violence on television) (Column)
The Christian Science Monitor (1983) June 18, 1993, v. 85 n. n142 p. 14
LC Call Number: Newspaper
Business Index Micro Film: None
Violence in television - Moral and ethical aspects / Television broadcasting industry - Moral and ethical aspects

Came, Barry
A child's crusade: more than a million Canadian's back a young Quebecer who abhors TV violence. (Cover Story)
Maclean's, Dec. 7, 1992, v. 105 n. n49 p. 46(2)
LC Call Number: AP5.M2; Microfilm (0) 84/200 (1909-1982) MicRR
Magazine Index Micro Film: None
Violence in television - Public opinion / Canada - Social aspects. Canada

Carter, Bill
Police drama under fire for sex and violence. (television program 'N.Y.P.D. Blue') (Living Arts Pages)
The New York Times, June 22, 1993, v. 142 p. B1(N) pC13
LC Call Number: Not in LC Collection
Magazine Index Micro Film: None
American Family Association - Social policy / N.Y.P.D. Blue (Television program) - Criticism, interpretation, etc. / Violence in television - Public opinion

Cassidy, J. Warren
Here we stand. (guns on television) (column)
American rifleman, March 1989, v. 137 n. n3 p. 7(1)
LC Call Number: SK1.A52
Magazine Index Micro Film: None
Firearms - television use / Violence in television - public opinion / National Rifle Association - public relations / Gun control - public opinion

Centerwall, Brandon S.
Television and violent crime. Public interest, no. 111, spring 1993: 56-71.
"We do not address the problem of motor vehicle fatalities by calling for a ban on cars. Instead, we emphasize safety seats, good traffic signs, and driver education. Similarly, to address the problem of television-inspired violence, we need to promote time-channel locks, program rating systems, and viewer education about the hazards of violent programming. In this way we can protect our children and our society."
Television and children [U.S.] / Violence in television [U.S.]

Cheung, C.K. & Chan, C.F. (1996)
Television Viewing and Mean World Value in Hong Kong's Adolescents. Social Behavior and Personality 24(1996)4, pp. 351-364, ISSN 0301-2212.

Christian leaders intensify their efforts against TV violence
Christianity Today (Washington), June 13, 1986, v. 30 p. 46(2)
LC Call Number: BR1.C6418; Microfilm (0) 83/406 (1981-   ) MicRR
Magazine Index Micro Film: 34F3870
Donald Wildmon. (portrait)
Wildmon, Donald E. - political activity
Christian leaders for Responsible Television - Management / violence in television - public opinion

Coe, Steve
Iger defends networks' record. (ABC Network Group President Bob Iger on TV Violence) (Brief Article)
Broadcasting and Cable, Jan. 17, 1994, v. 124 n. n3 p. 115(1)
LC Call Number: TK6540B85
Business Index Micro Film: None
Iger, Robert - Attitudes
Violence in television - Public opinion / Television broadcasting industry - Censorship

Coe, Steve
No warnings for fall, says Sagansky. (CBS Entertainment President Jeff Sagansky; advisories about violence on television programs)
Broadcasting and Cable, July 26, 1993, v. 123 n. n30 p. 20(2)
LC Call Number: TK6540B85
Business Index Micro Film: None
Accusations of excessive violence on television programs broadcast by CBS Entertainment have been exaggerated, according to Jeff Sagansky, president. During the press tour of the Television Critics Assn, Sagansky admitted that violence exists on TV, but he called for cable broadcasting to accept its share of responsibility. Also, he expressed hope that Congress will attack the roots of violence in our society, including the proliferation of guns.

Sagansky, Jeff - Addresses, essays, lectures
Violence in television - Public opinion / Television broadcasting industry - Social policy

Colson, Charles
Prime-time executives. (column)
Christianity Today (Washington), July 22, 1991, v. 35 n. n8 p. 64(1)
LC Call Number: BR1.C6418; Microfilm (0) 83/406 (1981-   ) MicRR
Magazine Index Micro Film: 60L3471
Capital punishment - Moral and ethical aspects / Violence in television - Moral and
ethical aspects / Criminal justice, Administration of - Moral and ethical aspects / KQED,
San Francisco, California (Radio) - Public opinion

Conway, M. Margaret, and others.
The news media in children's political socialization. Public opinion quarterly, v. 45,
summer 1981: 164-178.
Considers "the impact of news media use on children's political information, political
participation, and attitudes toward the political regime."
Television and children [U.S.] / Political socialization [U.S.]

Cook, Thomas D.; Kendziersski, Deborah A.; Thomas, Stephen V.
The implicit assumptions of television research: an analysis of the 1982 NIMH report on
Television and Behavior (television research)
Public opinion quarterly, Summ 1983, v. 47 p. 161 (41)
LC Call Number: HM261.A1P8; Microfilm 06208 (1959; 1977-1978) MicRR
Magazine Index Micro Film: None
Himmelweit's model of television and its influences. (chart) Results of LISREL analyses
for elementary boys and girls. (table) Relationship between lagged television coefficients
and delay between measurement waves. (graph) Results of the LISREL analyses for
teenage boys. (table)
Television in education - research / television in health education - research / television -
research / violence in television - research / crime in television - research / television and
youth - research / television and children - research

Cooke, Patrick
TV causes violence? Says who? (criticism of accusations of social harm of television)
(Column)
The New York Times, August 14, 1993, v. 142 p. 11(N) p19
LC Call Number: Not in LC Collection
Magazine Index Micro Film: None
Violence in television - Public opinion / Television - Psychological aspects / Television
and children - Public opinion

Corlin, Richard F.; Clegg, Legrand H., II; Stowe, Fred
Limiting violence on television. (Letter to the Editor)

The Los Angeles Times, Dec. 26, 1992, v. 112, p. B7
LC Call Number: Newspaper 7114-X
Business Index Micro Film: NONE
Violence in television - Prevention / Television broadcasting industry - Social policy

Critics' hour. (hypocrisy of government officials who want to censor what is offered by
the entertainment industry to protect society from violent programs) (Editorial)
National review (New York); Nov. 15, 1993, v. 45, n. n22 p 21(2)
LC Call Number: AP2.N3545; Microfilm 06959 (1967-1974) MicRR
Magazine Index Micro Film: None
Reno, Janet - Social policy / Simon, Paul (Politician) - Social policy
Violence in mass media - Social aspects / Violence in television - Social aspects /
Violence in motion pictures - Social aspects

Dempsey, John
Sponsor backlash catches first run syndie shows. (exploitive TV shows)
Variety, May 10, 1989, v. 335, n. n4 p. 71(2)
LC Call Number: PN2000.V3 Folio; Microfilm 03722 (1905-   ) MicRR
Magazine Index Micro Film: None
Violence in television - public opinion / Sex in television - public opinion /
Sensationalism in television - public opinion / Syndication of television programs -
marketing / Crimes of Passion 2 (television program) - marketing / Scandals II (television
program) - marketing

Dissatisfied customers in televisionland. (survey of attitudes) (Brief Article)
ADWEEK Eastern Edition, Sept. 12, 1994, v. 35 n. n37 p. 19(1)
LC Call Number: May or May Not Be in LC. Search further.
Business Index Micro Film: None
Television viewers - Attitudes / Violence in television - Surveys / Sex in television -
Surveys

Duclos, D. (1994)
Le complexe du loup-garou: la fascination de la violence dans la culture américaine.
Paris: Editions la Découverte, 1994, 272 p., ISBN 2-70712-323-4.

Eighty Eight percent say TV violence makes kids violence. (results of readership survey)
Glamour, Feb. 1987, v. 85 p. 89(1)
LC Call Number: TT500.G46
Magazine Index Micro Film: 37K5561
Television and children - public opinion / Glamour (Periodical) - surveys / Violence in
television - public opinion

Farewell, trash, goodbye, Nielsens. (lack of sponsorship for television programs with sex
and violence)

U.S. News & World Report, May 15, 1989, v. 106 n. n19 p. 14(2)
LC Call Number: JK1.U65; Microfilm 06106 (1933-) MicRR
Magazine Index Micro Film: 49K0281
Violence in television - public opinion / Corporate sponsorship - Moral and ethical aspects / Television broadcasting - Moral and ethical aspects / Sex in television - public opinion

Feirstein, Bruce
I'm no prude, but... (luridness in TV)
TV guide, Jan. 1, 1994, v. 42, n. n1 p. 22(4)
LC Call Number: Microfilm 06378 (1953-   ) MicRR
Magazine Index Micro Film: None
Sensationalism in television - Public opinion / Violence in television - Public opinion

Flint, Joe
Criticism of TV violence grows. (Brief Article)
Broadcasting and Cable March 29, 1993, v. 123 n. n13 p. 14(1)
LC Call Number: TK6540B85
Business Index Micro Film: 70T1103
Foundation to Improve Television - Political activity / Violence in television - Public opinion/ Television broadcasting - Censorship

Flint, Joe
MTV moves 'Beavis and Butt-Head.' (moves controversial cartoon to late-night time slot) (Brief Article)
Broadcasting and Cable, Oct. 25, 1993, v. 123 n. n43 p. 29(1)
LC Call Number: TK6540B85
Business Index Micro Film: None
Cartoon television programs - Public opinion / Violence in television - Public opinion / Cable television broadcasting industry - Calendars, schedules, etc.

Foote, Susan Bartlett; Mnookin, Robert H.
The "kid vid" crusade. Public interest, no. 61, fall 1980: 90=105.
Evaluates where the FTC made a disastrous political miscalculation in its campaign to protect children from exploitation by television advertising.
Television advertising [U.S.] / Television and children [U.S.] / Government regulation [U.S.] / U.S. Federal Trade Commission

Forshey, Gerald E.; Mahan, Jeffery
Critique of media lacks imagination. (letter)
The Christian century (1902) Jan. 1, 1986, v. 103 p. 20(2)
LC Call Number: BR1.C45; Microfilm 01962 (1900-   ) MicRR
Magazine Index Micro Film: 32B5910
violence in television - analysis

Foster, Catherine
After outcry, Australian TV agrees to limit adult programs. (3 major networks agree to limit violent and sexually graphic movies)
The Christian Science Monitor (1983), Dec. 2, 1992, v. 85 n. n5 p. 7
LC Call Number: Newspaper
Business Index Micro Film: NONE
Television broadcasting - Production and direction / Violence in television - Australia / Sex in television - Australia / Television programs - Production and direction / Australia - Social aspects
Australia

Frink, Gary; Fulenwider, Geraldine S.
Television: society's smoking gun. (responses to September 7 Opinion page article) (Letter to the Editor)
The Christian Science Monitor (1983), Oct. 12, 1993, v. 85 n. n221 p. 18
LC Call Number: Newspaper
Business Index Micro Film: None
Violence in television - Social aspects / Cable television broadcasting industry - Laws, regulations, etc.

Gaddy, Gary D.
Television's impact on high school achievement. Public opinion quarterly, v. 50, fall 1986: 340-359.
Considers that the nature of activities displaced by television viewing determines how this viewing affects academic achievement.
Television and children [U.S.] / Educational television [U.S.] / Social surveys [U.S.] / Academic performance [U.S.]

Gay, Verne
Rev. Wildmon's 'hit parade:' Mennen, Clorox make list; ClearTV declares a year-long boycott on the 'worst offenders.' (Christian Leaders for Responsible TV)
Variety, July 19, 1989, v. 336, n. n1 p. 45(1)
LC Call Number: PN2000.V3 Folio; Microfilm 03722 (1905-) MicRR
Magazine Index Micro Film: None
Wilmon, Donald E. - political activity
ClearTV - political activity / Religion and politics - personalities / Violence in television - public opinion / Sex in television - public opinion / Fundamentalism - Political aspects / Television broadcasting - public opinion

Glasser, Ira
TV causes violence/ Try again. (response to a June 1 letter) (Letter to the Editor)
The New York Times, June 15, 1994, v. 143 p. A14 (N) pA2
LC Call Number: Not in LC Collection

Magazine Index Micro Film: None
Violence in television - Demographic aspects / Crime prevention - Social aspects

Goodman, Walter
How harmful is viewing violence? (questions about research on television violence)
(Living Arts Pages)
The New York Times, March 22, 1994, v. 143 p. B3(N) pC22
LC Call Number: Not in LC Collection
Magazine Index Micro Film: None
Violence in television - Public opinion

Groller, Ingrid
Should TV be censored? Yes, Americans say, standards are needed. (Parents Poll)
Parents (Bergenfield) April 1990, v. 65 n. n4 p. 34(1)
LC Call Number: HQ768.P33
Magazine Index Micro Film: 54E0963
Parents - attitudes / Parents' Magazine (Periodical) - surveys / sex in television - public
opinion / Violence in television - public opinion / Censorship - public opinion /
Television broadcasting - censorship

Gunter, B. & Stipp, H. (1992)
Attitudes about Sex and Violence on Television in the United States and in Great Britain:
A Comparison of Research Findings. Medienpsychologie 4(1992)4, pp. 267-286, ISSN
0936-7780.

Gunter, Barrie
Violence on television: what the viewers think / Barrie Gunter, Mallory Wober. -
London: J. Libbey: IBA, c1988
xiii, 73 p.: ill.; 25 cm. (Television research monograph, ISSN 0951-3582) Bibliography:
p. 72.
Violence in television - Great Britain. Television broadcasting - Social aspects - Great
Britain. Television programs - Great Britain - Public opinion. Television and children -
Great Britain. Public opinion - Great Britain. I. Wober, J.M. (J. Mallory) II. Title. III.
Series.

Guttman, Monika
A kindler, gentler Hollywood. (Violence in Entertainment)
U.S. News & World Report, May 9, 1994, v. 116 n. n18 p. 38(8)
LC Call Number: JK1.U65; Microfilm 06106 (1933-   ) MicRR
Magazine Index Micro Film: None
Violence in television - Public opinion / Violence in motion pictures - Public opinion /
Entertainment industry - Social policy

Harriott, John
Death-dealing heroes are not "good guys." (In my view) (column)

Reader's Digest (Canadian edition), Nov. 1986, v. 129 p. 145(2)
LC Call Number: AP5
Magazine Index Micro Film: None
Violence in television - public opinion / Heroes - public opinion / Violence in motion
pictures - public opinion

Have it your way. (Notebook - Burger King succumbs to Christian pressure group on
'family values' TV policy, then sponsors violent show)
The New Republic, Dec. 24, 1990, v. 203 n. n26 p. 7(1)
LC Call Number: AP2.N624; Microfilm 03363 (1914-   ) MicRR
Magazine Index Micro Film: 57L0224
Violence in television - Public opinion / Christian Leaders for Responsible Television -
Anecdotes, cartoons, satire, etc. / Religion and politics - Anecdotes, cartoons, satire, etc. /
The Stranger Within (Television program) - Public opinion

Henry, William A., III
Another kind of ratings war. (campaign against TV sex violence)
Time (Chicago), July 6, 1981, v. 118 p. 17(3)
LC Call Number: AP2.T37; Microfilm 02914 (1923-   ) MicRR
Magazine Index Micro Film: None
Wildmon, Donald - aims and objectives
Coalition for Better Television - aims and objectives / Television - Advertising -
economic aspects / television serials - public opinion / conservatism - television use / sex
in television - public opinion / violence in television - public opinion

Hickey, Neil; Range, Peter Ross
Clinton on TV's clout. (President Clinton) (Interview)
TV Guide, March 26, 1994, v. 42 n. n13 p. 16(4)
LC Call Number: Microfilm 06378 (1953-   ) MicRR
Magazine Index Micro Film: None
Clinton, Bill - Interviews
Violence in television - Public opinion / Presidents - Interviews

Holtzman, Joseph M.; Akiyama, Hiroko
What children see: the aged on television in Japan and the United States. Gerontologist,
v. 25, Feb. 1985: 62-68.
"In this cross-national comparison of Japanese and American television programs most
often watched by children, the frequency and quality of the portrayal of older characters
were evaluated. Surprisingly, American television was found to portray older characters
more frequently and more positively than did Japanese television."
Television and children [U.S.] / Television and children [Japan] / Aged - Public opinion /
Public opinion [U.S.] / Public opinion [Japan]

Hudis, Mark
Hotter than they think? Will a claim that Beavis & Butt-Head made a kid burn down his
home change the state of today's cartoons? Probably not.
MEDIAWEEK, Oct. 18, 1993, v. 3 n. n42 p. 10(1)
LC Call Number: HF6146.T42M43
Business Index Micro Film: None
A woman in Moraine, OH, claims that an episode of the 'Beavis and Butt-Head'
television program inspired her five-year-old son to burn down the family's house, killing
his two-year-old sister. MTV Networks Inc., producer of the show, denies responsibility
for the tragedy, but is modifying the program to prevent such occurrences in the future.
'Beavis and Butt-Head' is a cartoon that attracts children who are definitely influenced
by violence on television, according to some psychologists.
Beavis and Butt-Head (Television program) - Public opinion / Violence in television -
Public opinion / Television programs for children - Social aspects

Hughes, John
Cleaning up the small screen. (Bill Clinton should use influence in Hollywood to clean
up pornography and violence in movies and on television) (Column)
The Christian Science Monitor (1983) June 3, 1993, v. 85 n. n131 p. 18
LC Call Number: Newspaper
Business Index Micro Film: None
Clinton, Bill - Social policy
Motion picture industry - Moral and ethical aspects / Television production companies -
Moral and ethical aspects / Violence in television - Moral and ethical aspects / Violence
in motion pictures - Moral and ethical aspects / Sex in mass media - Moral and ethical
aspects

Hughes, Michael
The fruits of cultivation analysis: a reexamination of some effects of television watching.
Public opinion quarterly, v. 44, fall 1980: 287-302.
"A set of items from the General Social Survey for 1975 and 1977 measuring alienation
and fear of walking near one's home at night, which were claimed by Gerbner et al.
(1978a) to be related to heavy television watching, are reanalyzed with simultaneous
controls for age, sex, race, income, education, hours worked per week outside the home,
church attendance, membership in voluntary associations and population size. The effects
of television watching on responses to these items which were claimed by Gerbner et al.
are largely absent in this analysis."
Television program [U.S.] / Human behavior [U.S.] / Violence in television [U.S.] /
Social surveys [U.S.]

In search of a knockout. (National Coalition on Television Violence vs. Olympic boxing)
Christianity Today (Washington), April 7, 1989, v. 33 n. n6 p. 50(1)
LC Call Number: BR1.C6418; Microfilm (0) 83/406 (1981-   ) MicRR
Magazine Index Micro Film: 49D3336

Thomas Radecki. (portrait)
Radecki, Thomas - political activity. National Coalition on Television Violence - Management / Boxing - public opinion / Violence in television - political aspects

Jablonski, C.M. & Zillmann, D. (1995)
Humor's Role in the Trivialization of Violence. Medienpsychologie (1995)7, pp. 122-133, ISSN 0936-7780.

Jacobsen, B. (1994)
Film- og videogramrett [Film and Video Legislation]. Oslo: TANO, 1994, 276 p., ISBN 82-518-3265-9.

Jarvis, Jeff
Witness to the Execution. (TV show)
TV guide, Feb. 12, 1994, v. 42 n. n7 p. 6(1)
LC Call Number: Microfilm 06378 (1953-   ) MicRR
Magazine Index Micro Film: None
Witness to the Execution (Television program) - Public opinion / Violence in television - Public opinion

Jessell, Harry A.
FCC chairman urges psychologists to speak out against TV violence; Hundt tells APA: 'There is on one better-suited to guide our thinking... than you.' (Reed Hundt, American Psychological Association) (Brief Article)
Broadcasting and Cable, August 22, 1994, v. 124 n. n34 p. 32(1)
LC Call Number: TK6540B85
Business Index Micro Film: None
Hundt, Reed - Attitudes
United States. Federal Communications Commission - Officials and employees / American Psychological Association - Political activity / Violence in television - Public opinion

Jessell, Harry A.
Quello lauds 'marketplace' curbs on indecency: says broadcasters, advertisers should listen to citizen groups or face government action. (Federal Communications Commissioner James Queelo) (Brief Article)
Broadcasting and Cable Jan. 27, 1992, v. 122 n., n5 p. 39(2)
LC Call Number: TK6540B85
Business Index Micro Film: 63R0808
Quello, James H. - Attitudes
United States. Federal Communications Commission - Officials and employees / Sex in television - Prevention / Violence in television - Prevention / Political participation - Management / Broadcasting industry - Social aspects

Jillette, Penn
Warning: this is a violent article. (violence in television) (The Playboy Forum)
Playboy (Chicago) Sept. 1994, v. 41 n. n9 p. 46(2)
LC Call Number: AP2.P69 Rare Bk
Magazine Index Micro Film: None
Reno, Janet - Public opinion
Violence in television - Analysis

Krumplitsch, Kellie Brower, Allison
Sex and violence roundly abhorred; large majority voices indignation in latest
'MediaWeek' poll. (Brief Article)
ADWEEK Eastern Edition, Nov. 1, 1993, v. 34 n. n44 p. 16(1)
LC Call Number: May or May Not Be in LC. Search further.
Business Index Micro Film: None
Television programs - Social aspects / Violence in television - Social aspects / Sex in
television - Social aspects / Television viewers - Surveys - Television broadcasting
industry - Statistics

Krumplitsch, Kellie; Brower, Allison
Public enemy no. 1? Most adults are offended by television's sex and violence.
MEDIAWEEK, Nov. 1, 1993, v. 3, n. n44 p. 18(4)
LC Call Number: HF6146.T42M43
Business Index Micro Film: None
A MediaWeek survey reveals that most adults find it offensive to watch sex and violence
in television programs, and even advertisers are nervous about sponsoring such shows.
About 50% of television viewers would not buy products from advertisers of these
shows, according to the survey. The survey backs up Pres Clinton and his
administration's views on television sex and violence, but advertisers do not want the
government to rate shows.
Violence in television - Surveys / Sex in television - Surveys / Television programs -
Public opinion / Television viewers - Attitudes

Leahy, Michael
To Grants, New Mexico, our cities are big, bad places - if you believe prime-time TV
TV Guide, May 3, 1986, v. 34 p. 4(6)
LC Call Number: Microfilm 06378 (1953-   ) MicRR
Magazine Index Micro Film: 33M0007
violence in television - public opinion / Cities and towns - Media coverage / crime in
television - public opinion / rural youth - attitudes

Leonard, John
TV and the decline of civilization. (Editorial)
The Nation (New York, N.Y.) Dec. 27, 1993, v. 257 n. n22 p. 785(5)
LC Call Number: AP2.N2; Microfilm 03323 (1965-1979) MicRR

Magazine Index Micro Film: None
Violence in television - Analysis / Television programs - Social aspects

Lichter, Linda S.; Lichter, S. Robert; Rothman, Stanley
Hollywood and America: the odd couple. Public opinion, v. 5, Dec. 1982-Jan. 1983: 54-58.
Reports results of an interview survey of 104 television producers, executives, and others who "represent the cream of television's creative community." The authors find that members of this elite group "view TV entertainment largely as we might expect on the basis of their social attitudes. Like many other liberal, cosmopolitan, upper status Americans, they believe sex is less of a problem than violence on television, and they see the medium as a source of needed social reform."
Television programs [U.S.] Public opinion / Television industry [U.S.] / Elite (Social sciences) [U.S.] / Liberalism in politics [U.S.] / Public opinion [Los Angeles] / Social surveys [Los Angeles] / Violence in television [U.S.] Public opinion

Louis Harris and Associates
Attitudes about television, sex and contraception: a survey of a cross-section of adult Americans. New York, Planned Parenthood Federation of America, 1987, 86 p.
At head of title: Study no. 874005.
Reports results of a Jan.-Feb. 1987 telephone survey of 1250 adults. "By a substantial 60-37% majority most Americans believe that television stations should be allowed to show contraceptive advertising... The overwhelming majority of Americans (82%) believe that contraceptive advertising on television would encourage more teenagers to use contraceptives... A modest 52-42% majority reject the argument that contraceptive advertising on television would encourage more teenagers to have sex... A huge majority (72%) of Americans say they would not be offended by contraceptive advertising on television."
Television advertising [U.S.] Public opinion / Television and children [U.S.] Public opinion / Contraceptives [U.S.] Public opinion / Public opinion [U.S.]

Lynn, Barry
How to separate the men from the boycotts. (Rev. Donald Wildmon's National Federation for Decency; includes sidebar and excerpts from N.F.D. Journal)
Playboy (Chicago), April 1988, v. 35 n. n4 p. 45(4)
LC Call Number: AP2.P69 Rare Bk.
Magazine Index Micro Film: None
Rev. Donald Wildmon E. - attitudes
Censorship - Societies, clubs, etc. / Sex in television - public opinion / Violence in television - public opinion / Fundamentalism - popular culture

MacIntyre, D.I. & Cantrell, P.J. (1995)
Punishment History and Adult Attitudes Towards Violence and Interpersonal Aggression

in Men and Women. Journal of Social Behavior and Personality 23(1995)1, pp. 23-28, ISSN 0886-1641.

Maddox, William S.; Handberg, Roger
Children view the new President. Youth & Society, v. 12, Sept. 1980: 3-16.
Questions, "does reliance on television as the major source of political information significantly affect how children perceive a new president in the first weeks of his administration?" Concludes from a Feb. 1977 survey of sixth graders in Seminole County, Florida, that children are influenced by partisan identification and general chauvinistic attitudes but not by the source of their political information.
Television and children [U.S.] / Political socialization [U.S.] / Carter Administration - Public opinion / Presidents - Public opinion / Public opinion [Seminole County, Fla.]

Mandese, Joe
Quality-TV group comes to defense of 'NYPD Blue.' (Viewers for Quality Television) (Brief Article)
Advertising Age, April 11, 1994, v. 65 n. n15 p. 8(1)
LC Call Number: HF5801.A276
Magazine Index Micro Film: None
Viewers for Quality Television - Management / American Family Association - Management / NYPD Blue (Television program) - Public opinion / Violence in television - Public opinion

Mann, Judy
A warning label for TV. (About the amount of violence in programs) (Column)
The Washington Post, July 2, 1993, v. 116, p. E3
LC Call Number: Newspaper
Business Index Micro Film: None
Violence in television - Laws, regulations, etc. / Television and children - Social aspects / Television broadcasting industry - Social policy

Meadow, Robert G.
Information and maturation in children's evaluation of government leadership during Watergate. Western political quarterly, v. 35, Dec. 1982: 539-553.
Using data from interviews with 356 elementary students in Philadelphia, the author examines "which children were most affected by Watergate at the time - and who may have been scarred politically - by exploring the relative contributions of mass media information and personal maturation to the evaluation of the President during the crisis."
Watergate affair - Public opinion/ Child psychology [U.S.] / Political socialization [U.S.] / Presidents - Public opinion / Leadership [U.S.] Public opinion / Television and children [U.S.] Elementary school students [Philadelphia] / Public opinion [Philadelphia]

Merlo-Flores, T. (1998)
Why Do We Watch Television Violence? Argentine Field Research. In: Carlsson, U. &

von Feilitzen, C. (Eds.): Children and Media Violence: Yearbook from the UNESCO International Clearinghouse on Children and Violence on the Screen 1998, pp. 155-179, Göteborg: Nordicom, Göteborgs universitet, 1998, 387 p., ISBN 91-630-6358-1.

Mills, Mike
TV violence: Hill may not wait for more industry action. (legislation on television violence)
Congressional Quarterly Weekly Report, Sept. 4, 1993, v. 51 n. n35 p. 2338 (4)
LC Call Number: See Catalogs or Staff
Magazine Index Micro Film: None
As the expiration date approaches for a Congressional antitrust waiver allowing networks to agree on voluntary reduction of TV violence, legislators will be considering several bills to institute further controls. So far NBC, ABC, CBS, Fox, and 15 major cable networks have agreed to air parental advisories before evening prime-time shows which the networks decide are violent. Critics contend that the limited advisories are insufficient. Lawmakers are likely to support proposed legislation such as HR 2888, which would require new TVs to have a device allowing owners to block violent programs. Sen. Paul Simon, who supports voluntary controls, is one of the few choices opposing such legislation.
Violence in television - Political aspects

Mondale, Lester
The stupidity of violence. (column)
The Humanist (Buffalo, N.Y.), Nov.-Dec. 1985, v. 45 p. 31(1)
LC Call Number: B821.A1H8
Magazine Index Micro Film: 33M5952
Violence - social aspects / fighting (psychology) - social aspects / violence in television - public opinion

More violence. (Citizens Task Force to fight video violence) (Brief Article)
Variety, June 21, 1993, v. 351 n. n7 p. 24 (1)
LC Call Number: PN2000.V3 Folio; Microfilm 03722 (1905-   )MicRR
Business Index Micro Film: None
Violence in television - Public opinion / Violence in motion pictures - Public opinion

Muck, Terry
Prime time for discernment. (television viewing) (editorial)
Christianity Today (Washington), Jan. 13, 1989, v. 33 n. n1 p. 19(1)
LC Call Number: BR1.C6418; Microfilm (0) 83/406 (1981-   ) MicRR
Magazine Index Micro Film: 48B3084
Violence in television - analysis / Television viewers - attitudes / Parent and child - Social aspects

Murray, Karen
Striking out at violence on TV. (Canada) (Brief Article)

Variety, May 17, 1993, v. 351 n. n3 p. 61(2)
LC Call Number: PN2000.V3 Folio; Microfilm 03722 (1905-   ) MicRR
Business Index Micro Film: None
Josephson, Wendy - Addresses, essays, lectures
Canadian Cable Television Association - Conferences, meetings, seminars, etc. /
Violence in television - Addresses, essays, lectures / Television broadcasting industry -
Social aspects

Music videos rapped for 'senseless violence.'
Variety, Dec. 12, 1984, v. 317 p. 1(2)
LC Call Number: PN2000.V3 Folio; Microfilm 03722 (1905-) MicRR
Magazine Index Micro Film: None
National Coalition on Television Violence - social policy / violence in television -
Societies, clubs, etc. / Music videos - public opinion

NBC alone of major networks aired graphic footage of Emilio Nunez shooting to death
his ex-wife, Maritza Munoz (National Broadcasting Co.)
Television Digest, Jan. 25, 1993, v. 33 n. n4 p. 7(1)
LC Call Number: May or May Not Be In LC. Search further.
Business Index Micro Film: 69T1059
Television broadcasting industry - Social policy / Violence in television - Moral and
ethical aspects

Neff, David
Prime-Time shoot-out; now that the networks have fired their censors, it is up to the
public to fight bad taste and impropriety on TV. (editorial)
Christianity Today (Washington); Oct. 6, 1989, v. 33 n. n14 p. 14(1)
LC Call Number: BR1.C6418; Microfilm (0) 83/406 (1981-) MicRR
Magazine Index Micro Film: 51J2731
Sex in television - Moral and ethical aspects / Violence in television - Moral and ethical
aspects / Christian Leaders for Responsible Television - political activity / Evangelists -
political activity

Neff, David
Why trust TV execs? (legislation planned for television violence) (Editorial)
Christianity today (Washington), August 16, 1993, v. 37 n. n9 p. 15(1)
LC Call Number: BR1.C6418; Microfilm (0) 83/406 (1981-   ) MicRR
Magazine Index Micro Film: None
Markey, Edward J. - Political activity / Simon, Paul (Politician) - Political activity
Violence in television - Laws, regulations, etc./ Television and children - Public opinion

Newhagen, J.E. (1998)
TV News Images That Induce Anger, Fear and Disgust: Effects on Approach-Avoidance and Memory. Journal of Broadcasting and Electronic Media 42(1998)2, pp. 265-276, ISSN 0883-8151.

Oliver, James
Washington report. (column)
Guns & Ammo, March 1980, v. 24 p. 6(2)
LC Call Number: TS535.G83
Magazine Index Micro Film: None
Hawaii Five-O (television program) - production and direction / violence in television - sociological aspects

Olson, Caity
Ad boycott concern is real; marketers urge offended TV views to just press 'off.' (advertisers tell consumers concerned about sex and violence in television programs to change the channel rather than boycott their products) (Brief Article)
Advertising Age, June 13, 1994, v. 65 n. n25 p. 3(1)
LC Call Number: HF5801.A276
Magazine Index Micro Film: None
Advertising Age (Periodical) - Surveys / Sex in television - Public opinion / Violence in television - Public opinion / Boycotts - Planning / Television advertising - Contracts

Oster, Jerry; Thackray, Barbara M.; Fox, Sanford, J.; Perron, Wendy
TV violence is the thing that never dies. (continuation of violence on television) (Letter to the Editor)
The New York Times, July 16, 1993, v. 142 p. A10(N) pA1
LC Call Number: Not in LC Collection
Magazine Index Micro Film: None
Violence in television - Public opinion / Television programs - Rating

Philips, Christopher Lee
Task force on TV violence formed. (Citizens Task Force on TV Violence) (Brief Article)
Broadcasting and Cable, June 14, 1993, v. 123 n. n24 p. 69(1)
LC Call Number: TK6540B85
Business Index Micro Film: 71Z2349
Citizens Task Force on TV Violence - Management/ Violence in television - Political aspects

Playing Reno Roulette. (Janet Reno's attempt to control violence on television) (Editorial)
MEDIAWEEK, Oct. 25, 1993, v. 3 n. n43 p. 8(1)
LC Call Number: HF6146.T42M43
Business Index Micro Film: None

US Attorney General Janet Reno's threat to regulate television broadcasting for depictions of violence represents a threat to the freedom of information in a democracy. Television broadcasters are not protected from this threat as much as print media because stations are licensed by the government. The public has the right to watch whatever it chooses on television and can vote its approval by changing channels or turning sets off. Regulation of television content would set a precedent that can lead to increased government censorship.
Reno, Janet - Social policy
Violence in television - Public opinion / Television broadcasting - Censorship

Pollak, Richard
Videotic maniacs. (violence in video games) (editorial)
The Nation (New York, N.Y.) Dec. 19, 1988, v. 247 n. n19 p. 673 (1)
LC Call Number: AP2.N2; Microfilm 03323 (1965-1979) MicRR
Magazine Index Micro Film: 47J0302
National Coalition on Television Violence - research / Violence in television - research / Video games - evaluation

Postrel, Virginia I.
TV or not TV? (Congress deliberates on censorship) (Editorial)
Reason, August-Sept. 1993, v. 25 n. n4 p. 4(2)
LC Call Number: H1.R35
Magazine Index Micro Film: None
Television - Censorship / Violence in television - Analysis

Powers, Run
The new 'holy war' against sex and violence.
TV Guide, April 18, 1981, v. 29 p. 6(5)
LC Call Number: Microfilm 06378 (1953-   ) MicRR
Magazine Index Micro Film: None
Wildmon, Don - interviews
Violence in television - public opinion / crime in television - public opinion / television broadcasting - moral and religious aspects / sex in television - public opinion / Coalition for Better Television - aims and objectives

Reel violence. (television violence) (Editorial)
The Lancet, Jan. 15, 1994, v. 343 n. n8890 p. 127 (2)
LC Call Number: R31.L3
Magazine Index Micro Film: None
Regulation of television and movie violence is poorly managed in the U.S. By the time they are 11 years old, children watching US television will have seen 100,000 violent acts in addition to 8,000 murders. In the 1950s, only 15% of prime-time television shows featured crime and violence. By 1990, 70% to 80% of prime-time programs featured at least one threat to hurt or kill a person. A noticeable change in television violence

occurred in the 1980s when violence in weekend programming for children increased by 36%. In June 1993, the television networks began broadcasting warnings to parents about the violent content of the programs. This step does not affect the large amount of cable-based programming. The Ratings Board of the Motion Picture Association of America assigns ratings by age category to US films. The only requirement to be appointed to the Board is to be a parent. Members receive fees from the movie industry. The Ratings Board bases its recommendations only on the violent actions that are seen and not on what can be imagined. It does not consider the psychological effects of violence or the maturity levels of different age classifications. The Board also assumes that responsible parents regulate movie viewing

Violence in television - Laws, regulations, etc./ Television and children - Psychological aspects / Violence in motion pictures - Rating

Reno endorses bills to deal with TV violence. (Attorney General Janet Reno)
Television Digest, Oct. 25, 1993, v. 33 n. n43 p. 1(2)
LC Call Number: May or May Not Be in LC. Search further.
Business Index Micro Film: 74N0532
Attorney Gen. Janet Reno testified before the Senate Commerce Committee that the regulation of violence on TV is constitutionally sound. Although Reno praised the entertainment industry's use of programming advisories, she maintained that considerable work needs to be done to curb violence. A major stumbling block in this task is the exact definition of what can be constructed as violent. A listing of the bills before the Senate committee are presented.

Reno, Janet - Public opinion
United States. Congress. Senate. Committee on Commerce, Science and Transportation - Laws, regulations, etc. / Violence in television - Laws, regulations, etc. / Television broadcasting industry - Laws, regulations, etc.

Rev. Wildmon pushes Mazda to pull ads. (Donald Wildmon of the American Family Association; Mazda Motors of America Inc.) (News Briefs: Advertisers) (Brief Article)
MEDIAWEEK Oct. 28, 1991, v. 1n, n40 p. 37(1)
LC Call Number: HF6146. T42M43
Business Index Micro Film: NONE
Wildmon, Donald E. - Influence
American Family Association - Officials and employees / Saturday Night Live (Television program) - Public opinion / Automobile industry - Advertising / Violence in television - public opinion / Television advertising - Planning / Sex in television - Public opinion

Righteous watcher of the airwaves. (Reverend Donald Wildmon)
Time (Chicago), July 6, 1981, v. 118 p. 20(1)
LC Call Number: AP2.T37; Microfilm 02914 (1923-   ) MicRR
Magazine Index Micro Film: None
Wildmon, Donald - aims and objectives

Coalition for Better Television - aims and objectives / National Federal of Decency - aims and objectives/ sex in television - public opinion / violence in television - public opinion

Robinson, Deanna C.; Medler, Jerry F.; Genova, B.K.L.
A consumer model for TV audiences: the case of TV violence. Communication research, v. 6, April 1979: 181-202.
"A consumer behavior model is used to explore attitudes toward TV violence and censorship. Five viewing groups with distinct media use characteristics and TV attitudes were found in two separate samples. Findings suggest support for the anti-TV-violence campaign is not universal and that excessive violence is only one of four distinct viewer complaints about television programs." Other areas of dissatisfaction were objectionable content other than violence, low level programming and lack of sufficiently diverse programming.
Censorship [U.S.] Public opinion / Violence in television [U.S.] Public opinion / Public opinion [U.S.] / Market surveys [U.S.]

Rubens, William S.
Sex and violence on TV. Journal of advertising research, v. 21, Dec. 1981: 13-20.
NBC's vice-president for research reports results of an NBC/Roper survey designed "to determine the extent to which the adult American public finds specific entertainment programs objectionable because of sex, profanity, and/or violence content," and to correlate responses with the religious beliefs of those polled. Whereas general questions were found to produce complaints of "too much sex and violence on television," questions on specific programs found only a minority critical of treatment of these themes."
Television programs [U.S.] Public opinion / Violence in television [U.S.] Public opinion / Pornography [U.S.] Public opinion / Television and children [U.S.] Public opinion / Church and social problems [U.S.] / Public opinion polls [U.S.] Evaluation / Public opinion [U.S.] / National Broadcasting Company, Inc.

Scheer, Robert
Violence is us. (Editorial)
The Nation (New York, N.Y.) Nov. 15, 1993, v. 257 n. n16 p. 555 (3)
LC Call Number: AP2.N2; Microfilm 03323 (1965-1979) MicRR
Magazine Index Micro Film: None
Violence in television - Psychological aspects / Television programs for children - Social aspects

Scully, Sean
Turner backs violence guidelines. (Ted Turner) (Brief Article)
Broadcasting and Cable, June 28, 1993, v. 123 n. n26 p. 12(1)
LC Call Number: TK6540B85
Business Index Micro Film: 72P1435

Turner, Ted - Attitudes
Violence in television - Public opinion / Broadcasting industry - moral and ethical aspects

Sprafkin, Joyce N.; Silverman, L. Theresa; Rubinstein, Eli A.
Reactions to sex on television: an exploratory study. Public opinion quarterly, v. 44, fall
1980: 303-315.
"The findings of this study strongly suggest that adults are uneasy about children being
exposed to televised sex."
Television programs [U.S.] / Sex [U.S.] / Television and children [U.S.]

Spring, Beth
As TV violence grows, the campaign against it alters course
Christianity today (Washington), Nov. 25, 1983, v. 27 p. 49(2)
LC Call Number: BR1.C6418; Microfilm (0) 83/406 (1981-   ) MicRR
Magazine Index Micro Film: 16F4199
Thomas Radecki. (portrait)
Koop, C. Everett - addresses, essays, lectures violence in television - public opinion /
National Coalition in Television Violence - social policy / American Medical Association
- social policy / United States. National Institute of Mental Health - reports

Stein, Ben
"Miami Vice." It's so hip you'll want to kill yourself. Public opinion, v. 8, Oct.-Nov.
1985: 41-43.
Examines the world view of the popular television program Miami Vice that "is soaked
up so regularly and so widely by... an impressionable audience" of younger viewers. The
author finds its messages are "anti business, anti-minority, anti-woman, pro-despair,
wildly materialistic."
Television programs [U.S.] Social aspects / Television and children [U.S.] / Minorities in
mass media [U.S.] / Women in mass media [U.S.] / Social life and customs [U.S.] /
Miami Vice (Television program)

Sweeny, Louise
Senator lights fire under TV industry over violence. (Senator Paul Simon threatens to
hold hearings to investigate television violence)
The Christian Science Monitor (1983) August 26, 1992, v. 84 n., n192 p. 9
LC Call Number: Newspaper
Business Index Micro Film: NONE
Simon, Paul (Politician) - Social policy
United States. Federal Communications Commission - Social policy / Violence in
television - Political aspects / Television broadcasting industry - Social policy

Tale of the tape. (murder caught on film by Telemundo, a Spanish network, airs on NBC
Nightly News) (Brief Article)
Time (Chicago), Feb. 1, 1993, v. 141 n. n5 p. 22(1)

LC Call Number: AP2.T37; Microfilm 02914 (1923-   ) MicRR
Magazine Index Micro Film: None
Violence in television - Public opinion / Murder - Reports

Television Violence and Public Policy
James Hamilton (ed.)
Hardcover//Illustrated. 400 pages.Language: English. Pub Date: March 1998
Pub: University of Michigan Press

The experts speak out. (violence in television) (includes advice on controlling the effects
of TV violence) (Panel Discussion)
TV Guide, August 22, 1992, v. 40 n. n34 p. 12(12)
LC Call Number: Microfilm 06378 (1953-   ) MicRR
Magazine Index Micro Film: None
Violence in television - Public opinion

TV violence: more objectionable in entertainment than in newscasts. Washington, Times
Mirror Center for the People and the Press, 1993, 53 p.
"For release, Wednesday, March 25, 1993, A.M."
"Many more Americans express concern about the amount of violence on entertainment
television programs than about the increasingly violent content of broadcast news. TV
news, while seen as containing more graphic violence than in the past, is also seen as
reflecting the reality of a violent society. Further, a large sector of the public appears
desensitized to violent video in newscasts because of the graphically brutal movies and
entertainment television programs it watches. These are the principal findings of a recent
Times Mirror nationwide survey... of 1,516 Americans conducted February 20-23."
Violence in television [U.S.] Public opinion / Television news [U.S.] Public opinion /
Public opinion [U.S.] / Violence research [U.S.]

Tyrer, Kathy
Nets wary as watchdog feds bark about TV violence.
ADWEEK Western Advertising News March 29, 1993, v. 43 n. n13 p. 2(1)
LC Call Number: May or May Not Be In LC. Search further.
Business Index Micro Film: None
Media buyers attending the annual fall program previews by the TV networks were wary
amid reports that the US Senate is planning to force the networks to create industry-wide
standards for sex and violence in programming. Two fall 1993 shows that caused a stir
were 'NYPD Blue,' which contains semi-nudity, and CBS' 'Walker Texas Ranger,'
which contains a graphic exhibition of martial arts. Despite the concern over such shows,
they usually result in only minimal ad revenue losses.
Violence in television - Public opinion / Sex in television - Public opinion / Television
advertising - Social aspects

University of California; Center for Communication and Social Policy (1997)
National Television Violence Study: Volume 1. Thousand Oaks: Sage Publications,
1996, XXI, 568 p., ISBN 0-7619-0802-1.

University of California; Center for Communication and Social Policy (1998)
National Television Violence Study: Volume 2. Thousand Oaks: Sage Publications,
1998, XVIII, 424 p., tab., fig., chart., bibl., ISBN 0-7619-1088-3.

University of California; Center for Communication and Social Policy (1998)
National Television Violence Study: Volume 3. Thousand Oaks: Sage Publications,
1998, 368 p., ISBN 0-7619-1654-7.

Violence and EEO major concerns. (cable television broadcasters express concern over
violence and equal employment opportunity)
Television Digest, March 7, 1994, v. 34 n. n10 p. 7(1)
LC Call Number: May or May Not Be in LC. Search further.
Business Index Micro Film: 76X0665
The National Assn of Broadcasters (NAB) has urged the Federal Communication
Commission to reconsider its policy statements on equal employment opportunity (EEO).
NAB stressed that the EEO statements must be subjected to industry comments and court
review. Meanwhile, broadcasters favored the cable networks' decision to conduct an
independent monitoring system for violence. These broadcasters believed that voluntary
industry efforts at monitoring television violence is much preferable to government
action.
National Association of Broadcasters - Attitudes / Discrimination in employment - Public
opinion / Violence in television - Public opinion/ Cable television broadcasting industry -
Social policy

Violent reactions. (regulating violence on television) (Editorial)
Economist (London), August 13, 1994, v. 332, n. n7876 p. 20(1)
LC Call Number: HG11.E2; Microfilm 03394 (1843-) MicRR
Business Index Micro Film: None
Preliminary evidence that children's exposure to violent media images may be harmful
has prompted critics of TV violence to call for stringent regulations. Rather than censor
violent shows, policy makers should help develop a ratings system that would let parents
restrict access to objectionable material.
Violence in television - Laws, regulations, etc. / Violence in children - Psychological
aspects / Television programs - Rating

Wall, James M.
Rights clash between children and television. (editorial)
The Christian Century (1902), June 19, 1985, v. 102 p. 603(2)
LC Call Number: BR1.C45; Microfilm 01962 (1900-) MicRR
Magazine Index Micro Film: 27L1428

violence in television - social aspects / sex in television - social aspects / television and children - social aspects / National Council of Churches of Christ. Communication Commission - investigations / United States. Constitution. 1st Amendment - interpretation and construction.

William M. Young and Associates
The national PTA public hearing report on "The Effects of Television on Children and Youth." [Chicago] National Congress of Parents and Teachers, 1977, 336 p.
Analyzes testimony from a wide cross section of the American public concerning the effect of television on children.
Television and children [U.S.] Public opinion / Public opinion [U.S.] / Violence in television [U.S.] Public opinion / Television programs [U.S.] Public opinion / Child psychology [U.S.] Public opinion / Censorship [U.S.] Public opinion / Quality of life [U.S.] Public opinion

Wilson, B.J.; Linz, D. & Randall, B. (1990)
Applying Social Science Research to Film Ratings: A Shift from Offensiveness to Harmful Effects. Journal of Broadcasting and Electronic Media 34(1990) 4, Fall, pp. 443-468. ISSN 0883-8151.

Wilson, B.J.; Linz, D.; Donnerstein, E. & Stipp, H. (1992)
The Impact of Social Issue Television Programming on Attitudes Toward Rape. Human Communication Research 19(1992)2, pp. 179-208, ISSN 0360-3989.

Winbush, Don
Bringing Satan to heel: tired of sex and violence on the air, the Rev. Donald E. Wildmon has discovered that the quickest, most effective route to the networks' conscience is through their pocketbooks. (interview)
Time (Chicago), June 19, 1989, v. 133 n. n25 p. 54(2)
LC Call Number: AP2.T37; Microfilm 02914 (1923-   ) MicRR
Magazine Index Micro Film: 50D0707
Donald Wildmon. (portrait)
Wildmon, Donald E. - Interviews
Sex in television - public opinion / Violence in television - public opinion / Television advertising - public opinion

Witkowsky, Kathy
Up in arms over guns in toyland.
Mother Jones, April-May 1986, v. 11 p. 12(1)
LC Call Number: AP2.M79193
Magazine Index Micro Film: 33B3655
Toy firearms - public opinion / toy industry - public opinion / violence in television - public opinion

Wober, J.M.
Televised violence and paranoid perception: the view from Great Britain. Public opinion quarterly, v. 42, fall 1978: 315-321.
Basing his conclusion on two surveys, the authors says "there is no evidence for a paranoid effect of television [violence] on British viewers." Wonders whether Gerbner has convincingly demonstrated the "paranoid effect" in America.
Television viewers [Great Britain] / Violence in television [Great Britain] / Social surveys [Great Britain]

Yahn, Steve
No! To feds monitoring TV. (advertising community responds to attorney general's warning about TV violence)
Advertising Age, Oct. 25, 1993, v. 64 n. n45 p. 1(2)
LC Call Number: HF5801.A276
Business Index Micro Film: 74R3892
Sixty-eight percent of ad professionals responding to an Advertising Age Fax Poll condemned legislative attempts to curb TV violence. But an equal number criticized broadcasters for depicting violence, citing not specific shows, but categories of shows. Twenty percent cited news shows, fifteen percent, cartoons. Violence must be censored by parents, they said, not be broadcasters or the government. The poll was conducted the day after Attorney General Janet Reno endorsed anti-violence legislation.
Violence in television - Public opinion / Advertising industry - Social policy

Young, K. & Smith, M. (1989)
Mass Media Treatment of Violence in Sports and It's Effects. Current Psychology 7(1989)4, Winter, pp. 298-311, ISSN 1046-1310.

Zinsmeister, Karl
Families. Public opinion, v. 10, March-April 1988: 2-19, 51-60.
Partial contents. Having children, helping children, by Karl Zinsmeister and others [at an AEI policy conferences] New family ties: how well are we coping? Thoughts of youth. TV and the family.
Families [U.S.] Public opinion / Social conditions [U.S.] / Television and children [U.S.] / Public opinion [U.S.]

Zipperer, John
Violence foes take aim. (television and media violence)
Christianity today (Washington), Feb. 7, 1994, v. 38 n. n2 p. 40(3)
LC Call Number: BR1.C6418; Microfilm (0) 83/406 (1981-) MicRR
Magazine Index Micro Film: None
American Family Association - Political activity / Violence in television - Public opinion / Television broadcasting industry - Laws, regulations, etc. / Television and children - Moral and ethical aspects

Laws, Guidelines and Standards

Andersen, Kurt
The great TV violence hype. (backlash against violence in television) (Column)
Time (Chicago), July 12, 1993, v. 142 n. n2 p. 66(1)
LC Call Number: AP2.T37; Microfilm 02914 (1923-) MicRR
Business Index Micro Film: None
Violence in television - Standards / Television broadcasting industry - Standards

Andres, Edmund L.
Mild slap at TV violence; Congress seems pleased at industry effort, leaving a slim
chance for stronger action. (Fox Broadcasting, CBS Inc., National Broadcasting Co., and
American Broadcasting Co. agree to warning announcements regarding violent progr
The New York Times, July 1, 1993, v. 142 p. A1(N) pA1
LC Call Number: Not in LC Collection
Business Index Micro Film: None
Violence in television - Laws, regulations, etc. / Television broadcasting industry - Laws,
regulations, etc.

Andrews, Edmund L.
A chip that allows parents to censor TV sex and violence; it's cheap. It's easy. It's
controversial; the broadcasters hate it. (computer chip installed in television could read
electronic coding of offensive programs)
The New York Times, July 18, 1993, v. 142 p. F14 (N) pF1
LC Call Number: Not in LC Collection
Business Index Micro Film: None
Television sets - Innovations/ Television broadcasting industry - Social policy / Cable
television broadcasting industry - Social policy / Violence in television - Standards

Andrews, Edmund L.
TV violence gets a warning. (advisories planned) (June 27-July 2)
The New York Times, July 4, 1993, v. 142 p. E2 (N)pE2
LC Call Number: Not in LC Collection
Magazine Index Micro Film: None
Violence in television - Standards / Television broadcasting industry - Standards

Antitrust exemption on violence. (extension of congressional exemption from antitrust laws for TV networks)
Television Digest, Dec. 6, 1993, v. 33 n. n49 p. 7(1)
LC Call Number: May or May Not Be in LC. Search further.
Business Index Micro Film: 74Y0534
The Justice Dept. granted legislators requests to extend congressional exemption for TV networks from antitrust laws that seeks to reduce TV violence. The original 3-year extension would have expired on Dec. 1, 1993. Since the extension was adopted, TV networks have provided violence warnings for programs and have developed standards aimed at reducing TV violence. Legislators are urging industry officials to make more self-regulatory measures to curb violence on TV.
United States. Department of Justice - Powers and duties / Antitrust law - Evaluation / Violence in television - Laws, regulations, etc.

Antiviolence 'chip.' (TV circuitry for blocking violent programs)
Television Digest, July 5, 1993, v. 33, n. n27 p. 16(1)
LC Call Number: May or May Not Be in LC. Search further.
Business Index Micro Film: 72Q0077
Another TV receiver legislation is expected following the firm endorsement of House Telecommunications Subcommittee Chairman Edward Markey for a TV circuitry capable of blocking violent programs. The system is based on Field 2 of line 21 of vertical blanking interval, which has already gained FCC approval for enhance captioning and extended data service. However, the system still relies on the cooperation of parents to select the appropriate programs for their children.
Markey, Edward J. - Laws, regulations, etc.
Violence in television - Laws, regulations, etc. / Television sets - Innovations

Attorney General addresses TV violence. (Janet Reno said she would support legislation curbing television violence if the industry does not regulate itself) (Brief Article)
Facts on File, Oct. 28, 1993, v. 53 n. n2761 p. 809(1)
LC Call Number: Not in LC Collection
Magazine Index Micro Film: None
Reno, Janet - Social policy
United States. Congress - Social policy / Violence in television - Laws, regulations, etc. / Television broadcasting industry - Laws, regulations, etc.

Auletta, Ken
The electronic parent. (media responsibility concerning depictions of violence)
The New Yorker, Nov 8, 1993, v. 69 n. n37 p. 68(6)
LC Call Number: AP2.N6763; Microfilm 06192 (1925-1978) MicRR
Magazine Index Micro Film: None
Violence in motion pictures - Laws, regulations, etc. / Violence in television - Laws, regulations, etc. / Television and children - Social aspects

Australian Broadcasting Tribunal; Inquiry into Violence on Television (1990)
Decisions and Reasons, Volume I. Sydney: Australian Broadcasting Tribunal, 1990,
XXVI, 174 p., ill., ISBN 0-64214-950-X.

Australian Broadcasting Tribunal; Inquiry into Violence on Television (1990)
Research Findings, Volume II. Sydney: Australian Broadcasting Tribunal, 1990, 259 p.,
ill., fig., tab., ISBN 0-64214-950-X.

Australian Broadcasting Tribunal; Inquiry into Violence on Television (1990)
Summary of Submissions, Volume III. Sydney: Australian Broadcasting Tribunal, 1990,
548 p., ISBN 0-64214-951-8.

Australian Broadcasting Tribunal; Inquiry into Violence on Television (1990)
Conference and Technical Papers, Volume IV. Sydney: Australian Broadcasting
Tribunal, 1990, 245 p., ISBN 0-64214-952-6.

Barak, G. (Ed.) (1994)
Media, Process, and the Social Construction of Crime: Studies in Newsmaking
Criminology. New York: Garland, 1994, XVIII, 322 p., bibl., tab., ISBN 0-8153-1259-3.

Barker, M. & Petley, J. (Eds.) (1997)
Ill Effects: The Media/Violence Debate. London: Routledge, 1997, X, 181 p., ISBN 0-
415-14673-9.

Beeb's new rules on sex, violence. (British Broadcasting Corp.)
Variety, March 8, 1989, v. 334 n. n7 p. 44(2)
LC Call Number: PN2000.V3, Folio; Microfilm 03722 (1905-   ) MicRR
Magazine Index Micro Film: None
Violence in television - Laws, regulations, etc. / Television broadcasting policy - United
Kingdom / Sex in television - Laws, regulations, etc.
Great Britain

Berns, Walter; van den Haag, Ernest
Learning to live with sex and violence. (Congress reluctance to regulate sex and violence
on television and in other entertainment media) (includes related article that defends the
right of pornographic expression as simply another form of dehumanization
National review (New York), Nov. 1, 1993, v. 45, n. n21 p. 56(4)
LC Call Number: AP2.N3545; Microfilm 06959 (1967-1974) MicRR
Magazine Index Micro Film: None
United States. Congress-Social policy / Television broadcasting - Moral and ethical
aspects / Sex in television - Laws, regulations, etc. / Violence in television - Laws,
regulations, etc. / Censorship - Laws, regulations, etc. / Pornography - Laws, regulations,
etc.

Bessant, J. (1995)
Violence, the Media and the Making of Policy: The Closure of Richmond Secondary School. Journal of Australian Studies 43(1995), pp. 45-58, ISSN 0314-769X.

Bill summaries. (Senate Commerce Committee's proposed bills regarding violence on television) (Violence on Television)
The Congressional digest, Dec. 1993, v. 72 n. n12 p. 297(2)
LC Call Number: JK1.C65
Magazine Index Micro Film: None
United States. Congress. Senate. Committee on Commerce, Science and Transportation - Laws, regulations, etc. / Violence in television - Laws, regulations, etc. / Television programs for children - Laws, regulations, etc.

Biocca, F.; Brown, J.; Makris, G.; Bernhardt, J.M. & Gaddy, G. (1998)
Improving Anti-Violence Public Service Announcements Through Systematic Analysis and Design: University of North Carolina, Chapel Hill Study. In: Federman, J. (Ed.): National Television Violence Study. Volume 2, pp. 323-424, Thousand Oaks: Sage Publications, 1998, 424 p., ISBN 0-7619-1088-3.

Boot, Max
New technology shifts debate on TV violence. (microchip in televisions would allow locking out of violent programs, if television broadcasting industry agrees to label them as such)
The Christian Science Monitor (1983), July 6, 1993, v. 85 n. n153 p. 7
LC Call Number: Newspapers
Business Index Micro Film: None
Violence in television - Standards / Television broadcasting industry - Standards / Television sets - Innovations

Bragg, Dabney Elizabeth
Regulation of programming content to protect children after Pacifica. Vanderbilt law review, v. 32, Nov. 1979: 1377-1417.
"This Note examines the 'protect the children' rationale as justification for the regulation of program content to determine if it is likely to withstand future challenges. Initially, the Note reviews the Pacifica decisions to illustrate how the rationale recently has been employed. The Note then considers this rationale in light of traditional first amendment analysis and the interface of that analysis with the rights of children, concluding that the rationale does not justify abridgment of the first amendment."
Television programs [U.S.] Legal cases / Television and children [U.S.] Legal cases / Freedom of speech [U.S.] Legal cases / Radio broadcasting [U.S.] Legal cases/ Censorship [U.S.] Legal cases / Pacifica Foundation v. FCC

Braxton, Greg
TV industry warned: curb violence or Congress will.

The Los Angeles Times, August 3, 1993, v. 112 p. D1
LC Call Number: Newspaper 7114-X
Business Index Micro Film: None
Violence in television - Standards / Television broadcasting industry - Standards / Cable television broadcasting industry - Standards

Broadcasters may accept violence monitoring. (violence in television)
Television Digest, Jan. 24, 1994, v. 34 n. n4 p. 1(2)
LC Call Number: May or May Not Be In LC. Search further
Business Index Micro Film: 75Y0791
Broadcasters prefer independent monitoring for violence in television over the use of V-chip. House Telecom Subcommittee Chmn. Ed. Markey has proposed the use of V-chip, which calls for the installation of a circuitry into televisions that would permit the blocking of violent contents in programming. Broadcasters emphasize that the V-chip could lead to the blocking of programs on controversial issues such as animal rights, sexual content and abortion.
Violence in television - Laws, regulations, etc. / Cable television broadcasting industry - Laws, regulations, etc.

Brodie, John; Robins, J. Max
Webs mad as hell over Capitol crix. (legislation on television violence)
Variety, August 2, 1993, v. 351 n. n12 p. 1(2)
LC Call Number: PN2000.V3 Folio; Microfilm 03722 (1905-) MicRR
Magazine Index Micro Film: None
Violence in television - Political aspects / Television broadcasting industry - Political activity

Calmes, J.C. (1997)
La pornographie et les représentations de la violence en droit pénal: Etude des articles 197 et 135 du code pénal suisse. Francfort sur le Main: Helbing und Lichtenhahn, 1997, XV, 363 p., ill., fig., Diss., ISBN 3-7190-1702-8.

Can't get enough of that sugar crisp: the First Amendment right to advertise to children.
New York University Law Review, v. 54, June 1979: 561-599.
Comment "examines the proposed ban on children's advertising in light of recent developments in the constitutional doctrine of commercial free speech. It concludes that the proposed regulations are overly broad and, therefore, unconstitutional."
Television and children [U.S.] / Television advertising/ Government regulation [U.S.] / Freedom of speech [U.S.] Legal cases / Supreme Court decisions

Canadians come down hard on television violence. (Brief Article)
Broadcasting and Cable, Nov. 8, 1993, v. 123 n. n45 p. 12 (1)
LC Call Number: TK6540B85
Business Index Micro Film: 74T1085

Canada. Canadian Radio - Television and Telecommunications Commission - Social
policy / Canadian Association of Broadcasters - Standards / Violence in television -
Laws, regulations, etc. / Television programs for children - Laws, regulations, etc.

Cerone, Daniel; Shiver, Jube Jr.
Cable, networks offer different violent plans. (plan to reduce violent programming)
The Los Angeles Times, Feb. 2, 1994, v. 113 p. 3
LC Call Number: Newspaper 7114-X
Business Index Micro Film: None
United States. Congress - Social policy / Cable television broadcasting industry - Laws,
regulations, etc. / Television broadcasting industry - Laws, regulations, etc. / Violence in
television - Laws, regulations, etc.

Chadwell, Teena
Local programming fine-tuned to comply with law; warnings to be broadcast for violent
shows. (Focus on Television and Radio)
The Business Journal - Serving Phoenix and the Valley of the Sun, July 30, 1993, v. 13 n.
n39 p. 17(1)
LC Call Number: May or May Not Be in LC. Search further.
Business Index Micro Film: 74Z4928
Television stations - Laws, regulations, etc. / Television programs - Laws, regulations,
etc. / Violence in television - Laws, regulations, etc. / Arizona - Social policy
Arizona

Charren, P.; Szulc, P. & Tchaicha, J. (1995)
A Public-Policy Perspective on Televised Violence and Youth: From a Conversation with
Peggy Charren. Harvard Educational Review 65(1995)2, Summer, pp. 282-291, ISSN
0017-8055.

Chiricos, T.; Eschholz, S. & Gertz, M. (1997)
Crime, News and Fear of Crime: Toward an Identification of Audience Effects. Social
Problems 44(1997)3, August, pp. 342-357, ISSN 0037-7791.

Clayton, Mark
Canadian broadcasters set violence standards for TV. (Canadian Association of
Broadcasters; Canadian Radio-Television and Telecommunications Commission)
The Christian Science Monitor (1983), Dec. 20, 1993, v. 86 n. n17 p. 15
LC Call Number: Newspaper
Business Index Micro Film: None
Canada. Canadian Radio-television and Telecommunications Commission - Standards /
Canadian Association of Broadcasters - Standards / Violence in television - Canada /
Freedom of speech - Canada

Cockburn, Alexander
When US politicians get fired up about screen violence, it has to be election year.
New Statesman & Society, May 17, 1996 v9 n403 p27(1)

Colford, Steven W.
Anti-violence hearing lashes TV advertisers.
Advertising Age. August 2, 1993, v. 64 n. n32 p. 26(1)
LC Call Number: HF5801.A276
Business Index Micro Film: 73R4215
Television advertisers were lambasted at a congressional hearing on TV violence, as
House members proposed that companies were not being selective enough in their choice
of programs. Reps. Ed Markey, D-Mass., and Mike Oxley, R-Ohio, suggested that
advertisers should pull commercials from programs considered violent. Rep. Markey is
sponsoring a bill which would include a microchip in TVs which could block violent
programming. An invitation to the hearing had been extended to twelve major US
advertisers, including AT&T, Ford, Kellogg and Philip Morris, but only AT&T accepted.
Television advertising - Moral and ethical aspects / Violence in television - Laws,
regulations, etc.

Colford, Steven W.
FCC nominee sees merit in ad boycotts. (Federal Communications Commissioner
Rachelle Chong)
Advertising Age, May 16, 1994, v. 65 n. n21 p. 8(1)
LC Call Number: HF5801.A276
Business Index Micro Film: 78U3213
FCC Commissioner Rachelle Chong endorsed consumer boycotts of violent TV show
sponsors, in her Senate confirmation hearing. Chong said Sen. Byron Dorgan's bill
requiring programmers to publish quadrennial lists of violent shows and their sponsors
would aid such efforts. Both Chong and fellow nominee Susan Ness were more reticent
on other issues, most notably the fairness doctrine.
Chong, Rachelle - Evidence / Ness, Susan - Evidence. United States. Federal
Communications Commission - Officials and employees / Violence in television - Laws,
regulations, etc.

Colford, Steven W.
Foes of TV violence persist.
Advertising Age, Feb. 7, 1994, v. 65 n. n6 p. 6(2)
LC Call Number: HF5801.A276
Magazine Index Micro Film: None
Congressional critics of violence on television will persist in their efforts to control the
medium's content even though the television and cable television broadcasting industries
have agreed to independent monitoring of their programs. This monitoring proposal
satisfied Senator Paul Simon's concerns, and it convinced Simon that his proposal to
have the government regulate television content was unnecessary. However,

congressmen such as Edward Markey and Byron Dorgan believe more regulation will be needed.
Simon, Paul (Politician) - Science and technology policy United States. Congress - Science and technology policy / Violence in television - Management / Television broadcasting industry - Management / Cable television broadcasting industry - Management

Colford, Steven W.
Foes of TV violence persist.
Advertising Age, Feb. 7, 1994, v. 65 n. n6 p. 6(2)
LC Call Number: HF5801.A276
Business Index Micro Film: 76S1476
Congressional critics of violence on television will persist in their efforts to control the medium's content even though the television and cable television broadcasting industries have agreed to independent monitoring of their programs. This monitoring proposal satisfied Senator Paul Simon's concerns, and it convinced Simon that his proposal to have the government regulate television content was unnecessary. However, congressmen such as Edward Markey and Byron Dorgan believe more regulation will be needed.
Simon, Paul (Politician) - Science and technology policy. United States. Congress - Science and technology policy / Violence in television - Management / Television broadcasting industry - Management / Cable television broadcasting industry - Management

Colford, Steven W.
Reno lowers boom on violent TV shows. (US Attorney General Janet Reno)
Advertising Age, Oct. 25, 1993, v. 64 n. n45 p. 59(1)
LC Call Number: HF5801.A276
Business Index Micro Film: 74R3972
Attorney General Janet Reno, appearing before a Senate committee, admonished advertisers to reconsider the values they are helping transmit to children when they subsidize violent programming, and she urged parents to boycott the products of such sponsors. Reno also expressed support for the Senate's Jan. 1, 1994 deadline on broadcaster self-regulation. One highlight of the hearing was a clip from the sitcom 'Love and War,' which became the focus of a heated debate over the fine line between legitimate and gratuitous violence.
Reno, Janet - Social policy
Violence in television - Laws, regulations, etc./ Television broadcasting industry - Laws, regulations, etc.

Colford, Steven W.
Senator passes out TV violence grades. (Senator Bryon Dorgan or North Dakota) (Brief Article)
Advertising Age, Dec. 20, 1993, v. 64 n. n53 p. 3(2)

LC Call Number: HF5801.A276
Magazine Index Micro Film: None
Dorgan, Byron L. - Social policy
Violence in television - Rating / Television programs - Rating

Colford, Steven W.
Senator wants to measure TV violence and sponsors. (Byron Dorgan)
Advertising Age, May 17, 1993, v. 64 n. n21 p. 3 (2)
LC Call Number: HF5801.A276
Business Index Micro Film: None
Sen. Byron Dorgan is expected to propose a bill that would require the FCC, or perhaps
another agency, to measure television violence. Under the law, a list of particularly
violent programs and their advertisers would be released. A House version of the bill will
be introduced by Reps. Richard Durbin and George Miller.
Plans for the legislation were disclosed during May 1993
House Energy and Commerce Committee subcommittee on telecommunications and
finance hearings on television violence
United States. Congress - Social policy / Violence in television - Laws, regulations, etc. /
Television broadcasting industry - Laws, regulations, etc.

Colford, Steven W.
TV violence is hit again on Hill. (Congressional action)
Advertising Age, Sept. 12, 1994, v. 65 n. n38 p. 60(1)
LC Call Number: HF5801.A276
Business Index Micro Film: None
Congress is mounting new efforts to control television program and advertising violence.
Sen. Bob Graham has proposed a bill that would prohibit federal bodies from advertising
on violent programs, and Sen. Byron Dorgan has proposed a law that would mandate the
listing of violent programs and their sponsors. The television and advertising industries
are developing strategies to combat the bills.
United States. Congress. Senate - Social policy / Television broadcasting industry -
Political activity / Advertising industry - Political activity / Violence in television - Laws,
regulations, etc. / Television advertising- Laws, regulations, etc.

Colford, Steven W.
TV violence, ad deductibility, food labeling out front (Marketing and Media Outlook: 10
Topics to Watch in 1994)
Advertising Age, Nov. 1, 1993, v. 64 n. n46 p. S10 (2)
LC Call Number: HF5801.A276
Business Index Micro Film: 74Y4324
Several regulatory proposals that could affect advertising are receiving Congressional
attention, including one to limit television commercials and one to control television
violence. The advertising industry is also concerned about attempts to limit tax

deductibility for advertising. Rep Joe Moakley of Massachusetts favors amending the Nutrition Labeling and Education Art to specifically cover food advertising. Sen. Strom Thurman and Rep. Joe Kennedy are sponsoring legislation to put health warnings on all alcoholic beverage advertising. The death of Thurmond's daughter by a drunk driver adds urgency to the bill and may get sympathy votes.

Violence in television - Laws, regulations, etc. / Food - Labeling / Tax deductions - Laws, regulations, etc. / Alcoholic beverages - Advertising / Television advertising - Laws, regulations, etc.

Colford, Steven W.
TV-violence commission sought; Congressman urges action. (Charles Schumer)
Advertising Age, June 14, 1993, v. 64 n. n25 p. 49(1)
LC Call Number: HF5801.A276
Business Index Micro Film: 72S4170
Rep. Charles Schumer proposes a commission to study television violence, which burgeons during semiannual 'sweeps weeks.' The commission, to be headed by the surgeon general and attorney general, would treat TV violence as a health issue and emulate the government campaign to reduce dependence on tobacco. Both houses of Congress are looking for ways to protect children from exposure to excessive violence in television portrayals, and the television and motion picture industries plan a joint meeting to explore solutions.

United States. Congress - Social policy / Violence in television - Laws, regulations, etc. / Broadcasting industry - Social policy

Congress to focus on TV violence.
Television Digest, May 17, 1993, v. 33 n. n20 p. 1(2)
LC Call Number: May or May Not Be in LC. Search further.
Business Index Micro Film: 71S0797
The House Telecom Subcommittee held its initial hearing on violence in programming last May 12, 1993. The hearing was characterized by demands for TV rating standards on violence and criticisms on the persistence of violence in the broadcasting industry despite efforts to control it. Another hearing is slated for June 1993. Meanwhile, Sen. Durenberger has introduced a legislation requiring broadcasters and cable operators to include adequate warnings on programs with violent themes.

Violence in television - Laws, regulations, etc. / Television broadcasting industry - Laws, regulations, etc. / Cable television broadcasting industry - Laws, regulations, etc.

Congressional skeptics challenge violence agreement. (Violence ratings on television programs)
Television Digest, July 5, 1993, v. 33, n. n27 p. 1(3)
LC Call Number: May or May Not Be in LC. Search further.
Business Index Micro Film: 72Q0062
Television network officials disclosed last June 30, 1993, an agreement on voluntary ratings for prime-time television programs. However, the House Telecommunications

Subcommittee belittled the development saying that it was only an initial step. The legislators reiterated that the real focus should be on less violence on television and not merely the imposition of violence ratings.
Violence in television - Laws, regulations, etc. / Television broadcasting industry - Management / Television programs - Rating

Cowan, Geoffrey
See no evil: the backstage battle over sex and violence on television / Geoffrey Cowan. - New York: Simon and Schuster, c1979
323 p.; 23 cm. Bibliography: p. [311]-313. Includes index.
Television - Law and legislation - United States. Violence in television - Law and legislation - United States. Sex in television - Law and legislation - United States. Writers Guild of America. Lear, Norman. United States. Federal Communications Commission. I. Title.

Cumberbatch, G. (1994)
Legislating Mythology: Video Violence and Children. Journal of Mental Health U.K. 3(1994)4, pp. 485-494, ISSN 0963-8237.

Cunningham, S. (1992)
TV Violence: The Challenge of Public Policy for Cultural Studies. Cultural Studies 6(1992)1, January, pp. 97-115, ISSN 0950-2386.

Cutler, Jonathan
Assault on Hollywood. (proposed legislative efforts to control broadcasting violence on television)
Mediaweek, April 4, 1994, v. 4, n. n14 p. 18(6)
LC Call Number: HF6146.T42M43
Business Index Micro Film: 77W0834
Public opposition to television violence has led to proposed federal legislation that would allow the government to regulate the content of television programs. Television producers and others in Hollywood are generally opposed to government regulation of programming but are in disagreement about possible solutions. The lack of a unified opposition to government regulation of programming leaves the television industry at odds with itself over this issue.
Violence in television - Censorship / Television broadcasting industry - Political activity

Dee, Juliet Lushbough
Media accountability for real-life violence: a case of negligence or free speech? Journal of communication, v. 37, spring 1987: 106-138.
Focuses on legal cases, the first six in which "someone was harmed by a third party whose dangerous conduct was allegedly triggered by the media. In the last nine cases, children or teenagers injured or killed themselves while enacting something they had ready about, heard, played in a game, or seem on television."

Violence in television [U.S.] / Violence in mass media [U.S.] Legal cases / Negligence [U.S.] Legal cases / Freedom of speech [U.S.] Legal cases

Diamond, Edwin
The Miami riots: did TV get the real story? TV guide, v. 28, August 30, 1980: 18-22. Argues that the national television network guidelines for "safe, neutral, responsible" coverage of racial disturbances hindered reporting of the Miami riots by focusing only on events, discouraging examination of underlying causes.
Racial violence [Miami, Fla.] / Riots [Miami, Fla.] / Blacks in urban areas [Miami, Fla.] / Television news [U.S.] Standards / Blacks in mass media [U.S.] Standards / Violence in television [U.S.]

Durkin, K. (1992)
Young People, Crime and the Media: Proceedings of the Censorship Conference, 1992. Sydney, N.S.W.: Office of Film and Literature Classification, 1992.

Edwards, Ellen
Cable networks agree to regulate violence. (plan for violence ratings system and technology that would allow viewers to block certain programs)
The Washington Post, Jan. 21, 1994, v. 117 p. A1
LC Call Number: Newspaper
Business Index Micro Film: None
United States. Congress - Social policy / Cable television broadcasting industry - Laws, regulations, etc. / Violence in television - Laws, regulations, etc.

Edwards, Ellen
Violent vs. vapid? (television executives warn that legislation to curb violence on television will result in less intelligent programming)
The Washington Post, Oct. 29, 1993, v. 116 p. B1
LC Call Number: Newspaper
Business Index Micro Film: None
Violence in television - Laws, regulations, etc./ Television broadcasting industry - Laws, regulations, etc. / Television producers and directors - Attitudes

Eggerton, John
Hundt hits television violence. (Federal Communications Commission Chairman Reed Hundt)
(includes related article on response from National Association of Television Program Executives)
Broadcasting and Cable, Jan. 31, 1994, v. 124 n. n5 p. 10(2)
LC Call Number: TK6540B85
Business Index Micro Film: 75Y1356
Hundt, Reed - Social policy

Violence in television - Laws, regulations, etc. / Television broadcasting industry - Laws, regulations, etc.

EIA treads lightly on 'V Chip' issue. (Electronics Industries Association; Violence Chip) Television Digest, Feb. 7, 1994, v. 34 n. n6 p. 15(1)
LC Call Number: May or May Not Be in LC. Search further.
Business Index Micro Film: 76R0176
The Electronics Industries Assn. (EIA), acting as a television set manufacturer's association, has assumed a low profile over a pending bill regarding television program violence still scheduled to undergo legislation by the US Congress. Television set manufacturers are resentful over the proposed legislation that directs them to design sets to respond to transmitted violence ratings by using TV's new extended data service system. The proposal is disadvantageous to the EIA's efforts of luring TV stations and Cable programmers into using the system for program identification.
Electronic Industries Association - Laws, regulations, etc. / Television broadcasting industry - Laws, regulations, etc. / Television equipment and supplies industry - Laws, regulations, etc. / Violence in television - Laws, regulations, etc.

Ericson, R.V.; Baranek, P.M. & Chan, J.B.L. (1991)
Representing Order: Crime, Law, and Justice in the News Media. Milton Keynes: Open University Press, 1991, XII, 383 p., ISBN 0-33509-753-7.

Fabianic, D. (1997)
Television Dramas and Homicide Causation. Journal of Criminal Justice 25(1997)3, pp. 195-203, ISSN 0047-2352.

Ferell, J. & Sanders, C.R. (Eds.)
(1995)
Cultural Criminology. Boston: Northeastern University Press, 1995, 375 p., ISBN 1-55553-236-5.

Ferris, C.F. (1996)
Cultivating Violence. Annals of the New York Academy of Sciences 20(1996)794, pp. 318-328, ISSN 0877-8923.

Field, Laurence
The new commercial speech doctrine and broadcast advertising. Harvard civil rights - civil liberties law review, v. 14, summer 1979: 385-484.
Comment contends that commercial speech is entitled to full protection, on a parity with that accorded political or religious messages and that broadcast advertising should not be accorded less protection than that granted print ads. Also argues that "the FTC's proposed ban on advertising directed at children would violate the first amendment."
Advertising [U.S.] Legal cases / Freedom of speech [U.S.] / Supreme Court decisions / Television and children [U.S.] Law and legislation / Television advertising [U.S.] /

Independent regulatory commissions / U.S. Federal Trade Commission. / Virginia State
Board of Pharmacy v. Virginia Citizens Consumer Council

Fischer, Raymond L.
Is it possible to regulate television violence? USA today (magazine), v. 123, July 1994:
72-75
"The Clinton Administration and Federal Communications Commission's efforts are
facing a mighty challenge from supporters of a strict interpretation of the First
Amendment."
Violence in television [U.S.] / Government regulation [U.S.] / Freedom of Speech [U.S.]
Legal cases / U.S. Federal Communications Commission

Fischer, Raymond L.
Suffer the little children: the FCC does it again. USA today, v. 115, Jan. 1987: 84-86
Argues that the December 1983, Federal Communications Commission order granting
television broadcasters "wide discretion in meeting the programming needs of children"
indicates that "clearly, the FCC has failed to meet its obligation to serve children."
Compares the current policy of the FCC under Mark Fowler to the FCC under Richard E.
Wiley.
Television and children [U.S.] Evaluation / Television and children [U.S.] Standards /
Television and children [U.S.] / Government regulation [U.S.] Evaluation / Fowler, Mark
/ Wiley, Richard E. / Action for Children's Television / U.S. Federal Communications
Commission

Flint, Joe
Quello decries 'siphoning,' TV violence. (Federal Communications Commission
Chairman James
Quello, monopolization of TV sports by pay-per-view TV) (Brief Article)
Broadcasting and Cable March 29, 1993, v. 123 n. n13 p (33(1)
LC Call Number: TK6540B85
Business Index Micro Film: 70T1122
Quello, James H. - Science and technology policy Violence in television - Standards /
Pay per view television - Standards / Television broadcasting of sports - Standards

Flint, Joe
Rakolta enlists ART against TV violence. (Terry Rakolta; Americans for Responsible
Television)
Broadcasting and Cable, March 22, 1993, v. 123 n. n12 p. 37(2)
LC Call Number: TK6540B85
Business Index Micro Film: 70T1058
Americans for Responsible Television Press Terry Rakolta has begun lobbying Congress
for legislation to reduce television violence during children's viewing hours, 4:00 PM to
9:00 PM. In a letter to Rep. John Dingell, she asked that gratuitous violence on network
television be limited by law, just as indecent material has been. Sen. Paul Simon has

already introduced anti-violence legislation in the Senate.

Rakolta, Terry - Political activity / Simon, Paul (Politician) - Political activity / Dingell, John D. - Political activity

Americans for Responsible Television - Political activity / Violence in television - Laws, regulations, etc.

Flint, Joe

Simon delivers violence ultimatum. (Senator Paul Simon; regulating violence on television) (includes related article listing additional proposals on how to reduce TV violence) (Cover Story)

Broadcasting and Cable, August 9, 1993, v. 123 n. n32 p. 18(3)

LC Call Number: TK6540B85

Business Index Micro Film: 72X0635

Sen. Paul Simon told television production executives that Congress would pass regulation on television violence unless the industry monitors itself through the formation of a committee within 60 days. His suggestions were not well received, but the executives did not arrive at any better solution at the one-day conference on TV violence sponsored by the Council for Families & Television. Opinions from television programming executives present at the conference regarding how to reduce television violence are quoted.

Simon, Paul (Politician) - Addresses, essays, lectures

Violence in television - Conferences, meetings, seminars, etc. / Television production companies - Conferences, meetings, seminars, etc.

Foisie, Geoffrey; Sukow, Randy

Schumer wants violence rating for TV shows.

(Representative Charles Schumer)

Broadcasting and Cable, Dec. 21, 1992, v. 122 n. n52 p. 38(2)

LC Call Number: TK6540B85

House Crime and Criminal Justice Subcommittee Chmn Charles Schumer has suggested a system of special warnings or ratings concerning the violence level of television. However, television industry does not favor these types of warnings for parents, fearing that the idea would cause problems with advertisers. Schumer has been frustrated by cable's violent programming and its apparent lack of cooperation with network efforts to set voluntary standards. However, it was revealed that the three major networks did not seek support from others in the television industry in formulating their agreement on curbing violence.

Schumer, Charles E. - Social policy

Television broadcasting industry - Social policy / Cable television broadcasting industry - Social policy / Legislators - Social policy / Violence in television - Standards

Follow-up hearings (on videogame violence)

Television Digest, Dec. 20, 1993, v. 33, n. n51 p. 7(1)

LC Call Number: May or May Not Be in LC. Search further.

Business Index Micro Film: 75P0696
Video games - Laws, regulations, etc. / Video game industry - Laws, regulations, etc. /
Violence in television - Laws, regulations, etc.

French government. (policy on television violence)
Television Digest, Dec. 13, 1993, v. 33, n. n50 p. 9(1)
LC Call Number: May or May Not Be in LC. Search further.
Business Index Micro Film: 75N0098
Violence in television - Laws, regulations, etc. / Television broadcasting industry - Laws,
regulations, etc. / France - Science and technology policy
France

Gerbner, G. (1994)
The Politics of Media Violence: Some Reflections. In: Hamelink, C.J. & Linné, O.
(Eds.): Mass Communication Research: On Problems and Policies: The Art of Asking the
Right Questions: In Honour of James D. Halloran, pp. 133-145, Norwood: Ablex, 1994,
XVIII, 417 p., ISBN 0-89391-738-9.

Gerbner, G. (1995)
Television Violence: The Power and the Peril. In: Dines, G. & Humez, J.M. (Eds.):
Gender, Race, and Class in Media: A Critical Text Reader, pp. 547-557, Thousand Oaks:
Sage Publications, 1995, 648 p., ISBN 0-8039-5164-7.

Gillespie, Nick
Meek previews (federal government's call for less violence in television)
Reason, May 1994, v. 26 n. n1 p. 42(2)
LC Call Number: H1.R35
Magazine Index Micro Film: None
Violence in television - Analysis / Television programs - Analysis

Gilliam, F.D. Jr.; Iyengar, S. & Simon, A. et al. (1996)
Crime in Black and White: The Violent, Scary World of Local News. Harvard
International Journal of Press/Politics 1(1996)3, pp. 6-23, ISSN 1081-180X.

Glogauer, W. (1994)
Kriminalisierung von Kindern und Jugendlichen durch Medien: Wirkungen gewalttätiger,
sexueller, pornographischer und satanischer Darstellungen. Baden-Baden: Nomos Verlag,
1994, 184 p., bibl., ISBN 3-7890-3391-X.

Goldman, Kevin
Networks' plan for TV programs warnings may backfire. (advertisers may pull out of
risky programming) (Column)
The Wall Street Journal, July 1, 1993, p. B1(W) pB
LC Call Number: See Catalogs or Staff

Business Index Micro Film: None
Television advertising - Contracts / Television broadcasting - Laws, regulations, etc. /
Violence in television - Laws, regulations, etc.

Goodman, Walter
About the new labels on TV violence: meanings and motives. (Living Arts Pages)
The New York Times, July 7, 1993, v. 142 p. B1(N) pC13
LC Call Number: Not in LC Collection
Business Index Micro Film: None
Violence in television - Standards / Television broadcasting industry - Standards

Goodman, Walter
About the new labels on TV violence: meanings and motives. (Living Arts Pages)
The New York Times, July 7, 1993, v. 142 p. B1(N) pC13
LC Call Number: Not in LC Collection
Magazine Index Micro Film: None
Violence in the television - Standards / Television broadcasting industry - Standards

Government action. (violence in television)
CQ Researcher, March 26, 1993, v. 3 n. n12 p. 277(2)
LC Call Number: H35.E35
Magazine Index Micro Film: None
A commission appointed by Pres Lyndon Johnson determined television viewing as a
contributory factor in social unrest. Since then, various political and social initiatives
have focused on the industry's self-regulation to reduce portrayals of violence during
broadcast hours when children are most likely to be among the viewers. This would
fulfill a commitment made by the industry as a counterproposal to FCC regulation. Even
in view of industry's inaction, legal motions filed by parents against networks for
broadcasts which resulted in children's deaths were not upheld.
Violence in television - Laws, regulations, etc. / Mass media policy - History / Violence
in children - Cases

Grabe, M.E. (1996)
Tabloid and Traditional Television News Magazine Crime Stories: Crime Lessons and
Reaffirmation of Social Class Distinctions. Journalism and Mass Communication
Quarterly 73(1996)4, Winter, pp. 926-946, ISSN 1077-6990.

Graham would bar federal ads on violent shows. (Senator Robert Graham; television
advertising by the armed forces and federal agencies) (Brief Article)
Advertising Age, May 23, 1994, v. 65 n. n22 p. 2(1)
LC Call Number: HF5801.A276
Magazine Index Micro Film: None
Graham, Robert K. - Social policy / Dorgan, Byron L. - Social policy

Violence in television - Laws, regulations, etc. / Administrative agencies - Advertising /
Armed Forces - Advertising

Graham would bar federal ads on violent shows. (Senator Robert Graham; television
advertising by the armed forces and federal agencies) (Brief Article)
Advertising Age, May 23, 1994, v. 65 n. n22 p. 2(1)
LC Call Number: HF5801.A276
Business Index Micro Film: 78V3900
Graham, Robert K. - Social policy / Dorgan, Byron L. - Social policy
Violence in television - Laws, regulations, etc. / Administrative agencies - Advertising /
Armed Forces - Advertising

Grant, J. (1992)
Prime Time: Television Portrayals of Law Enforcement. Journal of American Culture
15(1992)Spring, pp. 57-68, ISSN 0191-1813.

Guild, Hazel
German court sez violent TV footage property of police. (from television station ZDF-
TV)
Variety, Nov. 25, 1987, v. 329 n. n5 p. 1(2)
LC Call Number: PN2000.V3 Folio; Microfilm 03722 (1905-) MicRR
Magazine Index Micro Film: None
Television broadcasting policy - Germany, West / Violence in television - Germany,
West Germany, West

Hagiwara, S. (1990)
Violence on Television in Asia: Japanese Study. KEIO Communication Review
(1990)11, pp. 3-23.

Hamilton, J.T. (Ed.)
(1998)
Television Violence and Public Policy. Ann Arbor: University of Michigan Press, 1998,
XIV, 394 p., ill., bibl., ISBN 0-47210-903-0.

Harris, Paul
House passes bill to curb TV violence
Variety, August 9, 1989, v. 336 n. n4 p. 53(1)
LC Call Number: PN2000.V3 Folio; Microfilm 03722 (1905-) MicRR
Magazine Index Micro Film: None
United States. Congress. House - Science and technology policy / Television
broadcasting policy - Laws, regulations, etc. / Violence in television - Laws, regulations,
etc.

Harris, Paul
NAB approves guides for sex, violence and drugs. (National Association of Broadcasters)
Variety, June 27, 1990, v. 339, n. n12 p. 50(1)
LC Call Number: PN2000.V3 Folio; Microfilm 03722 (1905-   ) MicRR
Magazine Index Micro Film: None
Sex in television - standards / Violence in television - standards / Television broadcasting
- standards / National Association of Broadcasters - social policy

Harris, Paul; Wharton, Dennis
Next move industry's as TV violence law expires. (Brief Article)
Variety, Dec. 13, 1993, v. 353 n. n6 p. 30(1)
LC Call Number: PN2000.V3 Folio; Microfilm 03722 (1905-   ) MicRR
Business Index Micro Film: None
Violence in television - Laws, regulations, etc. / Television broadcasting industry - Laws,
regulations, etc.

Harris, Paul; Wharton, Dennis
Next move industry's as TV violence law expires. (Brief Article)
Variety, Dec. 13, 1993, v. 353 n. n6 p. 30(1)
LC Call Number; PN2000.V3 Folio; Microfilm 03722 (1905-   ) MicRR
Magazine Index Micro Film: none
Violence in television - Laws, regulations, etc. / Television broadcasting industry - Laws,
regulations, etc.

Hayes, Diane Aden
The children's hour revisited: the Children's Television Act of 1990. Federal
communications law journal, v. 46, Mar. 1994: 293-328.
Article reviews the Children's Television Act, and advises that the Federal
Communications Commission's call for comments on implementation should be heeded.
"Congress appears to want to create more rules for promoting educational programs, but
more rules will not necessarily solve the problems of the overcommercialization of
children's television and the lack of quality shows for children. Instead, better definitions
of what broadcasters should be doing will help if the Commission can ever decide exactly
what educational television includes."
Television and children [U.S.] Law and legislation / Children's Television Act / Federal
Communications Commission

Henderson, Keith
Activists say need is less violence in TV, not more warnings about it. (Dorothy Singer of
Yale University Family Television Research and Consultation Center; Susan Ginsberg of
Bank Street College Work and Family Program; Linda Braun of Families First
The Christian Science Monitor (1983) July 6, 1993, v. 85 n. n153 p. 7
LC Call Number: Newspaper
Business Index Micro Film: None

Violence in television - Standards / Television broadcasting industry - Standards /
Television viewers - Social aspects

Heuton, Cheryl
Congress shall make no law… (proposed legislation to regulate violence in television
may not survive legal challenges)
Mediaweek, April 4, 1994, v. 4 n. n14 p. 26(2)
LC Call Number: HF6146.T42M43
Business Index Micro Film: 77W0842
Legal experts observe that any laws passed by Congress to regulate violence in television
programs may be ruled to be unconstitutional by the Supreme Court. One legal counsel
noted that the current Supreme Court is a strong supporter of free speech based on a
number of decisions. Current legislation being discussed in Congress to curb television
violence would be viewed as a violation of the First Amendment by the Supreme Court
according to one legal expert.
United States. Congress - Political activity / Violence in television - Political aspects /
Television broadcasting policy - Laws, regulations, etc.

Heuton, Cheryl
Congress targets film trailers in debate over TV violence. (legislation to regulate violence
in television commercials)
Mediaweek, Feb. 14, 1994, v. 4 n. n7 p. 1(2)
LC Call Number: HF6146.T42M43
Business Index Micro Film: 76S0369
Three bills circulating in Congress would regulate the violence in television programs,
but some legislators feel additional legislation should be introduced to regulate violence
in commercials as well. The targeted ads would be those in top money-making
action/adventure television movies, which tend to feature shoot-outs, guns and bombings.
A bill sponsored by Sen. Byron Dorgan, one of the three in Congress, touches on
commercial violence.
United States. Congress - Social policy / Violence in television - Laws, regulations, etc. /
Television advertising - Laws, regulations, etc.

Hickey, Neil
Hollywood violence summit: much talk, some action (standards for violence on TV)
TV guide, August 14, 1993, v. 41 n. n33 p. 33(2)
LC Call Number: Microfilm 06378 (1953-   ) MicRR
Magazine Index Micro Film: none
Violence in television - Standards / Television broadcasting industry - Standards

Hickey, Neil
Sen. Simon sets January deadline on violence. (Senator Paul Simon's policy on violence
in television)
TV guide, Dec. 25, 1993, v. 41 n. n52 p. 37(1)

LC Call Number: Microfilm 06378 (1953-) MicRR
Magazine Index Micro Film: None
Simon, Paul (Politician) - Social policy
Violence in television - Standards / Television broadcasting industry - Standards

Hickey, Neil
Showdown for TV violence. (proposed standards for limiting TV violence) (includes list
of ten points that summit on TV violence should address) (Special Hollywood Issue)
TV guide, July 17, 1993, v. 41 n. n29 p. 16(5)
LC Call Number: Microfilm 06378 (1953-) MicRR
Magazine Index Micro Film: None
Violence in television - Standards / Television broadcasting industry - Standards

Hickey, Neil
TV violence; the controversy that refuses to go away.
TV guide, Feb. 12, 1994, v. 42 n. n7 p. 41(1)
LC Call Number: Microfilm 06378 (1953-) MicRR
Magazine Index Micro Film: None
Simon, Paul (Politician) - Social policy / Violence in television - Standards / Television
broadcasting industry - Standards / Cable television

Hickey, Neil; Rudolph, Ileane
Cable industry says 'OK' to Simon on violence measure. (Senator Paul Simon's
legislation on monitoring TV violence)
TV Guide, Jan. 22, 1994, v. 42 n. n4 p. 35(1)
LC Call Number: Microfilm 06378 (1953-) MicRR
Magazine Index Micro Film: None
Violence in television - Standards / Cable television broadcasting industry - Standards /
Television broadcasting industry - Standards

Hilker, Anne K.
Tort liability of the media for audience acts of violence: a constitutional analysis.
Southern California law review, v. 52, Jan. 1979: 529-571.
Comment contends "that media liability for damage caused in imitation of a media
message could arise under traditional tort doctrine, but that the first amendment
protections enunciated by the United States Supreme Court in Brandeburg v. Ohio should
be applied when tort actions are brought against media defendants for audience acts of
violence."
Television programs [U.S.] / Liability (Law) [U.S.] / Supreme Court decisions / Violence
in television [U.S.] / Brandenburg v. Ohio

Hill resolution hits TV violence. (legislation)
Television Digest, June 21, 1993, v. 33 n. n25 p. 7(1)
LC Call Number: May or May Not Be in LC. Search further.

Business Index Micro Film: 71Z1079
Violence in television - Laws, regulations, etc. / Television broadcasting industry - Laws, regulations, etc.

House Telecommunications Subcomittee Chairman Ed Markey (D-Mass) is not giving up. (Edward J. Markey, television program blocking technology bill) (Brief Article)
Broadcasting and Cable, Feb. 21, 1994, v. 124 n. n8 p. 65(1)
LC Call Number: TK6540B85
Business Index Micro Film: 76U1287
Markey, Edward J. - Social policy
Violence in television - Laws, regulations, etc. / Television broadcasting policy - Social aspects

Howitt, D. (1998)
Crime, the Media and the Law. Chichester: Wiley, 1998, X, 233 p., ISBN 0-47196-905-2.

Ignore the risk at your peril; it's self regulation - or government regulation. (violence in television) (Editorial)
The Los Angeles Times, Oct. 21, 1993, v. 112, p. B6
LC Call Number: Newspaper 7114-X
Business Index Micro Film: None
United States. Congress - Social policy / Violence in television - Laws, regulations, etc. / Television broadcasting industry - Social policy

Industry to approve standard blocking violent TV shows. (technical standard for new television sets to block out shows parents don't want their children to see; Electronics Industry Association)
The Wall Street Journal, July 11, 1994, p. B6(W) pB5
LC Call Number: See Catalogs or Staff
Magazine Index Micro Film: None
Electronic Industries Association - Standards / Television sets - Safety and security measures / Violence in television - Rating

Iyengar, S. (1991)
Is Anyone Responsible? How Television Frames Political Issues. Chicago: University of Chicago Press, 1991, VIII, 195 p., ISBN 0-22638-854-9.

Jackson, Robert J.; Hall, Jane
Reno warns TV industry; cut violence. (Attorney General Janet Reno)
The Los Angeles Times, Oct. 21, 1993, v. 112 p. A1
LC Call Number: Newspaper 7114-X
Business Index Micro Film: None
Reno, Janet - Social policy

Violence in television - Laws, regulations, etc. / Television broadcasting industry - Social policy

Jackson, Robert L.; Cerone, Daniel
TV violence label criticized as not enough. (network executives defended advisories)
The Los Angeles Times, July 1, 1993, v. 112 p. A1
LC Call Number: Newspaper 7114-X
Business Index Micro Film: None
Television broadcasting - Labeling / Violence in television - Laws, regulations, etc. / Television and children - Laws, regulations, etc.

James Slattery introduced a House Resolution expressing serious concerns about the quality of TV programming. (wants broadcasters to classify programs based on violence content) (Brief Article)
Broadcasting and Cable, June 21, 1993, v. 123 n. n25 p. 77(1)
LC Call Number: TK6540B85
Business Index Micro Film: 71Z2465
Slattery, Jim - Social policy

United States. Congress. House - Social policy / Violence in television - Laws, regulations, etc. / Television broadcasting industry - Laws, regulations, etc. / Cable television broadcasting industry - Laws, regulations, etc.

Janet Reno's heavy hand. (Attorney General's warning to television industry to show less violence in their programs is akin to censorship) (Editorial)
The New York Times, Oct. 22, 1993, v. 143 p. A14 (N) ppA
LC Call Number: Not in LC Collection
Magazine Index Micro Film: None
Reno, Janet - Social policy
Violence in television - Laws, regulations, etc. / Television broadcasting industry - Moral and ethical aspects / Television and children - Laws, regulations, etc. / Censorship - Moral and ethical aspects

Jensen, Elizabeth
Simon imposes deadline on TV industry to take further steps on violence issue. (Senator Paul Simon warns of congressional intervention against violence on television, announces 60-day mandate)
The Wall Street Journal, August 3, 1993, p. B7(W) pB7
LC Call Number: See Catalogs or Staff
Magazine Index Micro Film: None
Simon, Paul (Politician) - Social policy
Violence in television - Management / Television broadcasting policy - Social aspects / Television broadcasting industry - Social policy

Jensen, Elizabeth
Violence advisory set for unveiling by four networks. (Capital Cities / ABC Inc., CBS
Inc., General Electric Co., News Corp.)
The Wall Street Journal, June 30, 1993, p. B7 (W) pB6
LC Call Number: See Catalogs or Staff
Business Index Micro Film: None
Television broadcasting industry - Laws, regulations, etc. / Violence in television -
Laws, regulations, etc.

Jensen, Elizabeth; Mark, Robichaux
Television industry agrees on a plan to check violence. (television programming)
The Wall Street Journal, Feb. 1, 1994, p. B12 (W) pB1
LC Call Number: See Catalogs or Staff
Magazine Index Micro Film: None
United States. Congress - Social policy / Violence in television - Standards / Television
broadcasting industry - Standards / Cable television broadcasting industry - Standards

Jensen, Elizabeth; Mark, Robichaux
Television industry agrees on a plan to check violence (television programming)
The Wall Street Journal, Feb. 1, 1994, p. B12(W) pB1
LC Call Number: See Catalogs or Staff
Business Index Micro Film: None
United States. Congress - Social policy / Violence in television - Standards / Television
broadcasting industry - Standards / Cable television broadcasting industry - Standards

Jessell, Harry A.
Cable promises to curb violence; NCTA adopts four-point plan to assuage Washington
concerns that includes urging members to adopt standards and practices policies limiting
violence. (National Cable Television Association)
Broadcasting and Cable, Feb. 1, 1993, v. 124 n. n5 p. 33(2).
LC Call Number: TK6540B85
Business Index Micro Film: 69V0488
The National Cable Television Association (NCTA) has pledged to reduce the amount of
violence in television by urging its member cable networks to accept new standards. The
NCTA commissioned a study that reports low levels of violence in children's
programming, but acknowledged that certain types of violence are harmful to society.
The NCTA also proposes to join television broadcasters in a conference on television
violence and will begin a study in 1995 to monitor the effect of the cable industry's anti-
violence stance.
National Cable Television Association - Standards / Cable television broadcasting
industry - Standards / Violence in television - Standards

Jessell, Harry A.
Hundt sees role for FCC in limiting TV violence. (Reed Hundt)

Broadcasting and Cable, Sept. 27, 1993, v. 124 n. n39 p. 14(1)
LC Call Number: TK6540B85
Business Index Micro Film: 73U0967
Reed Hundt, nominated to be FCC chairman, said in written comments would like to limit television violence. He also said that there is convincing evidence that TV violence affects behavior. He acknowledged that First Amendment considerations make the issue challenging and expressed hopes that technological breakthroughs would provide effective violent-program access-control solutions.
Hundt, Reed - Social policy
United States. Federal Communications Commission - Officials and employees / Violence in television - Laws, regulations, etc.

Jessell, Harry A.
Turner supports efforts to reduce violence. (Ted Turner tells Congress that his networks will adopt television broadcasting industry violence standards) (Brief Article)
Broadcasting and Cable, June 21, 1993, v. 123 n. n25 p. 76(1)
LC Call Number: TK6540B85
Business Index Micro Film: 71Z2464
Turner, Ted - Management
Cable television broadcasting industry - Standards / Violence in television - Standards

Jessell, Harry
Senator Simon's message. (Paul Simon; suggestions for reducing violence in television) (includes related article outlining Simon's seven-point plan) (Interview)
Broadcasting and Cable, August 9, 1993, v. 123 n. n32 p. 25(2)
LC Call Number: Tk6540B85
Business Index Micro Film: 72X0642
Sen. Paul Simon defends his idea of the television industry forming its own advisory committee to monitor and decrease violence on television. He says that this would not encroach on free speech and that warning messages previewing shows are not enough. He would exempt news broadcasts but not cable television. He prefers such self-monitoring by the industry to government regulations. He declines to define the make-up of a self-monitoring council or the precise extent that violence would be eliminated.
Simon, Paul (Politician) - Interviews
Violence in television - Laws, regulations, etc.

Joffee, Linda
Sex, violence and Lord Rees-Mogg. (British television violence)
World Monitor, Jan. 1989, v. 2 n. n1 p. 14(3)
LC Call Number: AP2.W74839
Magazine Index Micro Film: None
Lord Rees-Mogg. (portrait)
Charles, Prince of Wales - Social policy / Rees-Moog, Lord - Social policy

United Kingdom. Broadcasting Standards Council - Laws, regulations, etc. / Sex in
television - Laws, regulations, etc. / Violence in television - Laws, regulations, etc.

Johnstone, J.W.C.; Hawkins, D.F. & Michener, A. (1995)
Homicide Reporting in Chicago Dailies. Journalism Quarterly 71(1995)4, pp. 860-872,
ISSN 0196-3031.

Keating, Susan Katz
Taking action on youth programs. Insight (Washington Times), v. 5, Feb. 27, 1989: 46-
47.
"Twenty years ago Peggy Charren decided to do something about the poor quality of
children's programming. So she formed [Action for Children's Television] to lobby for
change. Her efforts have led to a bill, expected to pass this year, that will put restrictions
on the networks. And she is due to receive an Emmy for her work."
Television and children [U.S.] Law and legislation / Lobbyists [U.S.] / Charren, Peggy /
Action for Children's Television

Keeffe, Arthur John; Valpey-Toussignant, Gregory W.
They're holding the party without Pertschuk. American Bar Association journal, v. 65,
Sept. 1979: 1407-1411
Examines the arguments in the district court's disqualification of the FTC chairman from
participating in the children's television advertising rule-making proceeding and
considers the parties' statements before the appellate court.
Administrative procedure [U.S.] / Judicial review of administrative acts [U.S.] /
Television advertising [U.S.] / Television and children [U.S.] / Pertschuk, Michael / U.S.
Federal Trade Commission

Kelly, Brendan
Beating up on TV violence. (Canada)
Variety, March 8, 1993, v. 350 n. n6 p. 40(2)
LC Call Number: PN2000.V3 Folio; Microfilm 03722 (1905-   )MicRR
Business Index Micro Film: NONE
Violence in television - Laws, regulations, etc. / Television broadcasting industry -
Canada / Canada - Social policy
Canada

Kelly, Brendan
Beating up on TV violence. (Canada)
Variety, March 8, 1993, v. 350 n. n6 p. 40 (2)
LC Call Number: PN2000.V3, Folio; Microfilm 03722 (1905-   ) MicRR
Magazine Index Micro Film: none
Violence in television - Laws, regulations, etc. / Television broadcasting industry -
Canada / Canada - Social policy
Canada

Kelmenson, Leo-Arthur
'Vast wasteland' revisited. (television programming)
Harvard business review, Nov.-Dec. 1980, v. 58 p. 28(7)
LC Call Number: HF5001.H3; Microfilm 06068 (1922-   ) MicRR
Magazine Index Micro Film None
Television industry - management / mass media - management / violence in television - standards

Gelman, Morrie
Era of intimidation in TV is back, Hollywood panel told
Variety, May 20, 1981, v. 303 p. 72(22)
LC Call Number: PN2000.V3 Folio; Microfilm 03722 (1905-   ) MicRR
Magazine Index Micro Film: None
Ross, Michael - reports / Schneider, Alfred - reports
Television - Advertising - standards / television programs - advertising / violence in television - standards / sex in television - standards

Kidd-Hewitt, D. & Osborne, R. (Eds.)
(1995)
Crime and the Media: The Post Modern Spectacle., London: Pluto, 1995, 266 p., ISBN 0-7453-0911-9.

Killias, M. (1990)
Vulnerability: Towards a Better Understanding of the Key Variable in the Genesis of Fear of Crime. Violence and Victims 5(1990)
pp. 97-107, ISSN 0886-67608.

Kolbert, Elizabeth
Canadians act to restrict violence on TV. (Living Arts Pages)
The New York Times, Jan. 11, 1994, v. 143 p. B1 (N) pC15
LC Call Number: Not in LC Collection
Magazine Index Micro Film: None
Violence in television - Laws, regulations, etc. / Television broadcasting industry - Laws, regulations, etc. / Canada - Social policy

Kolbert, Elizabeth
Canadians act to restrict violence on TV. (Living Arts Pages)
The New York Times, Jan. 11, 1994, v. 143 p. B1 (N) pC15
LC Call Number: Not in LC Collection
Business Index Micro Film: None
Violence in television - Laws, regulations, etc. / Television broadcasting industry - Laws, regulations, etc. / Canada - Social policy

Krattenmaker, Thomas G.; Power, L.A., Jr.
Televised violence: First Amendment principles and social science theory. Virginia law review, v. 64, Dec. 1978: 1123-1345.
Partial contents. The social scientists look at televised violence. First Amendment considerations. Application of general principles.
Violence in television [U.S.] / Television programs [U.S.] / Social science research [U.S.] / Government regulation [U.S.]

Kurtz, Steve
Deja viewing. (congressional hearings on TV violence)
Reason, Feb 1994, v. 25 n. n9 p. 44(3)
LC Call Number: H1.R35
Magazine Index Micro Film: None
Violence in mass media - Social aspects / Entertainment industry - Censorship / Mass media - Political aspects / Violence in television - Laws, regulations, etc.

Landler, Mark
Congress is screaming bloody murder. (violence on television)
Business Week, August 23, 1993, n n3333 p. 30(2)
LC Call Number: HF5001.B89; Microfilm 01956 (1929-   ) MicRR
Business Index Micro Film: None
Violence in television - Laws, regulations, etc. / Television broadcasting industry - Laws, regulations, etc.

Landler, Mark
Congress is screaming bloody murder. (Violence on television)
Business Week, August 23, 1993, n. n3333 p. 30 (2)
LC Call Number: HF5001.B89; Microfilm 01956 (1929-   ) MicRR
Magazine Index Micro Film: none
Violence in television - Laws, regulations, etc. / Television broadcasting industry - Laws, regulations, etc.

Lawton, Kim A.
A flurry of activity ends the Congressional year. (legislation affecting church organizations; includes related article)
Christianity Today (Washington), Dec 17, 1990, v. 34 n. n18 p. 42(3)
LC Call Number: BR1.C6418; Microfilm (0) 83/406 (981-   ) MicRR
Magazine Index Micro Film: 58A4196
George Bush (portrait)
Church charities - Laws, regulations, etc. / Church work with prisoners - Laws, regulations, etc. / Federal aid to the arts - Laws, regulations, etc. / Religious institutions - Laws, regulations, etc. / Abortion - Laws, regulations, etc./ Violence in television - Laws, regulations, etc. / Day care centers - Laws, regulations, etc. / Church work with immigrants - Laws, regulations, etc.

Levi, Richard P.
Violence on television: an old problem with a new picture. North Carolina law review, v. 58, Oct. 1979: 97-136.
Comment argues that "both current psychological knowledge and the first amendment preclude holding the networks accountable for violent acts by viewers; that, although some forms of indirect government regulation could be justified consistent with the first amendment, government regulation should not be used because of the impediments to free speech."
Television and children [U.S.] Legal cases / Violence in television [U.S.] / Social psychology [U.S.] / Freedom of speech [U.S.] / Government regulation [U.S.]

Lieb, Rebecca
German pols can't digest heavy dose of reality. (politicians object to reality programs on television)
Variety, March 15, 1993, v 350, n. n7 p. 41 (2)
LC Call Number: PN2000.V3 Folio; Microfilm 03722 (1905-   ) MicRR
Magazine Index Micro Film: None
Violence in television - Laws, regulations, etc. / Television broadcasting industry - Germany

Lippman, John
4 networks agree to TV violence warnings. (parental advisories)
The Los Angeles times, June 30, 1993, v. 112 p. A1
LC Call Number: Newspaper 7114-X
Business Index Micro Film: None
Violence in television - Laws, regulations, etc. / Television broadcasting - Laws, regulations, etc. / Television and children - Laws, regulations, etc.

Markey violence ratings. (Congressional Subcommittee on Telecommunications Chairman Edward Markey)
Television Digest, May 24, 1993, v. w33 n. n21 p. 6(1)
LC Call Number: May or May Not Be in LC. Search further.
Business Index Micro Film: 71T0698
Congressional Subcommittee Chairman Edward Markey has been soliciting inputs from network executives regarding the development of a system for evaluating violence on television similar to the MPAA ratings for movies. Markey acknowledged the difficulty of rating television compared to movies, but he insisted that the rating system would be more effective if it were established by the industry. The rating system would respect the First Amendment rights of television producers as well as parents.
Markey, Edward J. - Laws, regulations, etc.
United States. Congress. Senate. Subcommittee on Communications - Laws, regulations, etc. / Violence in television - Laws, regulations, etc. / Television broadcasting industry - Laws, regulations, etc.

Masters, Brooke
No TV violence cease - fire; big guns balk at Senate's threat.
The Washington Post, June 9, 1993, v. 116 p. D2
LC Call Number: Newspaper
Business Index Micro Film: None
Valenti, Jack - Political activity
United States. Congress. Senate - Social policy / Television broadcasting industry -
Social policy / Violence in television - Laws, regulations, etc.

McAvoy, Kim
'Report card' proposed by Dorgan; Senator to attach amendment authorizing NTIA to
fund violence rankings. (Senator Byron Dorgan, National Telecommunications and
Information Administration, violent programming)
Broadcasting and Cable, August 22, 1994, v. 124, n. n34 p. 11(1)
LC Call Number: TK6540B85
Business Index Micro Film: None
Senator Byron Dorgan (D-ND) is proposing that an amendment be attached to National
Telecommunications and Information Administration that would enable the agency to
finance grants to nonprofit organizations that want to research and report the amount of
violent television programming on broadcast networks and cable systems. The resulting
'report cards' would be made public. In one sample survey, Fox Broadcasting ranked
highest in broadcasted violent acts.
Dorgan, Byron L. - Social policy. United States. National Telecommunications and
Information Administration - Finance /Violence in television - Research / Television
broadcasting industry - Research

McAvoy, Kim
Chong: 'demerits' may reduce TV violence. (FCC nominee Rachelle Chong) (includes
related article where the Nominees Stand)
Broadcasting and Cable, May 16, 1994, v. 124 n. n20 p. 51(2)
LC Call Number: TK6540B85
Business Index Micro Film: 78S1697
FCC nominees Rachelle Chong and Susan Ness addressed a number of questions related
to the telecommunications industry in a Senate panel on May 11, 1994. Both Ness and
Chong, who have strong experience in the telecommunications field, expressed concern
about the violence on television. Chong proposed that television stations that broadcast
violent programs be awarded demerits that would be factored into the decision on
whether to approve a renewal of a television license. Chong also believes that the FCC
should take a proactive stance should networks be unable to eliminate violence in
television.
Chong, Rachelle - Evidence / Ness, Susan - Evidence. United States. Congress. Senate -
Investigations / United States. Federal Communications Commission - Officials and
employees / Violence in television - Investigations

McAvoy, Kim
Hill keeps up antiviolence pressure. (Congressional bills against television violence;
includes related article)
Broadcasting and Cable, Feb. 7, 1994, v. 124 n. n6 p. 7(1)
LC Call Number: TK6540B85
Business Index Micro Film: 76R1306
Congress is discussing various bills to control television violence, despite promises by
cable and broadcast television networks to monitor themselves. Sen. Ernest Hollings does
not believe that the television industry will keep its promise, and he plans to hold
hearings on a bill to prohibit broadcast of violence during hours when children are
watching. Sen. Byron Dorgan introduced a bill to require the use of V-chips in television
sets so that parents can block out violent programs. Sen. Paul Simon, however, opposes
any regulation and praised the plan of cable companies to monitor themselves.
Hollings, Ernest F. - Science and technology policy / Simon, Paul (Politician) - Science
and technology policy / Dorgan, Byron L. - Science and technology policy / Violence in
television - Laws, regulations, etc. / Television broadcasting industry - Laws,
regulations, etc.

McAvoy, Kim
Hill to revisit violence. (Congress to examine television violence)
Broadcasting and Cable May 3, 1993, v. 123 n. n18 p. 52(2)
LC Call Number: TK6540B85
Business Index Micro Film: 71Q1437
Congressional concern over the increase of television violence has prompted three House
and Senate committees to plan hearings. Members may be worried by reports that May
sweeps programming will include more violence than usual. They will have noted a
March 1993 Times-Mirror survey which indicated that 80% of the participants believed
that television violence had a damaging influence on society. The networks highlight
another survey in which the public found cable to be more violent than broadcast
television.
United States. Congress - Social policy / Violence in television - Standards / Television
broadcasting - Censorship

McAvoy, Kim
Hill wants FCC to issue violence report card. (new bills aimed at limiting violence in TV)
(Brief Article)
Broadcasting and Cable, May 24, 1993, v. 123 n. n21 p. 66(2)
LC Call Number: TK6540B85
Business Index Micro Film: 71U1334
Violence in television - Laws, regulations, etc. / Television broadcasting industry -
Censorship

McAvoy, Kim
Markey suggests violence 'lockbox.' (Edward Markey, House Telecommunications

Subcommittee hearing on TV violence)
Broadcasting and Cable, May 17, 1993, v. 123 n. n20 p. 41(2)
LC Call Number: TK6540B85
Business Index Micro Film: 71S1851
House Telecommunications Subcommittee Chairman Edward Markey says that Congress
should place restrictions on violence in TV programs because broadcasters have failed to
do so voluntarily. Markey is in favor of a rating system similar to that used by the motion
picture industry. He also recommends that TV sets be equipped with technology that
allows parents to block out programs at their discretion and that broadcasters be denied
the right to unscramble R-rated programs for promotional purposes.
Markey, Edward J. - Social policy
Violence in television - Laws, regulations, etc. / Television broadcasting industry -
Censorship

McAvoy, Kim
Networks close to violence plan. (television networks, TV violence) (Brief Article)
Broadcasting and Cable, Jan. 24, 1994, v. 124 n. n4 p. 11(1)
LC Call Number: TK6540B85
Business Index Micro Film: none
Violence in television - Standards / Television broadcasting industry - Mediation and
arbitration

McAvoy, Kim
Reno to head lineup at violence hearing. (Attorney General Janet Reno, violence on
television)
Broadcasting and Cable, Oct. 18, 1993, v. 123 n. n42 p. 43(1)
LC Call Number: Tk6540B85
Business Index Micro Film: 73Z0346
The Senate Committee on Commerce, Science and Transportation is conducting an
investigation on the increasing violence in television. Attorney General Janet Reno will
be the star witness, and her testimony is expected to help define any impending
regulations. The television broadcasting industry is hoping they will be allowed to
voluntarily regulate the problem before any legislation is passed by Congress.
Reno, Janet - Evidence
United States. Congress. Senate. Committee on Commerce, Science and Transportation -
Investigations / Violence in television - Investigations / Television broadcasting industry
- Investigations

McAvoy, Kim
Television violence legislation: the handwriting is on the wall. (includes related article on
possible Congressional revenge against network news programs)
Broadcasting and Cable, August 16, 1993, v. 123 n. n33 p. 31(2)
LC Call Number: TK6540B85

Business Index Micro Film: None

Congress is expected to pass some kind of legislation against television violence by the end of 1993. As of August 1993, eight bills were under consideration, including two that would revoke broadcasters' licenses if they violated Federal Communications Commission standards against violence. Another bill would require television sets to have technology that would allow parents to blockprograms. The National Association of Broadcasters and the Electronic Industries Association oppose such measures.

United States. Congress - Social policy / Violence in television - Laws, regulations, etc.

McAvoy, Kim

TV dominates agenda of returning Congress. (television regulation issues)

Broadcasting and Cable, Sept. 6, 1993, v. 124 n. n36 p. 51(1)

LC Call Number: TK6540B85

Business Index Micro Film: 73Q1696

A number of telecommunication issues will be addressed by Congress upon their return to session in Sept. 1993. The Aug court decision permitting telephone companies in the cable television business has raised the issue of a cross-ownership bill that had previously been stalled. In response to television violence, a bill has been introduced requiring TV set manufacturers to install a 'V chip' so parents can disable the set. Other legislation on the agenda includes the fairness doctrine in political broadcasting, performance rights fees and cable television rates.

Television broadcasting - Laws, regulations, etc. / Cable television - Laws, regulations, etc. / Violence in television - Laws, regulations, etc. / Telecommunications industry - Laws, regulations, etc. / Television broadcasting policy - Forecasts

McAvoy, Kim

TV industry to Senate: self-regulation, not legislation, the answer to violence

Broadcasting and Cable, May 24, 1993, v. 123 n. n21 p. 14(1)

LC Call Number: TK6540B85

Business Index Micro Film: 71U1282

Network and cable representatives told skeptical Senate Constitution subcommittee members that they were doing their best to curtail TV violence. Of the four networks, only Fox was willing to implement the voluntary ratings system proposed by House Telecommunications Subcommittee Chairman Edward Markey, who also testified before the Senate committee. Markey has also suggested that the Electronic Industries Assn. include ratings information in its extended data services standard.

Violence in television - Laws, regulations, etc. / Television broadcasting industry - Censorship

McAvoy, Kim

TV violence debate heats up: House, Senate and FCC all appear to be getting into the act. (special section: Action Hours)

Broadcasting and Cable, August 29, 1994, v. 124 n. n35 p. 40(2)

LC Call Number: TK6540B85

Business Index Micro Film: None
Anti-TV violence initiatives are a priority in the Senate and House, and even at the FCC.
Sen. Byron Dorgan plans to introduce a bill that would enable the National
Telecommunications and Information Administration to bestow grants on nonprofit
organizations that prepare violence report cards. Rep. Edward Markey says he will
proceed with a V-block bill if the Electronic Industries Assn does not adopt the
technology voluntarily.
Dorgan, Byron L. - Social policy / Markey, Edward J. - Social policy / Hundt, Reed -
Social policy / Violence in television - Laws, regulations, etc. / Television broadcasting
industry - Censorship

McAvoy, Kim
Violence regs wait as Hill watches. (regulators assess broadcasters' efforts to self-
regulate) (Brief Article)
Broadcasting and Cable, May 16, 1994, v. 124 n. n20 p. 16(1)
LC Call Number: TK6540B85
Business Index Micro Film: 78S1645
Violence in television - Laws, regulations, etc. / Television broadcasting industry -
Management

McAvoy, Kim; Coe, Steve
TV rocked by Reno ultimatum. (Attorney General Janet Reno tells broadcasters to clean
up violence; includes related article)
Broadcasting and Cable, Oct. 25, 1993, v. 123 n. n43 p. 6(3)
LC Call Number: TK6540B85
Business Index Micro Film: None
Attorney General Janet Reno gave her blessing to legislation curbing TV violence and
admonished broadcasters to make significant changes in program content by Jan. 1994.
Sen. Paul Simon says broadcasters must establish an Advisory Office on Television
Violence by this date or risk sanctions. The industry is vowing to fight back by joining
with the ACLU and other interest groups to challenge the constitutionally of anti-violence
legislation. Reno says the three bills currently in Congress are constitutional.
Violence in television - Laws, regulations, etc. / Television broadcasting industry -
Laws, regulations, etc.

Medved, Michael; Custer, C.D.
Curbing violence on television. (Letter to the Editor)
The Los Angeles Times, July 17, 1993, v. 112 p. B7
LC Call Number: Newspaper 7114-X
Business Index Micro Film: None
Violence in television - Control / Television broadcasting, Laws, regulations, etc.

Metts, Wally Jr.
TV violence: will a new bill help? (legislation; includes related article)

Christianity Today (Washington), Feb. 17, 1989, v. 33 n. n3 p. 47(2)
LC Call Number: BR1.C6418; Microfilm (0) 83/406 (1981-   ) MicRR
Magazine Index Micro Film: 48G2422
Simon, Paul (Politician) - Science and technology policy
Violence in television - Laws, regulations, etc. / Television programs for children - Laws,
regulations, etc. / National Coalition on Television Violence - Management

Meyer, Karl E.; Brown, Les; Schiefelbein, Susan
Is television dangerous? Saturday review, v. 5, Sept. 16, 1978: 19-20, 22-28.
Consists of 3 articles: a survey of legal battles based on TV violence, current and
prospective technological developments (2 way cable TV, satellite transmission, and
expansion of television channels), and efforts to improve programming.
Violence in television [U.S.] Legal cases / Television broadcasting [U.S.] Technological
innovations / Television programs [U.S.]

Mills, Mike
TV violence: Hill may not wait for more industry action. Congressional Quarterly weekly
report, v. 51, Sept. 4, 1993: 2338-2341.
"Wary of industry promises to tone down television mayhem, lawmakers are readying
their own solutions. But entertainment writers and producers fears the specter of
censorship, and some in Congress agree."
Violence in television [U.S.] Law and legislation / Television and children [U.S.] Law
and legislation / Censorship [U.S.] / Television industry [U.S.]
Minow, Newton N., 1926-
Abandoned in the wasteland : children, television, and the First Amendment / Newton N.
Minow and Craig L. LaMay. 1st ed., New York : Hill and Wang, 1995. xi, 237 p. ; 22
cm.
KF2840.M56 1995
0809023113
Includes bibliographical references (p. 209-224) and index. Television programs for
children -- Law and legislation -- United States.
Television advertising -- Law and legislation -- United States.
Violence on television -- Law and legislation -- United States.
Sex in television -- Law and legislation -- United States.
LaMay, Craig L.
32012613

Minow, Newton N., 1926-
Abandoned in the wasteland : children, television, and the First Amendment / Newton N.
Minow and Craig L. LaMay.
1st Hill and Wang paperback ed.
New York : Hill and Wang, 1996, c1995.
xi, 237 p. ; 21 cm.
KF2840.M56 1996

Mishra, Vishwa Mohan
Law and disorder: Law enforcement in television network news / V.M. Mishra. - New York: Asia Pub. House, c1979.
x, 127 p.; 22 cm. Bibliography: p.95-119. Includes index.
Television and broadcasting of news - United States. Journalism - Objectivity. Crime and the press - United States. Police and the press - United States. Violence in television - United States. I. Title.

More attacks on TV violence; licenses to be challenged.
Television Digest   March 29, 1993, v. 33 n. n13 p. 1(3)
LC Call Number: May or May Not Be In LC. Search further.
Business Index Micro Film: 70T0448
The Foundation to Improve Television (FIT) criticized televised violence last March 25, 1993, and demanded the FCC to restrict violence in television during children's viewing hours. FIT also pledged to hinder the license renewals of those stations that broadcast violence before 9 p.m. FCC Chairman James H. Quello has also proposed the imposition of 'safe harbor' time segment for televising violence similar to indecent programming. The National Telecommunications and Information Administration will also launch an inquiry on the effects of telecommunications on the occurrence of crimes and violence. United States. Federal Communications Commission - Laws, regulations, etc. / Violence in television - Laws, regulations, etc.

Morganthau, Tom
Can TV violence be curbed? (Congressional hearings)
Newsweek, Nov. 1, 1993, v. 122 n. n18 p. 26(2)
LC Call Number: AP2.N6772; Microfilm 01125 (1933-   ) MicRR
Magazine Index Micro Film: None
United States. Congress. Senate. Committee on Commerce, Science and Transportation - Investigations / Violence in television - Investigations / Violence in television - Investigations / Violence in mass media - Laws, regulations, etc. / Violence in motion pictures - Investigations

Mundy, Alicia
The Capital gang rides again. (Congressional leaders in the fight against violence in television) (includes related article on proposed legislation)
Mediaweek, April 4, 1994, v. 4 n. n14 p. 28(4)
LC Call Number: HF6146.T42M43
Business Index Micro Film: 77W0844
The debate in Congress over proposed legislation to control violence in television has escalated, placing increased pressure on the entertainment industry. A number of bills are pending in Congress which would control the amount of violence permitted to be broadcast on television. Attorney General Janet Reno's unexpected opposition to television violence and the emergence of crime as a national political issue have placed the entertainment industry on the defensive.

Reno, Janet - Political activity
Violence in television - Political activity / Television broadcasting policy - Laws,
regulations, etc.

Murray, J.P. (1994)
The Impact of Televised Violence. Hofstra Law Review 22(1994)4, pp. 809-825, ISSN
0091-4029.

Murray, J.P. (1995)
Children and Television Violence. Kansas Journal of Law and Public Policy 4(1995)3,
pp. 7-14, ISSN 1055-8942.

NAB still concerned. (National Association of Broadcasters)
Television Digest July 8, 1991, v. 31 n., n27, p. 4(1)
LC Call Number: May or May Not Be In LC. Search Further.
Business Index Micro Film: 59X0571
Simon, Paul (Politician) - Political activity National Association of Broadcasters -
Political activity/ Television broadcasting policy - Evaluation / Violence in Television -
Laws, regulations, etc. / Cable Television broadcasting industry - Political activity.

Sen. Simon (D-Ill). (Paul Simon: television broadcast industry guidelines on televised
violence)
Television Digest August 3, 1992, v. 32 n., n31 p. 7(1)
LC Call Number: May or May Not be in LC. Search further.
Business Index Micro Film: 66W0595
Simon, Paul (Politician) - Political activity
Violence in television - Laws, regulations, etc. / Television broadcasting industry - Social
policy

Wharton, Dennis
Simon says nets will create violence rules. (Senator Paul Simon, television violence)
(Brief Article)
Variety Dec. 14, 1992, v. 349 n. n8 p. 22(1)
LC Call Number: PN2000.V3 Folio; Microfilm 03722 (1905-   ) MicRR
Business Index Micro Film: NONE
Simon, Paul (Politician) - Political activity
Violence in television - Laws, regulations, etc.

Nelson, Eric M.
Communications law. Annual survey of American law, v. 1984, no. 2, 1984: 401-434.
"This article will examine developments in three areas of communications law that
illustrate [a] laissez-faire trend. The following discussion will include the recent
challenges to both broadcaster control and state and federal regulation of political
advertising, the reluctance of the federal courts to allow content regulation of cable

television programming, and the weakening of broadcasters' obligations in the area of children's programming."
Television in politics [U.S.] Legal cases / Television advertising [U.S.] / Cable television [U.S.] / Television and children [U.S.]

Networks vow TV violence warnings. (television networks agree to put warnings on violent programs)
Facts on File, July 15, 1993, v. 53 n. n2746 p. 524 (1)
LC Call Number: Not in LC Collection
Business Index Micro Film: None
Violence in television - Laws, regulations, etc. / Television broadcasting industry - Laws, regulations, etc.

O'Connor, John J.
Labeling prime-time violence is still a band-aid solution. (plan to warn parents of violent television content)
The New York Times, July 11, 1993, v. 142 p. H1(N) pH1
LC Call Number: Not in LC Collection
Magazine Index Micro Film: none
Violence in television - Laws, regulations, etc. / Television programs - Laws, regulations, etc.

Ohlenforst, Cindy Morgan
Big brother's war on television advertising: how extensive is the regulatory authority of the Federal Trade Commission? Southwestern law journal, v. 33, June 1979: 683-701.
Comment doubts that the FTC can formulate a rule on television advertising directed to children which would be effective and would comply with recent case law protecting commercial speech.
Television advertising [U.S.] Law and legislation / Television and children [U.S.] Law and legislation / Administrative procedure [U.S.] / Trade regulations [U.S.] / Freedom of speech [U.S.] / Deceptive advertising [U.S.] / U.S. Federal Trade Commission
Organization for Economic Cooperation and Development. Committee on Consumer Policy.
Advertising directed at children [and] endorsements in advertising. [Paris] 1982, 64 p.
"Both reports examine the various methods of advertising employed, the major areas of concern, the existing regulatory frameworks and voluntary arrangements, and suggest a number of policy solutions for consideration by member countries."
Advertising [OECD countries] Law and legislation / Children [OECD countries] / Trade regulation [OECD countries] / Consumer protection [OECD countries] / Television and children [OECD countries] / Deceptive advertising [OECD countries] / Endorsements in advertisements [OECD countries]

Philips, Christopher Lee
Hollywood takes Hill heat on violence. (Senate hearings on TV violence)

Broadcasting and Cable, June 14, 1993, v. 123 n. n24 p. 68(1)
LC Call Number: TK6540B85
Business Index Micro Film: 71Z2348
The Senate's second hearing on violence in TV featured the usual delaying tactics by TV industry representatives, in this case Jack Valenti and Kerry McCluggage. The Senate panel invited the industry to either come up with ways to curtail gratuitous violence or face government regulation. Particularly objectionable, said Sen. Carl Levin, are family programs that contain violent promotional ads. Sen. Charles E. Schumer proposed the creation of a presidential commission to address the problem.
Violence in television - Laws, regulations, etc. / Television broadcasting industry - Censorship

Pressuring the FCC. (violence in television)(Current Situation)
CQ Researcher, March 26, 1993, v. 3 n. n12 p. 280(2)
LC Call Number: H35.E35
Magazine Index Micro Film: None
The FCC is constrained from regulating media portrayal of violence by Section 36 of the Federal Communications Act of 1934 which provides against censorship. To decimate violent scenes and acts in television, a violence rating system may be needed and may be favorable over legislative motions. Additionally, cooperation between the television, cable and film industries is vital to the success of anti-violence campaigns. Several companies and groups are also solidifying efforts to produce non-violent children's shows and promote a code of ethics among producers.
United States. Federal Communications Commission - Powers and duties / Television broadcasting industry - Social policy / Violence in television - Laws, regulations, etc.

Quello would restrict TV violence. (FCC Chmn. James Quello)
Television Digest, March 15, 1993, v. 33 n. n11 p. 6(1)
LC Call Number: May or May Not Be In LC. Search further.
Business Index Micro Film: 70R4296
FCC Chmn James Quello verified that more complaints regarding televised violence are sent to public officials than those concerning indecency. Quello also expressed his support for a campaign being launched by the Americans for Responsible TV for the regulation of violence on television. Quello, however, admitted that FCC has virtually no authority to confront the complaints and that restrictions might go against the 1st Amendment.
Quello, James H. - Attitudes
United States. Federal Communications Commission - Powers and duties / Americans for Responsible Television - Social policy / Violence in television - Laws, regulations, etc.

Rainie, Harrison; Streisand, Betsy; Guttman, Monika, Allman, William F.
Warning shots at TV. (violence on television; includes related article)
U.S. news & world report, July 12, 1993, v. 115 n. n2 p. 48(3)
LC Call Number: JK1.U65; Microfilm 06106 (1933-   )MicRR

Business Index Micro Film: 69K1135
Television broadcasting industry - Laws, regulations, etc. / Violence in television - Laws, regulations, etc.

Real violence and TV. (TV violence and ratings debate still going on in Congress)(Editorial)
The Washington Post, March 3, 1997 v120 pA18 col 1 (II col in)

Recent action in the Congress. (television programming regulation) (Violence on Television)
The Congressional Digest, Dec. 1993, v. 72 n. n12 p. 299(1)
LC Call Number: JK1.C65
Magazine Index Micro Film: None
United States. Congress - Powers and duties / Violence in television - Laws, regulations, etc. / Television broadcasting policy - Planning

Reno urges TV violence be cut by industry or laws. (Attorney General Janet Reno)
The Wall Street Journal, Oct. 21, 1993, p. A18 (W)
LC Call Number: See Catalogs or Staff
Business Index Micro Film: None
Reno, Janet - Social policy
Violence in television - Laws, regulations, etc. / Television broadcasting industry - Social policy

Reno urges TV violence be cut by industry or laws. (Attorney General Janet Reno)
The Wall Street Journal, Oct. 21, 1993, p. A18 (W)
LC Call Number: See Catalogs or Staff
Magazine Index Micro Film: None
Reno, Janet - Social policy. Violence in television - Laws, regulations, etc. / Television broadcasting industry - Social policy

Response to antiviolence bills. (opponents of antiviolence bills take action)
Television Digest, Dec. 27, 1993, v. 33 n. n52 p. 5(1)
LC Call Number: May or May Not Be in LC. Search further.
Business Index Micro Film: 75N0114
Several groups belonging to the umbrella organization Media Coalition will take various measures to oppose legislation regulating violence on television when Congress resumes its sessions following winter recess. The groups, which number around 50 and include those from broadcasting and publishing, plan to raise First Amendment issues through print advertisements, news conferences and other methods. They content that the antiviolence bills will encroach on their constitutional rights and constitute a first step towards censorship.
Violence in television - Laws, regulations, etc. / Television broadcasting industry - Political activity

Rosin, Hanna
The producers. (Congress fights TV violence)
The New republic, Dec. 13, 1993, v. 209 n. n24 p. 12(2)
LC Call Number: AP2.N624; Microfilm 03363 (1914-) MicRR
Magazine Index Micro Film: None
Television broadcasting policy - Laws, regulations, etc. / Violence in television - Laws,
regulations, etc. / Sex in television - Laws, regulations, etc. / Television and children -
Laws, regulations, etc.

Rowe, Jonathan
Imagebusters, the sequel: why TV violence matters. American prospect, no. 17, spring
1994: 108-114.
Also includes "The Either/Or Fallacy" by Sissela Bok.
For Part I see LRS94-90.
Violence in television [U.S.] Law and legislation / Television and children [U.S.] /
Television industry [U.S.] / Censorship [U.S.]

Sacco, V.F. (1995)
Media Constructions of Crime. The Annals of the American Academy of Political and
Social Science 539(1995), pp. 141-154, ISSN 0002-7162.

Salgado, Richard P.
Regulating a video revolution. Yale law and policy review, v. 7, no. 2, 1989: 516-537.
Comment argues that state and local "legislatures are certainly free to draft statutes that
classify videos as indecent for children, but they must do so consistently with the
standards set forth by the Supreme Court." The author contends that drafting statutes
"that purport to regulate obscenity or indecency by referring to the [movie rating]
standards beet by the Motion Picture Association of America" is "abdicating the
responsibility for doing the 'dirty work' of video evaluations to private organizations
which are virtually immune from judicial scrutiny." The author argues that this "is not the
answer."
Home video systems [U.S.] / Television and children [U.S.] / Motion pictures [U.S.] /
Pornography [U.S.] Standards / Violence in mass media [U.S.] Standards / Government
regulation [U.S.] / Supreme Court decisions / Motion Picture Association of America

Saunders, K.W. (1996)
Violence as Obscenity: Limiting the Media's First Amendment Protection. Durkham:
Duke University Press, 1996, VIII, 246 p., ISBN 0-8223-1767-2.

Schlesinger, P. & Murdock, G. (1994)
Reporting Crime: The Media Politics of Criminal Justice. Oxford: Clarendon Press, 1994,
287 p., ISBN 0-19-825839-9.

Schlesinger, P. & Tumber, H. (1993)
Fighting the War Against Crime: Television, Police, and Audience. British Journal of
Criminology 33(1993)1, pp. 19-32, ISSN 0007-0955.

Schmuckler, Eric
Network buyers wait to see if ratings plan will affect programming or pricing
MEDIAWEEK, July 5, 1993, v. 3, n. n27 p. 4(1)
LC Call Number: HF6146.T42M43
Business Index Micro Film: None
Advertising buyers for television networks maintain that an eight-word warning label
recent required for violent shows will not affect their business. Media buyers have always
screened television shows for clients to determine suitability and will continue to do so.
The withdrawal of advertising from shows with warning labels could have the effect of
increasing rates for all other shows. Only a few shows will be affected by the label
requirements and buyers will continue to evaluate the shows independently of the
networks.
Violence in television - Laws, regulations, etc. / Television advertising - Censorship

Schrier, Helene T.
A solution to indecency on the airwaves. Federal Communications law journal, v. 41,
Nov. 1988: 69-107.
"This Comment demonstrates that the FCC's new indecency standard violates the First
Amendment because it is not sufficiently narrowly tailored to achieve the goal of
protecting children from harmful material where parents are unable to do so."
Censorship [U.S.] Legal cases / Television programs [U.S.] Legal cases / Television and
children [U.S.] Legal cases / Freedom of speech [U.S.] Legal cases

Scully, Sean
Violence laws would violate law, say lawyers. (Senate bills curbing TV violence are
unconstitutional) (Brief Article)
Broadcasting and Cable, Oct. 25, 1993, v. 123 n. n43 p. 14(1)
LC Call Number: TK6540B85
Business Index Micro Film: None
Violence in television - Laws, regulations etc. / Television programs - Censorship

Sen. Conrad seeks voluntary 'safe harbor' on violence.
Television Digest, Dec. 20, 1993, v. 33, n. n51 p. 2(2)
LC Call Number: May or May Not Be in LC. Search further.
Business Index Micro Film: 75P0691
Senator Conrad is battling for a 'tough and voluntary' antiviolence code for American
television, citing as example Canada's broad voluntary code that restricts violent shows.
Conrad has called on broadcasters, the cable industry as well as the government to adopt
new guidelines that would limit 'gratuitous, dramatized' violence from 6 a.m. to 10 p.m.
The senator and the code's proponents have sent their recommendations to Attorney

General Janet Reno.
Violence in television - Laws, regulations, etc./ Television broadcasting industry - Laws, regulations, etc.

Sen. Simon says law needed. (Paul Simon on television violence)
Variety, Dec. 17, 1990, v. 341 n. n10 p. 30(1)
LC Call Number: PN2000.V3 Folio; Microfilm 03722 (1905-   ) MicRR
Magazine Index Micro Film: None
Simon, Paul (Politician) - Political activity. Violence in television - Laws, regulations, etc. / Television programs - Laws, regulations, etc.

Sen. Simon. (feedback on Sen. Simon's appeal to curb TV violence)
Television Digest, Nov. 8, 1993, v. 33, n. n45 p. 3(1)
LC Call Number: May or May Not Be in LC. Search further.
Business Index Micro Film: 74T0676
Violence in television - Laws, regulations, etc. / Television broadcasting - Management

Senate hearing dissects violence. (on television) (Brief Article)
Variety, June 21, 1993, v. 351 n. n7 p. 24 (1)
LC Call Number: PN2000.V3 Folio; Microfilm 03722 (1905-   ) MicRR
Business Index Micro Film: None
United States. Congress. Senate - Social policy / Violence in television - Political aspects / Television broadcasting industry - Political activity

Senate hearing dissects violence. (on television) (Brief Article)
Variety, June 21, 1993, v. 351 n. n7 p. 24(1)
LC Call Number: PN2000.V3 Folio; Microfilm 03722 (1905-   ) MicRR
Magazine Index Micro Film: None
United States. Congress. Senate - Social policy / Violence in television - Political aspects / Television broadcasting industry - Political activity

Senate panel asks TV violence curb.
Television Digest, June 14, 1993, v. 33 n. n24 p. 7(1)
LC Call Number: May or May Not Be in LC. Search further.
Business Index Micro Film: 71X0384
Violence in television - Laws, regulations, etc. / Television broadcasting industry - Laws, regulations, etc. / Motion picture industry / Laws, regulations, etc.

Senate presses on violence. (television violence)
Television Digest, May 24, 1993, v. 33 n. n21 p. 5(1)
LC Call Number: May or May Not Be In LC. Search further.
Business Index Micro Film: 71T0697
The Senate Judiciary Committee has threatened the television broadcasting industry with harsh action if the industry fails to regulate violence in its programming. However,

network executives claimed that some violence was needed in television programming to remain competitive with cable and syndicated programs. But even while network representatives pointed to improvement in terms of less-violent program schedules, they also insisted that eliminating violence from television shows would be unrealistic. Executives also pointed out the need for cable, independents and the production sector to cooperate with their efforts.

United States. Congress. Senate - Social policy / Violence in television - Laws, regulations, etc. / Television broadcasting industry - Social aspects

Senator addresses TV violence. (Paul Simon urges television industry to set up an advisory panel that would monitor violent programming) (Brief Article)
Facts on File, Sept. 30, 1993, v. 53 n. n2757 p. 728(1)
LC Call Number: Not in LC Collection
Business Index Micro Film: None
Simon, Paul (Politician) - Addresses, essays, lectures
Violence in television - Laws, regulations, etc. / Television broadcasting industry - Laws, regulations, etc.

Senator addresses TV violence. (Paul Simon urges television industry to set up an advisory panel that would monitor violent programming) (Brief Article)
Facts on File, Sept. 30, 1993, v. 53 n. n2757 p. 728(1)
LC Call Number: Not in LC Collection
Magazine Index Micro Film: None
Simon, Paul (Politician) - Addresses, essays, lectures
Violence in television - Laws, regulations, etc. / Television broadcasting industry - Laws, regulations, etc.

Senator Bob Graham (D-Fla) introduced a bill last week to prohibit government agencies from advertising on violent tv shows (Brief Article)
Broadcasting and Cable, May 23, 1994, v. 124 n. n21 p. 124(2)
LC Call Number: TK6540B85
Business Index Micro Film: 78V2786
Graham, Bob - Economic policy. Television advertising - Laws, regulations, etc. / Administrative agencies - Laws, regulations, etc. / Violence in television - Laws, regulations, etc. / Television broadcasting industry - Laws, regulations, etc.

Sens Graham (and Dorgan introduce bill to prevent television advertising violence)
Television Digest, May 23, 1994, v. 34 n. n21 p. 13(1)
LC Call Number: May or May Not Be in LC. Search further.
Business Index Micro Film: 78V0039
Violence in television - Laws, regulations, etc. / Television advertising - Laws, regulations, etc.

Shiver, Jube Jr.
Lawmakers act to impose controls on TV violence. (Representative Edward Markey introduces legislation)
The Los Angeles Times, August 6, 1993, v. 112, p. D5
LC Call Number: Newspaper 7114-X
Business Index Micro Film: None
United States. Congress. House - Social policy / Violence in television - Laws, regulations, etc. / Television broadcasting - Laws, regulations, etc.

Skrzycki, Cindy
Reed Hundt of the FCC, mum on what he sees on TV. (Commissioner of the Federal Communications Commission)
The Washington Post, April 12, 1994, v 117 p. C1
LC Call Number: Newspaper
Business Index Micro Film: None
Hundt, Reed - Interviews. United States. Federal Communications Commission - Officials and employees / Violence in television - Laws, regulations, etc. / Television programs - Laws, regulations, etc.

Smith, Joan
Mrs. Mary Whitehouse's private member. (Winston Churchill Jr. and television)
New Statesman (1975), Dec. 13, 1985, v. 110 p. 10(2)
LC Call Number: AP4.N64; Microfilm (0) 83/132 (1981-1983) MicRR
Magazine Index Micro Film: None
Churchill, Winston Jr. - Social policy / Whitehouse, Mary   Social policy
Obscenity (Law) - Laws, regulations, etc. / Television - Laws, regulations, etc. / Violence in television - United Kingdom

Snyder, S. (1995)
Movie Portrayals of Juvenile Delinquency: Epidemiology and Criminology. Adolescence 30(1995)117, pp. 53-64, ISSN 0001-8449.

Son of captain law - nonviolent TV sets. (installation of blocking chips in television sets)
Television Digest, August 9, 1993, v. 33 n. n32 p. 14(1)
LC Call Number: May or May Not Be in LC. Search further.
Business Index Micro Film: 72W1327
Sen. Edward J. Markey has forwarded the bill entitled 'TV Violence Reduction Through Parental Empowerment Act of 1993,' in an effort to limit exposure of minors to violence in television. The bill proposes that television manufacturers be required to include a blocking chip feature in all sets 13 in and larger. Television manufacturers have complained that against government legislation on their manufacturing features. Manufacturers cite that legislators have shifted the responsibility for curbing television violence on them.
Markey, Edward J. - Laws, regulations, etc.

Television equipment and supplies industry - Laws, regulations, etc. / Violence in television - Laws, regulations, etc.

Spak, Michael I.
Predictable harm: should the media be liable? Ohio State Law Journal, v. 42, no. 3, 1981: 671-687.
Because "this article suggests that, in certain circumstances, television and movie producers should be able to predict with reasonable certainty that a harmful, violent act is likely to result from showing a unique act of violence," the author recommends either a "new judicially created tort theory of recovery, or the adoption of a statute designed to impose liability on the television or movie industry."
Violence research [U.S.] / Violence in mass media [U.S.] Legal cases / Television and children [U.S.] / Torts [U.S.] / Motion pictures [U.S.] Legal cases / Violence in television [U.S.] Legal cases

Sparks, R. (1996)
Masculinity and Heroism in the Hollywood 'Blockbuster': The Culture Industry and Contemporary Images of Crime and Law Enforcement. British Journal of Criminology 36(1996)3, pp. 348-360, ISSN 0007-0955.

Stern, Christopher
Broadcasters may have to accept cable violence plan. (after failing to come up with their own) (Brief Article)
Broadcasting and Cable, Jan. 17, 1994, v. 124 n. n3 p. 120(1)
LC Call Number: TK6540B85
Business Index Micro Film: None
Violence in television - Laws, regulations, etc. / Television broadcasting industry - Censorship / Cable television broadcasting industry - Censorship

Supreme Court nominee Stephen Breyer refused to talk specifically about TV violence and the First Amendment. (at Senate Judiciary Committee confirmation hearing) (Brief Article)
Broadcasting and Cable, July 25, 1994, v. 124 n. n30 p. 88(1)
LC Call Number: TK6540B85
Business Index Micro Film: None
Breyer, Stephen G. - Attitudes
United States. Supreme Court - Officials and employees / Violence in television - Laws, regulations, etc.

Surette, R. (1998)
Media, Crime, and Criminal Justice: Images and Realities. Belmont: Wadsworth Publications, 1998, XIV, 318 p., ill., bibl., ISBN 0-53450-863-4.

Surette, R. (Ed.) (1990)
The Media and Criminal Justice Policy: Recent Research and Social Effects. Springfield: C.C. Thomas Publisher, 1990, XX, 312 p., ill., ISBN 0-39805-687-0.

Sutil, C.R.; Esteban, J.L. & Takeuchi, M. (1995)
Televised Violence: A Japanese, Spanish, and American Comparison. Psychological Reports 77(1995)3, pp. 995-1000, ISSN 0033-2941.

Technology and television
The Congressional digest, Dec. 1993, v. 72 n. n12 p. 294 (2)
LC Call Number: JK1.C65
Magazine Index Micro Film: None
Violence in television - Laws, regulations, etc. / Television programs - Rating / Television - Social aspects

The '80s explosion. (violence in television) (Background)
CQ Researcher, March 26, 1993, v. 3n. n12 p. 278(2)
LC Call Number: H35.E35
Magazine Index Micro Film: None
Television portrayal of violence was boosted in the 1980's by availability of new technology and media deregulation. In spite of the far-reaching repercussions of media expansion, lawmakers were constrained against legislation on television violence. As a result, subsequent laws such as the Television Program Improvement Act of 1990 could not mandate television stations to reduce portrayals of violence. The Act could only make suggestions for and encourage reduced violence in television programs so as not to be criticized as a legislative attempt at censorship.
Violence in television - Laws, regulations, etc. / Mass media policy - Analysis

The antitrust exemption the television industry was granted so that its officials could meet and develop a voluntary approach to curbing violent programming expires this Wednesday. (Dec. 1: Justice Department might grant extension) (Brief Article)
Broadcasting and Cable, Nov. 29, 1993, v. 123 n. n48 p. 93(1)
LC Call Number: TK6540B85
Business Index Micro Film: 74W2464
Violence in television - Laws, regulations, etc. / Television broadcasting industry - Laws, regulations, etc.

The Portrayal of violence on television: BBC & IBA guidelines. [London]: British Broadcasting Corporation: Independent Broadcasting Authority, [1980]
52 p.; 23 cm.
Violence in television. I. British Broadcasting Corporation. II. Independent Broadcasting Authority.

Three new anti-violence bills on the table. (proposed broadcast television regulations) (Brief Article)
Broadcasting and Cable, August 9, 1993, v. 123 n. n32 p. 10(1)
LC Call Number: TK6540B85
Business Index Micro Film: 72X0627
United States. Congress - Social policy / Violence in television - Laws, regulations, etc. / Television broadcasting - Laws, regulations, etc.

Trueheart, Charles
Hear no evil, see no evil: Canada gets tough on TV violence.
The Washington Post, Nov. 23, 1993, v. 116, p. B1
LC Call Number: Newspaper
Business Index Micro Film: None
Violence in television - Laws, regulations, etc. / Television broadcasting policy - Canada / Canada - Social policy

Tucker, David E.; Saffelle, Jeffrey
The Federal Communications Commission and the regulation of children's television.
Journal of broadcasting, no. 3, summer 1982: 657-669.
"This paper takes a specific issue, the regulation of children's television, and shows how that issue might best be examined. The method of analysis used is the Krasnow-Longley-Terry systems approach to broadcast regulation."
Television and children [U.S.] / Television programs [U.S.] Law and legislation / U.S. Federal Communications Commission

Turner Bcstg. System. (violence ratings system for TV)
Television Digest, June 21, 1993, v. 33 n. n25 p. 6(1)
LC Call Number: May or May Not Be in LC. Search further
Business Index Micro Film: 71Z1078
Television broadcasting industry - Standards / Violence in television - Standards

TV blocking is endorsed. (technology that would allow viewers to automatically block violent television programs)
The New York Times, July 13, 1994, v. 143 p. C2 (N) pD2
LC Call Number: Not in LC Collection
Magazine Index Micro Film: None
Electronic Industries Association - Laws, regulations, etc. / Violence in television - Laws, regulations, etc.

TV stations in Britain told to curb violence. (Independent Television Commission request) (International Pages)
The New York Times, July 23, 1993, v. 142 p. A5 (N)
LC Call Number: Not in LC Collection
Magazine Index Micro Film: None

United Kingdom. Independent Television Commission - Social policy / Violence in television - Laws, regulations, etc. / Television broadcasting policy - United Kingdom.

TV violence standards. (television)
Television Digest Dec. 14, 1992, v. 32 n. n50 p. 6(1)
LC Call Number: May or May Not Be In LC. Search further.
Business Index Micro Film: 68X1254
Violence in television - Standards / Television broadcasting - Standards

TV's sickos, shooters - and kids. (2 main stations agree to warning system for violent programming) (Editorial)
The New York Times, July 1, 1993, v. 142 p. A12 (N) pA1
LC Call Number: Not in LC Collection
Business Index Micro Film: None
Television broadcasting - Laws, regulations, etc. / Violence in television - Laws, regulations, etc. / Television and children - Laws, regulations, etc.

U.K.'s Independent TV Commission. (called for reduction of TV violence)
Television Digest, July 26, 1993, v. 33 n. n30 p. 8(1)
LC Call Number: May or May Not Be in LC. Search further.
Business Index Micro Film: 72V0588
United Kingdom. Independent Television Commission - Laws, regulations, etc. / Violence in television - Laws, regulations, etc. / Television stations - Laws, regulations, etc. / United Kingdom - Business and industry
United Kingdom

U.S. Congress. House. Committee on Energy and Commerce. Subcommittee on Telecommunications and Finance.
Children's television. Hearing, 101st Congress, 1st session on II.R. 1677. April 6, 1989. Washington, G.P.O., 1989. 209 p.
"Serial no. 101-32"
Television and children [U.S.] Law and legislation / Television advertising [U.S.] Law and legislation / Television stations [U.S.] Licenses / Children's Television Act (Proposed)

U.S. Congress. House. Committee on Energy and Commerce. Subcommittee on Telecommunications and Finance.
Children's television. Hearing, 103d Congress, 1st session. Mar. 10, 1993, Washington, G.P.O., 1993, 78 p.
"Serial no. 103-27"
Television and children [U.S.] / Educational television [U.S.] / Children's Television Act.

U.S. Congress. House. Committee on Energy and Commerce. Subcommittee on Telecommunications and Finance.

Commercialization of children's television. Hearings, 100th Congress on H.R. 3288, H.R. 3966, and H.R. 4125. Washington, G.P.O., 100th 1988. 350 p.
Hearings held Sept. 15, 1987 and March 17, 1988.
"Serial no 100-93"
Television and children [U.S.] Law and legislation / Television advertising [U.S.] Law and legislation / Educational television [U.S.] Law and legislation / Television stations [U.S.] Licenses / U.S. Federal Communications Commission / Children's Television Act (Proposed) / Children's Television Practices Act (Proposed) / Children's Television Advertising Practices Act (Proposed)

U.S. Congress. House. Committee on Energy and Commerce. Subcommittee on Telecommunications and Finance.
Violence on television. Hearing, 103d Congress, 1st session. May 12-Sept. 15, 1993. Washington, G.P.O., 1994. 390 p.
"Serial no. 103-79"
Violence in television [U.S.] / Children and television [U.S.]

U.S. Congress. House. Committee on Energy and Commerce. Subcommittee on Telecommunications, Consumer Protection, and Finance.
Broadcast regulation: quantifying the public interest standard. Hearing, 98th Congress, 1st session. May 24, 1983. Washington, G.P.O., 1983. 163 p.
"Serial no. 98-61"
Radio broadcasting [U.S.] Law and legislation / Television broadcasting [U.S.] Law and legislation / Telecommunication law and legislation [U.S.] / Radio broadcasting [U.S.] Licenses / Television broadcasting [U.S.] Licenses / Radio programs [U.S.] Law and legislation / Television programs [U.S.] Law and legislation / Government regulation [U.S.] / Television and children [U.S.] / Television industry [U.S.] / Broadcasting Public Responsibility Deregulation Act (Proposed)

U.S. Congress. House. Committee on Energy and Commerce. Subcommittee on Telecommunications, Consumer Protection and Finance.
Children and television. Hearing, 98th Congress, 1st session. March 16, 1983. Washington, G.PO., 1983. 217 p.
Television and children [U.S.]
U.S. Congress. House. Committee on Energy and Commerce. Subcommittee on Telecommunications, Consumer Protection, and Finance.
Children's television programming. Hearings, 99th Congress, 1st session on H.R. 3216; a bill to amend the Communications Act of 1984 to increase the availability of educational and informational television programs for children. Washington, G.P.O., 1986. 143 p.
"Serial no. 99-66"
Hearings held Oct. 25, 1985 - Dallas, TX [and] Oct. 28, 1985 - Houston, TX
Television and children [U.S.] Law and legislation / Television programs [U.S.] / Government regulation [U.S.] / Communications Act / U.S. Federal Communications Commission

U.S. Congress. House. Committee on Energy and Commerce. Subcommittee on
Telecommunications, Consumer Protection and Finance.
Potential of television in educating children. Joint hearing before the Subcommittee on
Telecommunications, Consumer Protection and Finance of the Committee on Energy and
Commerce and the Subcommittee on Elementary, Secondary and Vocational Education
of the Committee on Education and Labor, House of Representatives, 98th Congress, 1st
session. Oct. 5, 1983. Washington, G.P.O., 1984. 104 p.
"Serial no. 98-86 (Committee on Energy and Commerce)"
Television and children [U.S.] / Learning [U.S.] / Educational television [U.S.] /
Television programs [U.S.]

U.S. Congress. House. Committee on Energy and Commerce. Subcommittee on
Telecommunications, Consumer Protection and Finance.
Social/behavioral effects of violence on television. Hearing, 97th Cong., 1st sess. Oct. 21,
1981. Washington, U.S. Govt. Print. Off., 1982. 248 p.
"Serial no. 97-84"
Television programs [U.S.] / Violence in television [U.S.] / Television and children
[U.S.]

U.S. Congress. House. Committee on Energy and Commerce.
Children's Television Act of 1989: report together with dissenting views to accompany
H.R . 1677 including cost estimate of the Congressional Budget Office. [Washington,
G.P.O.] 1989, 22 p. (Report, House, 101st Congress, 1st session, no. 101-385)
Television and children [U.S.] Law and legislation / Government regulation [U.S.] Law
and legislation / Children's television Act (Proposed)

U.S. Congress. House. Committee on Interstate and Foreign Commerce. Subcommittee
on Communications.
Federal Communications Commission oversight. Hearings, 94th Cong., 2d sess., on the
functions and duties of the Federal Communications Commission. March 2-3, 1976.
Washington, U.S. Govt. Print. Off., 1976. 105 p.
"Serial no. 94-89"
Independent regulatory commissions / Television news [U.S.] / Television programs
[U.S.] / Television and children [U.S.] / Television in politics [U.S.] / Fairness doctrine /
Citizens band radio [U.S.] / U.S. Federal Communications Commission

U.S. Congress. House. Committee on Interstate and Foreign Commerce. Subcommittee
on Communications.
Sex and violence on TV. Hearing, 95th Congress, 1st session, March 2, 1977.
Washington, U.S. Govt. Print. Off., 1978. 481 p.
"Serial no. 95-130"
Television programs [U.S.] / Sex [U.S.] / Violence in television [U.S.] / Television and
children [U.S.]

U.S. Congress. House. Committee on Interstate and Foreign Commerce. Subcommittee on Communications. Sex and violence on TV. Hearings, 94th Cong., 2d sess. Washington, U.S. Govt. Print. Off., 1977, 378 .
Hearings held July 9... Aug. 18, 1976.
"Serial no. 94-140"
Television programs [U.S.] / violence in television [U.S.] / Sex [U.S.] / Television and children [U.S.]

U.S. Congress. House. Committee on Interstate and Foreign Commerce. Subcommittee on Communications.
Violence on television; report together with additional, dissenting and separate views. Washington, U.S. Govt. Print. Off., 1977, 35 p.
At head of title: 95th Cong., 1st sess. Committee print 95-28
Television programs [U.S.] / Violence in television

U.S. Congress. House. Committee on the Judiciary
Television Violence Act of 1989: report together with dissenting views to accompany H.R. 1391, including cost estimate of the Congressional Budget Office. Washington, G.P.O., 1989, 15 p. (Report. House, 101st Congress, 1st session, no. 101-123)
Violence in television [U.S.] Law and legislation / Television Violence Act (Proposed)

U.S. Congress. House. Committee on the Judiciary. Subcommittee on Crime.
Crime and violence in the media. Hearing, 98th Congress, 1st session. April 13, 1983. Washington, G.P.O., 1984, 305 p.
"Serial no. 83"
Television and children [U.S.] / Television programs [U.S.] / Violence in television [U.S.]

U.S. Congress. House. Committee on the Judiciary. Subcommittee on Crime and Criminal Justice.
Violence on television. Hearing, 102nd Congress, 2nd session. Dec. 15, 1992. Washington, G.P.O., 1993, 179 p.
"Serial no. 115"
Violence in television [U.S.] / Violence research [U.S.] / Television and children [U.S.] / Child psychology [U.S.]

U.S. Congress. House. Committee on the Judiciary. Subcommittee on Economic and Commercial Law.
Television Violence Act of 1989. Hearing, 101st Congress, 1st session on H.R. 1391. May 10, 1989, Washington, G.P.O., 1990, 182 p.
"Serial no. 34"
Violence in television [U.S.] Law and legislation / Television industry [U.S.] Law and legislation / Restrictive trade practices [U.S.] Law and legislation / Television and children [U.S.] / Television Violence Act (Proposed)

U.S. Congress. House. Committee on the Judiciary. Subcommittee on Monopolies and Commercial Law.
Television Violence Act of 1988. Hearing, 100th Congress, 2nd session on H.R. 3848. Oct. 5, 1988. Washington, G.P.O., 1989. 133 p.
"Serial no. 87"
Violence in television [U.S.] Law and legislation / Television industry [U.S.] Law and legislation / Restrictive trade practices [U.S.] Law and legislation / Television and children [U.S.] / Television Violence Act (Proposed)

U.S. Congress. Senate. Committee on Commerce, Science and Transportation. Children's Television Act of 1989; report together with minority views on S. 1992. Washington, G.P.O. 1989. 28 p. (Report, Senate, 101st Congress, 1st session, no. 101-227)
Television and children [U.S.] Law and legislation [U.S.] / Children's Television Act (Proposed)

U.S. Congress. Senate. Committee on Commerce, Science and Transportation.
National Endowment for Children's Educational Television Act of 1989; report on S. 797. Washington, G.P.O., 1989. 23 p. (Report, Senate, 101st Congress, 1st session, no. 101-66)
Educational television [U.S.] Law and legislation / Television and children [U.S.] Law and legislation / Federal aid to education [U.S.] Law and legislation / National Endowment for Children's Educational Television (Proposed)

U.S. Congress. Senate. Committee on Commerce, Science and Transportation.
Subcommittee on Communications.
Broadcasting Improvements Act of 1987. Hearing, 100th Congress, 1st session on S. 1277. July 17 and 20, 1987. Washington, G.P.O., 1987. 169 p. (Hearing. Senate. 100th Congress, 1st session, S. Hrg. 100-314)
Broadcasting [U.S.] Law and legislation / Broadcasting [U.S.] Licenses / Regulatory reform [U.S.] / Independent regulatory commissions / Television industry [U.S.] / Television and children [U.S.] / Minorities in the mass media industry [U.S.] / Broadcasting Improvements Act (Proposed) / U.S. Federal Communications Commission

U.S. Congress. Senate. Committee on Commerce, Science and Transportation.
Subcommittee on Communications. Television broadcast policies. Hearings, 95th Cong., 1st sess. May 9,10 and 11, 1977. Washington, U.S. Govt. Print. Off., 1977, 512 p.
"Serial no. 95-60"
Television programs [U.S.] / Television and children [U.S.] / Cable television [U.S.] / Violence in television [U.S.] / Fairness doctrine / Television industry [U.S.] / Television advertising [U.S.] / Discrimination in employment [U.S.] / U.S. Federal Communications Commission

U.S. Congress. Senate. Committee on Commerce. Science and Transportation.
Subcommittee on Communications.

Children's TV Act of 1989. Hearing, 101st Congress, 1st session on S. 707 and S. 1215.
July 12, 1989. Washington, G.P.O., 1989, 115 p. (Hearing. Senate. 101st Congress, 1st
session, S. Hrg. 101-221)
Television and children [U.S.] Law and legislation / Television advertising [U.S.] Law
and legislation / Educational television [U.S.] Law and legislation / Television stations
[U.S.] Licenses / Children's Television Act (Proposed) / Children's Television Education
Act (Proposed) / U.S. Federal Communications Commission

U.S. Congress. Senate. Committee on Commerce. Subcommittee on Communications.
Impact of television on children. Hearing, 94th Cong., 2d sess., Feb. 13, 1976.
Washington, U.S. Govt. Print. Off., 1976. 62 p.
"Serial no. 94-62"
Television and children [Utah]

U.S. Congress. Senate. Committee on the Judiciary. Subcommittee on Antitrust,
Monopolies and Business Rights.
Television violence antitrust exemption. Hearing, 100th Congress, 1st session o S. 844.
June 25, 1987. Washington, G.P.O., 1987. 182 p. (Hearing, Senate, 100th Congress, 1st
session, S. Hrg. 100-276)
"Serial no. J-100-27"
Violence in television [U.S.] Law and legislation / Television industry [U.S.] Law and
legislation / Restrictive trade practices [U.S.] Law and legislation / Television and
children [U.S.]

U.S. Congress. Senate. Committee on the Judiciary. Subcommittee on Juvenile Justice.
Media violence. Hearing, 98th Congress, 2nd session, Oct. 25, 1984. Washington,
G.P.O., 1985. 121 p. (Hearing, Senate, 98th Congress, 2nd session, S. Hrg. 98-1283)
"Serial no. J-98-147"
Violence in television [U.S.] / Television and children [U.S.] / Television programs
[U.S.]

U.S. Congress. Senate. Committee on the Judiciary. Subcommittee on the Constitution.
Implementation of the Television Program Improvement Act of 1990. Joint hearings
before the Subcommittee on the Constitution and the Subcommittee on Juvenile Justice
of the Committee on the Judiciary. United States Senate, 103d Congress, 1st session.
May 21 and June 8, 1994. Washington, G.P.O., 1994. 205 p. (Hearing, Senate, 103d
Congress, 2d session, S. Hrg. 103-657)
"Serial no. J-103-13"
Violence in television [U.S.] Law and legislation / Television programs [U.S.] / Antitrust
law [U.S.] / Television and children [U.S.] / Violence research [U.S.] Television
Program Improvement Act of 1990

U.S. Congress. Senate. Committee on the Judiciary.
Exempting certain activities from provisions of the antitrust laws; report together with

additional views to accompany S. 2323. [Washington, G.P.O.] 1986, 26 p. (Report, Senate, 99th Congress, 2nd session, no. 99-535)
"As amended by the Committee, S. 2323 grants an exemption from the antitrust laws to the television industry that is carefully limited both in time and scope. It permits certain parties in the industry to act jointly during a period of 36 months from the date the bill is enacted for the narrow purpose of developing and disseminating voluntary guidelines designed to alleviate the negative effects of televised violence on children and adults."
Antitrust law [U.S.] / Television broadcasting [U.S.] / Television programs [U.S.] Law and legislation / Violence in television [U.S.] Law and legislation

U.S. Congress. Senate. Committee on the Judiciary.
Exempting certain activities from provisions of the antitrust laws; report together with additional views to accompany S. 844. [Washington, G.P.O.] 1988, 11 p. (Report, Senate, 100th Congress, 2nd session, no. 100-365)
Antitrust law [U.S.] / Television programs [U.S.] Law and legislation / Violence in television [U.S.] Law and legislation / Television broadcasting [U.S.] Law and legislation
U.S. Congress. Senate. Committee on the Judiciary.
Exempting certain activities from provisions of the antitrust laws; report together with additional views to accompany S. 2323. [Washington, G.P.O.] 1986, 26 p. (Report, Senate, 99th Congress, 2nd session, no. 99-535)
"As amended by the Committee, S. 2323 grants an exemption from the antitrust laws to the television industry that is carefully limited both in time and scope. It permits certain parties in the industry to act jointly during a period of 36 months from the date the bill is enacted for the narrow purpose of developing and disseminating voluntary guidelines designed to alleviate the negative effects of televised violence on children and adults."
Antitrust law [U.S.] / Television broadcasting [U.S.] / Television programs [U.S.] Law and legislation / Violence in television [U.S.] Law and legislation

U.S. Congress. Senate. Committee on the Judiciary.
Exempting certain activities from provisions of the antitrust laws; report together with additional views to accompany S. 844. [Washington, G.P.O.] 1988, 11 p. (Report, Senate, 100th Congress, 2nd session, no. 100-365)
Antitrust law [U.S.] / Television programs [U.S.] Law and legislation / Violence in television [U.S.] Law and legislation / Television broadcasting [U.S.] Law and legislation

U.S. Congress. Senate. Committee on the Judiciary.
TV violence antitrust exemption. Hearing, 99th Congress, 2nd session on S. 2323. June 20, 1986. Washington, G.P.O., 1986. 111 p. (Hearing, Senate, 99th Congress, 2nd session, S. Hrg. 99-925)
"Serial no. J-99-111"
Violence in television [U.S.] Law and legislation / Television industry [U.S.] Law and legislation / Restrictive trade practices [U.S.] Law and legislation / Television and children [U.S.]

U.S. Congress. House. Committee on Energy and Commerce
Children's Television Practices Act of 1988: report together with dissenting views to
accompany H.R. 3966 including cost estimate of the Congressional Budget Office.
[Washington, G.P.O.] 1988, 23 p. (Report. House, 100th Congress, 2nd session, no. 100-
675)
Television and children [U.S.] Law and legislation / Television advertising [U.S.] Law
and legislation / Television programs [U.S.] / Government regulation [U.S.] / Children's
Television Act / U.S. Federal Communications Commission

United States. Congress. House. Committee on Interstate and Foreign Commerce.
Subcommittee on Communications. Sex and violence on TV: hearings before the
Subcommitttee on Communications of the Committee on Interstate and Foreign
Commerce, House of Representatives, Ninety-fourth Congress, second session, on the
issue of televised violence and obscenity, July 9, August 17 and 18, 1976. Washington:
U.S. Govt. Prin. Off., 1977. iv, 378 p.; 24 cm. "Serial no. 94-140." Includes
bibliographical references.
Violence in television - United States. Sex in television. I. Title.

United States. Congress. House. Committee on Interstate and Foreign Commerce.
Subcommittee on Communications. Sex and violence on TV: Hearings before the
Subcommittee on Communications of the Committee on Interstate and Foreign
Commerce, House of Representatives, Ninety-fifth Congress, first session March 2, 1977.
Washington: U.S. Govt. Print. Of., 1978.
iv, 481 p.: ill.; 24 cm. "Serial no. 95-130." Includes bibliographical references.
Violence in television - United States. Sex in television. Television - United States.

United States. Congress. House. Committee on Interstate and Foreign Commerce.
Subcommittee on Communications. Violence on television: report, together with
additional, dissenting, and separate views / by the Subcommittee on Communications of
the Committee on Interstate and Foreign Commerce, House of Representatives, Ninety-
Fifth Congress, first session. - Washington: U.S. Govt. Print. Off., 1977.
iii, 35 p.; 23 cm.
At head of title: 95th Congress, 1st session. Committee print. Committee print 95-28.
Includes bibliographical references.
Violence in television - United States. I. Title.

United States. Congress. House. Committee on the Judiciary. Subcommittee on Crime.
Crime and violence in the media: hearing before the Subcommittee on Crime of the
Committee on the Judiciary, House of Representatives, Ninety-eighth Congress, first
session... April 13, 1983. Washington, U.S. G.P.O., 1984.
iii, 305 p.: ill.; 24 cm.
Distributed to some depository libraries in microfiche. Includes bibliographies. "Serial
no. 83." Item 1020-A, 1020-B (microfiche). Supt. of Docs. no.: Y 4. J 89/1:98/83
Violence in television - United States. Crime in television - United States. I. Title.

United States. Congress. House. Committee on the Judiciary. Subcommittee on Economic and Commercial Law. Television Violence Act of 1989: hearing before the Subcommittee on Economic and Commercial Law of the Committee on the Judiciary, House of Representatives. One Hundred First Congress, first session, on H.R. 1391... May 10, 1989. Washington: U.S. G.P.O.: For sale by the Supt. of Docs., Congressional Sales Office, U.S. G.P.O., 1990.
iv, 182 p.; 24 cm. Distributed to some depository libraries in microfiche. Shipping list no.: 90-077-P. Includes bibliographical references. "Serial no. 34." Item 1020-A, 1020-B (MF) Supt. of Docs. no.: Y 4.J 89/1:101/34
Violence in television - Law and legislation - United States. Television - Law and legislation - United States. Antitrust Law - United States. I. Title.

United States. Congress. House. Committee on the Judiciary. Subcommittee on Monopolies and Commercial Law. Television Violence Act of 1988: hearing before the Subcommittee on the Judiciary, House of Representatives, One Hundredth Congress, second session, on H.R. 3848... October 5, 1988. Washington: U.S. G.P.O.: For sale by the Supt. of Docs., Congressional Sales Office, U.S. G.P.O., 1989
iii, 133 p.; 24 cm. Distributed to some depository libraries in microfiche. Shipping list no.: 89-148-P. "Serial no. 87." Item 1020-A, 1020-B (microfiche). Supt. of Docs. no.: Y 4.J 89/1:100/87.
Violence in television - Law and legislation - United States. Television - Law and legislation - United States. Antitrust law - United States. I. Title.

United States. Congress. Senate. Committee on Commerce. Subcommittee on Communications. Violence on television. Hearings, Ninety-third Congress, second session... April 3, 4 and 5, 1974. Washington, U.S. Govt. Print. Off., 1974.
iii, 194 p. illus. 24 cm. "Serial no. 93-76." Includes bibliographical references.
Violence in television - United States. Television and children. I. Title.

United States. Congress. Senate. Committee on the Judiciary.
TV violence antitrust exemption: hearing before the Committee on the Judiciary, United States Senate, Ninety-ninth Congress, second session, on S. 2323... June 20, 1986. Washington: U.S. G.P.O.: For sale by the Supt. of Docs., Congressional Sales Office, U.S. G.P.O., 1986.
iv, 111 p.: ill.; 24 cm. (S. hrg.; 99-925)
Distributed to some depository libraries in microfiche. Shipping list no.: 86-998-P. Bibliography: p.97-98. "Serial no. J-99-111." Item 1042-A, 1042-B (microfiche). Supt. of Docs. no.: Y 4.J 89/2:S.hrg. 99-925.
Violence in television - Law and legislation - United States. Television - Law and legislation - United States. Antitrust law - United States. I. Title. II. Series: United States. Congress. Senate. S. hrg.; 99-925.

United States. Congress. Senate. Committee on the Judiciary. Subcommittee on Antitrust, Monopolies, and Business Rights.
Television violence antitrust exemption: hearing before the Subcommittee on Antitrust, Monopolies, and Business Rights of the Committee on the Judiciary, United States Senate, One Hundredth Congress, first session on S. 844... June 25, 1987. Washington: U.S. G.P.O.: For sale by the Supt. of Docs., Congressional Sales Office, U.S. G.P.O., 1987 [i.e. 1989].
iv, 182 p.; 24 cm. (S. hrg.; 100-976)
Distributed to some depository library in microfiche. Shipping list no.: 89-126-P.
Includes bibliographies. "Serial no. J-100-27." Item 1042-A, 1042-B (microfiche). Supt. of Docs. no: Y 4.J 89/2:S.hrg.100-976.
Violence in television - Law and legislation - United States. Television - Law and legislation - United States. Antitrust law - United States. I. Title. II. Series: United States. Congress. Senate. S. hrg.; 100-976.

United States. Congress. House. Committee on Energy and Commerce. Subcommittee on Telecommunications and Finance.
Title: Violence on television : hearings before the Subcommittee on Telecommunications and Finance of the Committee on Energy and Commerce, House of Representatives, One Hundred Third Congress, first session, May 12, June 25, July 1, 29, and September 15, 1993
SuDocs Call No.: Y 4.EN 2/3:103-79
Published: Washington : U.S. G.P.O. : For sale by the U.S. G.P.O., Supt. of Docs., Congressional Sales Office, Date: 1994. Description: iii, 390 p. ; 24 cm. Item No.: 1019-A
1019-B (MF)

United States. Congress. Senate. Committee on Commerce, Science, and Transportation.
Children's Protection from Violent Programming Act of 1995 : report of the Committee on Commerce, Science, and Transportation together with additional and minority views on S. 470.
Washington : U.S. G.P.O., 1995. ii, 32 p. ; 23 cm. Report / 104th Congress, 1st session, Senate ; 104-171.

United States. Congress. Senate. Committee on Commerce, Science, and Transportation.
SuDocs Call No.: Y 4.C 73/7:S.HRG.103-852
Title: S. 1383, Children's Protection from Violent Programming Act of 1993 : S. 973, Television Report Card Act of 1993, and S. 943, Children's Television Violence Protection Act of 1993 : hearing before the Committee on Commerce, Science, and Transportation, United States Senate, One Hundred Third Congree, first session, October 20, 1993.

Published: Washington : U.S. G.P.O. : For sale by the U.S. G.P.O., Supt. of Docs., Congressional Sales Office, Date: 1994. Description: iv, 133 p. ; 24 cm. Series: S. hrg. ; 103-852 Item No.: 1041-A 1041-B (MF)

United States. Congress. Senate. Committee on Commerce, Science, and Transportation. Television Violence Report Card Act of 1995 : report of the Committee on Commerce, Science, and Transportation together with minority views on S. 772.
Published: Washington : U.S. G.P.O., Date: 1996. Description: ii, 19 p. ; 24 cm. Series: Report / 104th Congress, 2d session, Senate ; 104-234 Item No.: 1008-C 1008-D (MF)

United States. Congress. Senate. Committee on Governmental Affairs. Subcommittee on Oversight of Government Management, Restructuring, and the District of Columbia. SuDocs Call No.: Y 4.G 74/9:S.HRG.105-218
Title: Government and television : improving programming without censorship : hearings before the Subcommittee on Oversight of Government Management, Restructuring, and the District of Columbia of the Committee on Governmental Affairs, United States Senate, One Hundred Fifth Congress, first session, April 16 and May 8, 1997.
Published: Washington : U.S. G.P.O. : For sale by the U.S. G.P.O., Supt. of Docs., Congressional Sales Office, Date: 1997.

United States. Congress. Senate. Committee on the Judiciary. Subcommittee on the Constitution. United States. Congress. Senate. Committee on the Judiciary. Subcommittee on Juvenile Justice.
SuDocs Call No.: Y 4.J 89/2:S.HRG.103-657
Title: Implementation of the Television Program Improvement Act of 1990 : joint hearings before the Subcommittee on the Constitution and the Subcommittee on Juvenile Justice of the Committee on the Judiciary, United States Senate, One Hundred Third Congress, first session ... May 21 and June 8, 1993.
Published: Washington : U.S. G.P.O. : For sale by the U.S. G.P.O., Supt. of Docs., Congressional Sales Office, Date: 1994. Description: vi, 205 p. : ill. ; 24 cm. Series: S. hrg. ; 103-657 Item No.: 1042-A 1042-B (MF)

United States. Federal Communications Commission. Report on the broadcast on the broadcast of violent, indecent, and obscene material [Washington]: Federal Communications Commission, 1975.
10, [38] p.; 27 cm. "FCC 75-202; 30159."
Violence in television - Law and legislation - United States. Obscenity (Law) - United States. Television - Law and legislation - United States. I. Title.

Uscinski, Henry John
Deregulating commercial television: will the marketplace watch out for children?
American University Law review, v. 34, fall 1984: 141-173.
Comment "examines the background of the FCC's regulation of children's programming

and commercial advertising practices during children's programs; traces the shift in the FCC's regulatory perspective from a public trustee model to a marketplace model; [and] analyzes the [Children's Television Programming and Advertising Practices: Report and Order, Docket No. 19142] from both legal and policy standpoints."
Television and children [U.S.] Law and legislation / Television broadcasting [U.S.] Licenses / Television programs [U.S.] Standards / U.S. Federal Communications Commission

Valenti prods TV execs to restrict violence. (Jack Valenti)
The Los Angeles Times, Jan. 28, 1994, v. 113 p. D4
LC Call Number: Newspaper 7114-X
Business Index Micro Film: None
Valenti, Jack - Attitudes
Violence in television - Laws, regulations, etc / Television broadcasting industry - Social policy
Video violence. (regulation of video games and television) (Editorial)
The Washington Post, May 31, 1993, v. 116 p. A18
LC Call Number: Newspaper
Business Index Micro Film: None
Video games - Social aspects / Video game industry - Laws, regulations, etc. / Violence in television - Laws, regulations, etc.

Violence conference fails to calm Congress. (violence on television)
Television Digest, August 9, 1993, v. 33 n. n32 p. 1(2)
LC Call Number: May or May Not Be in LC. Search further.
Business Index Micro Film: 72W1314
Advocates of regulation violence on television in the US Congress have presented different proposals to this end, despite the entertainment industry's efforts to establish self-policing guidelines. House Telecommunication Subcommittee Chmn. Edward Markey proposed that television manufacturers by required to include a blocking chip which would allow parents to block off television programs and time slots considered too violent for young children. On the other hand, Reps. Bryant and Holling propose that the FCC should take a more direct approach by specifying the hours when programs cannot include violent scenes.
Markey, Edward J. - Laws, regulations, etc.
United States. Congress - Laws, regulations, etc. / Violence in television - Conferences, meetings, seminars, etc. / Television broadcasting industry - Laws, regulations, etc.

Violence on television: pros & cons. Congressional digest, v. 72, Dec. 1993: whole issue (289-314 p.)
Presents background information on and separate arguments for and against the passage of legislation regulating television violence.
Violence in television [U.S.] Pro and con / Violence in television [U.S.] Law and

legislation / Television and children [U.S.] Law and legislation / Censorship [U.S.] Pro
and con / Censorship [U.S.] Law and legislation

Violent home videogames are "extreme junk." (Brief Article)
Television Digest, Dec. 6, 1993, v. 33 n. n49 p. 7(1)
LC Call Number: May or May Not Be in LC. Search further
Business Index Micro Film: 74Y0534
Video games - Laws, regulations, etc. / Video game industry - Laws, regulations, etc. /
Violence in television - Laws, regulations, etc.

Violent reactions. (regulating violence on television) (Editorial)
Economist (London), August 13, 1994, v. 332 n. n7876 p. 18(1)
LC Call Number: HG11.E2; Microfilm 03394 (1843-) MicRR
Business Index Micro Film: None
Violence in television - Laws, regulations, etc./ Violence in children - Psychological
aspects / Television programs - Rating

Washington Gov. Mike Lowry (signs omnibus youth bill)
Television Digest, April 11, 1994, v. 34 n. n15 p. 15(1)
LC Call Number: May or May Not Be in LC. Search further.
Business Index Micro Film: 77Z0606
Lowry, Mike - Laws, regulations, etc.
Violence in children - Laws, regulations, etc. / Television and youth - Laws, regulations,
etc. / Violence in television - Laws, regulations, etc.

Weiss, H.J. (1997)
Extreme Right-Wing Racial Violence: An Effect of the Mass Media? European Journal
of Communication Research 22 (1997)1, pp. 57-68.

West, Woody
TV's bigwigs are a smash at the Capitol Hill comedy club. (congressional investigation
into violence on television) (The Last Word) (Column)
Insight, July 5, 1993, v. 9 n. n27 p. 40(1)
LC Call Number: AP2.I624
Magazine Index Micro Film: None
Stringer, Howard - Evidence
United States. Congress. Senate - Investigations / Violence in television - Social aspects

Wharton, Dennis
Bush likely to greenlight anti-violence TV bill.
Variety, Nov. 5, 1990, v. 341 n. n4 p. 41(1)
LC Call Number: PN2000.V3 Folio; Microfilm 03722 (1905-) MicRR
Magazine Index Micro Film: None

Bush, George - Political activity
Television - Laws, regulations, etc. / Violence in television - Laws, regulations, etc.

Wharton, Dennis
Congress back with a chip. (legislation on television violence) (Brief Article)
Variety, Sept. 13, 1993, v. 352 n. n5 p. 19(2)
LC Call Number: PN2000.V3 Folio; Microfilm 03722 (1905-   ) MicRR
Business Index Micro Film: None
Markey, Edward J. - Political activity
Violence in television - Laws, regulations, etc. / Television broadcasting industry - Laws,
regulations, etc.

Wharton, Dennis
Congress back with a chip. (legislation on television violence) (Brief Article)
Variety, Sept. 13, 1993, v. 352 n. n5 p. 19(2)
LC Call Number: PN2000.V3 Folio; Microfilm 03722 (1905-) MicRR
Magazine Index Micro Film: none
Markey, Edward J. - Political activity
Violence in television - Laws, regulations, etc. / Television broadcasting industry - Laws,
regulations, etc.

Wharton, Dennis
New anti-TV violence bill targets promos (Brief Articles)
Variety, Nov. 1, 1993, v. 352 n. n12 p. 28(1)
LC Call Number: PN2000.V3 Folio; Microfilm 03722 (1905-) MicRR
Magazine Index Micro Film: None
Levin, Carl - Social policy
Violence in television - Laws, regulations, etc. / Television broadcasting industry - Laws,
regulations, etc.

Wharton, Dennis
New anti-TV violence bill targets promos. (Brief Article)
Variety, Nov. 1, 1993, v. 352, n. n12 p. 28(1)
LC Call Number: PN2000.V3 Folio; Microfilm 03722 (1905-) MicRR
Business Index Micro Film: None
Levin, Carl - Social policy
Violence in television - Laws, regulations, etc./ Television broadcasting industry - Laws,
regulations, etc.

Wharton, Dennis
Simon says nets will create violence rules. (Senator Paul Simon, television violence)
(Brief Article)
Variety, Dec. 14, 1992, v. 349 n. n8 p. 22(1)
LC Call Number: PN2000.V3 Folio; Microfilm 03722 (1905-) MicRR

Magazine Index Micro Film: none
Simon, Paul (Politician) - Political activity
Violence in television - Laws, regulations, etc.

Wharton, Dennis
Violence on the train to Reno. (Attorney General Janet Reno's stance on television violence)
Variety, Nov. 1, 1993, v. 352, n. n12 p. 25 (2)
LC Call Number: PN2000.V3 Folio; Microfilm 03722 (1905-) MicRR
Business Index Micro Film: None
Reno, Janet - Social Policy
Violence in television - Laws, regulations, etc. / Television broadcasting industry - Laws, regulations, etc. / Attorneys general - Social policy

Wharton, Dennis
Violence on the train to Reno. (Attorney General Janet Reno's stance on television violence)
Variety, Nov. 1, 1993, v. 352 n. n12 p. 25(2)
LC Call Number: PN2000.V3 Folio; Microfilm 03722 (1905-) MicRR
Magazine Index Micro Film: None
Reno, Janet - Social Policy
Violence in television - Laws, regulations, etc. Television broadcasting industry - Laws, regulations, etc. / Attorneys general - Social policy

Wharton, Dennis; Lowry, Brian
Violence erupts in D.C., Hollywood (legislation on violence in the media)
Variety, August 16, 1993, v. 352 n. n1 p. 18(1)
LC Call Number: PN2000.V3 Folio; Microfilm 03722 (1905-) MicRR
Magazine Index Micro Film: None
Simon, Paul (Politician) - Political activity
United States. Federal Communications Commission - Laws, regulations, etc. / Violence in television - Laws, regulations, etc./ Television broadcasting industry - Laws, regulations, etc.

Wharton, Dennis; Lowry, Brian
Violence erupts in D.C., Hollywood. (legislation on violence in media)
Variety, August 16, 1993, v. 352 n. n1 p. 18(1)
LC Call Number: PN2000.V3 Folio; Microfilm 03722 (1905-) MicRR
Business Index Micro Film: None
Simon, Paul (Politician) - Political activity
United States. Federal Communications Commission - Laws, regulations, etc. / Violence in television - Laws, regulations, etc. / Television broadcasting industry - Laws, regulations, etc.

Wilhelm, William Banks, Jr.
In the interest of children: Action for Children's Television v. FCC improperly delineating the constitutional limits of broadcast indecency regulation. Catholic University law review, v. 42, fall 1992: 215-246.
'This Note explores the history of cases and regulations affecting the broadcast of indecent programming and analyzes how the court's reasoning in ACT II may affect the future of broadcast content regulation. The Note first examines the FCC's struggle to define 'indecency,' as well as the agency's more recent efforts to establish a liberal construction of the term. The Note then explores the agency's shift from the limited enforcement of indecency to a twenty-four-hour-a-day standard. Next, this Note examines how the United States Supreme Court's prohibition of a total ban on indecent telephone messages affected the outcome of ACT II. This Note considers the ACT II decision an concludes that the court's reasoning in ACT II was flawed because the court failed to consider all relevant issues in a manner wholly consistent with Supreme Court precedent."
Television and children [U.S.] Legal cases / Child psychology [U.S.] / Pornography [U.S.] / Censorship [U.S.] / Action for Children's Television v. FCC

Wines, Michael
Reno chastises TV executives over violence. (Attorney General Janet Reno testifies before Senate Commerce Committee)
The New York Times, Oct. 21, 1993, v. 143 p. A1(N) ppA1
LC Call Number: Not in LC Collection
Magazine Index Micro Film: None
Reno, Janet - Social policy
United States. Congress. Senate. Committee on Commerce, Science and Transportation - Social policy / Violence in television - Laws, regulations, etc. / Television broadcasting industry - Laws, regulations, etc.

Sex in Television

Clark, Charles S.
Sex, violence and the media.
CQ Researcher, Nov 17, 1995 v5 n43 p1019(17)
VII. Dreamworlds 2 [videorecording] : desire/sex/power in music video / written, edited & narrated by Sut Jhally.
[2nd ed.]
Northampton, MA : Media Education Foundation, c1995.
1 videocassette (57 min.) : sd., col. ; 1/2 in. + 1 information sheet.
PN1992.8.M87
VHS format.
Musicians, Paul Eggleston, Peter Cororan, Peter Muller, Joshua Thayer, Joseph Bartone ; musical director, Joe Bartone II.
Composer, Joe Bartone II.
Updated ed. of the 1991 program: Dreamworlds : desire/sex/power in rock video.
Warning: this video contains a very brutal and shocking scene of sexual violence. It is imperative that instructors view the tape beforehand, provide adequate warning to students, and ensure that they can leave the screening at any time, if they desire--cassette label. A controversial video that MTV tried to ban. Portrays the impact that sex and violence in media have on society and culture in our everyday life. Shows scenes from over 165 music videos to show how the media portrays masculinity, femininity, sex, and sex roles. Includes a scene of a brutal gang rape from the movie, The accused.

Coe, Steve
ABC to viewers: dial M for murder; network installs hotline. (American Broadcasting Companies Inc. violence warnings)
Broadcasting and Cable, August 2, 1993, v. 123 n. n31 p. 16(1)
LC Call Number: TK6540B85
Business Index Micro Film: 72V1387
American Broadcasting Companies Inc. (ABC) has installed a toll-free telephone number to inform viewers of violence in certain network programs. Viewers will learn of the service when the network beings broadcasting announcements on Aug. 1, 1993. ABC is also cutting some footage from its new program 'NYPD Blue' because of sexual content. No nude scenes have been eliminated, but ABC believes that all its affiliates will carry the program. While the show will carry an adult language and nudity warning, there will

be no violence warning.
Broadcasting industry - Management / Violence in television - Management/ Sex in television - Management

Coe, Steve; Jessell, Harry A.
'NYPD Blue;' rocky start, on a roll. (includes related interview with Steven Bochco and related article on indecency complaints against the show) (Cover Story)
Broadcasting and Cable, Nov. 1, 1993, v. 123 n. n44 p 18(3)
LC Call Number: TK6540B85
Business Index Micro Film: 74Z1975
'NYPD Blue' is the highest-rated new drama and the third highest-rated new series of the 1993 television season, despite the controversy that has surrounded it. Most of the discussion revolves around the show's purported violence, sexuality and profanity, but program creator Steven Bochco says viewers continue to watch because of the show's imagination and quality. Donald Wildmon, long time opponent of sex and violence in television, has mounted a campaign against Capital Cities/ABC Inc. for scheduling the show and against the show sponsors. Fewer advertising spots on 'NYPD Blue' than on other ABC hour-long programs could indicate that sponsors are wary.
Bochco, Steven - Interviews / Wildmon, Donald - Quotations NYPD Blue (Television program) - Rating / Television broadcasting industry - Rating / Sex in television - Analysis / Violence in television - Analysis

Donnerstein, E. & Linz, D. (1994)
Sexual Violence in the Mass Media. In: Costanzo, M. & Oskamp, S. (Eds.): Violence and the Law, pp. 9-36, Thousand Oaks: Sage Publications, 1994, 290 p., bibl., ISBN 0-80395-342-9.

DuRant, R.H.; Rich, M.; Emans, S.J.; Rome, E.S.; Allred, E. & Woods, E.R. (1997)
Violence and Weapon Carrying in Music Videos: A Content Analysis. Archives of Pediatrics and Adolescent Medicine 15(1997)5, pp. 443-448, ISSN 1072-4710.

Evjen, T.Å. & Bjørnebekk, R. (1997)
Voldspornografi på internett: en kartlegging av forekomst og tilgjenglighet: Delrapport II [Pornography of Violence on Internet: A Survey of Existence and Availability]. Oslo: Regjeringens handlingsplan mot vold i bildemediene, 1997, 27 p., ill.

Gubar, S. & Hoff, J. (Eds.)
(1989)
For Adult Users Only: The Dilemma of Violent Pornography. Bloomington: Indiana University Press, 1989, 248 p., ill., ISBN 0-253-32365-7.

Hansen, C.H. & Hansen, R.D. (1990)
The Influence of Sex and Violence on the Appeal of Rock Music Videos.
Communication Research 17 (1990)2, pp. 212-234, ISSN 0093-6502.

Henchman, K.G. (1995)
Sex-Typing as a Predictor of Adolescents' Responses to Television Violence. Boston:
Harvard University, 1995, Diss.

Huston, A.C.; Wartella, E. & Donnerstein, E. (1998)
Measuring the Effects of Sexual Content in the Media: A Report to the Kaiser Family
Foundation. Menlo Park: H.J. Kaiser Family Foundation, 1998, 85 p., bibl.

Jankowski, Gene F.
Something to lose. (network programming standards)
Broadcasting and Cable, Sept. 13, 1993, v. 123 n. n37 p. 32(1)
LC Call Number: TK6540B85
Business Index Micro Film: 73R0679
The controversy over the new American Broadcasting Companies Inc.'s television
programs 'NYPD Blue' underscores what is wrong with network television today.
Network television should not try to compete with cable television, which draws vastly
smaller audiences, by reducing its standards of tasteful, quality programming. Blatant
nudity especially should not be tolerated by commercial networks, unless they want to
encourage government censorship and control over programming. ABC affiliates should
exercise their right to pre-empt programs they find objectionable.
NYPD Blue (Television program) - Moral and ethical aspects / Television programs -
Moral and ethical aspects / Television broadcasting industry - Standards / Sex in
television - Moral and ethical aspects / Cable television broadcasting industry -
Standards)

Jones, K. (1997)
Are Rap Videos More Violent? Style Differences and the Prevalence of Sex and Violence
in the Age of MTV. Howard Journal of Communications 8(1997)4, pp. 343-356, ISSN
1064-6175.

Laver, Ross
Less sex please - we're European. (sex and violence on television)
Maclean's, Oct. 12, 1987, v. 100 p. 50(1)
LC Call Number: AP5.M2; Microfilm (0) 84/200 (1909-1982) MicRR
Magazine Index Micro Film: 41K2189
Sex in television - Laws, regulations, etc. / Violence in television - Laws, regulations, etc.
/ Television - Psychological aspects / European Community social policy
Europe, Western

Linz, D.; Fuson, I.A. & Donnerstein, E. (1990)
Mitigating the Negative Effects of Sexually Violent Mass Communications Through
Preexposure Briefings. Communication Research 17(1990), pp. 641-674, ISSN 0093-
6502.

Linz, D.; Wilson, B.J. & Donnerstein, E. (1992)
Sexual Violence in the Mass Media: Legal Solutions, Warnings and Mitigation Through
Education. Journal of Social Issues 48(1992), pp. 145-171, ISSN 0022-4537.

Malamuth, N.M. (1989)
Sexually Violent Media, Thought Patterns, and Antisocial Behaviour. In: Comstock, G.A.: Public Communication and Behavior. Vol. 2, pp. 159-204, San Diego: Academic Press, 1989, ISBN 0-12-543202-X.

Molitor, F. & Sapolsky, B.S. (1997)
Sex, Violence, and Victimization in Slasher Films. Journal of Broadcasting and Electronic Media 37(1997)2, pp. 233-242, ISSN 0883-8151.

Ohbuchi, K.I.; Ikeda, T. & Takeuchi, G. (1994)
Effects of Violent Pornography Upon Viewer's Rape Myth Belief: A Study of Japanese Males Psychology. Crime and Law 1(1994)1, pp. 71-82, ISSN 0925-4994.

Ozemhoya, Carol U.
Sex and sin pays for WSVN-TV. (local news on sex, sin and violence boosts WSVN-TV's ratings)
South Florida Business Journal August 12, 1991, v. 11 n., n51 p. 1(2)
LC Call Number: May or May Not be in LC. Search further.
Business Index Micro Film: 61W5829
Late news ratings. (table)
WSVN, Miami, Florida (Television) - Rating / Sex in television - Economic aspects / Television broadcasting of news - Economic aspects / Marketing research firms - Reports / Television broadcasting - Rating / Violence in television - Economic aspects

Perloff, R. (1997)
Social Effects: Violence, Pornography, and Stereotyping. In: Jeffres, L. & Perloff, R. (Eds.): Mass Media Effects, pp. 141-170, Prospect Heights: Waveland Press, 1997, 478 p., ISBN 0-88133-962-8.

Robins, J. Max
Webs put squeeze on small-screen sleaze. (television networks reduce sex and violence)
Variety, March 1, 1993, v. 350 n. n5 p. 1(2)
LC Call Number: PN2000.V3 Folio; Microfilm 03722 (1905-) MicRR
Business Index Micro Film: NONE
Television broadcasting industry - Moral and ethical aspects / Violence in television - Planning / Sex in television - Planning

Roland, H.A. (1993)
Relationships of Gender, Rape Myth Acceptance, Viewing Patterns, and Sexual Perceptions of Music Videos. Gainesville: University of Florida, 1993, 287 p., Diss.

Rowe, D. (1993)
Hard Copy, Soft Porn: Tabloid TV and the Sexualisation of Violence. Metro: Media & Education Magazine (1993)93, Autumn, pp. 34-42, ISSN 0312-2654.

Rudman, W.J. & Verdi, P. (1993)
Exploitation: Comparing Sexual and Violent Imagery of Females and Males in
Advertising. Women and Health 20(1993)4, pp. 1-14, ISSN 0363-0242.

Scholz, R. & Joseph, P. (1993)
Gewalt- und Sexdarstellungen im Fernsehen: Systematischer Problemaufriss mit
Rechtsgrundlagen und Materialien. Bonn: Forum Verlag, 1993, 352 p., bibl., ISBN 3-
927066-72-9.

Sex und Gewalt im Spielfilm der 70er und 80er Jahre: 1. Lüneburger Kolloquium zur
Medienwissenschaft. Bardowick: Wissenschaftler Verlag, 1991, 94 p., ill., bibl., ISBN 3-
89153-015-3.

Soothill, K. & Walby, S. (1991)
Sex Crime in the News. London: Routledge, 1991, VII, 181 p., tab., bibl., ISBN 0-415-
01815-3.

Spears, G. & Seydegart, K. (1993)
Les sexes et la violence dans les médias. Ottawa: Centre national d'information sur la
violence dans la famille, Santé Canada, 1993, 69 p., bibl., ISBN 0-66298-567-2.

St. Lawrence, J. & Joyner, D. (1991)
The Effects of Sexually Violent Rock Music on Males' Acceptance of Violence Against
Women. Psychology of Women Quarterly 15(1991), pp. 49-63, ISSN 0361-6843.

Stoutemyer, K.L.H. (1998)
The Effects of Media Portrayals of Sexual Violence on Female Viewers. Stanford:
Stanford University, 1998, 61 p., Diss.

Weisz, M.G. & Earls, C.M. (1995)
The Effects of Exposure to Filmed Sexual Violence on Attitudes Toward Rape. Journal
of Interpersonal Violence 10(1995)1, pp. 71-84, ISSN 0886-2605.

West, Donald V.
FCC reviews sex, wires and video topics; commissioners give their read on current state
of programming, prospects for S. 12, network-cable crossownership, PTAR and more.
(Federal Communications Commission; prime time access rule)
Broadcasting and Cable, Jan. 27, 1992, v. 122 n., n5 p. 14(1)
LC Call Number: TK6540B85
Business Index Micro Film: 63R0783
Members of the Federal Communications Commission called for stricter controls on the
airing of sex and violence on television. Commissioners Ervin Duggan, Sherrie Marshall
and James Quello, gave their opinions as part of a panel at the 1992 National Association
of Television Program Executives' conference. other subjects covered included proposed

cable television legislation, changes to the prime time access rule and foreign ownership of radio and television stations.

Duggan, Ervin S. - Science and technology policy / Marshall, Sherrie - Science and technology policy / Quello, James H. - Science and technology policy United States. Federal Communications Commission - Officials and employees / National Association of Television Program Executives - Conferences, meetings, seminars, etc. / Television broadcasting industry - Conferences, meetings, seminars, etc. / Sex in television - Public opinion / Violence in television - Public opinion / Television stations - International aspects

Zgourides, G.; Monto, M. & Harris, R. (1997)
Correlates of Adolescent Male Sexual Offense: Prior Adult Sexual Contact, Sexual Attitudes, and Use of Sexually Explicit Materials. International Journal of Offender Therapy and Comparative Criminology 41(1997)3, pp. 272-283, ISSN 0306-624X.

Zillmann, D. (1991)
Television Viewing and Psysiological Arousal. In: Bryant, J. & Zillmann, D. (Eds.): Responding to the Screen: Reception and Reaction Processes, pp. 103-134, Hillsdale: Lawrence Erlbaum, 1991, XIV, 407 p., ISBN 0-80580-033-6.

Zillmann, D. (1998)
Connections Between Sexuality and Aggression. Mahwah: Lawrence Erlbaum, 1998, XIII, 359 p., ill., bibl., ISBN 0-80581-906-1.

INDEX